INTEGRATING SERVICES IN SOUTH ASIA

INTEGRATING SERVICES IN SOUTH ASIA

TRADE, INVESTMENT, AND MOBILITY

RUPA CHANDA

OXFORD
UNIVERSITY PRESS

OXFORD
UNIVERSITY PRESS

YMCA Library Building, Jai Singh Road, New Delhi 110 001

Oxford University Press is a department of the University of Oxford. It furthers the
University's objective of excellence in research, scholarship, and education
by publishing worldwide in

Oxford New York

Auckland Cape Town Dar es Salaam Hong Kong Karachi Kuala Lumpur
Madrid Melbourne Mexico City Nairobi New Delhi Shanghai Taipei Toronto

With offices in
Argentina Austria Brazil Chile Czech Republic France Greece Guatemala
Hungary Italy Japan Poland Portugal Singapore South Korea Switzerland
Thailand Turkey Ukraine Vietnam

Oxford is a registered trademark of Oxford University Press
in the UK and in certain other countries

Published in India
by Oxford University Press, New Delhi

ISBN-13: 978-0-19-806995-9
ISBN-10: 0-19-806995-2

Typeset in Adobe Garamond 10.5/12.6 pt.
by HT Burda Media Limited, Greater Noida 201 306 (India)

Printed in India by De-Unique, New Delhi 110 018
Published by Oxford University Press
YMCA Library Building, Jai Singh Road, New Delhi 110 001

*I dedicate this book to my parents, Ramesh and Kabita Chanda,
for their love, encouragement, and moral guidance, and their many sacrifices.
They have taught me the values of integrity, diligence, and hard work.*

Contents

Tables and Figures

Tables

Annexure Tables

Figures

Annexure Figures

Acknowledgements

This book is the culmination of several years of work. I would like to thank the many people who have contributed to this book in various capacities.

I would like to express my gratitude to Biplove Choudhury of the UNDP, who requested me to undertake a study on services integration in South Asia, which then became the basis for this book. I am particularly grateful to Vidya Rangan, who not only helped me with the UNDP project but also inspired me to build on that report and to write this book. She did a substantial part of the background data gathering and analysis in the initial stages. Without her encouragement, this book might never have been conceived.

I am also grateful to many others who worked hard in the background and made this book possible. Thanks are due to Sasidaran Gopalan, Rituparna Roy, Pralok Gupta, and Shreekanth Mahendiran who worked over several months to collect reports and data and compiled this information into tables and charts and helped me meet my deadlines. Thanks also to Abhishek Srivastava who chipped in with additional information. I am also grateful to various practitioners, industry experts, and academics from different countries in the region who shared their insights with me. Their views helped in shaping and corroborating my analysis.

Last but not least, I thank my family—my husband Pradip, my two boys Anchit and Sattwik, and my aunt Gita for their constant support and patience throughout this endeavour. Without their love and understanding, this book could never have seen the light of day. And finally, a special word of thanks to my parents, Ramesh and Kabita, who gave me the motivation and confidence to write this book and kept me going with their moral support and constant guidance.

Abbreviations

2D	2 Dimension
2G	2nd Generation
3G	3rd Generation
ADB	Asian Development Bank
AF	Afghanistan
AMRI	Advanced Medicare and Research Institute Limited
APT	Asia Pacific Telecommunications
APTA	Asia-Pacific Trade Agreement
ASEAN	Association of Southeast Asian Nations
ASEAN+3	Association of Southeast Asian Nations + Japan, Korea, China
ATTA	Afghanistan Transit Trade Agreement
BBIN-GQ	Bangladesh–Bhutan–India–Nepal Quadrilateral Initiative
BD	Bangladesh
BDeIN	Bangladesh to India
BIMSTEC	Bay of Bengal Incentive for Multi-Sectoral Technical and Economic Cooperation
BITS	Birla Institute of Technology and Science
BLT	Build, Lease, and Transfer
BOI	Board of Investment
BOO	Build–Operate–Own
BOOT	Build, Own, Operate, and Transfer
BOT	Build–Operate–Transfer
BPL	Broadband over Power Lines
BSNL	Bharat Sanchar Nigam Limited
BT	Bhutan
BTO	Build–Transfer–Operate
CAGR	Compound Annual Growth Rate
CAREC	Central Asia Regional Economic Cooperation

CBSE	Central Board of Secondary Education
CEA	Central Electricity Authority
CEB	Ceylon Electricity Board
CECA	Comprehensive Economic Cooperation Agreement
CEPA	Comprehensive Economic Partnership Agreement
CIDA	Canadian International Development Agency
CII	Confederation of Indian Industry
CMIE	Centre for Monitoring Indian Economy
CoE	Committee of Experts
CPC	Central Product Classification
DEC	Distance Education Council
DHE	Department of Higher Education
DPR	Detailed Project Report
DSL	Digital Subscriber Line
ECA	Economic Cooperation Agreement
ECFMG	Education Commission for Foreign Medical Graduates
ECO	Economic Cooperation Organization
EIA	Energy Information Administration
EPA	Economic Partnership Agreement
ESCAP	Economic and Social Commission for Asia and the Pacific
ETFC	Electricity Tariff Fixation Commission
FDIR	Foreign Direct Investment Registration
FIPB	Foreign Investment Promotion Board
FMRP	Financial Management Reform Programme
FTA	Free Trade Agreement
G-22	Group of 22
G-33	Group of 33
G-90	Group of 90
GAIL	Gas Authority of India
GATS	General Agreement on Trade in Services
GATT	General Agreement on Tariffs and Trade
GE	General Electric
GENCO	Generation Company Limited (Power)
GET	Global Employment Trend
GMPCS	Global Mobile Personal Communications Services
GSM	Global System for Mobile
HFCL	Himachal Futuristic Communications Limited
HSMP	Highly Skilled Migrant Programme
ICRIER	Indian Council for Research on International Economic Relations

ICSE	Indian Certificate of Secondary Education
ICT	Information and Communication Technologies
IGG	Inter-Governmental Group
IN	India
INeBD	India to Bangladesh
INSEAD	Institut Européen d'Administration des Affaires
IOM	International Organization for Migration
IP	Infrastructure Provider
IPP	Independent Power Projects
IPR	Intellectual Property Rights
IRDA	Insurance Regulatory and Development Authority
ISLFTA	Indo-Sri Lankan Free Trade Agreement
ISP	Internet Service Provider
ISRO	Indian Space Research Organization
ITES	Information Technology Enabled Services
ITU	International Telecommunication Union
JV	Joint Venture
KW	Kilo Watt
LDC	Least Developed Countries
LECO	Lanka Electricity Company
LIRNE	Learning Initiatives on Reforms for Network Economies
LK	Sri Lanka
LLDC	List of Landlocked Developing Countries
MAAC	Maya Academy of Advanced Cinematics
MCOMS	Manipal College of Medical Science
MDG	Millennium Development Goals
MEB	Maldives Electricity Board
Mercosur	Mercado de Sur America
MFN	Most Favoured Nation
MICE	Meetings, Incentives, Conventions, and Exhibitions
MoE	Ministry of Education
MTI	Ministry of Trade and Industries
MTNL	Mahanagar Telephone Nigam Limited
MV	Maldives
NAMA	Non-Agricultural Market Access
NASSCOM	National Association of Software and Services Companies
NAVTEC	National Vocational and Technical Education Commission
NEA	Nepal Electricity Authority

NEPRA	National Electric Power Regulatory Authority
NIIT	National Institute of Information Technologies
NP	Nepal
NT	Nepal Telecom
NTB	Non-Tariff Barriers
NTDC	National Transmission and Dispatch Company
NTPC	National Thermal Power Corporation
OECD	Organization for Economic Cooperation and Development
ONGC	Oil and Natural Gas Corporation
PEPCO	Pakistan Electric Power Company Private Limited
PK	Pakistan
PMRTS	Public Mobile Radio Trunked Service
PPA	Power Purchase Agreement
PPI	Private Infrastructure Projects
PPIAF	Public–Private Infrastructure Advisory Facility
PPIB	Private Power and Infrastructure Board
PSTN	Public Switched Telephone Networks
PTA	Preferential Trade Agreements
RBI	Reserve Bank of India
RCA	Revealed Comparative Advantages
RoO	Rules of Origin
SAARC	South Asian Association for Regional Cooperation
SAF	South Asia Foundation
SAFAS	SAARC Framework Agreement on Trade in Services
SAFTA	South Asian Free Trade Agreement
SAHEA	South Asia Higher Education Area
SAPTA	SAARC Preferential Trading Agreement
SARI	South Asia Regional Initiative
SASEC	South Asia Sub-regional Economic Cooperation
SATIN	South Asian Trade and Investment Network
SATRC	South Asian Telecommunications Regulators Council
SAU	South Asian University
SCAAP	Special Commonwealth African Assistance Programme
SEB	State Electricity Board
SLASSCOM	Sri Lanka Association of Software and Service Companies
SLIATE	Sri Lanka Institute of Advanced Technological Education
SLIC	Sri Lanka Insurance Corporation
SLTDA	Sri Lanka Tourism Development Authority
STC	SAARC Tuberculosis Centre

STELCO	State Electric Company Limited
TAR	Total Accounting Rate
TCB	Tourism Council of Bhutan
TDP	Tourism Development Plan
TIFA	Trade and Investment Framework Agreement
TPTCL	Tata Power Trading Company Limited
TRAI	Telecom Regulatory Authority of India
TRE	Telecom Regulatory Environment
UGC	University Grants Commission
UNAIDS	United Nations Programme on HIV/AIDS
UNCTAD	United Nations Conference on Trade and Development
UNESCAP	United Nations Economic and Social Commission for Asia and the Pacific
UNESCO	United Nations Educational, Scientific, and Cultural Organization
UNFPA	United Nations Fund for Population Activities
UNWTO	United Nations World Tourism Organization
UR	Uruguay Round
USAID	United States Agency for International Development
USO	Universal Service Obligation
VAT	Value Added Tax
WAPDA	Water and Power Development Authority
WDR	World Development Report
WTTC	World Travel and Tourism Council

Introduction

There has been a spurt in regional and bilateral integration efforts in the past decade, particularly since the establishment of the World Trade Organization (WTO) in 1995. According to the WTO, there are over 400 agreements—bilateral, intra-regional, and cross-regional—that have been negotiated since 1995. One can debate whether this surge in regional and bilateral arrangements has been spurred by factors, such as the slow pace of negotiations in the WTO, or the sensitivities involved in making concessions on a most favoured nation (MFN) basis, or the fact that strategizing of mutual interests is easier under regional and bilateral arrangements than under the multilateral trading system. One can also debate, as many experts have done, whether these arrangements are stepping stones or stumbling blocks to multilateral liberalization and whether they may not ultimately undermine the multilateral trading system.

Whatever be the causes and consequences of such agreements, it is clear that every region in the world, and almost every country in the world, is pursuing some kind of integration arrangement with its own economic, geo-political, and strategic interests in mind. The nomenclature has grown as rapidly as the number of agreements, including Preferential Trade Agreements (PTAs), Free Trade Agreements (FTAs), Economic Cooperation Agreements (ECAs), Economic Partnership Agreements (EPAs), Trade and Investment Agreements (TIAs), and other variants to these, suggesting that these integration schemes have widely varying scope and objectives. Some are narrow, focusing only on goods trade liberalization. Others are very broad-ranging, going beyond goods to cover services, investment, people mobility, intellectual property rights (IPRs), scientific and technological cooperation, and other collaboration issues. The extent of liberalization under these different arrangements also varies from very shallow levels of integration to far-reaching, deep integration.

The member countries of the South Asian Association for Regional Cooperation (SAARC)—Bangladesh, Bhutan, India, the Maldives, Nepal, Pakistan, and Sri Lanka—have been no exception to these recent trends in regional integration efforts.[1] However, they have been relatively slow movers in the process of regional cooperation. SAARC was set up as far back as 1985 in order to provide a forum for regional cooperation and to foster greater social and economic development in the region. But it took SAARC a decade to shift its focus to trade promotion as a concrete means of achieving greater regional integration, starting with the signing of the SAARC Preferential Trade Agreement (SAPTA) in April 1993 and its entry into force in December 1995. The aim of SAPTA was to eventually pave the way towards progressively deeper levels of integration, moving from a preferential trade agreement to a free trade agreement, namely, the South Asian Free Trade Agreement (SAFTA), followed by a customs union, a common market, and ultimately an economic union. This first step towards deeper integration was achieved with the signing of SAFTA in January 2004 and its entry into force in January 2006, with the goal of achieving a fully operational regional FTA by 2013 for the non-least developed country (LDC) members of SAARC and by 2016 for the LDC members of SAARC. There were subsequent talks at various SAARC summits to further the idea of a South Asian Economic Union and to establish various regional institutions and frameworks. To date, however, little concrete has been achieved in these latter regards and in pushing further the process of regional integration in South Asia.

Many studies and experts have highlighted the failure of SAPTA, and later SAFTA, to promote greater intra-regional cooperation. The share of intra-regional trade for SAARC increased only marginally from 2.68 per cent in 1990 to 4.85 per cent in 2005, comparing very poorly with other regional groupings in Asia as well as comparable groupings in other parts of the world.[2] Likewise, the limited data that are available on intra-regional investment flows suggest that the SAARC member countries are by and large not important destinations or sources for foreign direct

[1] Throughout this book, South Asia refers to Bangladesh, Bhutan, India, Nepal, the Maldives, Pakistan, and Sri Lanka and excludes Afghanistan and Iran, which are considered by international agencies and others as part of South Asia. The terms 'South Asian countries' and 'SAARC members' are used interchangeably in this book.

[2] Based on data from Asian Development Bank (ADB), Asia Regional Integration Centre Integration Indicators online database. Available at http://aric.adb.org/indicator.php, accessed on 29 June 2009.

investment (FDI).[3] The SAARC region remains poorly integrated despite rapid growth and liberalization of trade and investment regimes in several SAARC member countries in recent years and despite the emergence of an important regional and global player like India which could provide the much-needed momentum to regional integration efforts.

Studies on regional integration in South Asia point to a variety of factors that have impeded progress under SAARC. These include the strained bilateral political relations between India and Pakistan, security concerns, competing trade baskets and similar trade structures, corruption, the poor state of transport and related services infrastructure, and the lack of political will. In addition, factors specific to the architecture of the agreements under SAARC, such as the narrow coverage of regional commitments, the limited trade interest and potential of the member countries in the products that were covered, and modalities of trade liberalization, have played a role. There are also factors inherent to the region, such as limited market size and lack of scale economies, which are seen to have impeded progress. Thus, most studies tend to be pessimistic about the prospects for integration in SAARC, concluding that the economic rationale for such a regional bloc is weak and that SAFTA can be beneficial only if it is seen as part of a move towards a full-fledged FTA in Asia, and for pan-Asian integration.[4]

However, such quantitative and qualitative analyses suffer from two limitations. The first and perhaps most important limitation is that political and security considerations, and in particular the constraints posed to regional integration by the poor relations between India and Pakistan, tend to take centre stage in any discussions on South Asia, thus clouding any independent economic analysis of the potential for regional integration in South Asia. A second key limitation is that existing analyses tend to be based on the existing framework and scope of SAFTA and the prevailing composition and pattern of trade flows, which is primarily dominated by traditional products such as textiles, leather, and agricultural goods. One could argue that the conclusions regarding the prospects for regional cooperation may be quite different if SAFTA were to take a different shape in terms of its ambit and its negotiating modalities. It is worth noting that the few studies that are positive in their outlook for SAFTA generally argue for widening the scope of SAFTA, in particular, to include services and cross-cutting issues, such as investment and movement of persons in the negotiating agenda.

---

[3] There are some exceptions with regard to FDI from India to some of the smaller SAARC countries, as discussed in Chapter 2.

[4] See ADB (2008a).

Successive SAARC summits have emphasized the need to implement SAFTA in letter and spirit as a stepping stone to broader regional cooperation, indicating that an eventually broader ambit may be needed if progress is to be made and if benefits are to be realized under this regional bloc. The 14th SAARC Summit Declaration is significant as it specifically states the need to integrate services into the agreement if SAFTA is to realize its full potential. It calls upon member countries to work towards an early conclusion of SAFAS—the SAARC Framework Agreement on Trade in Services. This point was also echoed at the subsequent August 2008 Colombo SAARC Summit Declaration which stated that, 'Extending SAFTA to include services would considerably broaden its scope and impact and boost competitiveness in key emerging sectors, such as banking, communications, and aviation.' A Regional Study on the Potential for Trade in Services under SAFTA was also recommended. The 2008 SAARC Summit further highlighted the need for regional cooperation on a variety of policy issues, including domestic regulations and regulatory frameworks, data, and standards to complement efforts at promoting services integration in the region.

These recent developments naturally raise questions about the potential role that could be played by services in SAFTA. Is there a strong case to be made for including services under SAFTA? Can the expansion of SAFTA to services and investment provide the dynamism that has been lacking to date in South Asian integration? As argued in this book, there is a convincing case to be made for including services under SAFTA and there are potential gains to be realized for the member countries. Recent performance and policy trends in services in South Asia have made conditions conducive to framing a services agreement in South Asia, perhaps more so than in the case of goods.

The single most important factor is the dynamism exhibited by the service sector in South Asia and its growing importance in overall economic activity, including output, employment, trade, and investment flows in this region. The ADB's *South Asia Economic Report 2008* notes that the high GDP growth rates of 7 per cent or more experienced by several countries in the region, and the overall improvement in the region's economic performance in recent years, is directly related to the growth in services which have performed better than other parts of the economy in almost all the SAARC countries. The rise of services, prior to sustained industrialization, has been a particular feature of the region, unlike that in other parts of Asia (ADB 2008b). Today, services constitute close to 50 per cent or more of GDP for all the South Asian economies. This growing significance of services in South Asia has been in line with the service sector's rising share in output in the world economy. Services today account for over 70 per cent of the national income and employment in the OECD countries and even in the lowest income countries, they account for around 35 per cent of GDP.[5] Thus, the South Asian experience with services output is not an outlier, and in fact the service sector in South Asia has by and large witnessed higher growth rates than in other parts of Asia and also in other countries with comparable levels of development.

The higher capacity of the SAARC countries in producing and trading certain services, the availability of high quality services in the region, and the role of new economic geography in driving tradability of certain services creates opportunities for trade and investment complementarities within the region (SATIN 2008). This potential is further enhanced by the recent focus on services as a thrust area for trade and investment liberalization and regulatory reforms in South Asia and the common goal of all economies in this region to upgrade their services infrastructure. Hence, there appears to be a certain convergence of interests and approach to the service sector and therefore possibly a greater willingness to negotiate regional liberalization and intra-regional collaboration possibilities in services. There is the added benefit of geographic proximity as well as cultural and linguistic ties, as relationship-based marketing, social networks, and cross-border movement of service providers play an important role in driving services trade and investment flows, and the SAARC countries are well placed in this regard. The recent entry by some of the South Asian countries into extra-regional economic cooperation, trade and investment, or other partnership agreements that extend beyond goods to services further highlights the growing recognition of the importance of services to these economies and the possibility of realizing their interests in services through more broad-based regional and bilateral arrangements.

It is again worth noting that these regional trade and investment opportunities in services in South Asia are in line with the general expansion in services trade and investment flows witnessed globally, with global commercial services exports estimated at $2.8 trillion in 2006 and services FDI accounting for around 60 per cent of the global stock of FDI, or $6 trillion in 2004.[6] The shift in policy orientation towards the service sector in South Asia also mirrors closely the large-scale changes in FDI and trade

---

[5] See Hoekman and Mattoo (2008) for a discussion on services trade and growth and contributing factors.

[6] See Hoekman and Mattoo (2008).

policies concerning the service sector around the world over the past two decades and the growing trend of including services in regional integration arrangements. Thus both global and regional factors have contributed to the dynamism witnessed in services in South Asia and also to the emerging opportunities for regional cooperation in services.

However, there are many issues that need to be addressed in the context of a South Asian services agreement. What shape should such an agreement take? What sectors and issues should be the thrust areas for negotiations? What are the likely benefits to the countries in this region from expanding the scope of SAFTA? What might be some of the challenges and sticky areas for negotiation and how feasible will it be to overcome these challenges given the political economy realities and resource and capacity constraints that characterize this region? To address such a wide range of questions, an in-depth analysis of the prospects for services integration in South Asia is clearly warranted. At present, there is hardly any literature that discusses the potential for services integration *within* the region, particularly from bottom-up, that is, based on an understanding of the opportunities and challenges in individual service sub-sectors and in key cross-cutting areas. It is this gap that this book aims to fill in the existing literature on South Asian integration. An understanding of these issues would not only help inform the on-going negotiations under SAFTA, but would also provide a much-needed stocktaking of the service sector in South Asia.

Outline and Objectives

This book has four broad objectives. The first is to highlight the role and performance of services within the region, taking a collective regional perspective, and to use this as a basis for identifying those services and areas which offer good and varied prospects for intra-regional integration. The second objective is to highlight the status of liberalization and reforms and current levels of intra-regional engagement in services in order to provide an overview of the policy environment as well as existing opportunities and interests in the regional market. The third objective is to provide an overview of multilateral as well as extra-regional/bilateral commitments made by the SAFTA member countries in services and their positions on key issues in order to assess their preparedness to commit under SAFTA. The fourth and final aim is to outline negotiating priorities in different services and on cross-cutting issues based on the earlier analysis of opportunities and constraints and to point out possible modalities for negotiation.

The chapter flow and development of arguments in this book closely follows these four broad objectives. Chapter 1 provides an overview of the chronology of regional integration efforts in South Asia and outcomes, developments on the services negotiation front, and a broad comparison of where SAFTA stands vis-à-vis other regional alliances, particularly within Asia. This discussion provides an understanding of the limited progress to date under SAFTA.

Chapter 2 discusses why services integration makes sense under SAFTA by providing a detailed account of trends in services growth, output, employment, trade, and investment in each of the countries in the region. On the basis of performance and contribution characteristics, it identifies a representative set of services and issues that hold most promise for discussion under SAFTA. These include two infrastructure or producer services—telecommunications and energy, one commercial service—tourism, and two social services—education and healthcare. In addition, important cross-cutting issues, namely, investment and movement of natural persons are also discussed.

Chapters 3 to 7 provide a detailed analysis of selected services covering these clusters. These include telecommunications, energy, tourism, health and education, respectively. The discussion in each chapter follows a similar pattern, starting with an overview of the status of the sector in terms of growth, value added, contribution to the economies, extent of reforms and liberalization, regulatory issues, and the status of intra-regional trade and investment relations based on existing projects or proposed initiatives. Primary insights based on discussions with sectoral experts and stakeholders in the region are also provided to highlight the perceived prospects for and challenges to intra-regional integration in services. The discussion in each chapter also highlights steps that could be taken to further integration in each of the selected services.

Chapter 8 summarizes the service sector commitments made by SAFTA member countries in the WTO and in their other bilateral or regional agreements. The discussion highlights the main characteristics of these commitments, how these relate to their unilateral liberalization in these areas, how their multilateral commitments compare with their regional/bilateral commitments in services, and essentially what this reflects about their willingness and preparedness to negotiate and liberalize services in the context of SAFTA. The status of these commitments is also mapped with the existing levels of liberalization to indicate the countries' willingness to liberalize unilaterally as opposed to multilaterally or regionally. This discussion thus provides a sort of reality check on where intra-regional integration is feasible and not just where there is potential.

Chapter 9 draws upon the analysis in the preceding chapters to outline some negotiating priorities and modalities. It highlights the need to adopt a gradual approach to services negotiations under SAFTA, arguing that the most promising and least contentious services be brought into the scope of the proposed services framework agreement to begin with, and to gradually broaden the scope of SAFTA to include more difficult and challenging services once there is greater institutional and regulatory capacity and proven outcomes to facilitate the process. In particular, it highlights a variety of cross-cutting issues, such as investment, regional mobility of service providers, taxes, transport, trade facilitation, research and development, information collection and dissemination within the region, and regulatory cooperation, all of which would need to be addressed if any progress is to be made with regional services integration. This chapter also outlines the nature of commitments that could be undertaken by individual member countries under SAFTA and the approach that could be taken on key cross-cutting issues. The possibility of a GATS-type architecture is also discussed.

The Epilogue looks at the strategic issues and considerations that are likely to shape progress or lack thereof in any agreement on services in South Asia. It highlights the geo-political, security, and political economy challenges to regional integration in South Asia. It discusses whether or not these can be overcome in the context of services negotiations, and if so, within what limitations. The discussion also addresses the larger question of whether services can indeed provide the much needed fillip to regional cooperation in South Asia and the larger role that they can play in promoting the national goals of poverty reduction, social and economic equity, and more rapid economic growth for the countries in this region.

The main contribution of this book is that it expands the existing work on South Asian integration to cover the service sector. Thus far, services have either not been the focus of most studies on South Asia or have been looked at from the national perspective or from the perspective of South Asia vis-à-vis the rest of the world, but not from the perspective of intra-regional trade, investment, and collaboration opportunities. This book also pulls together country level and regional information on services, at the aggregate level and in individual service sectors, to provide a consolidated picture of recent trends and liberalization in this region, which can serve as a useful factual basis for services negotiations and for future academic and policy work in this region.

The main message of this book is that there are significant commercial and collaboration opportunities in services within South Asia. One will need to look beyond the traditional paradigm of integration through merchandise trade to consider services, investment, labour mobility, and regulatory cooperation issues if one is to realize the full potential for economic integration in this region. Services integration could also potentially provide a boost to political, cultural, and social relations in the region. While some of the steps required for services integration may be difficult to undertake, through incremental, pilot-based, and innovative initiatives, often perhaps at the sub-regional level, the South Asian countries can lay the foundations and gradually move towards wider integration.

Scope and Limitations

A few words on the scope and coverage of this book are, however, warranted. The first concerns the geographic scope of the analysis. Afghanistan has been excluded from the analysis even though it has recently become a member of SAARC. This is due to reasons of limited availability and poor quality of data that would be available for Afghanistan, and the political circumstances that would make it difficult to compare Afghanistan with other countries in the region. A full-fledged analysis of South Asian integration would, however, need to include Afghanistan. It should be noted that the geographic terms 'South Asia' and 'SAARC' are at times used interchangeably but the countries always under consideration are Bangladesh, Bhutan, India, the Maldives, Nepal, Pakistan, and Sri Lanka.

A second issue concerns the time period under analysis, which is for the most part 1990 through 2007 or 2008. The impact of the crisis on services trade and output for the region is thus not captured. This is primarily due to the availability of consistent and common time series data for most of the required indicators across all the countries in this region. To some extent, this choice of years is also justified by the fact that the overall objective is to understand the general trends and characteristics of services growth in the region over a sufficiently long period, roughly the past two decades, which may otherwise be masked by aberrations in more recent data due to the fall-out of the recent global crisis on these economies and the performance of their service sectors. Of course, one cannot overlook the possible role South–South cooperation and regional integration among developing countries could play in mitigating the effects of such economic crises, by providing diversified markets and opportunities for regional investment flows and collaboration.

The third issue concerns the scope of services covered by this book. Although the service sector is characterized by a wide range of activities, this book discusses only five services and leaves out several others that one could argue are worthy of discussion in the South Asian context. This deliberate narrowing of scope is driven by the broader objective of providing an in-depth and detailed idea of the kinds of issues and concerns associated with a *representative* set of services which cut across different service clusters, namely, infrastructural, commercial, and social services, rather than trying to provide a wide ranging but cursory account of all possible services that may be of interest within South Asia. However, the discussion does focus indirectly on several other services, such as transport, IT, financial, and research and development services, among others, in terms of their bearing on opportunities and constraints in the selected services and in other areas. The fact that the coverage of services is not exhaustive does not mean that they are not of potential interest to the region. Moreover, the discussion clearly recognizes the interdependence of various services, and thus touches upon these linkages wherever relevant.

Another point worth noting is that the focus of the analysis in this book is largely intra-regional. Thus many issues which may also be analysed from a national perspective have been approached differently. However, once again, the links between national policies and preparedness and regional cooperation are highlighted, wherever relevant.

The analysis in this book has been constrained by the lack of quality data on services in the region. The availability of data on services, especially at the intra-regional and sub-sectoral levels, and a cross-section of these two, is extremely poor. This has greatly constrained any empirical analysis and modeling that would otherwise have been attempted to quantitatively assess the potential for services integration in South Asia and the resulting trade and growth implications for the region. Notwithstanding these limitations, it is hoped that this book will provide a better understanding of the prospects for, and challenges to, services integration in South Asia, the potential benefits and associated challenges, and the implications of such integration for the realization of broader goals under SAFTA and nationally.

And finally, as highlighted earlier, there has been a deliberate attempt to stay away from the politics of the region and specifically from India–Pakistan or India–Bangladesh relations, national security, and ethnic issues that usually dominate the discussion on South Asian integration. Such issues are touched upon only where they are directly relevant to the sectors under discussion, such as in the context of energy or tourism services or where they are directly relevant to the services trade modalities under discussion, such as in the context of intra-regional mobility of labour. But these issues are not discussed at a general geo-political level because there are many books and reports which already do that and would do that better than this author could. The objective here has been to maintain as independent an economic analysis of the potential for regional integration as possible and to assess the likely benefits arising from such integration, without losing sight of the practical difficulties in this process, and without getting bogged down by the usual debate on South Asia's geo-politics and the pessimism surrounding integration in this region. The concluding chapter (Chapter 9) does, however, examine some of these issues and turns the usual question around to ask if integration could lay the foundation for progress on the geo-political front.

———

In April 2010, the SAARC Agreement on Trade in Services (SATIS) was signed by all the SAARC member countries. Schedule negotiations will commence soon. This Agreement has been referred throughout this book by its earlier name, that is, the SAARC Framework Agreement on Trade in Services (SAFAS).

1

Regional Integration Efforts and Outcomes

Regional and bilateral trading arrangements have gained prominence in the past two decades, prompted by the slow progress of multilateral negotiations and competitive pressures amongst countries to enter into such arrangements lest they lose out. The economies of South Asia have, however, been relatively slow to recognize the importance of regional integration in furthering their trade, investment, and larger development objectives. SAARC was established as late as 1985. SAPTA came into effect only a decade later in 1996 and SAFTA entered into force another decade later, in 2006. Much work still remains unfinished and many issues remain unresolved. As a result, even after more than two decades of the SAARC's establishment, South Asia remains one of the least integrated regions in the world with less than 5 per cent of the region's trade being carried out within the region (UNCTAD (2007). The UNCTAD *Trade and Development Report 2007*, which focused on regional cooperation for development, concluded that in comparison with other developing country groups, particularly ASEAN, regional cooperation has been far less dynamic in South Asia and that, unlike ASEAN, the establishment of SAARC has not given a fillip to intra-regional trade (UNCTAD 2007).

The discussion in this chapter provides a brief history of regional integration efforts in South Asia in terms of the progression from SAARC to SAFTA and the contentious issues that have characterized this process. It highlights the outcomes of these regional integration efforts in terms of the extent of intra-regional trade and penetration of markets within the region and unresolved issues. Based on the observed outcomes and drawing upon the prevailing theoretical literature on regional integration, as well as available studies on South Asia, the discussion examines whether SAFTA holds much promise in its current form and whether the inclusion of services might make this agreement more meaningful.

From SAARC to SAFTA

In comparison with other regions of the world, South Asia's arrival on the economic integration scene has undoubtedly been late. SAARC consisting of seven countries in South Asia was set up in 1985. It was seen as a vehicle for fostering greater social, cultural, and economic development for the region through cooperation, and to present a unified voice to the rest of the world.[1] It was championed by the leaders of the time and it tried to overcome the absence of a favourable political and economic climate for regional integration in the member countries. SAARC's economic integration process had two phases. The first phase focused on expanding output through trade, investment, and technology collaborations under an integrated programme of action that aimed at poverty alleviation, welfare of women and children, social and cultural exchange, and improving the environment. The second phase focused on the promotion of a common market and macroeconomic coordination through various economic cooperation and institutional initiatives.[2]

It was during the second phase that the first concrete step was taken under SAARC towards trade promotion. An Inter-Governmental Group (IGG) was set up to establish a SAARC Preferential Arrangement (SAPTA) by 1997. The formulation of SAPTA was envisaged as a necessary step in the transition towards a South Asian Free Trade Area (SAFTA), which would subsequently lead to a customs union, a common market, and eventually an economic union. Given the consensus within SAARC, SAPTA was signed earlier on 11 April 1993 at the 7th SAARC Summit in Dhaka; it came into force on 7 December 1995. This was the first significant collaborative agreement under SAARC. One of the important features of SAPTA was the distinction it made between the least developed and other developing member countries in the bloc with the former consisting of Bangladesh, Nepal, Bhutan, and the Maldives and the latter India, Pakistan, and Sri Lanka. The agreement provided for Special and Differential Treatment for LDC members and also included a 'regional' MFN provision. There were several rounds of SAPTA negotiations on a product-by-product basis, with LDCs receiving preferential treatment in the form of lower tariffs. The negotiations resulted in a total of 5,550 tariff line concessions being included in the agreement and tariff concessions varying from 5 to 100 per cent.[3] However, the overall approach to trade liberalization under SAPTA

---

[1] See the SAARC website.

[2] Some of these initiatives included the establishment of the SAARC Chamber of Commerce and Industry, the Council of Development Finance Institutions, and the Project Development Facility.

[3] Based on Weerakoon (2008) and Krueger et al. (2004).

was cautious and hesitant, hampered by low product coverage, stringent rules of origin, an item-by-item approach to tariff concessions, and denial of concessions on products that were of trade interest to the member countries.[4] The latter was coupled with problems of mistrust, lack of political will, and growing imbalance within the region given India's growing importance in the global economy.

Notwithstanding these challenges, in 1996, the SAARC member countries agreed to enact SAFTA no later than 2005. Following several rounds of negotiations and delays in discussions due to the souring of relations between India and Pakistan during the 1999–2001 period, finally, a Committee of Experts (CoE) was set up at the 10th SAARC Summit in 1998. This committee drafted a comprehensive treaty framework to establish a free trade area within the region. It was also proposed to go beyond an FTA to include provisions on trade facilitation, harmonization of customs classification, and removal of restrictions on intra-regional investment flows, consultations on macroeconomic policies, and development of communication systems and transport infrastructure under SAFTA. The SAFTA accord was signed in January 2004 at the 12th SAARC Summit in Islamabad and following further work on tariff liberalization, rules of origin, and sensitive lists, came into effect on 1 January 2006. Under the trade liberalization component of SAFTA, member countries agreed to gradually harmonize and eventually bring down their import tariffs on intra-regional trade to 5 per cent or less. Also, unlike SAPTA's negative list approach, SAFTA aimed at phasing out import tariffs on all goods except those on member-specific sensitive lists.[5]

[4] As outlined in several studies, despite three rounds of preference negotiations, SAPTA's product coverage remained limited. SAPTA resulted in significant preferences for only the least developed member countries. The estimated annual value of all imports that entered the SAARC member countries under the SAPTA preferences amounted to approximately $480 million at the end of the 1990s. The share of intra-regional imports covered by the SAPTA preferences ranged from as low as 12 per cent in the case of Sri Lanka to around 40 per cent in the case of Pakistan, with marginal coverage in the case of Bangladesh and the Maldives. See studies on South Asian integration such as Mukherji (2000) and Weerakoon (2008).

[5] The trade liberalization programme committed to reducing tariffs in non-LDCs to 20 per cent within two years of the agreement and further to 0–5 per cent over the next five years. The LDC members would have to reduce their tariffs to 30 per cent in two years and to 0–5 per cent in the next eight years. The approach taken was one of convergence, though the liberalization programme was backloaded. The rules of origin stipulated 40 per cent value addition in the case of India and Pakistan, 35 per cent in the case of Sri Lanka, and 30 per cent for the LDCs along with a change in tariff heading at the 4 digit HS code. There is a cumulative Rule of Origin (RoO) provision with minimum aggregate content of 50 per cent, subject to 20 per cent minimum input from the exporting country. There is a

SAFTA is expected to be fully operational by 2013 for non-LDC members and by 2016 for LDC members in the region.[6]

Recent SAARC summits have recognized the need to extend SAFTA beyond goods to address additional issues to deepen integration and complement the trade liberalization programme. Some of the proposed initiatives include improving regional connectivity for imports, trade facilitation measures, setting up a world class South Asian University, promoting South Asian textiles through textile exhibitions and a SAARC fashion festival in Delhi, and setting up a SAARC food bank to collectively meet the region's emergencies and shortages. The 14th SAARC Summit held in New Delhi in April 2007 called for the early finalization of an agreement in services and a collective vision of South Asia with free flow of goods, services, and ideas and in March 2008, the SAFTA Ministerial Council directed the drafting of a SAARC Agreement on Trade in Services (SAFAS) by end 2009. Sub-regional Economic Cooperation working groups have since been formed on transport and tourism services and sub-sectors. The South Asian governments have specially recommended certain areas for action, many of which have a bearing on services. These include improving mobility of people, strengthening communication and transport links, fostering cross-border energy investments and regional energy trade, and implementing measures for trade facilitation. This extension of SAFTA to include services and investment is part of the on-going discussions to further regional cooperation, with proposals for an eventual South Asia Economic Union, though nothing concrete has been realized to date.

Independently, outside these regional efforts, several sub-regional initiatives for trade liberalization have also emerged amongst the member countries. One such case is the Bangladesh–Bhutan–India–Nepal Growth Quadrilateral Initiative (BBIN–GQ) under the SAARC framework, which aims at promoting rapid economic development through the identification and implementation of specific projects. There are other initiatives such as BIMSTEC which involve some of the SAARC member countries as well as non-member countries to foster cooperation in a variety of areas.[7] There are also several bilateral

---

negative list to deal with sensitive sectors, with around 20 per cent of the tariff lines retained on the negative list by all countries. (This discussion is based on various studies on South Asian regional integration.)

[6] In recent years, India has adopted a strong positive stance towards regional cooperation in South Asia. It has provided free market access to imports from the LDCs in the region and has also committed to reduce its negative list and unilaterally liberalize visas.

[7] These areas include trade and investment, technology, transport and communication, energy, tourism, and fisheries.

trade agreements among the SAARC member countries, such as the Indo-Bhutan treaty on economic cooperation, multiple treaties between India and Nepal (with regard to trade, transit, and unauthorized trade), the Pakistan-Sri Lanka FTA, and the Indo-Sri Lanka Free Trade Agreement (ISLFTA) signed in 1998 and effective since 2000. Unlike SAFTA these agreements are more liberal and have been implemented much faster.[8] Overall, South Asian countries are involved in 21 bilateral arrangements besides SAFTA indicating that bilateral efforts have been running concurrently with regional efforts.

Impact on Trading Patterns

SAFTA has been criticized on various accounts, including its large negative lists that keep large parts of the region's import basket outside the purview of tariff liberalization, back-loaded tariff liberalization, restrictive rules of origin, and failure to address non-tariff barriers explicitly. As a result, the agreement has had little or no impact on South Asia's trading pattern. Although the volume of trade and exports for the South Asian countries has increased significantly, the volume of intra-regional trade among the SAARC countries

Table 1.1   Intra-regional Trade Indicators for Select Groupings in Asia, 2005

Intra-regional Trade Intensity Index	1990	1995	2000	2005
SAARC	2.81	3.84	3.68	3.64
ASEAN	4.39	3.68	3.97	4.98
East Asia-15	2.22	2.11	2.17	2.27
Intra-regional Trade Share (%)	1990	1995	2000	2005
SAARC	2.68	3.91	3.87	4.85
ASEAN	18.85	24	24.7	28.09
East Asia-15	43.08	51.92	52.15	55.56

Source: Based on ADB Asia Regional Integration Centre Integration Indicators Database (online version).
Notes: (i) Intra-regional trade intensity index is the ratio of intra-regional trade share to the share of world trade with the region, calculated using exports data. An index of more than one indicates that trade flow within the region is larger than expected given the importance of the region in world trade. (ii) Intra-regional trade share is the percentage of intra-regional trade to total trade of the region, calculated using exports data. A higher share indicates a higher degree of dependency on regional trade. ASEAN = Brunei Darussalam, Cambodia, Indonesia, Lao PDR, Malaysia, Myanmar, Philippines, Singapore, Thailand, and Vietnam; East Asia-15 = ASEAN+ People's Republic of China, Republic of Korea, Japan, Hong Kong, and Taipei, China.

[8] For instance, compared to a negative list of 1,065 and 1,183 for Sri Lanka and Pakistan, respectively, under SAFTA, the negative list is 697 and 540, respectively under the bilateral FTA between these two countries. See, Weerakoon (2008).

has not increased much despite SAPTA and SAFTA. As shown in Table 1.1, the very low level of intra-regional integration in South Asia when compared to other regional groupings in Asia, especially ASEAN, is quite striking.

As the data given in Table 1.1 indicate, trade intensity for the SAARC region has increased only marginally over a period of 15 years, from 2.81 in 1990 to 3.64 in 2005. The overall intra-regional trade share also remains very low at 4.85 per cent and has increased only modestly over this period. In comparison, other groupings like ASEAN and East Asia-15 have very high intra-regional trade shares and this has increased by around 10 per cent over the 1990–2005 period. Hence, SAFTA has not been successful at fostering intra-regional trade. Table 1.2 shows that the same holds true for individual member countries of SAARC.

Table 1.2 indicates that while for India, none of the SAARC countries are significant trading partners (the highest trade share being that with Sri Lanka—1 per cent), for the others, India is significant. In the case of Bhutan and Nepal, India is the most significant trade partner. This indicates the dependence of other economies on trade with India while India's own dependence on them is very low, thus reflecting the fundamental asymmetry in trade relations within the region. Over 90 per cent of the regional trade for Nepal, Sri Lanka, and Bangladesh is with India indicating that regional integration in South Asia is driven by bilateral links with the main country in this region, India (Weerakoon 2008, based on IMF 2007).

On the other hand, SAARC accounted only for 5.65 per cent of India's total exports and 0.88 per cent of total imports.[9] This reflects an asymmetry in trading relations, obviously reflecting the large differences in size, endow-

Table 1.2 Intra-regional Trade in SAARC—Share of Individual Countries (per cent), 2005

Trade Share	Bangladesh	Bhutan	India	Maldives	Nepal	Pakistan	Sri Lanka
Bangladesh	–	0.06	9.26	0.03	0.03	0.88	0.08
India	0.75	0.08	–	0.03	0.52	0.34	1.03
Maldives	0	n/a	10.06	–	0	0.34	6.96
Nepal	0.25	n/a	49.02	n/a	–	0.3	0.02
Pakistan	0.45	0	2.05	0.01	0.02	–	0.5
Sri Lanka	0.11	n/a	14.94	0.33	0	0.99	–

Source: Based on ADB Asia Regional Integration Centre Integration Indicators Database (online version).

[9] Based on RBI (2008). Due to the lack of disaggregated data on the direction of trade for services, it is not possible to provide an estimate for the share of services in intra-regional trade in South Asia.

ments, capacity, and potential between India and the other countries. In fact, India's dominance in regional trade has also been growing over time and there does not appear to be any clear secondary leader. This asymmetry has posed challenges to regional integration efforts due to concerns over India's regional hegemony and economic dominance over the smaller countries in the region (an issue that emerges in the context of services as well as seen in the discussion that follows in the rest of this book).

Table 1.3 shows the trends in the share of intra-regional exports, intra-regional imports, and intra-regional trade for all the countries (except Bhutan), as well as the significance of India for each of the countries in their intra-regional trade. As is evident, intra-regional exports and imports constitute a very low share of total exports and imports, respectively for almost all the countries, excepting Nepal. These shares have remained virtually stagnant over the 1990–2006 period for almost all the countries.

Table 1.3 Trends in Intra-regional Exports, Imports, and Trade and India's Importance (per cent), 1990, 2000, 2006

Country	Years	Share of Intra-regional Exports	Share of India in Intra-regional Exports	Share of Intra-regional Imports	Share of India in Intra-regional Imports	Share of Intra-regional Trade	Share of India in Intra-regional Trade
Bangladesh	1990	2.94	35.76	6.5	66.17	5.29	60.37
	2000	1.24	56.12	10.93	89.46	6.79	86..86
	2006	1.73	68.54	13.48	91.11	8.38	89.09
India	1990	2.12	–	0.33	–	1.11	–
	2000	3.00	–	0.61	–	1.69	–
	2006	3.11	–	0.70	–	1.82	–
Maldives	1990	4.07	0.69	10.54	39.08	7.12	27.44
	2000	3.05	1.74	19.82	39.76	11.43	34.68
	2006	3.29	5.47	13.34	74.13	34.68	64.55
Nepal	1990	3.83	91.41	9.43	74.43	7.55	77.33
	2000	24.12	99.35	32.77	97.89	29.16	98.39
	2006	46.06	98.97	50.66	99.68	49.30	99.48
Pakistan	1990	3.26	22.0	1.19	37.52	2.02	27.49
	2000	2.79	20.47	2.07	70.49	2.40	44.04
	2006	3.47	58.61	2.43	83.57	2.81	72.23
Sri Lanka	1990	3.05	28.88	6.20	64.15	4.83	54.44
	2000	2.97	30.59	8.73	84.85	6.19	73.37
	2006	7.05	81.61	20.23	92.42	14.66	90.22

Source: Based on UNCTAD (2008).

Table 1.4　Relative Share of India's Trade with SAARC and ASEAN +3 (per cent), 2000–6

	2000	2001	2002	2003	2004	2005	2006
SAARC							
Exports	4.2	5.7	5.1	6.4	5.6	5.2	5.5
Imports	0.9	1.3	0.9	0.9	0.8	0.9	1.0
ASEAN +3							
Exports	13.5	18.1	16.7	18.2	18.9	20.6	21.9
Imports	17.1	24.9	19.3	21.4	20.6	19.9	27.0

Source: Reproduced from Weerakoon (2008), Table 6, p. 12.

Even where there has been a noticeable upward trend, this increase is largely due to India's increased share in intra-regional exports and imports. The data also indicate India's growing significance as a trading partner for all the countries. In contrast, it is worth noting India's particularly low dependence on the region, again reflecting an asymmetry in trade relations within the region, while the share of India's trade with Southeast Asia and East Asian countries (ASEAN +3) has increased sharply, as shown in Table 1.4.

The limited impact of SAFTA on the trading pattern within South Asia is also indicated by the narrow basket of commodities traded among the member countries. Disaggregated data on trade among the South Asian countries indicate that intra-regional trade is dominated by primary products, of which food and animal based products constitute the bulk. Moreover, this trade shows considerable volatility due to fluctuations in import demand and domestic supply conditions in the South Asian countries. Hence, regional integration has not resulted in either a diversified or a stable trade relationship among the member countries (Pitigala 2005).

SAFTA has also had a limited role in lowering protection levels in South Asia. In fact, trade liberalization in the region has mainly been undertaken unilaterally while regional liberalization in the context of SAFTA has been quite shallow and limited in coverage. Table 1.5 indicates the limited nature of trade liberalization under this agreement.

As noted in several studies on SAFTA, the main problem with this agreement is the unreasonably long sensitive lists/negative lists of member countries which reduce the scope for intra-regional trade (as shown in columns 2 and 3 of Table 1.5). Not only is the number of items on the negative list huge but, on average, around 50 per cent of the trade is outside the scope of SAFTA, significantly limiting the potential for fostering intra-regional trade. There are also no binding provisions on members to systematically reduce their negative lists as SAFTA only calls for a 'review'

Table 1.5 Trade Restrictions under SAFTA

	No. of Items in Negative List in SAFTA	Value of Imports from SAARC Subject to Negative List (%)	Value of Exports to SAARC Subject to Negative List (%)
Bangladesh	1,254 (1,249–LDCs)	65.0	22.0
Bhutan	157		
India	884 (763–LDCs)	38.4	56.5
Maldives	671	74.5	57.6
Nepal	1,310 (1,301–LDCs)	64.0	46.4
Pakistan	1,183	17.2	34.0
Sri Lanka	1,065	51.7	47.0

Source: Based on Weerakoon and Thennakoon (2008), Table 3, p. 141 and Table 4, p. 143.

of lists every four years; this is ambiguous in contrast to ASEAN, which explicitly requires that member countries phase out their negative list products in five installments. Thus, overall there appears to be little will and commitment to trade liberalization under SAFTA.

The Challenges and Future Prospects

Although it is evident that SAFTA has not been a successful agreement in terms of increasing intra-regional penetration, one needs to examine whether this failure is primarily due to the limitations of SAFTA mentioned earlier (that is, its modalities and scope), or whether there are region or country-specific characteristics which pose fundamental challenges to regional integration in South Asia. In other words, would SAFTA have been a success story had it involved wider product coverage and more extensive liberalization commitments, or does this region fail to fulfil certain basic preconditions for successful regional integration? Most studies on South Asian integration tend to conclude that many of these conditions are not met and that there are basic challenges to achieving deeper economic integration in this region which preclude success under SAFTA as it currently stands.

Some of the main preconditions for a successful FTA include geographical proximity and reduced transportation and communication costs, trade complementarity, low non-tariff barriers, political will and stability, and streamlined factor and product markets to enable smooth allocation decisions and speedy distribution. According to several studies on South Asian integration, barring the criterion of geographic proximity, the economies in this region fail to meet most of the other criteria and thus SAFTA cannot be expected to yield any major welfare gains in terms of improved allocation efficiency, increased production, and changes in trade pattern, especially in the smaller countries.

First and foremost, there is considerable overlap in the trade basket of the member countries. Currently, the South Asian countries trade in similar goods, exporting items, such as textiles and apparel and importing items, such as crude oil. (Coupled with this is the fact that where there are potential opportunities for increased trade, such as imports of raw materials for final goods production as in textiles, such items have generally not been granted concessions under SAFTA). An examination of the trade structure within the region shows an underlying mismatch between import and export structures for most of the member countries. The Revealed Comparative Advantage (RCA) indices for the main exported items are similar for many of the countries in this region indicating competition in exports rather than complementarities.[10] Hence, the South Asian countries fail to meet the natural trading partner hypothesis which states that members of a regional agreement should trade disproportionately with each other in order to be a successful bloc. Only the smaller landlocked countries of Bhutan and Nepal have a disproportionate share of trade with the region, that too mainly due to their dependence on trade with India, while none of the other economies account for a significant part of their trade with the region. Trade volume data (including conservative estimates of informal trade) suggest that the South Asian countries are not 'natural trading partners'. This is also supported by evidence on the trade intensity indices which are asymmetric and have been declining, except in the case of India and Nepal. Thus, due to similarities in trade and production structures, the South Asian countries are likely to remain dependent on other regions for sourcing key imports and for their export markets, posing challenges to increasing intra-regional trade.[11]

A second inherent challenge in deepening regional integration is that most of the markets in this region are small and relatively undeveloped. The

[10] The measure of the RCA, also known as the Balassa Index, is the ratio of the share of a country's exports of a particular product (or group of products) in a country's exports to another country/reference region/the world to the share of that same product in the other country/region/world's exports.

[11] A key driver would be India and the extent to which it provides greater access to its market and provides scope for product complementarities and diversification of trade profiles given its more diversified trade and production structure. The relatively high intra-regional trade shares for manufactured goods (automobiles, pharmaceuticals, and agricultural equipment) in the case of India indicate that there is potential for India to act as a source of industrial products for other countries in the region and to enable diversification in the intra-regional trade basket.

region constitutes less than 5 per cent of the world in terms of GDP and if India is excluded, its share drops to 0.4 per cent (Panagariya 2007). Although in terms of population, the region provides a significant market, the low per capita incomes and purchasing power remain a constraint. Trade flows are also very small relative to those in the rest of the world. Hence, barring India, most of the economies in this region are not inherently attractive markets for exports. Given such small markets, the scope for trade creation is limited and the probability of efficient suppliers being based within the region is low.

A third constraint to regional integration is poor connectivity in terms of transport and communication links and infrastructural bottlenecks which undermine the advantages of geographic and cultural proximity. The significance of these constraints is evident from the importance that has been given in recent years to the issue of trade facilitation and improved connectivity at SAARC summits. These bottlenecks constitute some of the most important non-tariff barriers to trade within the region. As argued in a recent study (Moinuddin 2008), the geographical proximity argument (that countries in relative geographical proximity tend to trade more with each other than with more distant countries owing to lower transport and communications costs), does not hold for South Asia in general. While there is regional trade centered around India, there is little or no trade among the smaller countries, such as Bhutan, the Maldives, and Nepal. It has been argued that apart from factors such as small markets, low purchasing power, and lack of trade complementarities other factors, such as transport and logistical impediments have raised transaction costs for intra-regional trade and contributed to the low levels of trade within South Asia. Thus, South Asia does not appear to fit the hypothesis that geography is an important determinant of trade.

A fourth factor impeding economic integration in South Asia is the relatively high and dispersed levels of protection in most of the South Asian countries, especially when compared to other developing countries. The simple average of the applied duties in non-agricultural goods ranges from 10 per cent in Sri Lanka to 21 per cent in Bangladesh. In India, this tariff is approximately 20 per cent. In agriculture, the level of protection is even higher and ranges from 25 per cent in Pakistan to 100 per cent in India.[12] Moreover, the political economy dynamics in South Asia have tended to take a defensive approach to trade liberalization within the region, with domestic interest groups lobbying for exclusions from tariff reductions and free trade, especially in those sectors where competition is more likely, and

---

[12] Based on various studies on trade in South Asia and on SAARC, for instance, Weerakoon and Thennakoon (2008) and Panagariya (2007).

for strict rules of origin. In contrast, the countries have been much more willing to liberalize trade vis-à-vis countries outside the region. Hence, the region is characterized by pressures that would result in trade diversion as opposed to trade creation.

Finally, political problems have been a major constraint to economic integration as countries (especially Pakistan and India) have been unwilling to increase interdependence, communication has often broken down among the major players in the region, and security concerns and political tensions have put a dampener on regional negotiations. Political will to fast track regional trade liberalization has been lacking and the currently agreed timeframe of 2016 for implementing the free trade area may be of little import given the liberalization that is likely to be undertaken by the SAARC member countries in multilateral and extra-regional contexts in the near future. As argued by some experts, SAFTA needs to follow the open regionalism approach of ASEAN and not allow political differences to stand in the way of economic goals.

Overall, the conditions and regional characteristics do not appear to be conducive to deeper economic integration in South Asia.[13] As has been argued in Pitigala (2005), the countries might be better off pursuing unilateral trade liberalization as the gains from regional trade liberalization are likely to be very limited and mostly confined to India.[14] Some studies also point to greater potential returns for South Asian countries from pursuing integration with other regional blocs, such as EU or ASEAN, rather than going ahead with SAFTA.[15] What then is the impetus for SAFTA? As noted in Panagariya (2007), the impetus for SAFTA is probably political, such as the need to enter into a regional trade agreement as most other regional blocs are doing so, or to respond to trade diversion effects on the region arising from the formation of other trade blocs in Europe and Latin America, and most importantly, to improve political relations among the members (Panagariya 2007).[16]

---

[13] It has been noted, however, that the sizeable amount of unrecorded trade among South Asian countries indicates that the level of complementarity may be better than that captured by data and that there may be scope for increased trade within the region.

[14] For SAFTA to be meaningful, there would need to be minimization of sectoral/product exclusions, simpler rules of origin, and MFN-based trade between India and Pakistan.

[15] See Rodriguez-Delgado (2007).

[16] A recent ADB report argues that SAFTA can serve as a stepping stone to a full-fledged FTA in Asia and for a pan-Asian trade bloc that can integrate the various sub-regional blocs (SAARC, ASEAN, CAREC, and East Asia) to achieve greater economic prosperity and stability in Asia. See ADB (2008a).

Can SAFTA Deliver More?

Although the evaluation of regional integration efforts and outcomes in South Asia is not encouraging, one must recognize that much of this assessment is based on the current trade pattern which is dominated by merchandise products, and based on the current modalities and coverage under SAFTA, with all the aforementioned limitations. Thus, one needs to ask if SAFTA might have better prospects and could potentially yield greater gains if it were to take a different shape, and if so, what shape it would need to take.

An indication to this effect is provided by the declarations at recent SAARC summits and proposed initiatives which suggest that SAFTA needs to move beyond goods to cover services and investment issues if it is to realize its full potential and be meaningful. The Declaration of the 14th SAARC Summit stressed that integration of services into the agreement is a necessity and that member countries should aim towards the conclusion of a service sector agreement (called SAFAS—the SAARC Agreement on Trade in Services) at the earliest. This point was also echoed at the recently held first South Asia Economic Summit (held alongside the SAARC summit from 28 to 30 August 2008 in Colombo). The Summit Declaration stated that 'There is a need to finalise the SAARC Agreement on Trade in Services (SAFAS) without further delay. Extending SAFTA to include services would considerably broaden its scope and impact and boost competitiveness in key emerging sectors such as banking, communications, and aviation.'[17] In recognition of the significance of the service sector for all countries in the region, initiatives have been proposed in key services such as energy, transport, communication, and healthcare.

The need to include services is consistent with a point made in several studies which note the exclusion of services as a serious limitation of SAFTA. These authors argue that the prospects for services integration are brighter than for goods in South Asia and that services trade is more likely to result in trade creation as opposed to trade diversion for a variety of reasons.[18] Some of the reasons highlighted include the higher capacity of the member countries in producing and trading services, the growing importance of services in all the South Asian countries, the relatively greater role of geographic, cultural, and linguistic ties in services as opposed to goods trade, and the relatively greater homogeneity among the South Asian countries with regard to trade and investment liberalization policies in services. These studies also

[17] This is the first South Asia Economic Summit Statement.
[18] See, for instance, SATIN (2008).

highlight the wide range of potential benefits that could accrue from the inclusion of services. Some of the identified potential benefits include helping upgrade the region's services infrastructure and services delivery thus reducing transaction costs and also bolstering goods trade; enabling joint projects in areas such as education and healthcare to promote social sector goals; leveraging the advantage of geographic proximity to build partnerships in areas such as banking, IT, telecommunications, ports, and aviation services; fostering cross-border energy investments and promoting a regional energy trade to take advantage of complementarities in energy resources within the region; and promoting cross-border flows of people to facilitate tourism and business activities. Interestingly, studies which outline a desirable agenda for furthering integration in South Asia typically involve five or six key elements which all relate to service sector integration, such as strengthening transport and communication linkages, or fostering cooperation in tourism, education, and healthcare.

Overall, there appears to be some ground to argue that while SAFTA may not be a successful agreement as it stands today, if it were to become broader in scope by including services and investment, it may be much more successful. It may provide the much needed dynamism to regional integration efforts in South Asia, and potentially also help overcome some of the factors that have constrained intra-regional trade in goods thus far. The following chapter examines the validity of these arguments regarding the potential role that services can play in South Asian integration, by examining recent trends in the service sector in this region.

2

Why Services Integration?

It is evident from the preceding discussion that there has been a general lack of dynamism and political will to push regional integration efforts within South Asia. Although there has been progress on the bilateral front between the SAARC member countries, such as under the ISLFTA between India and Sri Lanka, and more recently the bilateral Comprehensive Economic Partnership Agreement (CEPA) which includes services and investment, or the FTA between Pakistan and Sri Lanka, or the bilateral agreements between India and Nepal and India and Bhutan, a major stumbling block for the region has been the bilateral relationship between India and Pakistan. Trade and investment relations between these two largest member countries of SAARC, have hardly shown any progress, often souring due to deteriorating political relations and dampening prospects for deeper integration within the region. Added to these political dynamics are several characteristics inherent to this region, such as its limited market size and purchasing power, the competing production and trade structures of member countries, and inadequacies in physical infrastructure and governance, which have greatly constrained regional integration.

Given this background, is an expansion of SAFTA to include services justified? Would services integration be subject to these same problems or are there certain characteristics exhibited by the service sector in the SAARC countries that may enhance the prospects for regional integration? A close examination of recent trends in and various performance indicators for the service sector in individual SAARC member countries, and the region as a whole seems to suggest that the grounds for services integration may be much stronger than those for goods and that the potential for complementarities and congruence of interests and policy approaches is likely to be much greater in services than in the case of goods.

Services Growth and Contribution to Output[1]

In South Asia, services have clearly outperformed other sectors of the economy in terms of exhibiting higher growth combined with less volatility. The average annual growth rate in service sector output has consistently moved upward, from a little under 4.5 per cent in the 1970s, to a little over 6 per cent in the 1980s, over 6.5 per cent in the 1990s, and further to 8.3 per cent in 2000–7. Although the manufacturing sector in the region has also shown an upward trend in growth, its performance has been less steady than in the case of services, with the average annual growth rate rising to a little over 7 per cent in the 1980s, then dropping to less than 6 per cent in the 1990s, and rising to around 6.5 per cent in the current decade. Agricultural growth has not only been much lower but also highly volatile.

Services have been a key driver of overall economic growth in South Asia since the 1990s. Services have consistently outperformed overall GDP growth, thus helping pull up overall economic growth in the region and compensating for volatility in other sectors.[2] Figure 2.1 highlights trends

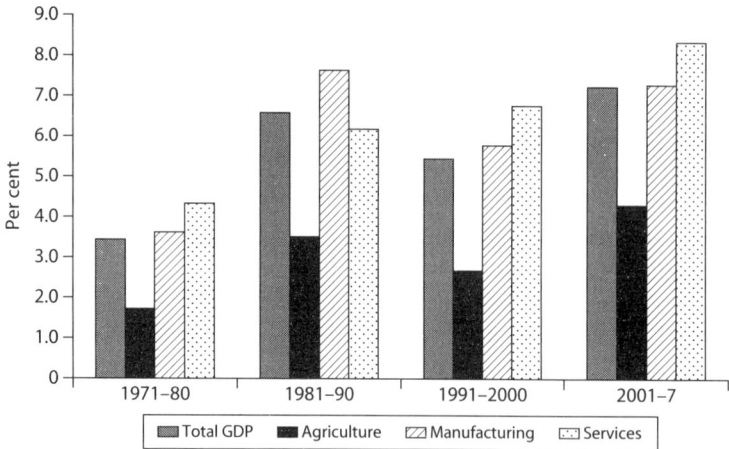

Figure 2.1   Trends in Overall and Sectoral Growth in South Asia, CAGR (constant 1991 prices)

Source: Author's calculations based on UN statistical database (online version).

---

[1] Most of the discussion in this section is based on data from the UN online statistical database and the UNCTAD *Handbook of Statistics 2008* (online version), unless otherwise indicated.

[2] The sector 'utilities', that is, electricity, gas, and water supply, has been included under the manufacturing sector. If utilities are to be considered as a part of the service sector (as the rest of this book does), there will accordingly be changes in the relative shares of manufacturing and service sectors in South Asia's GDP.

Table 2.1   Trends in South Asia's GDP and Sectoral Composition, 1980–
2006 (US$ mn and per cent shares)

	1980	1990	1995	2000	2006
Total South Asian GDP	245,722	429,139	511,555	619,201	1,155,549
Agriculture	33.0	26.9	24.3	21.9	18.3
Industry	21.4	23.9	24.5	51.8	25.0
Services	36.4	39.1	42.2	46.3	48.7

Source: Author's calculations based on the UN statistical database (online version).

in individual sectors and in total GDP for the South Asian region over the past three decades and in recent years.

The relatively superior performance of the service sector over the previous decades has also resulted in the sector's growing contribution to South Asia's GDP. Interestingly, this increased share has been directly at the expense of the agricultural sector, with agriculture's share in the region's GDP declining from 33 per cent to around 18 per cent and that of services increasing from 36 per cent to nearly 50 per cent over the 1980–2006 period, almost exactly offsetting the decline in agriculture. The industrial sector's contribution has increased only marginally over this period and has largely been stagnant. Table 2.1 shows the trends in the sectoral breakdown of GDP in South Asia.

If one compares the evolution of South Asia's sectoral composition and trends with that of other regions, developing and developed (with some exceptions), one finds broadly the same pattern, with the contribution of services showing an upward trend. However, what is interesting to note is that South Asia emerges as the region which, barring Southern Africa, has experienced the largest increase in the share of services in GDP in the past decade and a half, even though it does not have the highest contribution of services to total output. Between 1990 and 2006, services share in South Asia's GDP increased by nearly 10 per cent, while the increase in this sector's share in most of the other regions was quite marginal, less consistent in terms of the trajectory, and in some cases the sector also declined in importance in these other regions. South Asia is also the only region within Asia that has experienced an increase in services contribution and when compared with Sub-Saharan Africa, a region consisting of countries with comparable levels of income, the contribution of services is several percentage points higher. Thus, South Asia stands out in terms of the service sector's growing role in value added. The difference in sectoral trends between South Asia and other developing regions is evident from Table 2.2.

Similarly, a comparison of South Asia's growth performance vis-à-vis other regions shows a relatively higher growth rate for services output through the 1990s and in recent years, as shown in Table 2.3. Among

Table 2.2   Services Contribution to GDP in Different Regions, 1990–2006 (per cent)

Regions	1990	1995	2000	2006
World	**61.4**	**65.0**	**67.2**	**67.0**
Southern Africa	54.4	60.6	63.9	64.8
Sub-Saharan Africa	42.6	48.2	45.7	45.0
Caribbean	66.7	67.4	65.7	68.6
South America	56.7	58.1	58.4	53.4
Eastern Asia	44.5	47.7	50.2	49.0
Western Asia	47.5	49.8	46.5	45.6
Southeast Asia (ASEAN)	48.2	48.9	48.0	46.9
South Asia excluding Afghanistan	**43.5**	**46.4**	**50.2**	**52.9**
European Union (EU-27)	63.5	67.2	69.7	71.3
North America (Canada + USA)	68.2	69.5	70.0	71.5

Source: Author's calculations based on the UN statistical database (online version).

Table 2.3   CAGR of Services GDP in Different Regions, 1991–5 to 2001–6 (per cent)

		1991–5	1996–2000	2001–6
World	**GDP**	**5.062**	**1.009**	**7.416**
	Services	**5.852**	**1.789**	**6.939**
Southern Africa	GDP	4.741	−1.381	12.956
	Services	6.275	−0.774	13.159
Sub-Saharan Africa	GDP	0.252	0.668	12.942
	Services	2.009	0.014	12.552
Caribbean	GDP	5.025	5.454	6.916
	Services	3.791	5.348	7.531
South America	GDP	10.232	−2.002	8.694
	Services	9.061	−2.346	6.820
Eastern Asia	GDP	11.010	2.927	10.413
	Services	11.214	4.595	9.725
Western Asia	GDP	3.398	4.443	14.892
	Services	3.315	3.688	13.553
Southeast Asia (ASEAN)	GDP	11.277	−4.566	10.863
	Services	11.661	−4.303	10.184
South Asia (excl. Afghanistan)	**GDP**	**5.139**	**2.960**	**10.728**
	Services	**6.077**	**4.872**	**11.232**
of which India	**GDP**	**4.973**	**3.729**	**10.978**
	Services	**5.819**	**6.166**	**11.605**
European Union (EU-27)	GDP	4.075	−1.998	9.187
	Services	4.755	−1.488	9.455
North America (Canada + USA)	GDP	3.929	4.620	4.996
	Services	4.162	5.385	5.038

Source: Author's calculations based on the UN statistical database (online version).

the developing regions, it is the only one that has consistently exhibited a higher growth rate for services than for overall GDP, again indicating the importance of this sector in driving overall growth. A point to note is that the region's overall and service sector growth performance also closely mirrors India's overall and service sector specific growth experience as India has been the main driver of services growth in South Asia (an issue discussed in further detail later in this chapter).

The regional picture also holds at the individual country level. Although the relative performance of services in terms of the sector's growth rate and also how this compares to overall GDP growth varies across the seven countries, a broad common pattern emerges. Services have been growing faster than the rest of the economy in all these countries, thereby helping raise overall GDP growth, and increasing their contribution to domestic output over time.

Owing to these trends, services today occupy over half of GDP in all the countries of South Asia (Table 2.4), ranging from a low of about 53 per cent in the case of Nepal to over 80 per cent in the case of the Maldives. The sector's contribution has increased steadily in each of the South Asian economies through the 1990s and till recently, mainly

Table 2.4 Sectoral Composition of GDP in South Asian Countries (per cent)

		1980	1985	1990	1995	2000	2007
Bangladesh	Agriculture	40.70	38.28	34.65	30.06	29.52	24.49
	Manufacturing	13.66	12.95	14.35	17.81	18.00	20.88
	Services	45.64	48.77	51.00	52.13	52.48	54.62
Bhutan	Agriculture	55.16	51.19	39.03	31.07	22.30	16.81
	Manufacturing	3.12	5.51	18.82	19.67	13.05	12.71
	Services	41.72	43.30	42.15	49.26	64.65	70.48
India	Agriculture	37.15	33.80	30.20	25.93	21.99	17.83
	Manufacturing	17.88	19.72	21.87	23.26	22.11	21.57
	Services	44.98	46.47	47.93	50.81	55.90	60.60
Maldives	Agriculture	15.60	15.56	14.90	11.01	8.43	6.26
	Manufacturing	10.06	10.04	9.95	10.01	11.34	10.81
	Services	74.35	74.40	75.14	78.98	80.23	82.93
Nepal	Agriculture	47.54	48.78	47.21	39.58	36.80	37.05
	Manufacturing	4.85	6.48	6.94	9.70	10.47	9.94
	Services	47.61	44.74	45.86	50.72	52.73	53.01
Pakistan	Agriculture	30.11	26.57	24.89	25.38	24.26	20.90
	Manufacturing	18.79	20.59	22.81	22.40	22.93	25.39
	Services	51.10	52.84	52.30	52.23	52.81	53.71
Sri Lanka	Agriculture	30.64	28.71	25.33	21.98	18.76	15.59
	Manufacturing	20.59	20.59	23.72	26.39	28.95	28.80
	Services	48.77	50.70	50.94	51.63	52.29	55.61

Source: Author's calculations based on the UN statistical database (online version).

Table 2.5   Service Sector GDP and Growth in South Asian Countries (US$ mn at 1990 prices and per cent)

	Services Sector GDP				Compound Annual Growth Rate (%)		
	1980	1990	2000	2007	1980–90	1990–2000	2000–7
Bangladesh	9,244.02	15,039.03	24,711.07	37,959.77	5.0	5.1	6.3
Bhutan	47.19	115.53	364.66	790.08	9.4	12.2	11.7
India	76,046.83	140,299.83	285,647.78	516,334.77	6.3	7.4	8.8
Maldives	48.75	147.18	335.95	551.29	11.7	8.6	7.3
Nepal	1,181.78	1,789.93	3,352.04	4,106.86	4.2	6.5	2.9
Pakistan	14,400.86	26,731.11	39,841.91	62,070.44	6.4	4.1	6.5
Sri Lanka	1,944.10	3,247.38	5,711.42	8,376.43	5.3	5.8	5.6

Source: Author's calculations based on the UN statistical database (online version).

offsetting the declining contribution of agriculture, as seen at the overall regional level, with manufacturing remaining largely stagnant or increasing its share only marginally. The two smallest economies of the Maldives and Bhutan are highly dependent on services, reflecting the absence of a diversified economic base as well as heavy dependence on a few service sub-sectors (as seen later in this chapter).

There is, however, considerable asymmetry across the seven countries in terms of the relative size of the service sector, and also in terms of the relative growth performance over the last two decades (Table 2.5).

The service sector in India is almost 1,000 times that of the smallest economy in South Asia, the Maldives, and is around eight times larger than that of the second largest economy, Pakistan. This naturally reflects significant differences in capacity, scope, and potential in services across the countries in this region. The differences in growth performance are also quite revealing. While the comparatively higher growth rates for Bhutan and the Maldives can be explained by the small base of service sector output, they also reflect potential niches within the service sector as also captured earlier by the very high shares of services in their GDPs and as shown later in the disaggregated services data. The fluctuating trends in their growth rates also reflect the possible vulnerability of these economies to trends in specific segments of the service sector on which they are more dependent. In contrast, India exhibits a sustained high growth rate, which has also increased over time, reflecting the country's growing capacity and potential in this sector. For the remaining countries, the service sector exhibits more moderate and at times fluctuating growth rates. These are also countries where the service sector has not been as significant in driving the overall

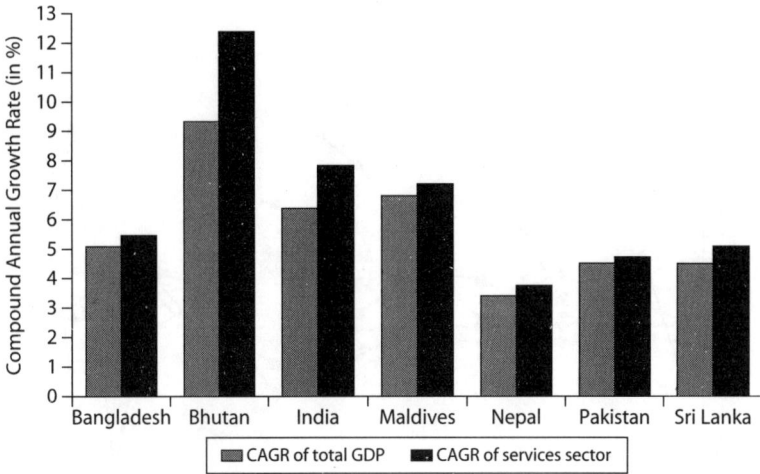

Figure 2.2   CAGR of Total GDP and in Service Sector in SAARC
             Countries, 1995–2007

Source: Author's calculations based on the UN statistical database (online version).

growth trajectory, as also seen in Figure 2.2. Nepal exhibits the weakest and most unsteady growth performance over the given time period.

This variability in growth rates is also evident from the annual growth performance in services for the countries in this region. Figure 2.3 illustrates that while for the larger countries, the annual growth rate has been relatively consistent in the range of 4–8 per cent, the smaller economies of Bhutan and the Maldives have exhibited very high and low growth rates, with extreme swings in some years. As noted earlier, these swings most likely reflect their over-dependence on a few services such as tourism that are susceptible to external conditions and exogenous shocks.

These significant differences in service sector performance are indicative of the potential complementarities in services within the region, which have a bearing on the scope for intra-regional integration and collaboration in services and likely asymmetries in the role to be played by the different countries in this integration process and also in the resulting distribution of costs and benefits.

Sub-sectoral trends in services output across the countries also highlight the differences in scope and potential. An examination of the disaggregated composition of services GDP indicates the areas where each of the countries has exhibited higher and relatively sustained growth, segments in which some of the South Asian economies are highly dependent and

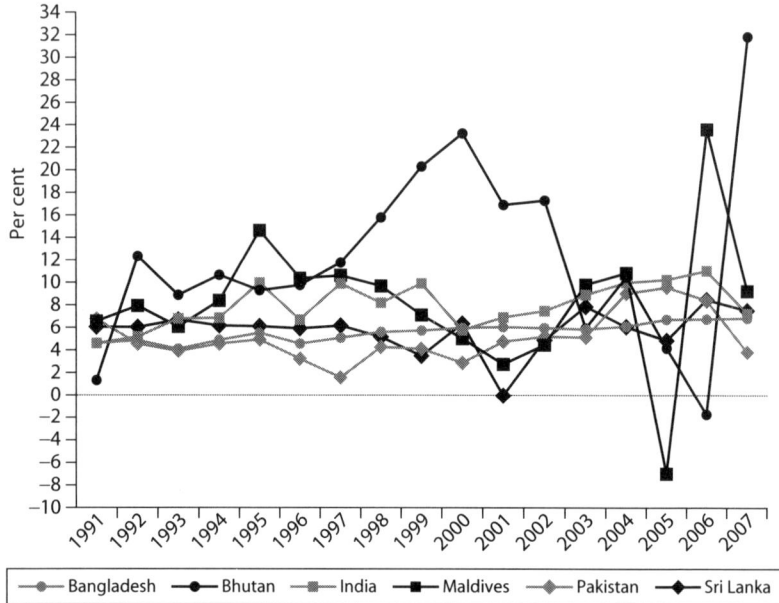

Figure 2.3   Annual Growth Rate of Services in SAARC Countries, 1991–2007 (constant 1991 prices)

Source: Author's calculations based on the UN statistical database (online version).

potential areas of complementarity and competition across countries in the South Asia region. Table 2.6 provides a detailed summary of the sub-sectoral composition of services GDP in each of the seven South Asian countries and their CAGRs for 2001–7.[3] Those sub-sectors that have registered growth rates of 8 per cent are highlighted to help identify commonalities and differences in these trends across the countries.

Table 2.6 shows that although the sub-sectoral composition of GDP varies considerably across the different countries in this region, there are also similarities. Notwithstanding differences in data classification and availability, by and large services, such as construction, wholesale and

[3] As the definition of services and sub-sectoral classification varies from country to country on account of differences in the national accounts tabulation and data collection procedures, no pooling together of sub-sectoral composition of services GDP has been attempted for the region. Such procedural differences in services statistics are a point to be noted as they do constrain a researcher's ability to synthesize available information in a standardized and statistically accurate manner. Initiatives taken by SAARC in recent meetings on this issue are indeed important.

Table 2.6 Sector-wise Composition of Services GDP in South Asian Countries (2001, 2007) and CAGR (2001–7)

Country	Service Sectors	Share in Services GDP (%)		CAGR (%)
		2001	2007	
BANGLADESH	**Total services**	**100.0**	**100.0**	**5.42**
1	Power and water supply	2.50	2.71	6.67
2	Construction	13.86	15.29	6.91
3	Wholesale and retail trade	23.12	23.65	5.76
4	Hotels and restaurants	1.10	1.16	6.23
5	Transport, storage, and communication	16.16	17.04	6.22
6	Financial intermediaries	2.70	2.89	6.47
7	Real estate renting and business activities	14.94	12.76	3.08
8	Public administration and defence	4.39	4.59	6.10
9	Education	3.84	4.24	6.94
10	Health and social work	3.75	3.82	5.66
11	Community, social, and personal services	13.65	11.84	3.30
		2000	2006	
BHUTAN	**Total services**	**100.0**	**100.0**	**8.01**
1	Electricity, gas, and water supply	13.80	15.86	10.17
2	Construction	16.90	15.17	6.35
3	Wholesale and retail trade	5.40	6.95	11.99
4	Hotels and restaurants	0.54	0.88	15.82
5	Transport, storage, and communication	11.02	11.24	8.32
6	Financial, insurance, and real estate			11.00
6.1	Finance and insurance	4.79	7.90	16.02
6.2	Real estate and dwellings	3.86	2.57	1.90
7	Community and social services	17.23	14.22	5.09
8	Public administration	12.55	10.69	5.56
9	Education and health	4.68	3.53	3.74
10	Private social, personal, and recreational services	0.59	0.52	6.17
		2001–1	2006–7	
INDIA	**Total services**	**100.0**	**100.0**	**8.05**
1	Electricity, gas, and water supply	4.16	3.31	4.51
2	Construction	9.93	11.24	9.66
3	Trade, hotels, and restaurants			7.59
3.1	Trade	22.30	21.71	7.29
3.2	Hotels and restaurants	2.18	2.31	8.55
4	Transport, storage, and communication			12.49
4.1	Railways	2.01	1.83	6.27
4.2	Transport by other means	8.13	8.23	7.89
4.3	Storage	0.14	0.10	2.24
4.4	Communication	3.30	7.67	21.46

(Contd . . .)

(*Table 2.6 contd . . .*)

Country	Service Sectors	Share in Services GDP (%)		CAGR (%)
5	Financing, insurance, real estate, and business services			8.25
5.1	Banking and insurance	9.49	10.43	9.17
5.2	Real estate and ownership of dwellings	12.78	11.92	6.63
6	Community, social, and personal services			5.18
6.1	Public administration and defence	11.42	8.80	3.77
6.2	Other services	14.16	12.45	5.74
		2001	2007	
MALDIVES	**Total services**	**100.0**	**100.0**	**6.91**
1	Electricity, gas, and water supply	4.00	4.94	10.20
2	Construction	4.07	6.84	15.14
3	Wholesale and retail trade	5.10	4.27	4.24
4	Tourism	36.97	30.97	4.24
5	Transport and communication	16.50	20.94	10.61
6	Finance	3.89	3.32	4.50
7	Real estate	8.96	6.76	2.69
8	Business services	3.33	2.65	3.48
9	Government administration	14.71	17.61	9.69
10	Education, health, and social services	2.47	1.71	1.46
		2002–3	2006–7	
NEPAL	**Total services**	**100.0**	**100.0**	**13.54**
1	Electricity, gas, and water	4.18	4.22	13.79
2	Construction	21.95	11.03	−1.07
3	Wholesale and retail trade	19.61	23.56	17.78
4	Hotels and restaurants	0.00	2.91	2.90
5	Transport, storage, and communication	14.82	15.74	14.91
6	Financial intermediation	19.65	7.17	−7.20
7	Real estate renting and business	0.00	13.53	3.17
8	Public administration and defence	0.00	3.36	3.46
9	Education	0.00	10.63	2.73
10	Health and social work	0.00	2.44	4.02
11	Other community, social, and personal services	19.79	5.40	−12.42
		2000–1	2007–8	
PAKISTAN	**Total services**	**100.0**	**100.0**	**5.44**
1	Electricity, gas, and water supply	5.81	2.97	−3.07
2	Construction	4.24	4.64	6.64
3	Transport, storage, and communication	20.38	17.44	3.40
4	Wholesale and retail trade	31.35	29.70	4.72
5	Finance and insurance	5.43	11.28	15.53

(*Contd . . .*)

(*Table 2.6 contd . . .*)

Country	Service Sectors	Share in Services GDP (%)		CAGR (%)
6	Ownership of dwellings	5.53	4.60	3.03
7	Public administration and defence	10.87	11.32	5.97
8	Community, social, and personal services	16.38	18.06	6.73
		2002	2007	
SRI LANKA	**Total services**	**100.0**	**100.0**	**5.97**
1	Electricity and water			
1.1	Electricity	2.76	3.16	8.40
1.2	Gas	0.35	0.30	3.11
1.3	Water	0.19	0.16	3.29
2	Construction	9.30	9.35	6.07
3	Wholesale and retail trade			
3.1	Import trade	13.87	13.28	5.20
3.2	Export trade	7.16	6.79	5.05
3.3	Domestic trade	15.01	15.63	6.69
4	Hotels and restaurants	0.32	0.60	17.70
5	Transport and communication			
5.1	Transport	14.21	15.80	7.86
5.2	Cargo handling—ports and civil aviation	0.95	0.97	6.21
5.3	Post and telecommunication	0.93	1.98	20.30
6	Banking, insurance, and real estate etc.	12.08	12.64	6.78
7	Ownership of dwellings	6.33	4.73	0.95
8	Government services	12.88	11.19	3.53
9	Private services	3.67	3.43	4.77

Source: Author's calculations based on National Accounts Statistics of all countries from Central Bank documents, Statistical Bureaus, and other official sources.

retail trade and distribution, communication, and transport are the most significant contributors to GDP (around 12–20 per cent) in the South Asian countries. One exception is the Maldives, where tourism services dominate, contributing over a third of GDP. It is also worth noting that government services or public administration related services, which are non-commercial in nature, occupy a significant share of GDP in several countries in this region, indicating that part of the growth of services is non-tradable in nature. In terms of growth trends, communication services tend to exhibit the highest growth, registering growth rates of over 10 per cent in most of the countries. Financial services have also grown rapidly in several of the countries.

These sub-sectoral trends in terms of GDP contribution and growth reflect the importance of a variety of factors in shaping service sector performance in South Asia. These factors include deregulation and policy reforms in areas, such as telecommunications and financial services, the role of rising incomes and domestic demand in driving growth in segments, such as trade and distribution services, and the lack of diversification in the case of smaller economies like the Maldives. The sub-sectoral composition also indicates the importance of non-commercial services, such as public administration, government services, and community, social and personal services in some of the countries. This reflects the role of domestically oriented provision and consumption in driving services growth in this region. Hence, one can infer that general growth dynamics of rising incomes and consumption, liberalization and reform measures undertaken in services, and the role of the public sector in services delivery are likely to play an important role in determining the scope for intra-regional trade, investment, and collaboration in services within South Asia.

Services Contribution to Employment

Official statistics for many of the countries suggest that the share of services in employment has increased in the last 20 years. However, the sector's role as a source of employment in South Asia has not been commensurate with its contribution to output and overall growth. The rate of growth of employment in services has been far lower than the rate of growth of GDP in services posing challenges for job creation. Although one could argue that there are problems with the availability of data on employment (particularly with regard to informal and contractual activities which cover many service sector transactions), thus making it difficult to properly capture the full contribution of services to employment, the limited national accounts and labour survey data that are available suggest that services growth in South Asia has not been very employment-intensive. As some studies have argued, services growth may in part reflect increased total factor productivity as opposed to increased factor accumulation.[4] Figure 2.4 shows the divergence between services contribution to GDP and its contribution to employment in each of the seven countries in this region.

As shown in Figure 2.4, in all seven countries, the contribution of services to GDP is greater than its contribution to employment by around 10 per cent or more. The discrepancy is highest in the case of Nepal where the service sector contributes to 53 per cent of GDP but only 18 per cent

---

[4] See Banga and Goldar (2004) and Singh (2006).

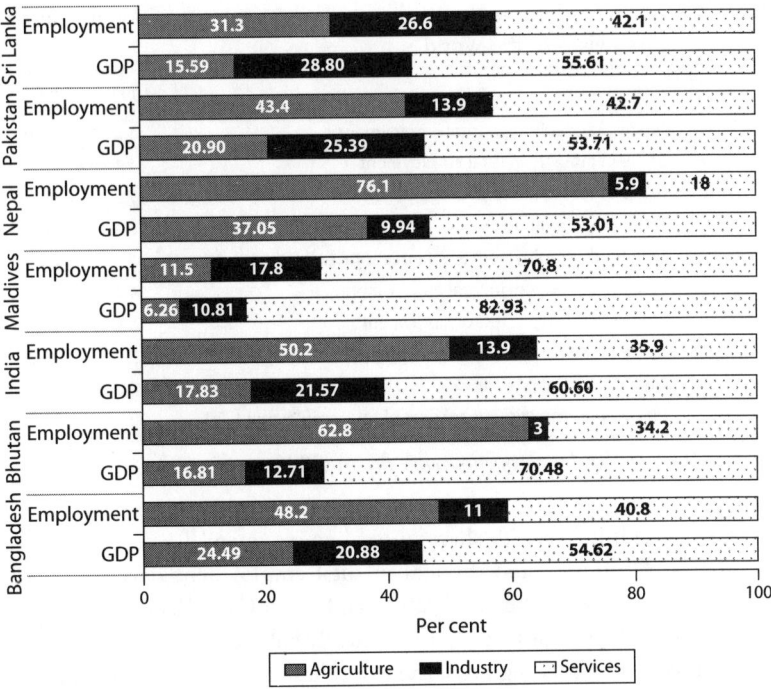

Figure 2.4 Services Contribution to GDP and Employment in South Asian Countries

Source: Based on National Accounts Statistics and labour surveys of various countries.

to employment. Likewise in India, which has shown the most consistent rise in the service sector's contribution to GDP, the sector's contribution to employment remains much lower, at 35 per cent. The only country where services constitute a significant share of employment is the Maldives, again reflecting the high dependence of this economy on certain service segments and the general lack of diversification. This divergence between services contribution to GDP as opposed to employment has led some researchers and analysts to term the growth of the service sector as 'jobless growth' and to raise questions about the sustainability of a services led growth paradigm given the sector's inability to generate jobs in a manner commensurate with its growing importance in output and overall growth.

If one compares the employment trends in services in South Asia with those seen in the rest of the world, however, a broad similar pattern emerges. Table 2.7 provides a comparison of the employment situation in South Asia vis-à-vis the world.

Table 2.7   Select Indicators Comparing the Employment Situation in South
Asia vis-à-vis the World

	Indicator	1997	2007
World	Share of agriculture in total employment	41.4	34.9
	Share of industry in total employment	21.1	22.4
	Share of services in total employment	37.5	42.7
	Unemployment rate (%)	6.1	6.0
	Vulnerable employment as share of total employment (%)	52.8	49.9
South Asia	Share of agriculture in total employment	59.4	48
	Share of industry in total employment	15.3	21.7
	Share of services in total employment	25.2	30.3
	Unemployment rate (%)	4.7	5.1
	Vulnerable employment as share of total employment (%)	80	77.2

Source: ILO, *Global Employment Trends Report* (2008).

The agricultural sector's share in total employment has declined while
the shares of industry and services in total employment have increased.
However, as noted by the ILO's 2007 and 2008 GET Reports, although
the agricultural sector still accounts for nearly half of the total employment
in South Asia, no other region of the world has seen a faster decline in agricultural employment over the past decade. It is interesting to note that the
industrial sector in South Asia has shown a greater increase in employment
than the service sector (6.4 per cent increase as opposed to 4.9 per cent
between 1997 and 2007), which contrasts with the industrial sector's much
lower contribution to GDP when compared to services. Hence, as pointed
out by the ILO, industry has tended to be more employment-intensive
compared to services in South Asia.

The ILO statistics further suggest that the service sector, despite its
significance in shaping overall growth in the South Asian economies, has
not been able to adequately address the need to create long-term quality
jobs in the South Asian region, and the millennium development goal
(MDG) to 'achieve full and productive employment and decent work for
all, including women and young people'.[5] According to the GET Reports,
77.2 per cent of those employed remain vulnerable. Moreover, available data on gender disaggregation of services employment indicate that
the share of males employed in services in most South Asian economies
exceeds that for females. The ILO, and several other studies, also note that
the share of informal and contract based employment in services is high,

[5] Millennium Development Goals Target 2, United Nations.

raising concerns about the long-term sustainability of jobs in the service sector and the vulnerability of those employed in services.

A sector-wise disaggregation of the trends in employment in the service sector reveals that those segments which constitute a larger share of GDP also tend to constitute a larger share of employment (Table 2.8). These include construction, wholesale and retail trade, and public administration services which account for around half or more of service sector employment in most of the South Asian economies. However, it is not necessarily the case that segments which have exhibited higher growth, such as financial services or hotel and restaurant services, also account for a high share of employment, again suggesting the point made earlier, that the pattern

Table 2.8 Sector-wise Disaggregation of Service Sector Employment in South Asian Countries (per cent)

Sector	Bangladesh (2005–6)	Bhutan (2006)	India (2006)	Maldives (2006)	Nepal (1998–9)	Pakistan (2005–6)	Sri Lanka (2007)
Electricity, gas, and water	0.61	6.27	0.92	1.68	1.85	1.55	17.07[g]
Construction	6.71	8.81	17.01	8.12	24.52	14.36	n/a
Wholesale and retail trade	n/a	14.78	n/a	16.03	29.08	34.36[d]	29.33
Hotels and restaurants	47.56	9.25	36.74[b]	16.55	8.13	n/a	3.73
Transport, storage, and communication	24.39	7.31	14.11	9.72	9.62	13.45	14.37
Financial intermediation	4.27	2.09	6.19[c]	0.80	1.35	2.58[e]	6.77[h]
Real estate and associated activities	31.10	3.58	n/a	1.58	2.28	n/a	n/a
Public administration, defence and compulsory social security	15.85[a]	25.97	n/a	21.83	4.99	33.61[f]	13.62
Education	n/a	10.30	n/a	13.51	11.69	n/a	8.16
Health and social work	n/a	4.33	n/a	5.73	2.42	n/a	3.65
Other community and personal services	15.85	7.31	25.01	4.45	4.06	n/a	3.29

Source: Labour surveys and censuses of the seven countries.

Notes: n/a—not available at all or separately; a—includes education and health; b—includes trade; c—includes real estate and related activities; d—includes hotels & restaurants; e—includes real estate and related activities; f—includes heath, education and other services; g—includes construction; and h—includes real estate.

of growth in services may not always have been very employment inten-sive and that growth in some service sub-sectors may reflect productivity growth as opposed to increased absorption of the factors of production.

Overall, services employment exhibits a mixed picture. While the sector has grown in importance in terms of its contribution to growth and output, its role in terms of creating gender neutral and quality employment remains more limited. Thus, from an intra-regional perspective, it would be important to assess the implications of intra-regional trade, investment, and collaboration efforts for the creation of quality long-term sustainable jobs in the service sector and any regional integration efforts in services would need to be cognizant of this issue.

Services Trade in South Asia

Although there is a divergence in the behaviour of services employment and services output both at the regional and at the individual country level, in the case of services trade, there is much greater convergence between the two. Data at the regional level indicate that the service sector's growth has not only contributed to increased services trade in South Asia, but also to this region's increased participation in world services trade.

Figures 2.5 and 2.6 show South Asia's growing share in world services trade over the past 15 years. From a share of around 1 per cent of world services exports as well as imports, the region's share increased to nearly 3 per cent for services exports and to around 2 per cent for services imports.

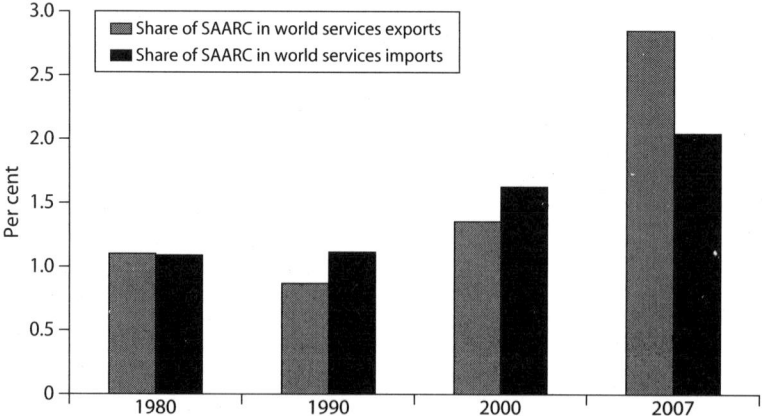

Figure 2.5   South Asia's Participation in World Services Trade

Source: Author's calculations based on UNCTAD (2008).

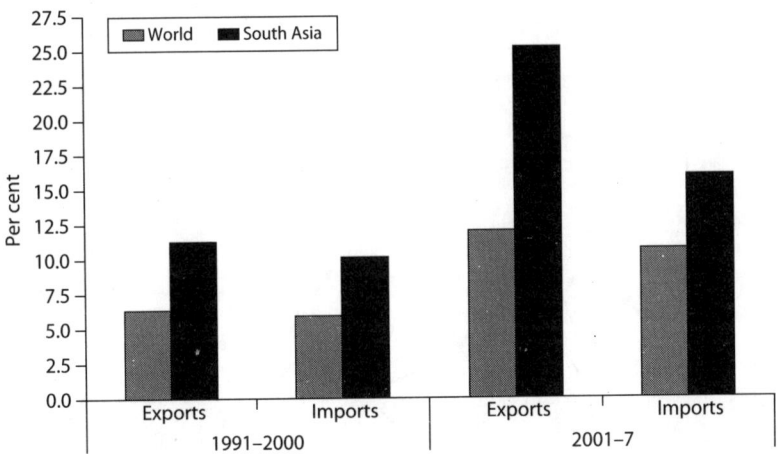

Figure 2.6 Average Annual Growth Rate of Services Trade in South Asia and the World

Source: Author's calculations based on UNCTAD (2008).

The trends suggest that services growth in South Asia has been trade oriented, particularly with regard to services exports. This trade orientation is also evident if one compares the growth in South Asia's services trade with that of the world. The average annual rates of growth for South Asia's exports and imports of services have exceeded those for the world economy during 1991–2000 and 2000–7. This difference is not only greater in the case of South Asia's services exports as opposed to its services imports, but this difference has also increased in the more recent period compared to the 1990s. The service sector appears to have a higher export as opposed to import orientation in South Asia.

The annual growth rates for South Asia's services exports when compared to those for the world similarly show the region's broadly sustained increase in its penetration of the world services market, particularly since the mid-1990s (Figure 2.7).

South Asia's performance in services trade is even more striking if one compares it with trends in services trade in other regions. South Asia's services exports showed a steady upward growth trend through the 1980s and the 1990s, with export growth accelerating in the post-2000 period. While all regions saw a spurt in services exports during 2001–7, most likely reflecting the general growth and dynamism seen in services around the world in recent years due to technological, regulatory, and structural factors, South Asia's performance is noteworthy as it registered the highest

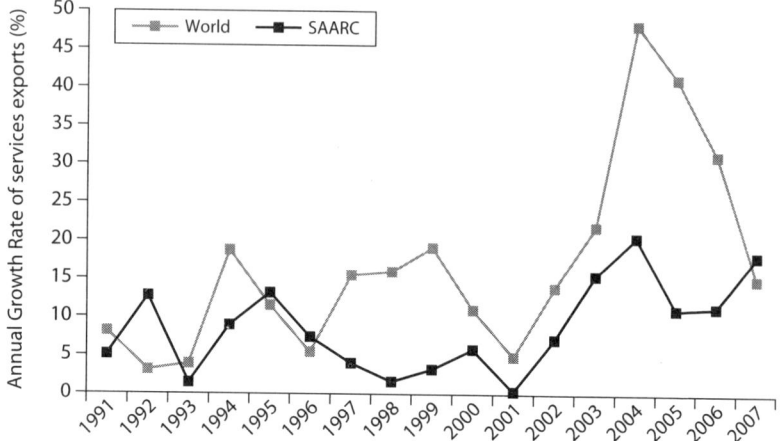

Figure 2.7 Annual Growth Rate of Services Exports in South Asia and
the World, 1991–2007

Source: Author's calculations based on UNCTAD (2008).

growth in services exports among all regions, with a CAGR of 23.5 per cent
during this period, much above the CAGR of 11.8 per cent for the world
and other high growth regions (Table 2.9).

The same picture emerges if one compares the growth trends for
South Asia's services imports with those in other regions (although South
Asia does not emerge as the region with the highest growth rates and the
difference is less striking than in the case of services exports). There is again

Table 2.9 CAGR of Services Exports in Different Regions, 1980–5
to 2001–7 (per cent)

Year	1980–5	1986–90	1991–5	1995–2000	2001–7
Region/Grouping					
World	**0.7**	**11.8**	**7.1**	**2.9**	**11.8**
Southern Africa	−5.1	11.8	7.9	0.7	15.5
Sub-Saharan Africa	−4.0	9.7	4.5	2.4	13.9
Caribbean	3.6	9.4	7.6	6.0	7.2
South America	−1.9	9.8	9.4	4.8	11.4
Eastern Asia	5.4	13.4	14.6	4.2	13.3
Western Asia	1.9	9.0	9.0	8.1	14.0
Southeast Asia (ASEAN)	4.0	17.9	16.7	−3.6	12.8
South Asia (excl. Afghanistan)	**2.4**	**8.3**	**7.2**	**12.1**	**23.5**
European Union (EU-27)	−1.8	12.0	5.3	2.4	12.3
North America (Canada + USA)	7.1	11.1	5.9	4.7	7.7

Source: Author's calculations based on UNCTAD (2008).

Table 2.10 CAGR of Services Imports in Different Regions, 1980–5 to 2001–7 (per cent)

Region/Grouping	1980–5	1986–90	1991–5	1996–2000	2001–7
World	**−0.3**	**12.2**	**6.7**	**2.9**	**10.3**
Southern Africa	−6.6	8.2	8.0	0.3	16.8
Sub-Saharan Africa	−6.1	7.8	4.5	−1.2	13.9
Caribbean	1.3	9.3	6.7	5.2	7.1
South America	−5.7	6.5	11.1	3.1	8.7
Eastern Asia	4.7	17.5	15.4	3.7	13.0
Western Asia	−1.2	4.9	−2.0	1.6	12.6
Southeast Asia (ASEAN)	2.2	14.6	19.0	0.0	9.7
South Asia (excl. Afghanistan)	**4.2**	**9.0**	**10.4**	**7.6**	**13.6**
European Union (EU-27)	−2.6	13.8	6.0	2.9	10.5
North America (Canada +USA)	8.9	8.7	3.3	7.3	7.9

Source: Author's calculations based on UNCTAD (2008).

an acceleration of services import growth in the post-2000 period (as is also seen in other regions) (Table 2.10). It is also worth noting that South Asia shows the least volatility in services import growth. Hence, although South Asia's services imports have grown less rapidly compared to its services exports, the trends are indicative of import liberalization in services and an overall trend towards greater openness in the service sector, which has been growing over time and is comparable to that seen in other regions in recent years.

Given the export and import growth in South Asia's service sector, the contribution of services to the region's total trade has increased over time, constituting around one-fourth of all trade flows (merchandise plus services) in recent years. This is comparable to the contribution of services to overall trade in developed regions such as the EU. The only other developing region which shows a higher share of services in total trade is the Caribbean, while all others show a much lower contribution of services in trade flows (at less than 20 per cent) (Table 2.11).

These trends are indicative of South Asia's growing competitiveness in services. This is also evident from trends in South Asia's Revealed Comparative Advantage (RCA) indices for services exports compared to those in other regions over the past two decades.[6] As seen in Figure 2.8, South Asia is one of only two developing country regions which have seen an increase

---

[6] The measure of the RCA, also known as the Balassa Index, is the ratio of the share of a country's exports of a particular product (or group of products) in a country's exports to another country/reference region/the world to the share of that same product in the other country/region/world's exports.

Table 2.11   Share of Services in Total Trade for Different Regions (per cent)

	1980	1985	1990	1995	2000	2005	2007
Southern Africa	13.0	14.4	17.0	17.8	15.5	16.8	16.5
Sub-Saharan Africa	17.1	18.5	21.5	22.0	19.1	18.6	19.3
Caribbean	10.9	18.1	27.6	33.6	31.8	30.9	29.9
South America	17.2	16.9	19.0	18.0	18.3	15.5	14.7
Eastern Asia	13.8	12.4	13.4	14.6	14.0	12.7	12.7
Western Asia	17.4	25.5	23.2	23.8	20.1	16.0	15.7
Southeast Asia (ASEAN)	14.2	16.5	16.0	18.0	16.2	17.0	16.7
South Asia excluding Afghanistan	19.2	21.3	20.5	20.5	24.1	27.5	25.4
European Union (EU-27)	18.4	17.9	20.3	20.2	20.8	21.5	21.3
North America (Canada + USA)	14.8	18.5	21.1	19.6	19.1	19.7	20.0

Source: Author's calculations based on UNCTAD (2008).

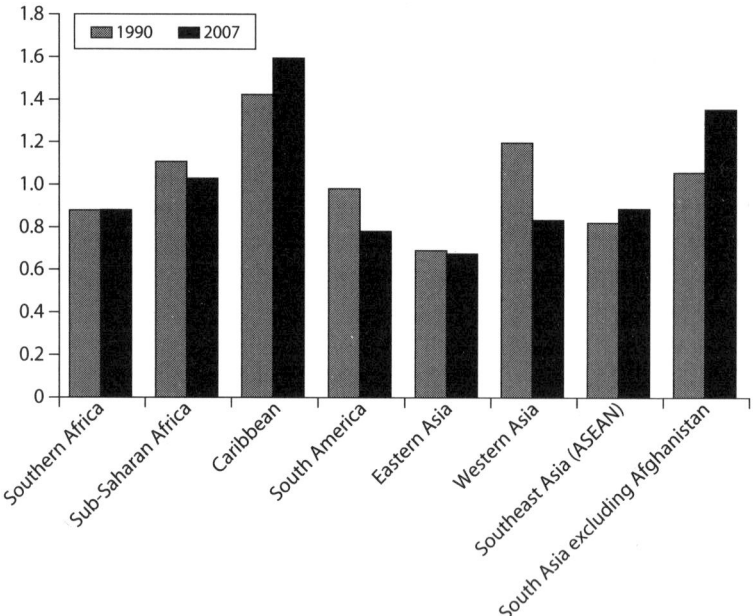

Figure 2.8   Revealed Comparative Advantage Indices for Services in Different Regions

Source: Author's calculations based on UNCTAD (2008).

in the RCA index for services between 1995 and 2007. It is also the region which has experienced the greatest increase in this index over this period, from 1.07 to 1.31 and ranked second in terms of the value of its RCA index, after the Caribbean.

It is also interesting to note that while South Asia's RCA in services has been rising, its RCA in merchandise declined over this period and the gap between merchandise and services exports has in fact widened (Figure 2.9). Such divergent trends between services and goods may also be indicative of the limited scope for intra-regional trade in commodities (as discussed earlier) compared to that in services.

Thus, taking the overall regional trends into consideration, that is, growth in services exports and imports, growing participation in world markets, and competitiveness indicators, South Asia's performance suggests that it has considerable trade potential in its service sector. However, one needs to ask whether these broad regional trends are also evident at the national level in each of the countries in South Asia and what kinds of asymmetries may be present here as well.

A cross-country examination of services trade trends in South Asia reveals that there are considerable asymmetries within the region in terms of magnitude, pattern, growth, and potential, quite akin to the asymmetries seen in the case of services output. Not all countries have experienced high growth rates for services exports and imports. Not all countries have witnessed a steady increase in the contribution of services to their trade flows, or in their own contribution to world services exports, or in their RCAs for services. There is also considerable variation across different segments within the service sector both across and within countries.

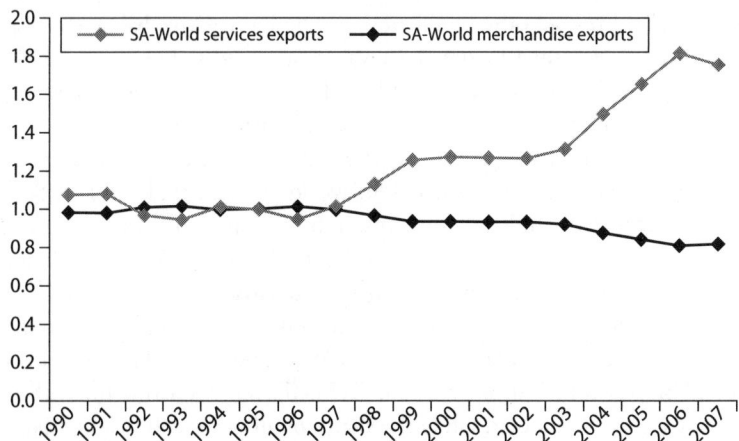

Figure 2.9   South Asia's Revealed Comparative Advantage in Services and Merchandise Trade, 1990–2007

Source: Author's calculations based on UNCTAD (2008).

Table 2.12   Trade in Commercial Services in South Asian Countries (US$ mn, in current prices)

		1980	1985	1990	1995	2000	2005	2006	2007
Bangladesh	Exports	172	207	296	469	283	474	603	679
	Imports	444	401	554	1,192	1,523	2,011	2,111	2,417
Bhutan	Exports		17	28	15	20	42	52	60
	Imports		39	28	27	28	82	65	57
India	Exports	2,861	3,274	4,609	6,763	16,030	55,508	75,057	86,366
	Imports	2,915	3,815	5,943	10,062	18,896	47,545	63,053	78,080
Maldives	Exports	52	61	101	230	345	317	470	544
	Imports	40	24	37	75	108	201	228	266
Nepal	Exports	118	92	166	592	410	271	252	
	Imports	84	112	159	305	193	424	488	
Pakistan	Exports	565	743	1,218	1,432	1,284	2,043	2,245	2,204
	Imports	734	1,011	1,863	2,431	2,109	7,206	8,094	8,410
Sri Lanka	Exports	223	234	425	800	915	1,519	1,604	
	Imports	344	440	620	1,169	1,592	2,051	2,359	

Source: WTO statistics database.

Table 2.12 shows the huge asymmetry in the magnitude of trade flows within South Asia, mirroring the asymmetry highlighted earlier for services output. India's services exports were over 1,000 times greater than those for Bhutan and around 40 times greater than that for the second largest service exporter, Pakistan. The magnitude of difference is similar in the case of services imports. It is also interesting to note that excepting India and the Maldives, all other countries have had a negative balance of trade in services. This range in the sheer value of services trade and the clear dominance of India is indicative of the likely asymmetries as well as scope for complementarities in services across the South Asian countries.

This stark difference in size is reflected in the relative importance of each of the South Asian countries in world services trade and in South Asia's services trade. India's dominance in both respects is clear as shown in Figures 2.10 and 2.11. India's share in South Asia's overall services exports has grown from around 64 per cent in 1990 to close to 90 per cent in 2007, while its share in the region's services imports has grown from around 62 per cent to around 76 per cent between 1990 and 2007. The share of the second biggest contributor, Pakistan, declined over this period for both services exports and imports, while the shares of all other countries remained stagnant and at negligible levels.

India is the only country within this region that significantly increased its share in world services exports as well as imports during 1990–2007, while the shares of all other countries remained at around the same levels

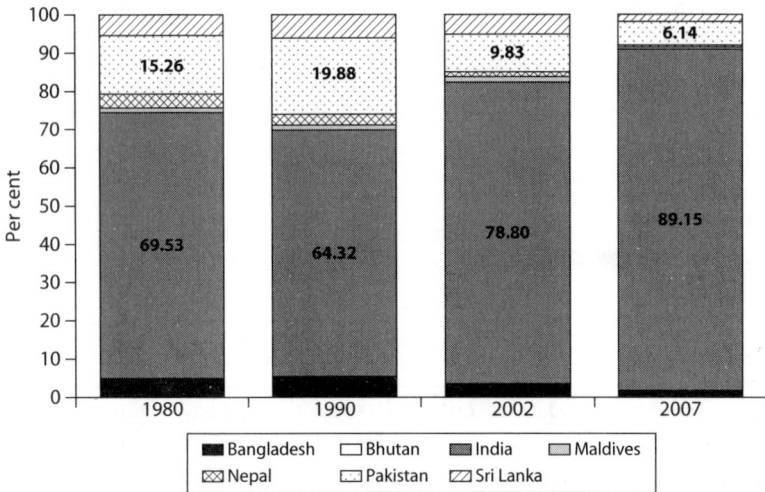

Figure 2.10   Share of Countries in South Asia's Services Exports
Source: Author's calculations based on UNCTAD (2008).

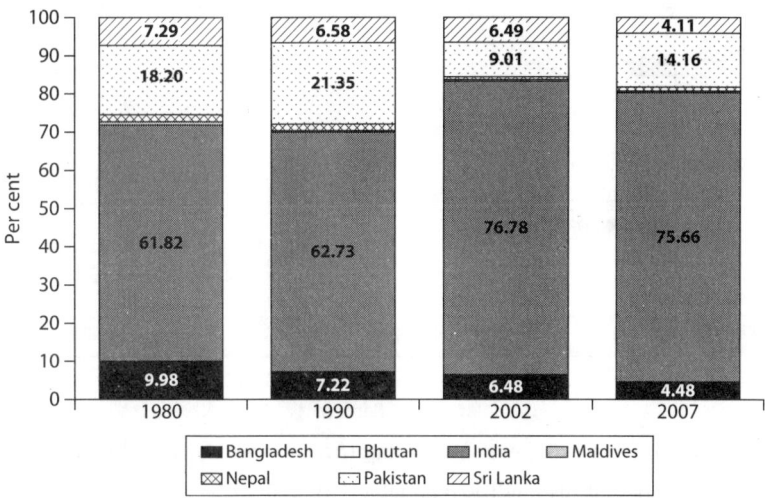

Figure 2.11   Share of Countries in South Asia's Services Imports
Source: Author's calculations based on UNCTAD (2008).

through this period. As shown in Figures 2.13 and 2.14, respectively, India's share in world services exports increased from less than 1 per cent in 2000 to 2.5 per cent in 2007 and likewise, its share in world services imports increased from a little over 1 per cent in 2000 to over 1.5 per cent in 2007.

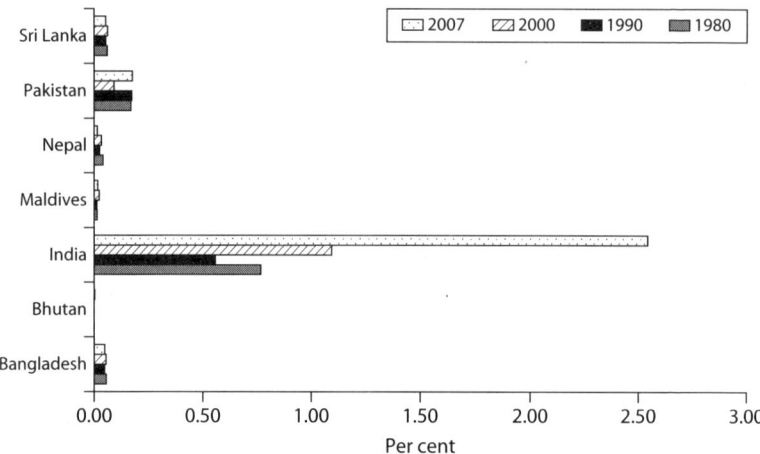

Figure 2.12   Share of South Asian Countries in World Services Exports
Source: Author's calculations based on UNCTAD (2008).

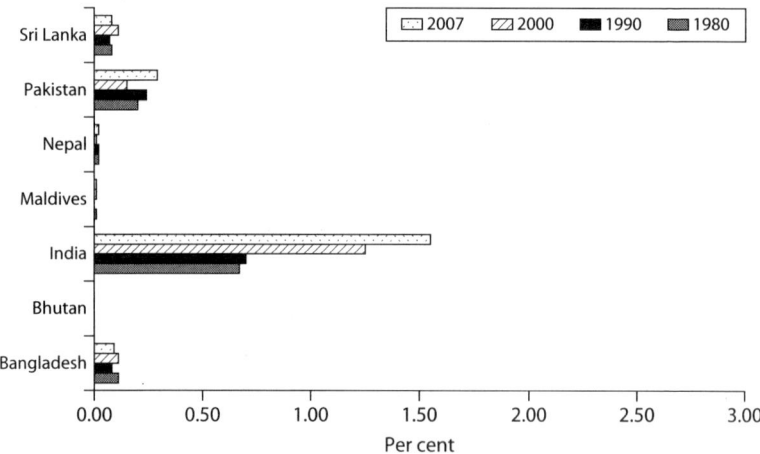

Figure 2.13   Share of South Asian Countries in World Services Imports
Source: Author's calculations based on UNCTAD (2008).

The shares in world services exports and imports for all the other countries in South Asia remained negligible at between 0–0.3 per cent throughout this period. Thus, the trends seen earlier in South Asia's services are largely a reflection of trends in India's services trade, which does raise issues about whether there would be a sufficient convergence of interest across the South Asian countries in pushing services integration.

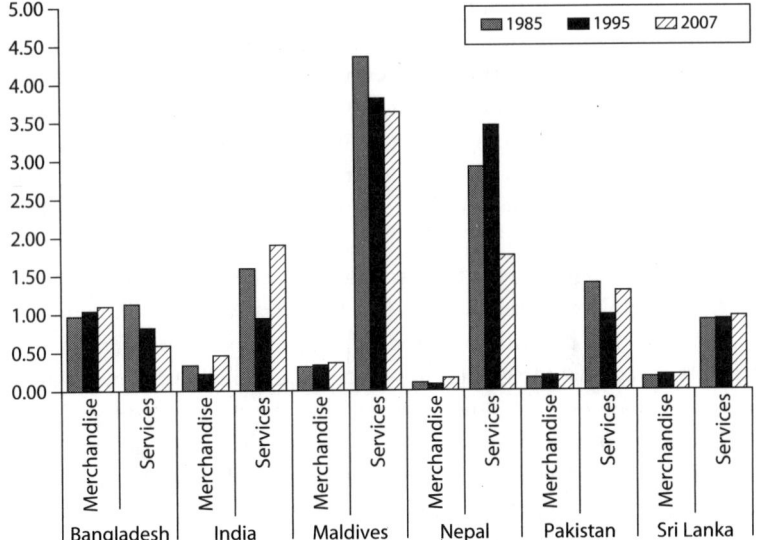

Figure 2.14 Trends in RCA Indices for Merchandise and Services in South Asian Countries

Source: Author's calculations based on UNCTAD (2008).

A similar picture emerges if one compares growth trends in services exports. As shown in Table 2.13, while the average annual growth rate for South Asia as a whole almost trebled between 1991–5 and 2001–7, only India experienced a consistent upward trend in its growth rate over this period. Several countries experienced a deceleration in their services exports during 1996–2000 before growth picked up post-2000. Also,

Table 2.13 Average Annual Growth Rate for Services Exports in South Asian Countries (per cent)

	1991–5	1996–2000	2001–7
South Asia	9.14	13.42	25.20
Bangladesh	12.31	3.57	10.51
Bhutan	0.00	0.00	18.88
India	8.12	20.02	27.51
Maldives	18.92	8.68	9.52
Nepal	28.86	−3.15	1.27
Pakistan	5.45	−5.23	26.10
Sri Lanka	13.52	3.01	10.35

Source: Author's calculations based on the UN statistical database (online version).

for many of the countries, the average growth rate was lower in 2001–7 than in 1991–5, indicating that the output growth that occurred in services in the post-2000 period, did not necessarily translate into increased competitiveness and exports for all the countries. This is also consistent with the fact that in some countries, several non-commercial services have grown in importance. Data also indicate that services exports have been quite volatile in most of the countries, particularly so in Nepal and Pakistan.

Overall, the figures show that growth in South Asia's services trade and the region's growing competitiveness and penetration of world markets in services is in large part driven by India's performance. This means that any attempts at regional integration in services would obviously involve asymmetries in trade potential and interests, that the dominant player, India, would need to play an important role in driving the intra-regional integration process, and that there may be very different distributional effects of such integration across the countries in this region.

Should one then conclude that there is not much of a basis for pursuing intra-regional integration in services within South Asia, and that there is not much benefit to be derived for countries other than India? Interestingly, an examination of the trends in competitiveness in services vis-à-vis merchandise trade in South Asia and a closer look at the sub-sectoral composition of services trade within South Asia suggest that there are potential complementarities that can be exploited within the service sector, with regard to particular sub-sectors as well as modes of delivery.

If one examines the trends in RCAs for services as opposed to merchandise for each of the countries in this region, then one finds that in all the countries, the RCA for services exceeds that for merchandise trade, although only India has experienced an increase in this RCA while all countries, other than Bangladesh, have remained at similar levels of competitiveness over the 1995 and 2007 period (Figure 2.14). What this suggests is that the South Asian countries may have greater trade prospects in services compared to merchandise where the RCAs are much below 1 in all the countries, except Bangladesh.

Thus, these figures suggest that there may be more scope for intra-regional trade in services than in goods from a competitiveness point of view, as also evident from the currently very low shares of intra-regional trade in goods despite integration efforts, and given the high degree of overlap in the merchandise trade structure within South Asia. An examination of the composition of services trade in the South Asian countries reveals that there are possible complementarities across the countries in this region in terms of their services trade structure, which could provide a basis for promoting intra-regional trade in services. Figures 2.15a, b and 2.16a, b show the breakdown of services exports and imports, respectively, for all the South Asian countries, except Bhutan (for which comparable disaggregated services trade statistics were not available) in 2006 and 1995, respectively.

There are various ways in which the services export and import composition figures can be analysed to assess the extent of complementarities and unexploited potential in services trade within South Asia. First, if one looks at the structure of services exports for each of the countries in 1995 and in 2006, it is evident that the export basket for all the countries has become a bit more diversified and more dissimilar, particularly in the case of India. In 2006, India's services exports consisted of traditional segments, such as transport and travel, as well as new areas such as computer and information services and other business services, the former having declined in importance over the 1995–2006 period.[7] In contrast,

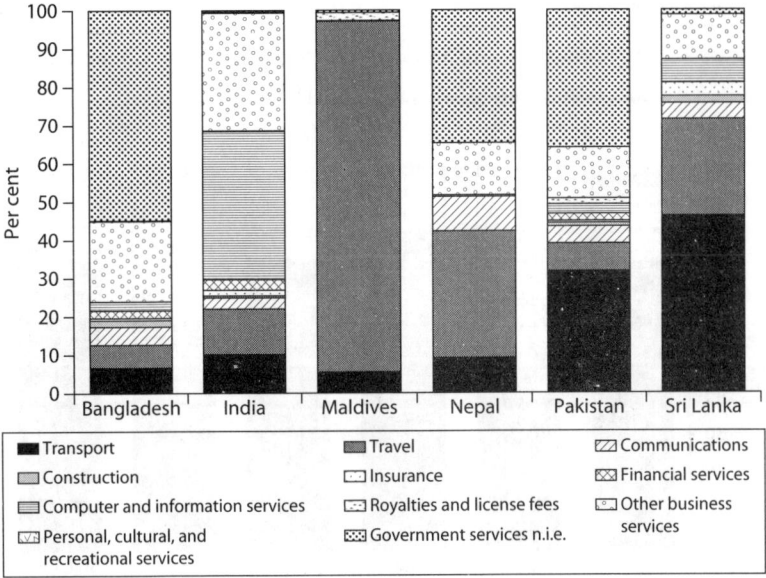

Figure 2.15a   Composition of Services Exports in South Asian Countries, 2006

Source: Author's calculations based on UNCTAD (2008).

[7] The UNCTAD defines 'other business services' as including merchant and other trade-related services; operational leasing services; and miscellaneous business, and professional and technical services.

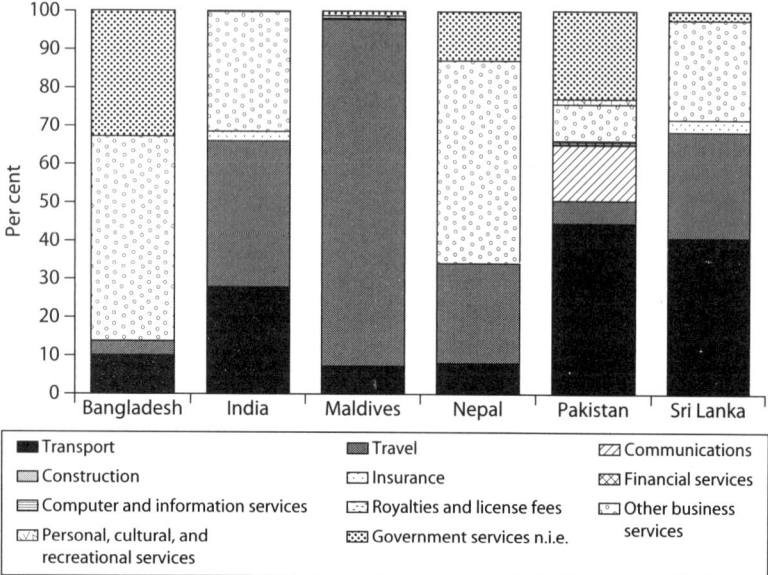

Figure 2.15b   Composition of Services Exports in South Asian Countries, 1995
Source: Author's calculations based on UNCTAD (2008).

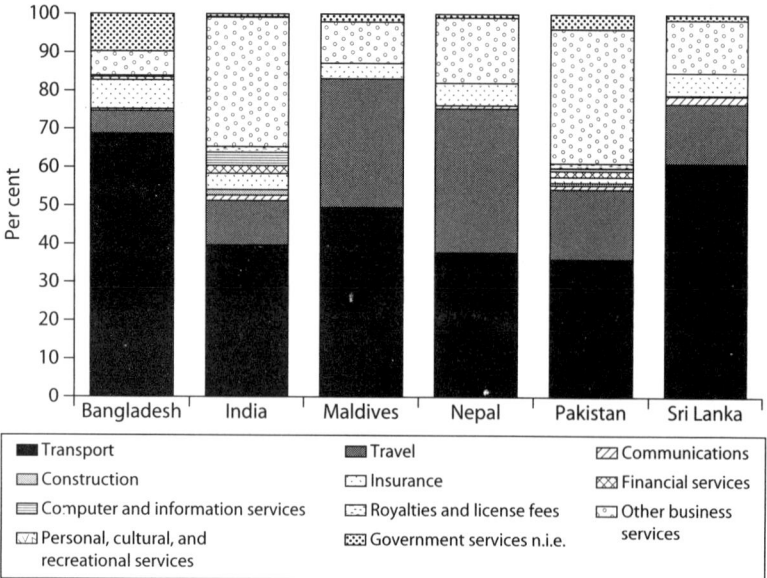

Figure 2.16a   Composition of Services Imports in South Asian Countries, 2006
Source: Author's calculations based on UNCTAD (2008).

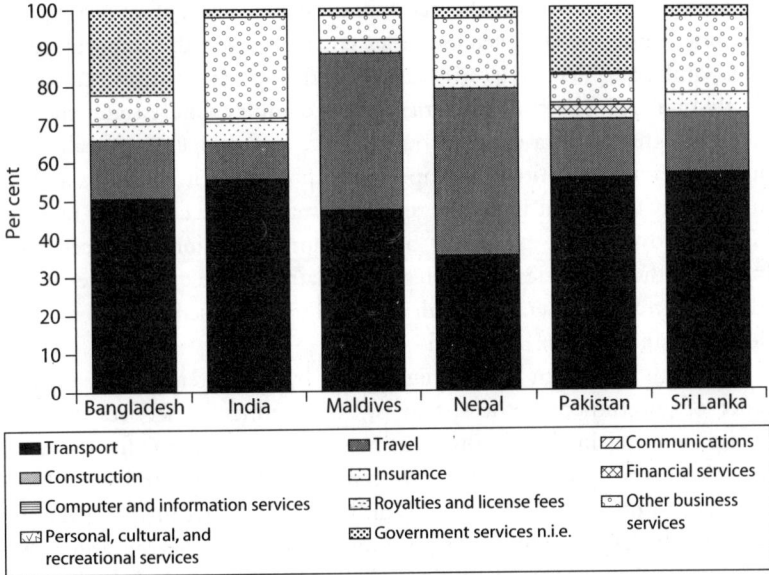

Figure 2.16b Composition of Services Imports in South Asian Countries, 1995
Source: Author's calculations based on UNCTAD (2008).

the Maldives's services exports consisted mainly of travel services, Nepal's basket consisted mainly of travel and government services, Pakistan's was dominated by transport and government services, Sri Lanka's by transport and travel services, and Bangladesh's by government services and, to a lesser extent, other business services. Thus India's orientation shifted towards professional and business services while most of the other countries are still more dependent on certain traditional commercial services, such as tourism and transport, though their export baskets today comprise of more activities than in 1995. Thus, there are complementarities in the export pattern, particularly between India and the other countries in the region.

Second, if one examines the composition of services imports in 1995 and 2006, one finds that although travel and transport services are the most important, services, such as business, financial, insurance, and communication have increased in importance in the import basket over the 1995–2006 period. This indicates some diversification of services imports, most likely reflecting the outcome of service sector liberalization and reforms.

Third, if one juxtaposes the trends in the composition of service exports and imports, some complementarities emerge. Given the importance of travel and transport services in exports and imports, tourism services is clearly one area where all countries have a common interest and there is scope for greater intra-regional trade and related cooperation. Likewise, business services constitute an important export segment for India and an increasingly important import segment for some of the countries, indicating the prospects for exports of business and professional services from India to other countries in the region. Related to these categories is the scope for greater cooperation in air and land transport services and facilitation of business and leisure travel.

A fourth important feature highlighted by these trends is the significance of government services, that is, non-commercial services in some of the countries in this region. This may have implications for the areas in which intra-regional integration occurs in South Asia and what form this integration takes. Although it is difficult to interpret further given the lack of sub-classification under government services, one can argue that given the significant role of public services in South Asia's trade basket, any regional agreement that covers services could potentially explore possibilities for collaboration, capacity building, and regulatory cooperation and that services such as healthcare, energy, education, and environment are potentially important areas to consider for regional discussions.

A sub-sectoral analysis of the RCA indices for each of the countries also reveals these potential complementarities. For most of the sub-sectors, the RCA indices are 1 or less. However, in several of the countries, there are specific sub-sectors which show a very high RCA, such as travel in the case of the Maldives and computer and information services in the case of India. The latter shows a particularly high RCA index of 8.5 reflecting the tremendous growth this segment has witnessed over the past decade and the very high export orientation of this sub-sector. Likewise, the high RCA value for travel services in the case of the Maldives reflects the high dependence of this economy on tourism services. What is difficult to interpret is the relatively high RCA index for communication services across most of the countries, even those countries which have not experienced high overall growth in services exports or output. The latter may reflect the deregulation of telecommunication services in recent years which has spurred growth in this segment in several countries in South Asia. However, without further sub-classification of what constitutes communication services, it is hard to assess what the competitiveness in this segment signifies. Interestingly, Sri Lanka exhibits the highest

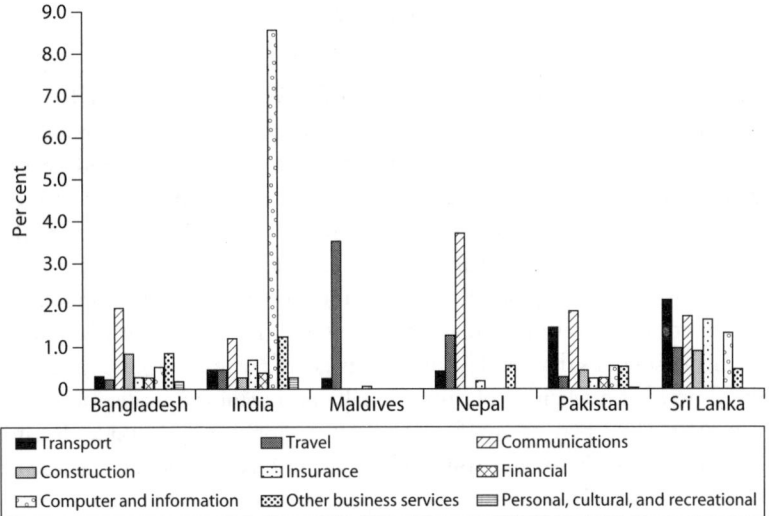

Figure 2.17 RCA Indices for South Asian Countries in Main Service Sub-sectors, 2006

Source: Author's calculations based on UNCTAD (2008).

RCA indices for most of the service sub-sectors, with index values of over 1 for transport, communication, computer and information, and insurance services. In contrast, although India has shown the most dynamism in its services exports and output, the RCA calculations indicate that this dynamism is not that widespread and is basically concentrated in software, business, and communication services (Figure 2.17).

It is important to point out that the commonalities or complementarities in the trading pattern highlighted earlier are vis-à-vis the world and thus do not necessarily mean that countries in South Asia would want to trade with one another in some of the identified service segments. They may be more interested in other markets than those within the region. Thus, this analysis of trade prospects and potential is valid only to the extent that the countries in South Asia see each other's markets as important enough to target in services. Here, the relatively small size of some of the South Asian economies is a likely impediment to growth in intra-regional services trade. In this context, a question that arises is the extent to which a regional agreement that covers services and investment can influence this dynamic and make the regional market more attractive to each of the players within the region, particularly in some of the services such as tourism, IT, and business.

Important Modes of Services Trade[8]

The sector-wise profile of trade interests and opportunities within the region are also indicative of the modes of services trade that are likely to be important in South Asia. For instance, the commonality of interest and high RCAs for some of the countries in tourism services would suggest that mode 2 or consumption abroad as per the GATS modal classification would be an important form of services trade in the region. Related to this would be the significance of air transport and other transport services across the countries, that is, mode 1. Likewise, the growing share of computer and information services or business services in the trade basket of some of the countries suggests that mode 1 in the context of outsourcing and mode 4 in the context of movement of professionals and business travellers across the countries could play an important role in regional services trade. Related investments in these, and some of the other services highlighted earlier, such as in financial, communication, and transport services would also be important for most of the countries in this region. Thus, all four modes of services delivery appear to be important for promoting intra-regional integration in South Asia.

The following discussion focuses on modes 3 and 4 specifically. It outlines the nature of temporary movement of service providers (or mode 4) from South Asia and trends in remittances to the South Asian countries to highlight the importance of mode 4 exports for South Asia. It also outlines the nature of investments (mode 3) in the service sector to highlight the scope for regional integration through investment flows. For both modes 3 and 4, to the extent permitted by data availability, the discussion also indicates the extent of intra-regional flows.

Examining Mode 4 Trade

As discussed in the recent World Migration Report, Bangladesh, Nepal, India, Pakistan, and Sri Lanka are major source countries for migrant workers, both permanent and temporary (mode 4) at various skill levels, to developed

---

[8] The GATS classifies services trade into four modes of supply. These are: mode 1 or cross-border supply which refers to services in the form of data and information flows or carriers actually flowing across borders; mode 2 or consumption abroad which occurs when a consumer goes abroad to consume a service as in the case of tourism services; mode 3 or commercial presence which refers to the setting up of a commercial establishment through a subsidiary, or joint venture, branch office, or affiliate office; and mode 4 or movement of natural persons which refers to the temporary cross-border movement of service suppliers to provide a service in another market (but not for permanent residence and entry into the labour market of the host country).

and developing countries. Although it is difficult to separate temporary movement of labour from permanent movement in the existing migration data in order to separately identify the significance of mode 4 exports, some broad trends and patterns are evident for South Asia's labour flows. These trends and patterns are captured in the figures and tables in Appendix 2A.

India is the main source country in South Asia. Moreover, its emigration levels increased the most during 2001–5, as is also evident from India's increased share in total labour inflows in several major OECD countries during the 2001–5 period compared to the 1990–2004 period (rising from 5 to 8 per cent in the case of Australia, from 7 to 11 per cent in the case of Canada, and from 5 to 8 per cent in the case of the US).[9]

The main destination markets for South Asia's migrants are the Gulf countries, Southeast Asia, and the English speaking OECD countries— US, UK, Australia, Canada, and New Zealand. Although the destination countries have become diverse over time, the Middle East remains the most important destination. An estimated 8.7 million temporary contractual workers from different South Asian countries live and work in the Middle East.[10] South Asia is an important source region for migrant workers to the Gulf countries.

The skill profile for South Asia's labour flows varies by destination. By and large, the bulk of unskilled migrant labour is headed towards the oil rich Gulf countries. Bangladesh, Pakistan, and India primarily supply workers for infrastructure projects in the Gulf region. Around 90 per cent of Pakistani temporary contractual workers to the Gulf countries are engaged in semi- and low-skilled jobs (IOM 2008: 443). Sri Lanka and Bangladesh are important source countries for domestic workers to the Middle East (and also Southeast Asia), which has also resulted in the feminization of migration from South Asia.

Table 2A.1 (see Chapter Appendix) illustrates the skill composition and market orientation of labour outflows from Sri Lanka in 2005. It shows that the Middle-Eastern countries feature amongst the top 10 destinations for Sri Lankan migrant workers and that most of this movement is in the unskilled and housemaids categories, which together account for over 70 per cent of all labour outflows from Sri Lanka.[11]

Likewise, if one examines the data for Pakistani and Bangladeshi migrants, one finds that a majority are engaged in production and service

[9] See IOM (2008: 442).
[10] See IOM (2008: 443).
[11] Based on estimates of the stock of Sri Lankan overseas contract workers from the Sri Lanka Bureau of Foreign Employment.

activities, in semi- and low-skilled occupations in the Middle East. However, what is worth noting in Table 2A.1 is that the Maldives features among the top 10 destinations for Sri Lankan workers and accounted for around 1 per cent of the country's outflows in 2005. The same holds true for Bangladeshi workers engaged in the hospitality industry in the Maldives. Hence, this is indicative of the scope for intra-regional movement of workers, with some of the smaller countries relying on migrant inflows from the relatively more populous countries in South Asia to serve their needs in specific segments, an issue discussed at greater length later.

The OECD countries, along with the Middle East, are also an important destination market for South Asian migrants (temporary and permanent), particularly skilled migrants (see Table 2A.2).

If one examines the profile of the South Asian immigrants in the OECD countries, then one finds that over two-thirds of them had tertiary level education, that is, they were skilled immigrants. For India, the proportion of highly educated immigrants in the total stock of immigrants for 2000 was over 75 per cent. For Pakistan and Sri Lanka, the share was over two-thirds, while for Bangladesh the share was slightly lower at around 50 per cent. Thus, for all the countries, nearly half or more of the immigrants in the OECD countries were skilled workers. It is also worth noting that the subcontinent is quite comparable to other source regions, such as East Asia and certain countries in Central Asia and the Middle East in terms of the size of its tertiary educated immigrant population, as well as the share of this segment in its overall immigrant base in the OECD market.

The significance of the larger South Asian countries as a source of skilled workers is particularly striking in the case of the UK's Highly Skilled Migrant Programme (HSMP), which admits thousands of South Asians every year into the UK. In 2005 alone, of the 17,631 persons hailing from over 100 countries who were admitted into the UK under the HSMP, Indians and Pakistanis accounted for half of all HSMP approvals. Indians alone accounted for 38 per cent of total admissions under this scheme. Indians dominated in most categories. Some 77 per cent of all HSMP approvals were for persons looking to pursue their careers in four main occupational categories—medical with a share of 33 per cent, financial with a share of 19 per cent, business with a share of 14 per cent, and information technology with a share of 12 per cent. With the exception of finance, the largest proportion of approvals in all the other occupational categories was for Indians, who constituted 59 per cent of all those admitted in the medical field and 45 per cent of those admitted in the IT sector (Salt 2006).

Table 2A.3 provides the distribution of Indians and Pakistanis receiving work permits in the UK by occupational category.

Knowledge workers constitute a particularly important category of migrant service providers for India, particularly to the OECD markets. According to a 2001 study, there were over 3 million Indian knowledge workers working and living in various countries around the world, with the US, UK, Canada, and Australia together accounting for around three-quarters of this workforce (D'Sami 2001: 3).

The importance of mode 4 exports for the South Asian region is reflected in the absolute size of remittances as well as their share in the South Asian economies. There has been a consistent increase in remittances in the 1985–2006 period for all the South Asian countries, with a more than doubling of remittances from $12 billion to over $24 billion between 2000 and 2006 in the case of India (see Figure 2A.3).

Within the Asian region, the four South Asian countries of India, Bangladesh, Pakistan, and Sri Lanka also feature among the top 10 recipients of remittances. India, in fact, is the country which receives the largest amount of remittances in the world.

Although India ranks first in terms of the absolute value of remittances, receipts from overseas workers constitute a significant share of GDP at over 7 per cent for Bangladesh, Sri Lanka, and Nepal (see Table 2A.4).

This data clearly indicate that remittances and associated labour outflows are important for all the South Asian economies. What is worth noting, however, is that for some countries in the region, there are also labour inflows, particularly from the rest of the region. Although other regions constitute the main destination markets, there is also some degree of intra-regional movement of workers (some of it irregular and undocumented as well). India is the main destination country in this region, with an estimated 5.7 million international migrants living and working in the country, although accounting for only 0.5 per cent of the total population.[12] A large number of these are migrant workers of Bangladeshi origin, followed by Nepali workers. The limited data available on intra-regional migration in South Asia indicates that the largest group of expatriate workers in the Maldives comprises of Bangladeshis (36,380), followed by Indians (23,985), and then Sri Lankans (9,754) who are largely employed in the construction and tourism sectors.[13]

Figures 2A.5 and 2A.6 indicate the stock of migrant workers in the South Asian countries in absolute and relative terms in recent years.

[12] See discussion on migration trends in South-Central Asia in IOM (2008: 441).
[13] Individual country reports.

They clearly highlight that some of the larger countries in South Asia are host to a relatively large number of migrant workers (over 5 million in the case of India and around 3 million in the case of Pakistan in 2005). The latter are likely to be underestimates given the porous borders within the region, and the large number of undocumented irregular workers from Nepal and Bangladesh in India. Data on remittance outflows from India by destination markets indicate that much of the migrant stock in India is from within the region, and this is also likely to be the case for other South Asian countries. Over 70 per cent of the remittances flowing out of India are to two other South Asian countries, Bangladesh and Pakistan, with Bangladeshi workers accounting for over half of these remittance outflows. It is also likely that Nepal features in the set of 'other countries', which account for another 22 per cent of remittances from India. Thus, the importance of India as a destination market for South Asian migrant workers is quite evident.

Once again, as with remittance receipts, although India is the most important destination market within the region given its large economy and demand for labour, in relative terms, remittance outflows constitute an insignificant part of GDP. It is again the Maldives which shows a very high dependence on migrant labour as revealed by its high share of remittance payments in GDP.

Thus, taking account of the migration trends and patterns, one can conclude that not only is South Asia significant as a source region for workers for the rest of the world, but that there is also considerable intra-regional movement of workers that takes place (documented or otherwise). These intra-regional flows are driven by employment opportunities in some of the larger markets, such as India, and by demand-supply mismatch in selected sectors in some of the smaller markets, such as the Maldives. Intra-regional labour flows thus reflect the asymmetries in relative size and labour market depth, as well as dynamics arising from poverty and social and cultural networks within the region. Thus, mode 4 related issues would have to play an important role in any intra-regional agreement that covers services in terms of liberalizing visa and immigration related regulations given its bearing on trade and investment flows across a wide range of services.

Investment Flows in Services

As highlighted earlier, the growth witnessed in several service sectors, such as communication, finance, and IT services is a reflection of the reforms undertaken and policies adopted in these areas. One of the main elements of reforms in this region has been overall FDI liberalization as well as in key services. Although data availability specifically for FDI in services is limited, the overall regional and country level trends for FDI clearly indicate that there is a growing role for investments in this region across most of the countries with some countries emerging as potential exporters of FDI as well. Moreover, a large part of this investment is moving to the service sector, with potential ramifications for intra-regional investment flows and related trade in services.

As per the 2008 UNCTAD *World Investment Report* statistics, FDI inflows into South Asia have grown sharply in the last 15 years, from less than US$ 3 billion in 1991 to over US$ 33 billion in 2007 (see Figure 2A.8). The average annual rate of growth of FDI inflows in South Asia stood at 31.5 per cent in 2000–7. As a result, South Asia's share in global FDI increased from 2.6 per cent in 2000 to 4 per cent in 2006, and the region's share of FDI in GDP rose from 4.7 per cent in 2000 to 6.5 per cent in 2006, although FDI's role in the region still remains much smaller than that in other Asian groupings (with a 25.1 per cent share for East Asia and 39.5 per cent share for Southeast Asia) (ADB 2008b). FDI outflows remain much smaller, but have increased significantly in the post-2000 period, from almost 0 to nearly US$ 15 billion.

The country-wise trends in FDI flows (inward and outward) show that almost all the South Asian countries have experienced a significant increase in FDI inflows during 1990–2007, with India receiving over 80 per cent of these inflows. Interestingly, there has also been increased FDI outflow from the region, for India, Pakistan, Bangladesh, and Sri Lanka, with a trebling of FDI outflows in the case of India from around US$ 500mn to over US $13.5 billion during 2000–7. India accounted for over 90 per cent of the region's FDI outflows in 2007.

India not only enjoys dominance as a destination but also as a source of FDI from a global perspective (see Figures 2A.9 and 2A.10). From a regional perspective, in addition to geographic and cultural proximity related factors that could facilitate intra-regional investment flows, to the extent that any regional agreement covering investment enables a more business friendly environment for regional investors, Indian companies could potentially increase their presence in the other South Asian countries. As pointed out in a recent article by *The Economist*, India is one of the most critical emerging markets for outward FDI.[14] Moreover, much of this outward FDI is to developing countries. Hence, the overall FDI trends and patterns suggest that there is scope for India to play a greater role in FDI

[14] See Economist Intelligence Unit (2007).

flows in South Asia as India becomes a more competitive source country for FDI and other countries in this region become more open to FDI.

Available data on the composition of outward FDI from India also indicate that services constitute around 40 per cent of such outflows, with non-financial services, namely computer and information services, constituting the bulk of outward FDI in services from India. Thus, the pattern of FDI from India reflects its competitiveness in business and professional services (as highlighted earlier in the trade data), and one can find a close mapping of trade and investment interests for the main driver of services growth in the region.

It is difficult to gauge how much intra-regional investment there is currently within South Asia, moreover so in services, given the limited information available in this regard. As per the ADB's South Asia Economic Report 2008, FDI flows between South Asia, East Asia, and Southeast Asia have risen in recent years and now account for almost 50 per cent of the Asian region's total FDI inflows. FDI flows between East Asia and Southeast Asia have been significant. However, FDI flows between South Asia and East and Southeast Asia are relatively small and in particular, cross-border FDI within South Asia is negligible. India is the only country in the region that is investing to any extent in its neighbours.

FDI flows from within South Asia account for a very small share of the total FDI inflows in the South Asian countries, and countries outside the region such as the US, UK, Japan, and Singapore continue to be the main sources for FDI (see Table 2A.8). The only noteworthy investor country is India, particularly in the case of Nepal and to a small extent, Sri Lanka. The latter fact most likely reflects the bilateral agreements between India and these two countries and the resulting implications for Indian investors in these particular markets. It is interesting to note that there is no FDI engagement between India and Pakistan, reflecting the political problems between the two countries. In essence, the pattern that emerges is that of the bigger countries as potential investors in the smaller countries in the region. Hence, one could conclude from the limited data that not only is there scope for India to play a bigger role in FDI flows to the rest of South Asia, but that an investment agreement could potentially facilitate this process, something the bilateral treaties appear to have done.

As bilateral-cum-service sector specific data are not available, it is difficult to assess the extent to which the service sector would be a recipient of any increased intra-regional investment. However, if overall data (not by source country) on the composition of FDI by different activities is an indicator, then the high share of services in total FDI, particularly in the likely recipient markets of Nepal, Bangladesh, and Sri Lanka would suggest that much of any increased intra-regional FDI would be in the service sector. Table 2A.9 provides the share of services in total inward FDI for select countries in South Asia, based on the UNCTAD's *World Investment Report* (2004), which focused on the global shift towards FDI in services. The data indicate that the post-1995 period has seen an increasing share of services in total inward FDI for countries in the region. Bhutan and the Maldives are excluded as comparable data is not available for these two countries.

There is another reason to believe that any increased intra-regional FDI would mainly be in the service sector. This is because trade and investment flows often tend to be closely linked, with investment serving the purpose of sourcing inputs and leveraging cost advantages to facilitate goods trade. To the extent that there is very limited intra-regional trade in goods, and the trade structures are similar (as discussed in Chapter 1), and given largely comparable wage and other production costs within South Asia and infrastructural and other constraints in the region, one would expect intra-regional FDI to be oriented more towards services as opposed to manufacturing. The purpose of such FDI is more likely to relate to reasons such as addressing resource gaps in the source country or establishing local presence to tap the export potential in a particular service segment rather than focusing on demand in the host country market given the relatively small size of most of the likely recipient markets in this region.

One can also draw some inferences about the sectors which show the most promise for intra-regional FDI based on disaggregated inward services FDI data for some of the countries. The disaggregated data for Bangladesh, India, and Pakistan reveal that the most important sub-sectors are communication, energy, and financial services. To a lesser extent construction and certain business services are also important.

Although similar data could not be obtained for Nepal and Sri Lanka, recent reports indicate that services have been the leading recipient sector for FDI in the case of Sri Lanka and that in 2000, services accounted for 55.6 per cent of the total FDI inflows, compared to 41.7 per cent for the manufacturing sector (UNCTAD 2004). The major sub-sectors that continue to attract large amounts of FDI in Sri Lanka are telecommunications and business process outsourcing, with telecommunications alone receiving about half of the total services FDI (World Bank 2007; UNCTAD 2004). In Nepal, although manufacturing accounts for a large share of FDI (around 49 per cent in 2003), tourism and communication services accounted for 24 and 21.4 per cent of total FDI inflows, respectively (Pant and Sigdel 2004). Similar information is not available for Bhutan and the Maldives. However, discussions suggest that the tourism sector attracts a large part of the services

FDI in the Maldives, while the tourism and energy services segments are the main recipients of FDI in the case of Bhutan. Overall, there is clearly scope for increased intra-regional FDI given some apparent complementarities in the service sector across investor and recipient countries and the continued deregulation of many services in the South Asian countries.[15]

Identifying Potential Services for Regional Integration

Drawing upon the earlier discussion on trends in output and trade performance, an attempt was made to identify at a broad level, without getting into sub-sectoral specificities, those services which are likely to hold the most promise for regional integration. This approach is based on identifying those high performing services which are common across three or more countries in the region (that is, where there is a critical mass of countries) to assess potential commonality of interest as well as to identify low performing services where some other countries could potentially contribute based on complementarities in performance.

Tables 2A.11, 2A.12, and 2A.13 categorize the output, export, and import performance of the service sector, respectively, in each of the South Asian countries. In each case, the categorization is done based on rates of growth for output and trade and the service sector's contribution to output or trade flows. A threshold growth rate of 8 per cent was taken to categorize services into high and low growth performers, and a threshold contribution of 10 per cent to categorize services into high and low contribution in GDP. These threshold rates were selected based on the performance of services across the different countries.

The sectors that exhibit high growth rates coupled with a high shares in GDP or trade for a critical mass of countries in the region, are those which potentially present the best prospects for regional integration. From the data on output trends, the one sector that shows high growth across the largest number of countries in the region is transport, storage, and communication services. If one also allows for high growth sectors with low shares of GDP, that is, those which are performing well and are likely to grow in importance in the overall activity in these economies, then energy services emerges as another prospective area where there is growth potential. There are also differences in the performance for these same services across the countries, with some of the countries showing lower growth rates or contributions to GDP in these sub-sectors. The latter may indicate complementarities

---

[15] These complementarities in selected services and trends in liberalization of services in the South Asian countries are discussed at length in later chapters.

in resource endowments or differences in the level of maturity of different services which create possibilities for trade flows from the high performing countries to the lagging countries possibly supported by investments from the larger deficit countries to the smaller countries. For instance, there is complementarity in the case of energy services with high growth performers like Bhutan and Nepal and slow growth performers like India and Pakistan, or in the case of communication services with high growth performers like India and low growth performers like Bangladesh. It is also interesting to note the generally low growth as well as low shares for social services such as healthcare and education, indicating the untapped potential in these areas and possibilities for future growth in these segments.

If one juxtaposes the trade related categorization of services with that for output, then the set of services where there are prospects for regional integration, expands. These include travel, transport, communication, financial, business, and computer and information services. Several of these services show high growth rates for exports and imports combined with low shares in trade, implying that these segments are likely to become important in trade (and investment) flows over time and that there is unrealized potential. The fact that both exports and imports show high growth rates indicates that the region shows a general openness to trade in these segments. It is also worth noting that some services, such as travel and transport appear to be the most promising, exhibiting high growth and high shares in almost all the countries.

Overall, there appear to be three factors that would propel regional integration in services in South Asia. The first factor relates to the possibility of leveraging of each other's resource endowments, such as in energy services and differences in size and demand-supply gaps are likely to be important in such services. The second factor relates to the unrealized potential and emerging commercial opportunities in some areas, such as telecommunication, tourism, and business services within the region, with some countries placed better within the region to export their expertise or investment or technology in these areas. Finally, it is also evident from the list of services that investment would have to play an important role in increased intra-regional penetration and that trade in services would need to be supported by investment and labour flows in services in many sub-sectors.

Implications for Regional Integration

The preceding discussion has highlighted several interesting trends and features about the service sector in South Asia, which suggest that there is scope for increased intra-regional trade and factor flows within the region.

It is worth summarizing some of the most salient points highlighted earlier and what they would imply regarding the likely nature of and scope for regional integration in services in South Asia and what a prospective regional agreement on services would need to consider.

First and foremost, all the countries in this region have seen a shift in the structure of their economies away from agriculture and towards services. There has similarly been increased growth in services trade and investment in all the economies and South Asia's contribution in global services trade has increased over the past decade. The growing role of services in GDP, the high output as well as trade growth witnessed in several service sub-sectors validate the contention that services (as well as investment since many services would only be tradable through FDI flows) are a potential thrust area for furthering regional integration.

Second, there is considerable variation across the countries in this region in terms of the size of their service economies, the output and export growth performance of services, the relative shares of individual economies in regional services trade and output, and in their revealed comparative advantage indices. Much of the superior performance of the region as a whole is attributable to the performance of India's service sector in terms of the growing diversification of its export basket and emergence of non-traditional service segments and India's increased penetration of the world market, particularly in computer and information services and in business services. Given such asymmetries, the South Asian countries are likely to have very divergent interests in each other's markets and there is likely to be a lot of asymmetry in the roles they would play in any regional integration process in services. India would probably need to act as the main driver of services integration in South Asia. Moreover, bilateral or plurilateral relations in certain areas where there is commonality of interest and complementarity in endowments, would also be an important driving force for any regional discussions on services.

Third, there are potential complementarities with regard to capital and labour flows across countries in the region. Some countries, such as India, with more established service sector companies which are also engaging in outward investment could emerge as sources of FDI in sub-sectors, such as energy, communication, and tourism services, while other countries in the region could clearly benefit from FDI inflows into these sub-sectors. Likewise, in the case of labour flows within the region, India provides an attractive destination market for migrant workers from the smaller and poorer countries in the region and the Maldives provides employment opportunities in niche segments. There is also scope for movement of professionals and intra-company transferees in business services, particular from India to the smaller countries given India's growing competitiveness in business services and the general openness of this segment in most countries. The sub-sectoral trends in growth, trade, and competitiveness suggest that there is a potential commonality of interests within the region in areas such as communication, tourism, and computer and information services. Given the factor-intensity of some of these sub-sectors, factor flows in the form of investments and movement of service providers are likely to be important for furthering intra-regional commerce in these areas.

Fourth, the significance of traditional and governmental services in the growth and trade pattern for some of the countries in this region suggests that discussions on services integration cannot overlook issues of regulatory cooperation and capacity building in services. Intergovernmental cooperation in the provision and delivery of services and collaboration amongst regulatory bodies, public sector institutions, and associations would have to be an important element of services integration in this region.

Finally, an important issue highlighted by the development of the service sector in the South Asian economies is its relatively smaller contribution to employment as opposed to trade and output. As highlighted earlier, this raises issues of sustainability of services growth given the large and young labour force and the need for employment creation for poverty alleviation and attaining the MDGs in this region. However, it also points to the possibility of using any regional services agreement to address employment and sustainability related concerns in the service sector, by facilitating the sector's contribution to employment, productivity growth, and its linkages with other sectors of these economies.

The following chapters examine some of the services identified in this chapter as having the most potential for trade, investment, and cooperation. These include telecommunications, energy, tourism, healthcare, and education services. Other areas, such as IT and transport services as well as cross-cutting issues of investment and mobility of service providers are highlighted in terms of their bearing on the selected set of services. For each of these services, the analysis focuses on recent performance, current and prospective regional initiatives, the extent and nature of liberalization, and issues to be addressed in any regional integration efforts. The aim of this sub-sectoral analysis is to assess the opportunities for and constraints to deepening regional integration in different services segments and the overall prospects for services integration in South Asia.

Appendix 2A:
Significance of Labour and Investment Flows in South Asia

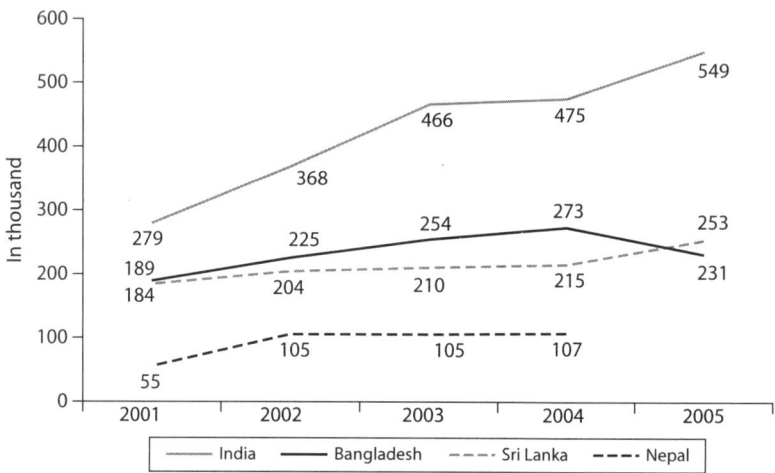

Figure 2A.1   Labour Migration Outflows for South Asia, 2001–5

Source: Reproduced from International Organization for Migration (IOM), *World Migration Report* (2008), Figure 3, p. 442.

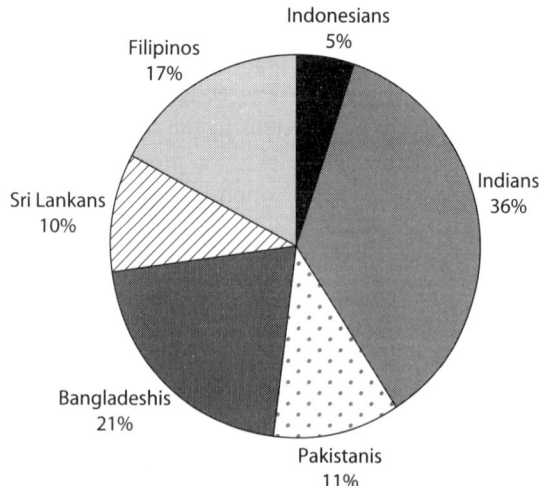

Figure 2A.2   Estimated Stock of Asian Origin Temporary Contractual Workers in the Middle East

Source: Reproduced from IOM, *World Migration Report* (2008), Figure 4, p. 443.

Table 2A.1 Departures for Foreign Employment from Sri Lanka for Top 10 Countries and by Manpower Level, 2005

Country	Professional Level	Middle Level	Clerical and Related	Skilled	Unskilled	Housemaid	Total
Saudi Arabia	314	1,802	1,432	12,411	10,063	50,091	76,113
Kuwait	58	470	410	4,395	2,203	28,563	36,099
UAE	408	2,269	3,014	8,179	8,790	13,646	36,306
Qatar	339	1,414	1,723	13,028	14,570	4,858	35,932
Lebanon	1	50	14	73	273	15,978	16,389
Jordan	16	99	163	2,917	221	4,859	8,275
South Korea	1,086	641	3	31	3,086	2	4,849
Oman	109	469	307	704	381	1,551	3,521
Bahrain	53	180	156	890	322	2,142	3,743
Maldives	163	305	374	921	802	154	2,719

Source: *Sri Lanka Bureau of Foreign Employment.*

Table 2A.2 Number of Immigrants (25 or Older) to the OECD by Level of Educational Attainment, 2000

Country	Total Immigrants	Educational Level		
		Primary or Less	Secondary	Tertiary
East Asia				
China	722,400	148,029	185,295	389,076
Indonesia	142,540	3,910	32,347	106,283
Philippines	356,134	27,604	70,079	258,452
Eastern Europe/Central Asia				
Turkey	1,913,782	263,078	534,429	1,116,275
Latin America/Caribbean				
Brazil	176,519	16,026	64,097	96,396
Jamaica	117,199	9,483	54,647	53,069
Middle East/North Africa				
Morocco	560,658	30,706	168,179	361,773
Tunisia	142,828	10,027	41,782	91,019
Egypt	20,373	733	3,796	15,844
South Asia				
Bangladesh	44,417	3,852	12,902	27,663
India	375,283	18,471	57,199	299,613
Pakistan	85,668	6,022	22,458	57,188
Sri Lanka	64,143	1,455	16,741	45,947
Total	4,721,944	539,396	1,263,951	2,918,597

Source: Adams (June 2003), Table 4, p. 26 (based on OECD, *Trends in International Migration*, Annual Report, 2001).

Table 2A.3   Work Permits and First Permissions by Occupation for Indians and Pakistanis in the UK, 2005

Country	India		Pakistan	
	Number of Work Permits	Proportions of Occupation by Nationality	Number of Work Permits	Proportions of Occupation by Nationality
Managers and senior officials	2,831	9.7	313	10.9
Professional occupations	17,053	58.3	807	28
Associate professional and technical occupations	7,156	24.5	926	32.1
Administrative and secretarial occupations	16	0.1	1	0
Skilled trades occupations	924	3.2	475	16.5
Personal service occupations	512	1.7	261	9.1
Sales and customer service occupations	4	0	1	0
Process, plant, and machine operatives	20	0.1	7	0.2
Elementary occupations	745	2.5	92	3.2
All occupations	29,261	100	2,883	100

Source: Based on Salt (2006).

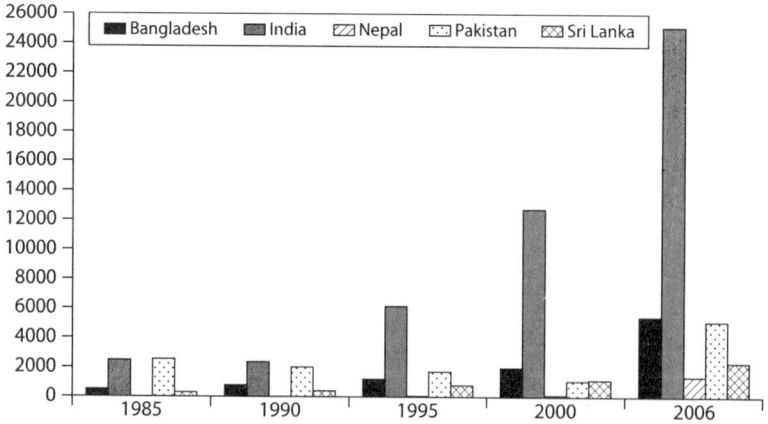

Figure 2A.3   Trends in Workers' Remittances in South Asian Countries, 1985–2006 (US$ mn, current prices)

Source: Based on UNCTAD (2008).

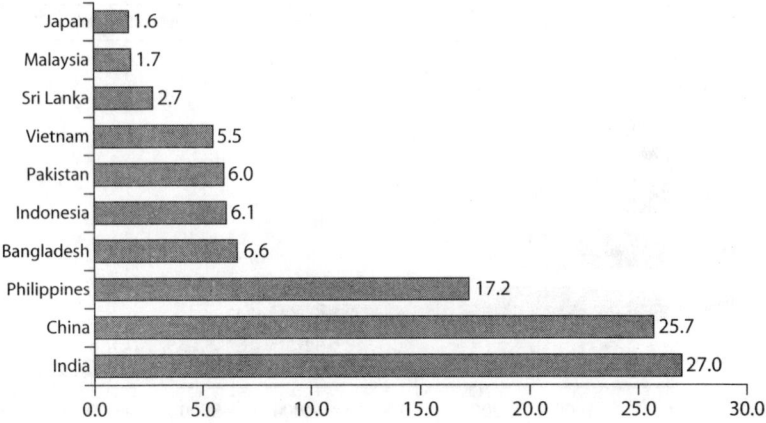

Figure 2A.4   Remittances Received in Asia by Main Countries of Origin, 2007 (US$ billion)

Source: Reproduced from IOM, *World Migration Report* (2008), Figure 15, p. 449.

Table 2A.4   Workers Remittances (Receipts) as Per cent of GDP for South Asian Countries

YEAR	1985	1990	1995	2000	2006
Bangladesh	2.29	2.45	2.91	4.03	7.94
India	1.09	0.72	1.66	2.72	2.78
Nepal	–	–	1.35	2.09	16.99
Pakistan	6.46	3.51	2.10	1.37	3.48
Sri Lanka	4.86	4.88	5.91	6.83	8.50

Source: Based on UNCTAD (2008).

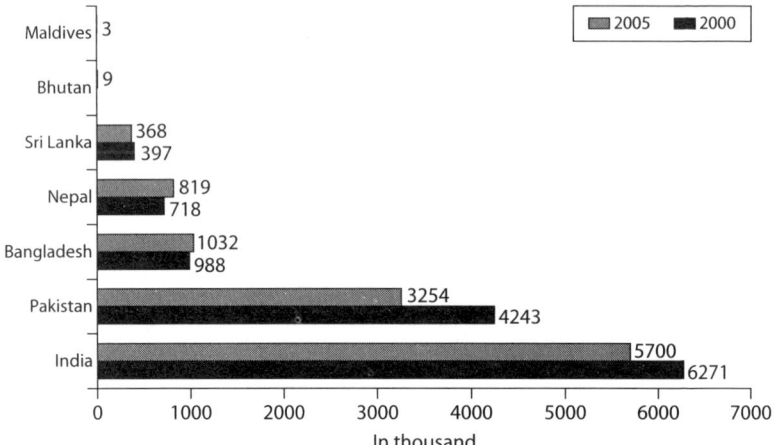

Figure 2A.5   Stock of Migrants in South Asian Countries by Destination, 2000 and 2005

Source: Reproduced from IOM, *World Migration Report* (2008), Figure 2: Part A, p. 441.

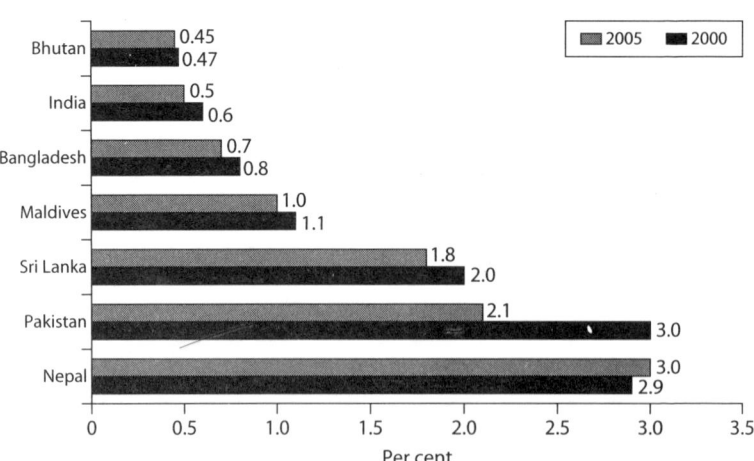

Figure 2A.6   Migrant Workers as a Share of Total Population

Source: Reproduced from IOM, *World Migration Report* (2008), Figure 2: Part B, p. 442.

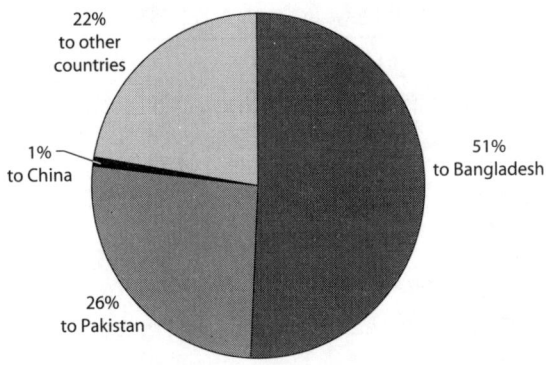

Figure 2A.7 Remittances Sent from India to Selected Countries, 2006 (US$ mn)
Source: Reproduced from IOM, *World Migration Report* (2008), Figure 16, p. 450.

Table 2A.5 Remittance Payments as a Share of GDP (per cent)

	1991	1995	2000	2006
Bangladesh	..	..	0.01	0.00
India	..	..	0.02	0.08
Maldives	6.78	6.66	7.41	9.17
Nepal	..	0.21	0.31	0.85
Pakistan	..	0.01	0.00	0.00
Sri Lanka	..	..	..	0.94

Source: UNCTAD (2008).

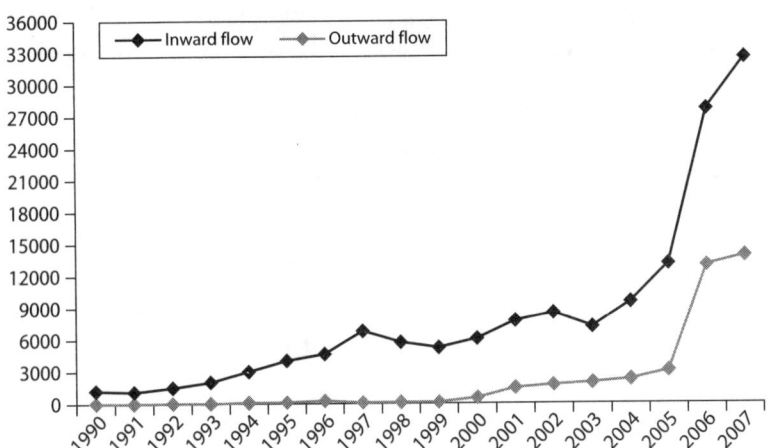

Figure 2A.8 FDI Inflows into South Asia, 1991–2007 (US$ mn at current prices)

Source: Based on UNCTAD (2008).

Table 2A.6   Trends in FDI Flows in South Asia (US$ mn at current prices)

	Inward FDI Flow				Outward FDI Flow			
	1990	1995	2000	2007	1990	1995	2000	2007
Bangladesh	3.2	92.3	578.7	666.4	0.5	1.7	2.0	21.0
Bhutan	1.6	0.1	0	78.3	0	0	0	0
India	236.7	2151	3585	22,950	6.0	119.0	509.0	13,649.0
Maldives	5.6	7.2	13.0	15.0	0.0	0.0	0.0	0.0
Nepal	5.9	0.0	−0.5	5.7	0.0	0.0	0.0	0.0
Pakistan	278.3	492.1	309.0	5,333.0	2.0	0.0	11.0	98.0
Sri Lanka	43.4	65.0	173.0	528.7	0.8	5.6	2.0	95.0

Source: UNCTAD (2008).

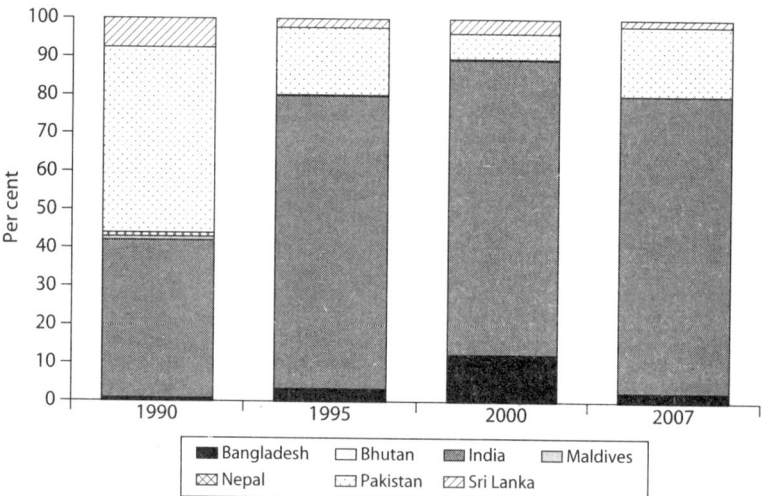

Figure 2A.9   Share of Countries in FDI Inflows in South Asia
Source: Based on UNCTAD (2008).

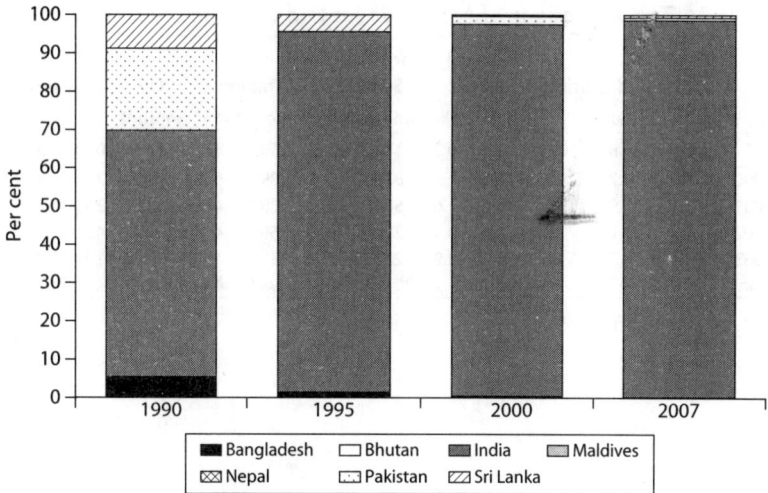

Figure 2A.10   Share of Countries in FDI Outflows in South Asia
Source: Based on UNCTAD (2008).

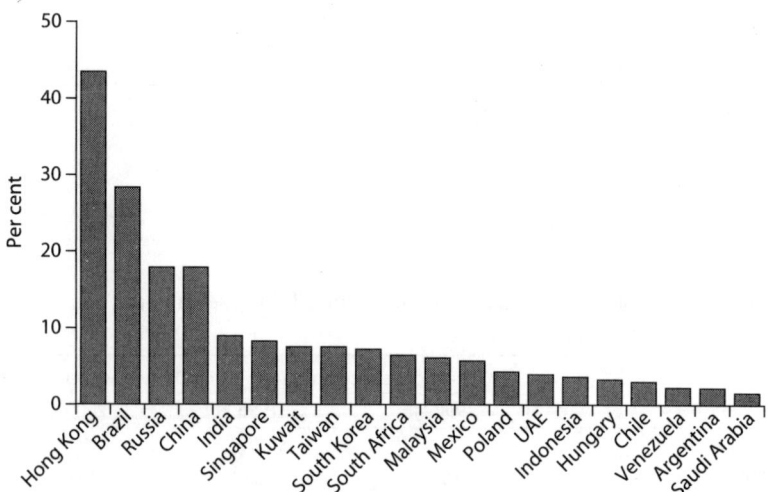

Figure 2A.11   FDI Outflows from Emerging Markets, 2006 (US$ billion)
Source: Reproduced from Economist Intelligence Unit, *World Investment Prospects to 2011*, p. 28.

Table 2A.7   Composition of Approved Outward FDI from India (US$ mn)

Year	Manufacturing Amount	%	Financial Services Amount	%	Non-financial Services Amount	%	Trading Amount	%	Others Amount	%	Total Amount
1999–2000	535.8	30.9	4.3	0.2	1130.7	65.3	58.3	3.4	2.3	0.1	1731.5
2000–1	370.7	26.8	16.6	1.2	876.5	63.4	89.2	6.5	29.1	2.1	1382.2
2001–2	2210.9	73.0	48.6	1.6	565.5	18.7	139.2	4.6	62.3	2.1	3027.0
2002–3	1056.7	71.8	1.8	0.1	280.2	19.0	69.9	4.7	63.7	4.3	1472.2
2003–4	504.5	55.7	35.1	3.9	223.3	24.6	37.0	4.1	106.3	11.7	906.3
Total	4678.7	54.9	106.4	1.2	3076.2	36.1	393.5	4.6	263.7	3.1	8519.2

Source: UNCTAD (2008).

Table 2A.8   Intra-regional FDI Flows in South Asia (Per cent of Total Regional FDI Inflows)

Source of FDI	Recipient of FDI India	Pakistan	Sri Lanka	Bangladesh	Nepal
India	x	–	2.60	0.20	51.00
Pakistan	–	x	0.60	0.10	0.03
Sri Lanka	–	–	x	0.10	–
Bangladesh	0.01	0.08	0.18	x	–
Nepal	–	–	–	–	x
Share of South Asia	0.04	–	2.10	0.40	37.60

Source: ADB, *South Asia Economic Report 2008*.

Table 2A.9   Share of Services in Total Inward FDI for Select South Asian Countries

	Share of Services in Total Inward FDI (avg. per cent) 1990–4	1995–9	2000–2
Bangladesh		28.5	45.7
India	10.5	28.3	20.97
Nepal	52.7	68.3	
Pakistan	64.6	69.1	56.6
Sri Lanka		75.4	48.1

Source: UNCTAD, *World Investment Report 2004*.

Table 2A.10 Composition of FDI Inflows into Services in Bangladesh, India, and Pakistan (Latest Year Available)

	Service Sector	Volume of Inward FDI (US$ mn)	Share in Total Inward FDI (%)
Bangladesh (2006)			
1	Power, gas, and petroleum	208.2	26.27
1.1	Power	21.2	2.68
1.2	Gas and petroleum	187.2	23.62
2	Manufacturing	104.9	13.24
2.1	Textile and wearing	17.1	2.16
2.2	Cement	2.6	0.33
3	Trade and commerce	130.2	16.43
3.1	Banking	117.7	14.85
4	Transport, storage, and communication	347	43.79
4.1	Telecommunications	346.5	43.72
5	Services	0.2	0.03
	Total inward FDI	792.5	100.00
	Share of services (3+4+5+6)	**86.54%**	
India (2007–8)			
1	Financial services	6615	26.91
2	Computer software and hardware	1410	5.74
3	Construction	1743	7.09
4	Telecommunications	1261	5.13
5	Housing and Real Estate	2179	8.87
6	Power	967	3.93
8	Petroleum and Natural Gas	1427	5.81
	Total inward FDI	24579	
	Share of services (1–8)	**52.19%**	
Pakistan (2008)			
1	Power	70.29	1.36
1.1	Thermal	61.56	1.19
1.2	Hydel	8.83	0.17
1.3	Coal-based	0.00	0.00
2	Trade	175.53	3.41
3	Tourism	41.48	0.81
4	Transport	38.22	0.74
5	Storage facilities	0.59	0.01
6	Communications	1625.42	31.54
6.1	Telecommunications	1438.65	27.92
6.2	Information technology	180.72	3.51
6.2.1	Software development	13.61	0.26
6.2.2	Hardware development	6.62	0.13
6.2.3	IT services	160.49	3.11
6.3	Postal and courier services	5.95	0.12
7	Financial business	1607.70	31.20
8	Social services	14.16	0.27
9	Personal services	92.99	1.80
	Total inward FDI	5152.80	
	Share of services (1–9)	**71.15%**	

Source: Bangladesh—Board of Investment; India—Department of Industrial Policy and Promotion, Ministry of Commerce and Industry; Pakistan—State Bank of Pakistan.

Table 2A.11 Categorizing Performance in Key Services in South Asian
Countries (Based on Latest Data)

Country	High Growth Rate with High Share in GDP	High Growth Rate with Low Share in GDP	Low Growth Rate with High Share in GDP	Low Growth Rate with Low Share in GDP
Bangladesh			• Construction • Wholesale and retail trade • Transport, storage, and communication • Real estate renting and business activities • Community, social, and personal services	• Power and water supply • Hotels and restaurants • Financial intermediaries • Public administration and defence • Education • Health and social work
Bhutan	• Electricity, gas, and water supply • Transport, storage, and communication	• Wholesale and retail trade • Hotels and restaurants • Finance and insurance	• Construction • Community and social services • Public administration	• Real estate and dwellings • Health and education • Private social, community, and recreational services
India	• Construction • Banking and insurance	• Communications • Hotels and restaurants	• Trade • Real estate and ownership of dwellings • Other services	• Electricity, gas, and water supply • Railways • Transport by other means • Storage • Public administration and defence
Maldives	• Transport and communication • Government administration	• Electricity, gas, and water supply • Construction	• Tourism	• Wholesale and retail trade • Finance • Real estate • Business services • Education, health, and personal services
Nepal	• Wholesale and retail trade • Transport, storage, and communication	• Electricity, gas, and water	• Construction • Real estate renting and business • Education	• Hotels and restaurants • Financial intermediation • Public administration and defence • Health and social work • Other community, social, and personal services

(*Contd . . .*)

(*Table 2A.11 contd...*)

Country	High Growth Rate with High Share in GDP	High Growth Rate with Low Share in GDP	Low Growth Rate with High Share in GDP	Low Growth Rate with Low Share in GDP
Pakistan	• Finance and Insurance		• Transport, storage, and communication • Wholesale and retail trade • Public administration and defence • Community, personal, and social services	• Electricity, gas, and water supply • Construction • Ownership of dwellings
Sri Lanka		• Electricity • Hotels and restaurants • Post and telecommunication	• Import trade • Domestic trade • Transport • Banking, insurance, and real estate • Government services	• Gas • Water • Construction • Export trade • Cargo handling: ports and civil aviation • Ownership of dwellings • Private services

Source: Computations based on National Accounts Statistics of all countries from central bank documents, statistical bureaus, and other official sources.

Table 2A.12   Summary of Key Services Exports Sectors for South Asian Countries, 2006

Exports	High Growth Rate with High Share in Exports	High Growth Rate with Low Share in Exports	Low Growth Rate with High Share in Exports	Low Growth Rate with Low Share in Exports
Bangladesh	• Other business services	• Communications • Construction • Transport • Insurance • Financial services • Computer and information services • Royalties and license fees • Personal, cultural, and recreational services	• Government services	• Travel
India	• Transport • Travel • Computer and information services	• Communications • Insurance • Finance • Other business services		• Construction • Royalties and fees • Government services
Maldives		• Royalties and license fees	• Travel	• Transport • Insurance • Government services
Nepal			• Travel • Other business services • Government services	• Transport
Pakistan	• Other business services • Government services	• Travel • Insurance • Financial • Computer and information services	• Transport	• Communications
Sri Lanka	• Transport • Travel		• Other business services	• Communications • Insurance • Government services

Source: Computations based on National Accounts Statistics of all countries from central bank documents, statistical bureaus, and other official sources.

Table 2A.13 Summary of Key Services Imports Sectors for South Asian Countries, 2006

Imports	High Growth Rate with High Share in Imports	High Growth Rate with Low Share in Imports	Low Growth Rate with High Share in Imports	Low Growth Rate with Low Share in Imports
Bangladesh	• Transport	• Communications • Insurance • Computer and information services • Other business services • Personal, cultural, and recreational services • Government services		• Travel • Construction • Financial • Royalties and license fees
India	• Transport • Travel • Other business services	• Communications • Construction • Insurance • Computer and information services • Royalties and license fees • Government services		• Financial
Maldives	• Transport • Travel	• Insurance • Other business services • Government services		
Nepal	• Transport • Travel		• Other business services	• Government services
Pakistan	• Transport • Travel • Other business services	• Communications • Insurance • Financial • Government services		
Sri Lanka			• Transport • Travel • Other business services	• Communications • Insurance • Government services

Source: Computations based on National Accounts Statistics of all countries from central bank documents, statistical bureaus, and other official sources.

3

Telecommunication Services
Need for a Pro-competitive Approach

Telecommunication services are recognized as a critical element in the development of a country's infrastructure. Improved communication facilities can play an important role in accelerating growth, improving access to markets, enhancing trade and investment prospects, and reducing poverty and inequality. All over the world, the telecommunication sector has witnessed rapid advancements in technology and the emergence of new segments and value added services. It has also undergone considerable liberalization, including corporatization of erstwhile government telecom providers, privatization, and entry of foreign investors. In the past decade or so, developing countries around the world have implemented national telecommunication policies that have restructured and deregulated their telecom service sectors with the ultimate objectives of lowering connectivity costs, improving the quality of telecom services, and meeting universal service obligations. Independent regulatory bodies have also been established in many countries, though often this process has been a complex one, fraught with challenges. The South Asian countries have also followed a similar trajectory in terms of their telecom sector policies and initiatives over the past decade.

As identified in the previous chapter, telecommunication services are a potential area where greater regional integration can be pursued in South Asia. A combination of factors makes this sector particularly appealing and conducive to regional discussions. These include the high growth rates and rising contribution of telecom services to GDP, the opening up of the sector to foreign ownership in several of the South Asian countries, the potential pooling of resources for investment and regulatory capacity building, and the common goal across all the countries in this region of augmenting investment in telecom infrastructure and establishing regulatory frameworks in order to improve efficiency, affordability, and access. Such commonalities in policy trends and objectives, combined with large resource gaps and investment requirements, create scope for both collaborative and commercial relations in telecom services within the region.

This chapter starts by providing a background overview of the telecom services sector in South Asia along various dimensions. It shows where South Asia is placed vis-à-vis the world in terms of key telecom sector indicators and performance measures, in order to highlight the overall infrastructure requirements and investment needs in this sector. This is followed by an overview of the trends in key indicators for telecom services in each of the South Asian countries to identify what has been the growth trajectory in this sector, and the differences and similarities across the countries in this regard. The chapter next highlights the trends observed in telecom sector policies and regulatory reforms in the South Asian countries over the past decade or so and relates these developments to their sectoral performance. This discussion is followed by an overview of the intra-regional initiatives and projects that are in place or planned in this sector. These include initiatives on regulatory cooperation and frameworks, and proposed or on-the-ground cross-border investments in telecom services between countries in the region. The discussion highlights the progress of such intra-regional efforts and commercial ventures. Next the chapter discusses the multilateral and other commitments made by the South Asian countries in the telecom services sector, in the context of the WTO and in various bilateral or extra-regional agreements, respectively to highlight the extent to which these countries are prepared for liberalization and reforms. The concluding section of this chapter draws on an analysis of trends, initiatives, and commitments to highlight the main opportunity areas for greater intra-regional integration, the challenges that exist, and specific issues that would need to be pursued in regional negotiations.

Overview of Telecommunication Services

The telecommunication services sector has witnessed rapid growth in the South Asian countries over the past decade. The total subscription base for the region increased from a mere 41.8 million in 2000 to around 540 million in 2008 and the teledensity (number of total subscriptions per 100 persons) in the region grew manifold from a median of 2.52 to around 32. There have been significant increases in the number of subscriptions, as well as penetration across the various segments of the telecom sector, including fixed line, mobile, and internet services. Tables 3.1 and 3.2 provide the current status of the telecom sector in South Asia and also

Table 3.1　Status of Fixed Line and Mobile Telephony in South Asia, Selected Other Countries and the World, 2008

Country	Total Telephone Subscriptions ('000s)	Total Teledensity (Subscribers per 100 Persons)	Total Fixed Subscription ('000s)	Fixed Teledensity (per 100)	Mobile Subscriptions ('000s)	Mobile Teledensity	Mobile as % of Total Telephone Subscriptions
World	**5,201,839.2**	**76.91**	**1,269,856.6**	**18.77**	**4,018,807.3**	**59.34**	**75.6**
South Asia							
Bangladesh	45,984.5	28.74	1,344.5	0.84	44,640.0	27.9	97.1
Bhutan	278.5	40.55	27.5	4	251	36.55	90.1
India	384,790.0	32.57	37,900	3.21	346,890	29.36	90.2
Maldives	482.6	158.2	46.9	15.38	435.6	142.82	90.3
Nepal	5,005.1	17.37	805.1	2.79	4200	14.58	83.9
Pakistan	92,436.2	52.24	4,416.4	2.5	88,019.7	49.74	95.2
Sri Lanka	14,528.7	72.42	3,446.4	17.18	11,082.2	55.24	76.3
Others							
Brazil	191,782.8	99.9	41,141.4	21.43	150,641.4	78.47	78.5
China	912,943	68.69	365,637	27.51	634,000	47.41	59.9
Malaysia	31,417	116.3	4,292	15.89	27,125	100.41	86.3
Singapore	8,232.6	178.39	1,857.1	40.24	6,375.5	138.15	77.4
South Africa	4,9425	99.51	4425	8.91	45,000	90.6	91
Thailand	69,024	102.43	7,024	10.42	62,000	92.01	89.8

Source: ITU World Telecommunications Regulatory Database.

for selected developing countries and the world to place the South Asian region in a comparative perspective. Table 3.1 provides the basic statistics for telephone services while Table 3.2 provides summary statistics for internet services.

Tables 3.1 and 3.2 clearly indicate that notwithstanding the growth of the telecom sector in South Asia, the region remains behind other developing countries and also compares poorly with available global averages. Although it is difficult to do a one-to-one comparison of SAARC member countries with other selected countries, given the wide variation in size and levels of development across the South Asian countries, a few features regarding the state of development of their telecom sectors are quite evident.

Overall, teledensity as well as fixed and mobile teledensity are lower in all South Asian countries, except for the Maldives and Sri Lanka, when compared to that in selected developing countries. They are also lower than the global average except in the case of the Maldives (which has very high teledensity ratios of over 100 per cent). It is worth noting that the indicators for the South Asian countries compare more favourably for mobile teledensity than for fixed teledensity. They show a higher share of

Table 3.2 Status of Internet and Broadband Use in South Asia, Selected Countries and the World, 2008

Country	No. of Internet Subscriptions ('000s)	Internet Subscribers per 100 Persons	Internet Users ('000s)	Internet Users per 100 People	Broadband Subscribers ('000s)	Broadband Subscribers per 100 Persons
World	**529,541**	**8.35**	**10,599,610.7**	**156.92**	**412,357**	**6.15**
South Asia						
Bangladesh	150	0.1	556	0.35	43.7	0.03
Bhutan	6	0.87	40	5.82	2.1	0.3
India	12,850.0	1.09	81,000.0	6.95	5,280.0	0
Maldives	17.9	5.86	71.7	23.52	15.7	5.15
Nepal	79.5	0.28	499	1.73	9.9	0.04
Pakistan	3,700.0	2.09	18,500.0	10.45	168.1	0
Sri Lanka	246.2	1.23	1,148.3	5.72	100.2	0.5
Others						
Brazil	11,401.9	5.94	64,948.0	33.83	10,098.0	5.26
China	150,264.0	11.31	298,000.0	22.28	83,366.0	6.23
Malaysia	5,21.6	19.33	16,02.6	62.57	1,301.6	4.82
Singapore	1,103.4	23.91	3,70.0	73.02	1,003.1	21.74
South Africa	3,566.0	7.51	4,187.0	8.43	378	0.77
Thailand	...	...	12,130.0	18	913	1.36

Source: ITU World Telecommunications Regulatory Database.

mobile subscriptions to total subscriptions than the world average and are either comparable to or higher than in the selected countries, indicating the much greater growth witnessed in their mobile telephony segment. The latter is also evident from the high CAGRs for mobile telephony, which are several times higher than those in the selected other countries and also the global average. This difference in relative performance between fixed and mobile segments in the South Asian countries is not only an indication of the growth potential in the mobile segment, but is also indicative of the regulation, policy, and infrastructure related factors which have affected the fixed line segment more than the mobile segment.

It is evident from the summary statistics on internet penetration and usage in Table 3.2 that all the South Asian countries are far behind other developing nations and also the global average in the internet services segment. The latter is indicative of the lack of related communications and electricity infrastructure, the low levels of literacy, per capita income, and urbanization in this region which adversely affect the ability to access and use internet services. The latter is also captured by the very low levels of computer ownership in this region—20 or less per 100 persons (ADB 2008c).

However, data from the World Bank's database on private sector participation shows that South Asia is comparable with other developing regions in terms of the value of private sector investment committed in recent

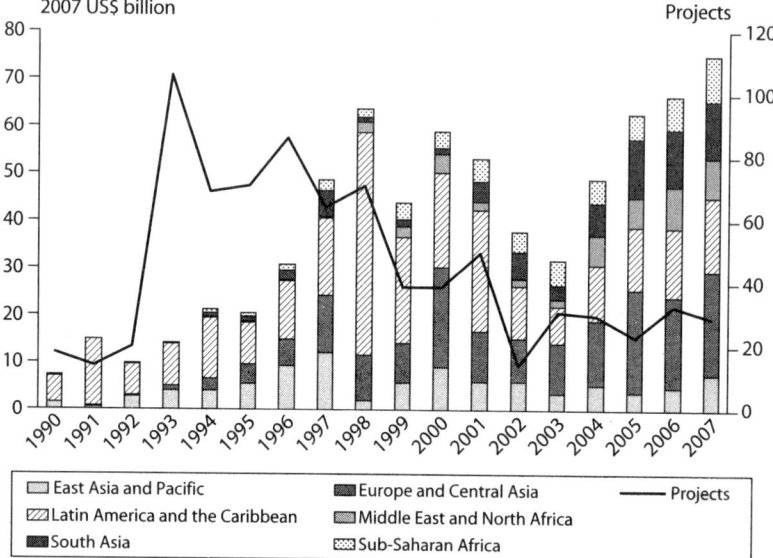

Figure 3.1   Investment Commitments in Telecom Projects with Private Participation in Developing Countries, by Region, 1990–2007

Source: Reproduced from World Bank and Public–Private Infrastructure Advisory Facility (PPIAF), Private Participation in Infrastructure (PPI) Project Database presentation on 'PPI in Developing Countries', p. 7. Available at http://ppi.worldbank. org/features/Dec2009/2008ECADataset.pptx, accessed on 2 October 2009.

years. The region's importance in this regard has increased, particularly since 2000, as shown in Figure 3.1. This growth has in a large part been driven by investments in the mobile telephony segment.

Overall, the telecom sector in South Asia, despite its rapid growth in recent years, remains underdeveloped. This is particularly so in the internet segment and the fixed line segment. However, there is a large untapped subscriber base in the region and there are considerable opportunities for further growth and infrastructure development.

Trends in Telecom Sector Performance

An examination of the trends in telecom services, as captured by the usual indicators of performance in this sector, reveals several common features. All the countries have experienced an increase of anywhere between 10 to 60 times in their total subscription base for telecom services (fixed and mobile) and anywhere between a 10 to 50-fold increase in their teledensities (although the region still lies much below the world average and below comparable developing countries). In all the countries, the main contributor to growth in subscriptions and teledensity has been the mobile segment.

There is, however, also a huge variation across the South Asian countries in the size and levels of penetration of their telecom sectors and in the rate of expansion. For instance, total teledensity ranged from a low of 17.27 for Nepal to 158.2 for the Maldives in 2008, with a median teledensity of 32.57. The magnitude of increase also varied within the region, with the Maldives experiencing a rapid increase in teledensity during 2000–8, followed by Sri Lanka.

Figures 3.2 and 3.3 and Table 3.3 and illustrate the growth in subscriptions, teledensity, and internet penetration in each of the South Asian countries over the past decade or more to highlight some of these common features as well as differences.

As seen in Table 3.3, mobile telephony has experienced particularly high growth. It has come to occupy a growing and significant share of total subscriptions in all the countries. Figure 3.3 further shows that across all the countries in the region, growth in teledensity has been driven by a huge increase in mobile subscriptions rather than in fixed line subscriptions.

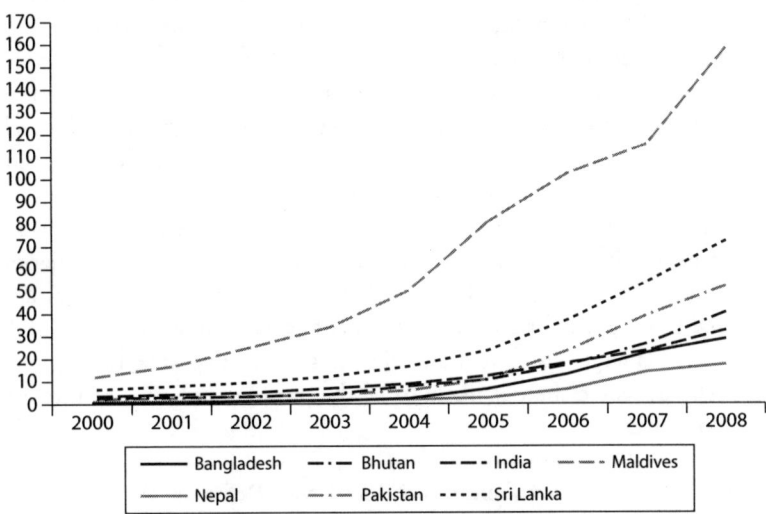

Figure 3.2   Trends in Total Teledensity in the South Asian Countries, 2000–8

Source: Based on ITU, World Telecom Regulatory Database.

Note: Total teledensity refers to the total number of fixed lines cum mobile connections, per 100 persons.

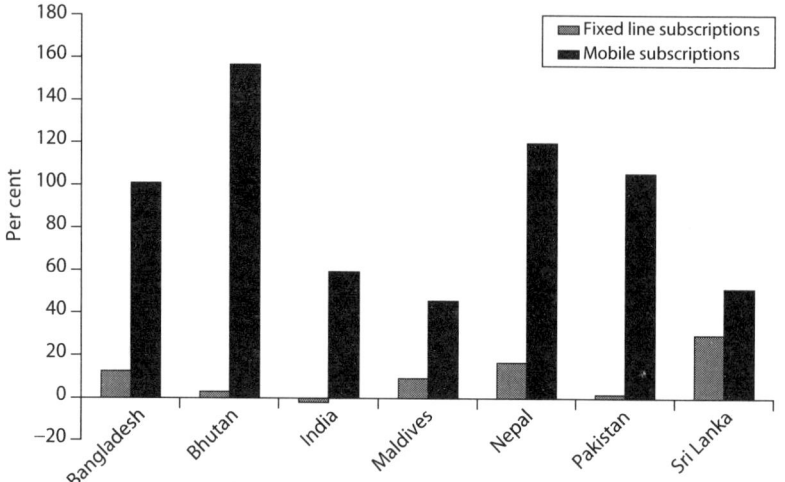

Figure 3.3   CAGR of Fixed Line and Mobile Subscriptions in the South Asian Countries, 2003–8

Source: Based on International Telecommunications Union ICT Indicators Database.

Internet penetration and subscribers have also grown manifold in all the South Asian countries, though in absolute terms the levels of usage still remain very low. Broadband penetration, however, is particularly low and stands below 1 for all the countries. Table 3.4 shows trends in internet subscriptions and penetration in the region. It clearly highlights the much more backward status of development in the internet services segment compared to basic and mobile telephony.

The expansion of scale and scope of services observed in the telecom sector in South Asia is a reflection of the liberalization and deregulation undertaken in this sector. The trends and performance indicators also highlight the need for further investment in certain segments. Mobile telephony emerges as potentially the most attractive area for regional discussions, where there is likely to be the most convergence of interests and objectives.

Policy Trends and Regulatory Reforms

All the South Asian countries have embraced the liberalization of telecom services, though to varying degrees and at varying paces. In almost all the countries, reforms began in the 1990s, starting with restructuring and partial privatization of state-owned incumbent operators, allowing entry into the

Table 3.3 Trends in Subscriptions, Teledensity, and Share of Mobile Subscriptions in South Asian Countries, 2000–8 ('000s and per cent)

Country	Indicator		1995	2000	2008
Bangladesh	Fixed telephone lines	No. of lines ('000s)	286.6	491.3	1,344.5
		Teledensity	0.25	0.38	0.84
	Mobile subscribers	No. of subscribers (000s)	2.5	279	44,640
		Mobile teledensity	n/a	0.22	27.9
		As % of total telephone subscribers	n/a	36.2	97.1
Bhutan	Fixed telephone lines	No. of lines ('000s)	5.2	14.1	27.5
		Teledensity	0.3	0.73	4.0
	Mobile subscribers	No. of subscribers ('000s)	n/a	n/a	251
		Mobile teledensity	n/a	n/a	36.55
		As % of total telephone subscribers	n/a	n/a	90.1
India	Fixed telephone lines	No. of lines ('000s)	11,978	32,436.1	37,900
		Teledensity	1.28	3.18	3.21
	Mobile subscribers	No. of subscribers ('000s)	76.7	3,577.1	346,890
		Mobile teledensity	n/a	0.35	29.36
		As % of total telephone subscribers	n/a	9.9	90.2
Maldives	Fixed telephone lines	No. of lines ('000s)	13.9	24.4	46.9
		Teledensity	5.51	8.42	15.38
	Mobile subscribers	No. of subscribers ('000s)	n/a	7.6	435.6
		Mobile teledensity	n/a	2.63	142.82
		As % of total telephone subscribers	n/a	23.8	90.3
Nepal	Fixed telephone lines	No. of lines ('000s)	83.7	266.9	805.1
		Teledensity	0.39	1.09	2.79
	Mobile subscribers	No. of subscribers ('000s)	n/a	10.2	4200
		Mobile teledensity	n/a	0.04	14.58
		As % of total telephone subscribers	n/a	3.7	83.9
Pakistan	Fixed telephone lines	No. of lines ('000s)	2,127.3	3,053.5	4,416.4
		Teledensity	1,69	2.14	2.5
	Mobile subscribers	No. of subscribers ('000s)	41	306.5	88019.7
		Mobile teledensity	n/a	0.21	49.74
		As % of total telephone subscribers	n/a	9.1	95.2
Sri Lanka	Fixed telephone lines	No. of lines (000s)	204.4	767.4	3,446.4
		Teledensity	1.08	3.87	17.8
	Mobile subscribers	No. of subscribers ('000s)	51.3	430.2	11,082.2
		Mobile teledensity	n/a	2.17	55.24
		As % of total telephone subscribers	n/a	35.9	76.3

Source: ITU, World Telecommunications Regulatory Database.

Table 3.4   Trends in Internet and Broadband Subscription and Penetration in South Asia, 2000 and 2008

Country	Indicator		2000	2008
Bangladesh	Internet penetration	No. of subscribers ('000s)	60	150
		Subscription per 100	0.4	0.1
	Broadband penetration	No. of subscribers ('000s)	n/a	43.7
		Subscription per 100	n/a	0.03
Bhutan	Internet penetration	No. of subscribers ('000s)	0.9	6
		Subscription per 100	0.13	0.87
	Broadband penetration	No. of subscribers ('000s)	n/a	2.1
		Subscription per 100	n/a	0.3
India	Internet penetration	No. of subscribers ('000s)	2,970	12,850
		Subscription per 100	0.28	1.09
	Broadband penetration	No. of subscribers ('000s)	n/a	5,280
		Subscription per 100	n/a	0
Maldives	Internet penetration	No. of subscribers ('000s)	1.1	17.9
		Subscription per 100	0.39	5.86
	Broadband penetration	No. of subscribers ('000s)	n/a	15.7
		Subscription per 100	n/a	5.15
Nepal	Internet penetration	No. of subscribers ('000s)	12	79.5
		Subscription per 100	0.05	0.28
	Broadband penetration	No. of subscribers ('000s)	n/a	9.9
		Subscription per 100	n/a	0.04
Pakistan	Internet penetration	No. of subscribers ('000s)	133.9	3,700
		Subscription per 100	0.09	2.09
	Broadband penetration	No. of subscribers ('000s)	n/a	168.1
		Subscription per 100	n/a	0
Sri Lanka	Internet penetration	No. of subscribers ('000s)	40.5	246.2
		Subscription per 100	0.22	1.23
	Broadband penetration	No. of subscribers ('000s)	n/a	100.2
		Subscription per 100	n/a	0.5

Source: ITU World Telecom Regulatory Database.

mobile telephony market and value added services, competition in the fixed line segment, adoption of national telecommunication policies, and establishment of regulatory commissions. By and large, mobile telephony, value added, and internet services have been opened up in most of the countries to full competition, while local and long distance landline services still remain subject to monopoly in a few countries. The objectives have been common across all the countries—to develop telecom infrastructure, provide universal access, and to improve the quality of telecom services. Table 3.5 gives the policy status in the telecom sector in the South Asian countries.

As indicated in Table 3.5, the South Asian countries are at different stages of liberalization in the telecom sector; the competitive scenario in this sector also varies. The two larger countries, Pakistan and India, have liberalized the most, allowing full competition in most segments while some of the

Table 3.5 Status of Competition and Liberalization in Telecommunication Services in South Asian Countries

Service[a]	Bangladesh (2005)	Bhutan (2007)	India (2005)	Maldives (2007)	Nepal (2007)	Pakistan (2007)	Sri Lanka (2007)
Local services	Full competition	Monopoly	Full competition	Monopoly	Partial competition	Full competition	Monopoly
Domestic fixed long dist.	Full competition	Monopoly	Full competition	Monopoly	Partial competition	Full competition	Partial competition
International fixed long dist.	Monopoly	Monopoly	Full competition	Monopoly	Partial competition	Full competition	Monopoly
Wireless local loop	Partial competition	Monopoly	Full competition	n/a	Partial competition	Full competition	Partial competition
Data	Full competition	Full competition	Full competition	Partial competition	Full competition	Full competition	Partial competition
DSL	Full competition	n/a	n/a	n/a	n/a	Full competition	Partial competition
Cable modem	n/a	n/a	Full competition	n/a	Full competition	n/a	Partial competition
VSAT	Full competition	Full competition	Full competition	n/a	Full competition	Full competition	Partial competition
Leased lines	n/a	Full competition	n/a	n/a	Full competition	Full competition	Partial competition
Fixed wireless broadband	n/a	Full competition	n/a	Partial competition	n/a	Full competition	Partial competition
Mobile	Full competition	Full competition	Full competition	Partial competition	Partial competition	Full competition	Partial competition
Paging	Monopoly	n/a	Full competition	n/a	n/a	n/a	n/a
Cable TV	n/a	Full competition	Full competition	Partial competition	Full competition	Full competition	Partial competition
Fixed sat	Monopoly	n/a	n/a	n/a	n/a	n/a	Partial competition
Mobile sat	n/a	n/a	n/a	n/a	Full competition	n/a	Partial competition
GMPCS	n/a	n/a	n/a	n/a	Full competition	Full competition	Partial competition
IMT 2000	n/a	n/a	n/a	Partial competition	Partial competition	n/a	Partial competition
Internet services	Full competition	Full competition	Full competition	Partial competition	Full competition	Full competition	Partial competition
International gateways	Monopoly	Full competition	Full competition	Partial competition	Partial competition	Full competition	Partial competition
Level of competition[b]	1.25	1.33	2	0.7	1.47	2	0.89
Comparison with regional average (1.38)	Below	Below	Above	Below	Above	Above	Below

Source: ITU World Regulatory Policies Database.

Notes: [a] Monopoly—least liberalized; Full competition—most liberalized.

[b] The level of competition is determined by putting a value of 0 for monopoly, 1 for partial competition, and 2 for full competition and then dividing the total sum by the number of applicable segments.

smaller countries still have monopoly state operators, particularly in their fixed line segment. They have the most competitive telecommunications markets in this region. The Maldives is the least liberalized, although it is also the country with the highest teledensity and penetration ratios within the region and also compared to the more liberalized countries, India and Pakistan. The same is true for Sri Lanka which emerges as less competitive than the regional average but has higher penetration ratios and teledensity than some of the more liberalized countries in the region. This would suggest that while the regulatory framework is important for promoting competition and increased services, other factors, such as income per capita also play an important role in improving access.

The extent of liberalization of FDI policies varies across the SAARC countries. Some, such as Pakistan, have permitted 100 per cent foreign ownership and also relaxed conditions on repatriation and licensing. The smaller countries of Bhutan and the Maldives have still not opened this sector to FDI. Yet others have permitted foreign presence up to specified foreign equity ceilings and subject to various approvals. The variations in the extent of liberalization are indicative of the fact that the countries are at different stages of development and did not embark on telecom reforms at the same time. Appendix Table 3A.1 provides estimated indices of restrictiveness in fixed telecom services for the four larger South Asian countries, following the usual methodology for quantifying services barriers in mode 3. Notwithstanding some element of subjectivity in the weights assigned to the various restrictions and regulatory requirements imposed on foreign telecom providers, the indices broadly reflect the fact that there was considerable liberalization in the fixed telephony segment during 2000–9 in South Asia.

The outcome of these reforms and FDI liberalization in the telecom sector is evident from the rise in teledensity and subscriber base in all the South Asian countries (as shown earlier), although other factors have also played a role in these improvements. These reforms have also spurred investments and greater competition, lower prices, and a wider range of telecom services in the region. In line with the earlier estimates for market competitiveness, India and Pakistan have the largest number of operators. Tables 3.6 and 3.7 highlight the increased investment and competition that have resulted in the telecom sector in the South Asian countries with its opening up to private and foreign players.

Table 3.7 is indicative of the growing number of operators in the telecom sector of these countries, particularly in the two largest markets which have also undertaken more liberalization.

Table 3.6 Total Private Investment in Telecommunications in South Asia (US\$ mn)

Year of Investment	Bangladesh	Bhutan	India	Maldives	Nepal	Pakistan	Sri Lanka
1990	110		0			20	0
1991	6		0			20	0
1992	0		0			20	0
1993	0		0			20	42
1994	0		97			502	2
1995	30		683			21	0
1996	165		1,229			18	140
1997	74		3,827			31	268
1998	26		673			6	38
1999	143		1,045			0	113
2000	74		682		15	77	159
2001	61		3,445			60	9
2002	61		4,615		5	170	122
2003	205		1,968			240	90
2004	420		3,731		43	1,684	120
2005	473		6,201	40	46	4,365	215
2006	1,113		7,271		12	2,473	233
2007	1,349		7,579		14	2,741	387
Total (US\$ mn)	4,310	18	43,045	40	135	12,466	1,937
Total no. of projects: primary sector	12	1	34	1	3	6	7

Source: World Bank PPI Database.

Table 3.7 List of Operators in Mobile and Fixed Line

		No. of Operators	Names of Operators and Year of License Issue
Bangladesh	Mobile operators	6	1. Grameen Phone Limited (1996) 2. Banglalink (Orascom Telecom Bangladesh Limited) (1996) 3. Citycell (Pacific Bangladesh Telecom Limited) (1989) 4. Teletalk (Teletalk Bangladesh Limited) (2004) 5. Aktel (TM International Bangladesh Limited) (1996) 6. Warid (Warid Telecom International Limited) (2005)
	PSTN (Public Switched Telephone Networks)	13	National licenses 1. Bangladesh Telecommunications Company Limited (2004) 2. Dhaka Telephone Company Limited (2007) 3. Ranks Telecom Limited (2007) 4. National Telecom Limited (2007) 5. Tele Barta Limited (2007) 6. People's Telecommunication and Information Service Limited (2008)

(*Contd . . .*)

(Table 3.7 contd . . .)

	No. of Operators	Names of Operators and Year of License Issue
		Zonal licenses 7. Bangla Phone Limited (2004) 8. Jalalabad Telecom Limited (2004) 9. Westec Limited (2004) 10. One Tel Communication Limited (2004) 11. SA Telecom System Limited (2005) 12. Worldtel Bangladesh Limited (2004) Rural 13. Shebanet (2004)
Bhutan	Mobile operators	2	1. B-Mobile (2002) 2. Tashi Infocomm (2007)
	PSTN (Public Switched Telephone Networks)	1	1. Bhutan Telecom Limited (2000)
India	Wireless services	18	1. BSNL/MTNL 2. Airtel—Bharti Hexacom Limited 3. Aircel Group 4. Idea—Idea Cellular Limited 5. Tata Tele Services Limited 6. Idea mobile Communications Limited 7. Reliance Telecom Limited 8. Reliance Infocomm 9. Reliance Group 10. Vodafone Essar 11. Shyam Telelink 12. BPL/Loop Telecom Private Limited 13. Datacomm Solutions Private Limited 14. Swan Telecom Pvt. Limited 15. Spice Communications 16. S-Tel Limited 17. HFCL 18. M/s Volga Properties Pvt. Ltd., M/s Hudson Properties Ltd., M/s Unitech Infrastructure Pvt. Ltd., M/s Azare Properties Ltd., M/s Aska Projects Ltd., M/s United Builders & Estates Private Ltd., M/s Adonis Projects Pvt. Ltd., M/s Nahan Properties P. Ltd.
	Wireline services	8 DIPP— licenses given to 31 operators	1. BSNL 2. MTNL 3. Bharti Airtel Limited 4. Tata Teleservices Limited 5. Tata Teleservices Maharashtra Limited 6. HFCL Infotel Limited 7. Shyam Telelink Limited 8. Reliance Communications Limited

(Contd . . .)

(Table 3.7 contd . . .)

		No. of Operators	Names of Operators and Year of License Issue
Maldives	Mobile operators	2	1. Dhiraagu (1988) 2. Wataniya Telecom Maldives (Pvt.) Limited (2005)
	Fixed telephone lines	1	1. Dhiraagu (Dhivehi Raajjeyge Gulhun Pvt. Limited) (1988)
Nepal	Basic telephone services	2	1. Nepal Doorsanchar Company Limited 2. United Telecom Limited
	Cellular mobile services	2	1. Nepal Doorsanchar (Pvt.) Limited 2. Spice Nepal Limited
Pakistan	Fixed telephony (Intl long distance)	13	1. Wateen Tekecom 2. Dancom 3. Redtone Communications 4. Link dial international 5. Telenor 6. Burraq Telecom. 7. Callmate Telips Telecom Limited 8. DV Com. 9. Telecard 10. Worldcall Telecom 11. Circle Net Communication 12. Wise Communication Systems (Pvt.) Limited 13. Multinet Pakistan (Pvt.) Limited
	Mobile operators	7	1. Instaphone (Pakcom Limited) 2. Mobilink (Pakistan Mobile Company Limited) 3. Paktel (CM Pak Limited) 4. Telenor (Telenor Pakistan Limited) 5. Warid (Warid Telecom Pakistan Limited) 6. Ufone (Pakistan Telecom Mobile Limited) 7. SCO (Special Communication Organization Limited)
Sri Lanka	Fixed telephony	4	1. Sri Lanka Telecom Limited (1991) 2. Suntel Private Limited (1996) 3. Lanka Bell Private Limited (1996) 4. Dialog Broadband Networks Private Limited (1996)
	Mobile telephony	5	1. Hutchison Telecommunications Lanka (Pvt.) Limited (1992) 2. Mobitel Pvt. Limited (1993) 3. Dialog Telecom Limited (1993) 4. Celltel Lanka Limited (1995) 5. Bharti Airtel Lanka Private Limited

Source: Based on telecommunication regulatory bodies/ministry websites of South Asian countries.

Note: Year when license was issued is given where available.

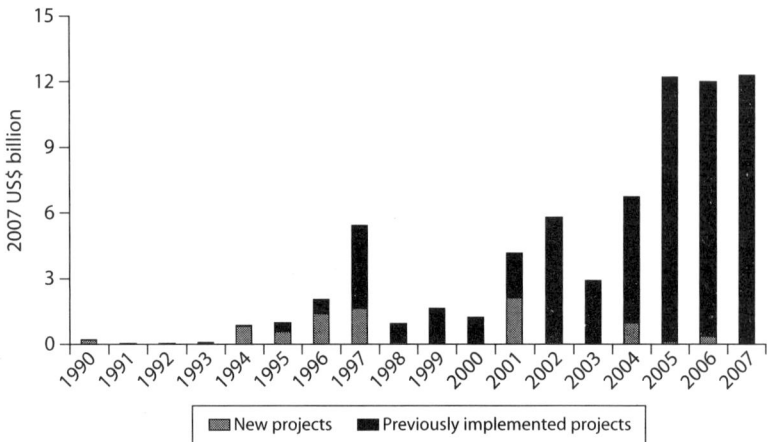

Figure 3.4   Investment Commitments in Telecom Projects with Private
Participation in South Asia, by Implementation Status, 1990–2007

Source: Reproduced from World Bank and PPIAF, PPI Project Database presentation on 'PPI in Developing Countries', p. 13.

Similarly, Figure 3.4 illustrates the significant increase in private sector
investment commitments in telecom, particularly after 2000. The data
further suggest that there has been a shift from greenfield projects which
characterized the early years of liberalization in the late 1990s to acquisi-
tion-related investment projects, as reflected by the larger share of previ-
ously implemented projects more recently.

This growth in investment reflects the entry of domestic and foreign operators. In Pakistan, which has gone furthest in opening up this
sector to FDI, there has been a huge increase in FDI inflows into telecom, including acquisitions of important domestic companies by foreign
operators. FDI inflows into Pakistan's telecom sector rose from $6.1 mil-
lion in 2001–2 to $1.9 bn in 2005–6 and in May 2007, China Mobile
acquired 100 per cent shares in Paktel. The telecom sector's contribution
to total FDI in Pakistan increased from a mere 1.26 per cent in 2001–2 to
54.per cent in 2005–6.[1] Thus, increased competition in telecom services,
particularly in the two larger markets, has resulted from growing domestic
and foreign private sector participation and both greenfield investments
and acquisitions.

[1] See Wilson (2008: 11, Table 4).

It is also worth noting that the objective of universal service obligation (USO) has featured very importantly in all the national telecommunication policies in this region, as the development of the telecom sector is seen as integral to overall development and equity goals. Table 3.8 highlights the status of USOs in each of the countries, in terms of its definition, coverage, and how it is to be achieved.

All the South Asian countries have defined universal service obligations, at a minimum, in terms of fixed line and mobile services, and some countries have extended this further to include internet services. The main sources of funding are additional levies on the sector, cross subsidization, and direct subsidies from the government.

Regulatory and Other Challenges

Notwithstanding the growth and improved performance that has been witnessed in the telecom sector in all the countries of South Asia, certain challenges remain as pointed out in recent surveys on the telecom regulatory framework in South Asia. These studies suggest that market entry is no longer a major barrier in the region. The challenges mainly pertain to institutional and regulatory practices. These include lack of institutional transparency, anti-competitive practices, a tendency to prefer incumbents, lack of independence of telecom regulatory authorities, political interference and lobbying by incumbents, regulatory uncertainties, policy gaps arising from differences between policies on paper and policies in practice, continued monopoly in certain segments, problems of infrastructure and in particular spectrum allocation, and high surcharges and levies on telecom operators due to a high dependence on this sector for revenues in some countries.

Figures A.1 to A.4 (see Annexure to the book) highlight the results from the Telecom Regulatory Environment Survey conducted in 2008 for Pakistan, Sri Lanka, the Maldives, and India, respectively, across a wide range of stakeholders. The scores range from 1–5 for each of the parameters that have been assessed for the regulatory environment—market entry, access to scarce resources, tariff regulation, universal service obligations, regulation of anti-competitive practices, and quality of service, with 5 being highly effective, 3 being average, and 1 being highly ineffective.[2]

It is evident from these Telecom Regulatory Environment (TRE) figures that the selected South Asian countries have done relatively better on market entry, interconnection measures, and tariff related measures, especially in

[2] See Telecom Regulatory Environment Surveys for India, Maldives, Pakistan, and Sri Lanka by Malik (2008), Galpaya (2008), Wilson (2008), and Knight-John (2008), respectively.

Table 3.8 Status of Universal Service Obligations in the Telecommunication Sector

	Bangladesh	Bhutan	India	Maldives	Nepal	Pakistan	Sri Lanka
Defined universal service access/service	Yes	Yes	Yes	Yes	Yes	Yes	No
Services for which USO defined	• Fixed line private residential service • Individual mobile cellular service	• Fixed line public payphone service • Dial-up internet access • Telecentres • Emergency services • Directory services	• Fixed line private residential service • Fixed line public payphone service • Individual mobile cellular service • Public mobile payphone service • Fax • Dial-up internet access • High-speed internet access: 0.125	• Other: Technology neutral basic telecom package including 90 minutes of national calls, 250 MB of internet access at minimum 56 Kbps to all by end 2008	• Fixed line public payphone service • Public mobile payphone service • Dial-up internet access • Emergency services • Directory services	• Fixed line private residential service • Fixed line public payphone service • Individual mobile cellular service • Public mobile payphone service • Fax • Dial-up internet access • Broadband • Tele centres • Emergency services • Special services for the impaired or elderly • Directory services	
How USOs are funded?	Providing 5 per cent of networking capacity in rural areas	Universal service funds	Universal service funds	Cross-subsidy between own services and universal service funds	Direct subsidy from government and universal service funds	Universal service funds	

Source: ITU Regulatory database.

the mobile segment. While the Maldives does relatively better on access to resources, reflecting its higher teledensity and penetration ratios, the other countries do not perform well on this parameter, particularly for fixed and broadband services. Thus, there are still challenges in terms of access to telecom infrastructure. Sri Lanka, interestingly, performs poorly across all the parameters, despite having opened up its telecom sector to partial competition in most services. This poor performance has been attributed to lapses in governance and problems with regulation.[3]

Overall, the common feature that emerges is that the South Asian countries perform poorly on anti-competitive practices, with scores below 3. This is mainly due to lack of independent regulation and protection of incumbent operators, which undermine the reforms undertaken in this sector. One could also argue that it also reflects a certain defensive policy orientation that still prevails in some of the countries in this region, an orientation that could have a bearing on the prospects for regional integration in this sector.

Intra-regional Initiatives

Telecommunication services is one sector where there has been an explicit recognition among the SAARC member countries of the need for greater intra-regional cooperation and initiatives to address common objectives and interests. There has been considerable discussion within the region on telecom services in inter-governmental and industry fora.

Inter-governmental Negotiations

ICT is designated as one of the priority sectors for cooperation under the South Asia Sub-regional Economic Cooperation (SASEC) programme. Lack of connections between the member countries, lack of strong infrastructure, and poor human resource capacity in this sector are seen as major barriers to regional penetration of telecom services in South Asia. To address these constraints, a working group on telecom and ICT was set up after the 12th SAARC Summit in January 2004. This working group identified five focus areas: enhancing regional connectivity; promoting information sharing and human resource development; establishing community information centres; strengthening and harmonizing regulations and standards; and developing common software tools to enhance content available on the internet. Multilateral support has been provided by the ADB for this working group. Some of the achievements of the SASEC sub-regional programme include the agreement on a SASEC Information

---

[3] See Knight-John (2008).

Highway Project to optimize the interconnection costs and to extend the reach of ICT services in this region.

An important inter-governmental initiative was the establishment of the South Asian Telecommunications Regulators' Council (SATRC) in 1998, following discussions between the ITU, the Asia Pacific Telecommunity (APT), and the respective governments in the region.[4] The SATRC is a permanent body that functions under the auspices of the APT. Its member countries include Afghanistan, Bangladesh, Bhutan, India, Iran, the Maldives, Nepal, Pakistan, and Sri Lanka. The SATRC is responsible for discussions and coordination of all issues relating to regulations in the telecommunication sector which are of common interest to the telecom regulators of the South Asian countries. The council also aims to identify and promote areas of potential cooperation in telecommunications among the South Asian countries and serves as a forum for mutual learning, sharing of experiences, and the harmonization of regulations. It facilitates the exchange of information through regional seminars, workshops, and training courses. Several SATRC meetings have been held since 1998. An action plan was drawn up at the SATRC meeting in 2004. This action plan reflects the common issues and concerns of the countries in South Asia.

The key issues that have been discussed by the SATRC under its action plan include licensing, service quality, universal service and access obligations, tariff rebalancing, interconnection, numbering plan, number portability, equal ease of access, intelligent network services, and broadband technology.[5] The plan aims to lower telecom tariffs within the SAARC region to the lowest levels possible, introduce special rates for transiting regional traffic, promote inter-country direct services, calling cards, cellular roaming, and liberalized leased lines and use of either direct links or hubbing or transit facilities to facilitate intra-regional communications, and to promote regulatory cooperation to improve performance. The common priority areas under this plan are universal access, development of rural services, optimal sharing of available resources, enhanced cooperation in technology transfer, and standardization.

In the context of USOs, the SATRC countries have adopted various kinds of schemes, the primary one being that of cross-subsidization supplemented

---

[4] The Asia Pacific Telecommunity (APT) was set up in 1979. It is a multi-government regional telecommunications organization based in Bangkok. Its goal is to facilitate the development of telecommunication services and information infrastructure in the Asia-Pacific region. It specifically focuses on the expansion of this sector in the less developed parts of this region.

[5] See APT (2004).

by revenues from telecom operators. The council has also completed case studies of universal access programmes in Nepal and Sri Lanka. It has further been decided to establish a Universal Service Fund and a monitoring mechanism to ensure that USOs are met, along with the possibility of a performance bond and possible future penal action for non-compliance.

With regard to numbering plans, the council has decided to review the issues of harmonization of emergency telephone numbers, mobile service access code, and satellite based mobile telephony and terrestrial mobile telephony. Mismatch of numbering schemes is recognized as affecting subscribers when they travel within the region. Harmonization is seen as important for enabling access to international telecom networks within the SATRC network and for simplification of the network. However, the council meetings have also noted the many constraints in implementing large-scale changes in numbering plans. New numbering formats have been proposed among the members and some flexible areas have been identified where harmonization can be achieved, the main such area being emergency services (police, fire, and medical assistance). Numbering formats have also been proposed for mobile, internet, public switched data networks, and intelligent networks.

On the issue of tariff rebalancing (that is, to move telecom service rates closer to their associated costs), there has been some discussion and analysis of incumbent operators within the region for various parameters such as licensing fees, benchmarking, return on capital, market competitiveness, and transparency, neutrality and independence of regulators. The working group has also carried out an analysis for determining national and international tariffs, collection charges, and interconnection charges, though no recommendation has been made yet.

There has also been some discussion on performance indicators, quality of services, licensing issues, and enforcement mechanisms to ensure adherence to network and service benchmarks, and identification of challenges in meeting the established quality benchmarks. Some of the constraints that have been identified by the council include shortage of spectrum, lack of sufficient interconnection capacity between operators, and technology. In addition, the SATRC has also discussed the classification and form of licenses, dispute resolution, and policies and regulations for broadband development in South Asia.

Several working groups have been formed under SATRC which have submitted their reports on several of these issues. The SAARC action plan of 2004 was a culmination of the reports by various working groups on key regulatory issues of concern among the SATRC member countries. Several resolutions have since been taken up for carrying forward the consultative process in these areas and for further work on technical, regulatory, and implementation issues, as well as an exploration of complementarities and synergies within the region. In the past few years, several SATRC projects have been under implementation and several workshops have been held on regulatory capacity building, licensing for convergence, mutual recognition agreements, and interconnection in convergence.

However, although some resolutions have been taken in specific areas, by and large, there has been more talk than action in SATRC and progress has been limited. Most of the discussions remain at a proposal or vision stage. But as is evident from the agenda of the various SATRC meetings, the significance of the telecom services sector within the region is well recognized, both in terms of its implications for furthering national goals and for addressing regional opportunities in other areas such as tourism, business, and IT and related applications.

Industry Level Initiatives

There is an annual meeting of a CEO conclave which consists of SAARC industry leaders in the telecom industry. This conclave has thus far completed seven summits. The key issues that have been discussed are the lowering of tariffs, roaming facilities, high speech services, sharing of regulatory best practices, building knowledge and capacity on latest technology in the sector, and standardization of telecom monitoring methods. Industry CEOs have acknowledged the untapped opportunities in the South Asian market and the need to leverage each other's abilities. A SAARC industry forum has also been launched for the telecom sector, with the Confederation of Indian Industry (CII) agreeing to host this platform. The industry forum will focus on network expansion and mobile security. The 6th Voice and Data CEO Conclave held in December 2007 hosted the first summit of the SAARC Telecom Advisory Council. A roadmap was drawn up for telecommunications in the region for 2008 and beyond by the council.

Some specific issues have been pointed out in the CEO conclave. One of the main issues on the agenda has been the need to lower roaming tariffs and improve roaming facilities among the SAARC countries. The discussions have highlighted the need to have cross-border availability of services and for cooperation among operators not only in voice services but also in data services. Possibilities for regional operators such as BSNL to service the regional market and the need for discussions among the major operators in the region to finalize roaming agreements have also been highlighted. It has also been pointed out that operating on a SAARC-wide level could provide the economies of scale which individual markets in this region do not provide. The superior performance of the smaller countries in the region in terms of teledensity, the possibility of the larger operators learning from their smaller counterparts in the region, and the potential gains for the smaller players from associating with the larger operators have also been identified. For instance, an association of the Maldivian companies with Sri Lankan operators and with Reliance Communications has been seen as a way for small players to operate at the regional level. Industry participants have also highlighted the need for standardization of products and services in the region in order to facilitate outsourcing and disaster recovery by IT firms within South Asia and to enable a spillover of opportunities from India's IT sector to other countries in the region.

Overall, industry leaders in the telecom sector have viewed regional cooperation in telecom as closely linked to the objectives of poverty alleviation and enhancing quality of life through the use of latest technologies in the SAARC region. An industry association that includes telecom operators, various regional industry associations, and regulators who would act on a SAARC level has also been proposed at the CEO conclave.

Private Sector Initiatives

The telecom sector has seen growing investments. According to a Frost and Sullivan study (2009), mobile services are expected to constitute the major capital expenditure in South Asia and technological advancements like 3G, broadband and value added services are expected to show the most promise. The Indian market, given its size, is expected to dominate telecom spending in the region and to act as a regional source of investment in the other SAARC member countries. There have been several large Indian telecom companies which have either entered the markets of the other South Asian countries or have announced plans to do so.

The Indian telecom giant, Bharti Airtel announced its entry into the Sri Lankan mobile phone sector in 2007 with an investment of US$ 200 million. Services were to begin by end 2007. However, the company delayed its entry till January 2009.[6] It has since set up a Sri Lankan subsidiary, Bharti Airtel Lanka Pvt. Ltd. It has so far invested US$ 100 million and

[6] It has been speculated that this delay was caused by the difficulties in getting frequencies from the Telecom Regulatory Council, which tends to be highly politicized in Sri Lanka. It has also been speculated that the company may have altered its focus to some Indian states which are equally large and as attractive as the Sri Lankan mobile phone market. The company, however, has cited infrastructure related requirements as the main reason for the delay rather than institutional and market attractiveness related factors.

will be investing further over the next three years. Within a few months its customer base had crossed one million. The company has entered into a three year managed network deal with China's Huawei Technologies. The company is offering 2G and 3G services in Sri Lanka.

The big telecom operators in India have similarly been eyeing other SAARC markets. Bharti Airtel has announced plans to expand its cable network to Bhutan to help develop ICT infrastructure, in partnership with the Bhutan government. This initiative to create a terrestrial cable network in Bhutan is expected to boost the IT and telecom infrastructure in that country. More generally, the company is also looking at the other SAARC countries in a move to expand its operations beyond India. Reliance Info-comm and Bharti Airtel have shown interest in bidding for a license for GSM 2D cellular services in Bhutan. In 2004, Airtel signed the first ever roaming agreement with Pakistan's Mobilink to provide mobile roaming facilities for its pre-paid and post-paid customers. There have also been attempts to lower tariff rates within the region. In November 2008, BSNL cut international call rates to SAARC countries by 15–35 per cent so as to enable BSNL customers, both mobile and landline, to make calls to Pakistan, Bangladesh, the Maldives, and Bhutan at cheaper rates.

There are similar initiatives by Indian companies in Bangladesh. Two major Indian telecom majors, Bharti Airtel and Reliance Communications, have submitted a joint proposal to the Bangladesh Telecommunications Regulatory Commission to establish a telecom corridor through Bangladesh to reach the northeastern part of India. Bharti Airtel and Reliance Communications are interested in linking with any Bangladeshi fibre optic operator to provide telecom services to the northeastern Indian states. In return they have offered a stand-by submarine cable to Bangladesh. There is likely to be mutual benefit to India and Bangladesh from this initiative. The northeastern states of India would benefit as they currently get telecom services through VSAT at very high price. Bangladesh would in turn be able to use this link as an alternative to its current lone submarine cable from Southeast Asia thus helping it to avoid disruptions of undersea cable which it faces at present. The Indian companies have already brought Pakistan, Nepal, and Bhutan under their submarine cable network and this initiative would benefit Bangladesh by connecting it to the rest of the region. Internet service providers in Bangladesh have endorsed this initiative. The Bangladesh government, however, has still to decide on this proposal.

But these ventures have not been without occasional roadblocks. The first challenge arose due to anti-competitive practices by incumbent operators, as is highlighted by the Bharti Airtel venture in Sri Lanka, discussed earlier. The company has complained of unfair competition from other players in the Sri Lankan market. The contention is that the incumbent mobile telecom operators in Sri Lanka have not provided adequate points of interconnect to them causing call congestion. This has been seen as an anti-competitive orientation.

A second challenge has been that of security as demonstrated by the case of Telenor Pakistan which is interested in entering India. The Indian Foreign Investment Promotion Bureau (FIPB) is expected to approve the entry of Telenor into India and to grant the necessary security clearances to increase its stake in Unitech Wireless to the maximum limit of 74 per cent. However, there have been security concerns in India about possible spying and subversion. Hence, Indian authorities have granted permission only on the condition that no employees from Telenor's Pakistan subsidiary work for the Indian company, keeping human resources of the Indian and Pakistani arms of the company separate. Interestingly, Telenor which is also a majority shareholder in Bangladesh's Grameen Phone, was not seen as posing any major security risk when it entered Bangladesh.

A third challenge is that of high roaming tariffs and termination charges for SAARC originated international traffic.[7] The SAARC region has one of the highest intra-regional mobile tariffs in the world. The cheapest intra-SAARC price from Pakistan is four times that of the cheapest extra-SAARC price from that country. The cheapest prices from Sri Lanka to neighbouring SAARC countries are 40 to 50 per cent more than that to the US. In almost all the countries, the lowest rates charged to SAARC countries are higher than those charged to countries outside the region, including the US, Europe, and Southeast Asia. High roaming tariffs are a deterrent to regional investment in the mobile telephony segment. The Telecom Regulatory Authority of India (TRAI) has raised this issue with the APT, to find ways to bring down global roaming rates within the region along the lines of the EU model. Reduced rates would enable Indian companies, such as Bharti Airtel which are interested in penetrating other markets in the region, to come out with attractive tariff packages for their subscribers in India when traveling to SAARC markets like Sri Lanka. It has been proposed to bring down the termination charges for international calls originating in SAARC countries either by lowering them to the lowest charges on offer or by eliminating surcharges and levies that currently apply to such calls.

Tables 3.9 and 3.10 provide the intra- and selected extra-SAARC per minute charges for international calls for fixed as well as mobile phones.

[7] See Samarajiva (2008).

Table 3.9 Intra- and Selected Extra-SAARC per Minute Charges for International Calls from Fixed Phones (US$ at current rate conversions), June 2008

Region	Country	From AF n/a	From BD Peak	From BD Off-peak	From BT Peak	From BT Off-peak	From IN	From MV	From NP Peak	From NP Off-peak	From PK	From Lk
SAARC	Afghanistan		0.35	0.26	0.98	0.98	0.28	0.7	0.29	0.22	0.22	0.94
	Bangladesh				0.59	0.59	0.28	0.3	0.29	0.22	0.14	0.32
	Bhutan		0.26	0.2			0.28	0.55	0.29	0.22	0.22	0.52
	India		0.26	0.2	0.31	0.3		0.3	0.29	0.22	0.12	0.32
	Maldives		0.26	0.2	0.59	0.59	0.28		0.29	0.22	0.36	0.32
	Nepal		0.26	0.2	0.59	0.59	0.28	0.46			0.22	0.32
	Pakistan		0.26	0.2	0.59	0.59	0.28	0.3	0.29	0.22		0.32
	Sri Lanka		0.26	0.2	0.59	0.59	0.17	0.3	0.29	0.22	0.22	
Southeast Asia	Malaysia		0.26	0.2	0.98	0.98	0.23	0.27	0.73	0.73	0.03	0.24
	Singapore		0.26	0.2	0.59	0.59	0.23	0.23	0.73	0.73	0.14	0.21
	Thailand		0.26	0.2	0.48	0.48	0.23	0.27	0.73	0.73	0.14	0.24
East Asia	China		0.35	0.26	0.79	0.79	0.28	0.23	0.73	0.73	0.03	0.24
	Hong Kong		0.26	0.2	0.59	0.59	0.23	0.27	0.73	0.73	0.03	0.24
	Japan		0.35	0.26	0.79	0.79	0.28	0.3	0.73	0.73	0.07	0.21
Australasia	Australia		0.35	0.26	0.59	0.59	0.28	0.3	0.73	0.73	0.03	0.24
Europe	France		0.35	0.26	0.79	0.79	0.23	0.38	0.73	0.73	0.03	0.21
	Germany		0.35	0.26	0.79	0.79	0.23	0.38	0.73	0.73	0.03	0.21
	Italy		0.35	0.26	0.59	0.59	0.23	0.38	0.73	0.73	0.03	0.21
	Sweden		0.4	0.31	0.59	0.59	0.23	0.38	0.73	0.73	0.07	0.24
	Switzerland		0.4	0.31	0.59	0.59	0.23	0.38	0.73	0.73	0.07	0.24
	UK		0.35	0.26	0.59	0.59	0.17	0.38	0.73	0.73	0.03	0.21
North America	Bahamas		0.4	0.31	0.98	0.98	0.28	0.7	0.73	0.73	0.14	0.94
	Canada		0.35	0.26	0.59	0.59	0.17	0.23	0.73	0.73	0.03	0.21
	Cuba		0.4	0.31	0.98	0.98	0.28	0.7	0.73	0.73	1.01	0.94
	Mexico		0.4	0.31	0.98	0.98	0.28	0.7	0.73	0.73	0.14	0.24
	US		0.35	0.26	0.59	0.59	0.17	0.23	0.73	0.73	0.03	0.21

Source: Reproduced from Samarajiva (2008), Table 1. See http://www.lankabusinessonline.com/fullstory.php?nid=1871648785, accessed on 13 October 2009.

Note: The cost of calls from a country must be read vertically, along the columns.

Table 3.10 Intra- and Selected Extra-SAARC per Minute Charges for International Calls from Mobile Phones (US$ at current rates), June 2008.

Region	Country	From AF	From BD	From BT Peak	From BT Off-peak	From IN	From MV	From NP Peak	From NP Off-peak	From PK	From Lk
SAARC	Afghanistan			–	–	0.22	0.7	0.36	0.36	0.29	0.74
	Bangladesh	0.49		0.59	0.59	0.22	0.3	0.36	0.36	0.12	0.32
	Bhutan	0.49				0.22	0.55	0.36	0.36	0.29	0.56
	India	0.49		0.31	0.31		0.3	0.29	0.22	0.16	0.14
	Maldives	0.49		0.59	0.59	0.22		0.36	0.36	0.29	0.23
	Nepal	0.49		0.59	0.59	0.22	0.46			0.29	0.32
	Pakistan	0.49		0.59	0.59	0.22	0.3	0.36	0.36		0.32
	Sri Lanka	0.49		0.59	0.59	0.22	0.3	0.36	0.36	0.29	
Southeast Asia	Malaysia	0.49		0.98	0.98	0.15	0.27	0.73	0.73	0.12	0.1
	Singapore	0.49		0.59	0.59	0.15	0.23	0.73	0.73	0.03	0.1
	Thailand	0.49		0.48	0.48	0.15	0.27	0.73	0.73	0.12	0.32
East Asia	China	0.49		0.79	0.79	0.22	0.23	0.73	0.73	0.03	0.1
	Hong Kong	0.49		0.59	0.59	0.15	0.27	0.73	0.73	0.03	0.1
	Japan	0.49		0.79	0.79	0.22	0.3	0.73	0.73	0.12	0.14
Australasia	Australia	0.54		0.59	0.59	0.15	0.3	0.73	0.73	0.03	0.14
Europe	France	0.54		0.79	0.79	0.15	0.38	0.73	0.73	0.03	0.23
	Germany	0.54		0.79	0.79	0.15	0.38	0.73	0.73	0.03	0.14
	Italy	0.54		0.59	0.59	0.15	0.38	0.73	0.73	0.03	0.23
	Sweden	0.54		0.59	0.59	0.15	0.38	0.73	0.73	0.03	0.23
	Switzerland	0.54		0.59	0.59	0.15	0.38	0.73	0.73	0.03	0.23
	UK	0.54		0.59	0.59	0.15	0.38	0.73	0.73	0.03	0.14
North America	Bahamas	0.54		0.98	0.98	0.22	0.7	0.73	0.73	0.29	0.1
	Canada	0.54		0.59	0.59	0.15	0.7	0.73	0.73	0.03	0.1
	Cuba	0.54		0.09	0.98	0.94	0.7	0.73	0.73	1.11	0.74
	Mexico	0.54		0.98	0.98	0.22	0.7	0.73	0.73	0.29	0.1
	US	0.54		0.59	0.59	0.15	0.7	0.73	0.73	0.03	0.1

Source: Reproduced from Samarajiva (2008), Table 2. See http://www.lankabusinessonline.com/fullstory.php?nid=1871648785, accessed on 13 October 2009.

Note: The cost of calls from a country must be read vertically, along the columns. BD prices from mobiles are fixed+.

The call rates clearly show that intra-SAARC rates are not necessarily competitive when compared with calls originating in SAARC countries to countries in Southeast Asia, North America, and Europe. As highlighted by experts, the lower rates from SAARC countries to other parts of the world are a reflection of the lower termination charges imposed by the foreign operators who receive the calls. Since the markets in the US and Asia-Pacific are much more competitive and the governments there do not keep termination charges artificially high, this results in lower call rates to those markets. These lower rates are evident in India, Sri Lanka, and Pakistan, where telecom reforms have gone the furthest. Given that the foreign operators are not likely to be charging higher prices for the remaining SAARC countries, the higher rates prevailing in the latter countries probably reflect the fact that their operators do not pass on the lower costs to their customers due to lack of competition in those markets. The call rates also indicate that there is greater competition in the mobile telephone segment than in the fixed line segment. Appendix Table 3A.2 provides the incoming and outgoing roaming rates within SAARC countries. On the whole, the call charges indicate that in the regional context, the South Asian region has not been able to leverage its ability to provide among the lowest mobile rates in the world. Thus, there is evidently lack of political will to bring down regional tariffs and much of the discussion under SATRC on this issue, remains only on paper.

Multilateral and Other Commitments in Telecommunication Services

This is a sector that has been scheduled by all the WTO member countries in SAARC, except the Maldives. Table 3.11 summarizes the Uruguay Round commitments as well as the initial conditional and revised offers made by the South Asian countries to highlight their willingness to negotiate telecom services and to bind in the liberalization policies discussed earlier.

Table 3.11 reflects the general orientation of the SAARC countries towards multilateral liberalization in telecom services. It shows that mode 3 has tended to be the most sensitive of all the modes, with mostly partial commitments, but for a few exceptions. These conditions typically include limits on foreign equity participation, on the number of licenses, and on the type of foreign presence that is permitted. Fixed line services tend to be more cautiously committed than value added services, such as internet and

Table 3.11 Status of Commitments Undertaken in Telecommunication Services by South Asian Countries under the WTO–GATS Framework

Sector/Sub-sector	Uruguay Round Commitments	Conditional Initial Offer	Revised Offer
Bangladesh	**April 1995**		
All sub-sectors	• Market Access Limitation: Mode 4—Employment of foreign nationals to be approved by the government and such personnel shall be employed in higher management and specialized jobs only. • National Treatment Limitation: Modes 1 and 3—Certain subsidies and tax benefits may only be extended to national operators.		
For public use international service	1. No bypass of network facilities of government operator; no call-back or refile allowed 2. No limitations 3. Reserved to exclusive supply by the government operator 4. Unbound		
For public use fixed network infrastructure, domestic long distance and local service	1. No bypass of network facilities of government operator 2. No limitations 3. Two licenses are issued to private operators each to serve designated administrative (rural) areas in competition with the government operator 4. Unbound		
The above for non-public use	1. No bypass of network facilities of government operator 2. None 3. Only on network facilities supplied by the government operator and other licensed public-service operators. Two-ended breakout and resale of excess capacity are not permitted 4. Unbound		

(Contd . . .)

(*Table 3.11 contd . . .*)

Sector/Sub-sector	Uruguay Round Commitments	Conditional Initial Offer	Revised Offer
Internet access services	1. No bypass of network facilities of government operator 2. None 3. Only on network facilities supplied by the government operator and other licensed public-service operators 4. Unbound except as indicated under 'All Sub-sectors'		
Cellular/mobile voice telephone services	1. No bypass of network facilities of government operator 2. None 3. Four licenses issued to private operators, in addition to the government operator 4. Unbound		
VSAT/gateway earth services/ teleconferencing	1. No bypass of facilities of government operator 2. None 3. Reserved to exclusive supply by the government operator 4. Unbound		
India	**April 1995**	**12 January 2004**	**24 August 2005**
Voice telephone services	1. Unbound 2. Unbound 3. Service permitted to be provided only after operator gets license from designated authority, subject to terms and conditions; FDI limit of 25 per cent on wire based services	1. No change 2. No change 3. No change Additional requirement of FIPB approval for foreign investors having prior collab-oration; FDI ceiling of 25 per cent for wire based services	1. No change 2. None 3. Licensing terms and conditions requirement removed; foreign equity limit on wire based services raised to 49 per cent
Cellular mobile services	1. Unbound 2. Unbound 3. As in voice telephony only digital (GSM) technology, terrestrial based, will be permitted	1. No change 2. No change 3. No change	1. No change 2. None 3. GSM technology requirement relaxed and FDI ceiling raised to 49 per cent

Data and message transmission services (e-mail, voice mail, etc.)	1. None 2. Unbound 3. Foreign equity ceiling of 51 per cent	1. No change 2. No change 3. No change	1. No change 2. None 3. Foreign equity ceiling increased to 74 per cent

NEPAL   **Date of submission: 30 August 2004**

Basic telecommunications (local telephone service, domestic telephone service, international telephone services, telex service, domestic and international telegraph service)	1. None 2. None 3. No limitation on number of service providers from January 2009; foreign equity limit on joint ventures—80 per cent 4. Unbound; consultants not available in Nepal may enter to work for 90 days

Mobile telecommunication services	1. None
	2. None
	3. None except:
	  • No limitation on number of service providers from January 2009. Foreign equity limit on joint ventures—80 per cent
	  • Mobile technology will not be prescribed but will be left to the choice of the operator upon the date of accession
	4. Unbound

Value-added telecommunications	1. None 2. None 3. None except foreign participation permitted through a joint venture with up to 80 per cent equity participation 4. Unbound except as indicated in the horizontal section

(Contd. . . .)

(*Table 3.11 contd . . .*)

Sector/Sub-sector	Uruguay Round Commitments	Conditional Initial Offer	Revised Offer
PAKISTAN	**April 1995**	**30 May 2005**	
All sub-sectors	• The number of operators, service providers and licensees may be limited due to technical constraints • The confidentiality of International Total Accounting Rate (TAR) shall be maintained • The bilateral agreements on accounting rates shall be in accordance with ITU guidelines • Up to 100 per cent foreign investment on licensed services may be permitted • Does not include any broadcasting services		
Voice telephone services	1. None since 2004 2. Alternative practices such as call back are not allowed; country direct card service can only be permitted by mutual agreement with the licensed operator 3. Unbound 4. Unbound	1. No change 2. No change 3. None	
Packet-switched data, e-mail, internet and intranet services, and circuit-switched data transmission services	1. None since 2003 2. None 3. Licensing restrictions on no of licenses granted 4. Unbound	1. No change 2. No change 3. None 4. No change	
VSAT for domestic data services/telegraph services	1. Licensing restrictions 2. None 3. None 4. Unbound	VSAT: 1. No change 2. No change 3. No change 4. No change Telegraph: 1. None	
Telex services/facsimile services	1. None 2. None 3. None 4. Unbound	1. No change 2. No change 3. No change 4. No change	

	April 1995	September 2003
Private leased circuit services/video conferencing /trunk radio dialling	1. None 2. None 3. None 4. Unbound	1. None, subject to technical constraints 2. None 3. None 4. Unbound
Mobile communication services	Sector not scheduled	

SRI LANKA

	April 1995	September 2003
International voice	1. Monopoly for Sri Lanka telecom till December 1999 and issuing of license thereafter based on satisfactory conclusion of tariff rebalancing 2. None 3. Monopoly for Sri Lanka telecom till December 1999 and issuing of license thereafter based on satisfactory conclusion of tariff rebalancing Foreign equity participation of up to 35 per cent permitted in Sri Lanka telecom 4. Unbound	1. Unbound 2. No change 3. None 4. No change
Domestic long distance and local–mobile cellular services	1. None 2. None 3. Only 4 licenses issued–number to be reviewed in 2000 4. Unbound	No change—4 licenses issued
Wireless local loop	1. None 2. None 3. Two licenses issued: duopoly guaranteed for 5 years—to be reviewed in 2000	No change—3 licenses issued

(Contd....)

(*Table 3.11 contd . . .*)

Sector/Sub-sector	Uruguay Round Commitments	Conditional Initial Offer	Revised Offer
Public pay phone services	1. None 2. None 3. Five service providers—number to be reviewed as per economic needs 4. Unbound	No change—5 licenses issued	
Radio paging services	1. None 2. None 3. Five licenses 4. Unbound except as indicated in the horizontal section	No change—5 licenses issued	
Data communication services	1. None 2. None 3. Six licenses only 4. Unbound except as indicated in horizontal section	No change—6 licenses issued	
Satellite-based services; GMPCS services supplied through own gateways	1. None 2. None 3. Issuing of licenses is under consideration. Foreign equity participation in these enterprises determined per the horizontal section 4. Unbound except as indicated in horizontal section	1. No change 2. No change 3. None 4. No change	
Trunk radio mobile services	Sector not scheduled	1. None 2. None 3. One license issued 4. Unbound except as indicated in the horizontal section	

Value added services, such as:	Sector not scheduled	1. None
		2. None
• electronic mail		3. None
• voice mail		4. Unbound except
• online information and		as indicated in the
data base retrieval		horizontal section
• enhanced/value added		
facsimile services		
• Code and protocol		
conversions		
• Online information		
and/or data processing		
EDI	Sector not scheduled	1. None
		2. None
		3. Unbound
		4. Unbound except
		as indicated in the
		horizontal section

Source: Based on WTO member countries' GATS Commitments and Offer Schedules.

Note: Broadcasting service is defined as a radio communication service in which the transmissions are intended for direct reception by the general public. This service may include sound transmission, television transmissions or other types of transmissions. In the Pakistan telecom law, like in many other countries, broadcasting is not part of basic telecommunication services.

data processing services. Mobile communications also tend to be more liberally scheduled than landline services. MFN exemptions have been sought for the application of different accounting rates for different operators or countries covered by international telecommunication services agreements between local operators and various foreign operators and for the countries which are covered by these agreements. This includes, for instance, the telecommunications agreements entered into with other countries in the region, hence providing scope for preferential rates to be given to operators within the region.

There are differences in the scope and extent of the liberalization that has been undertaken. Pakistan has scheduled most segments within telecom services and has also made very liberal commitments. It has placed no restrictions in modes 1 and 2, and has made relatively liberal commitments even in mode 3, permitting 100 per cent participation in some segments. This is in line with the greater degree of unilateral liberalization undertaken in that country. Nepal has for the most part made unrestricted commitments in all the segments it has scheduled, with mode 3 subject to a very liberal ceiling of 80 per cent foreign equity participation. Bangladesh and Sri Lanka's commitments reflect a defensive stance with regard to government monopoly operators and a desire to protect incumbents, again in line with their unilateral policy stance. Bangladesh's commitments are particularly restrictive with even mode 1 being subject to limitation. India's Uruguay Round (UR) commitments are also defensive. They are narrow in scope and exclude long distance and international voice services. The mode 3 commitments are quite restrictive with foreign equity ceilings capped at 25 or 51 per cent. Several of the modes remain unbound. However, India's revised offer is significantly more liberal, with a relaxation of the foreign equity ceiling and removal of conditions on foreign operators. This is unlike the case with the initial offers made by Pakistan and Sri Lanka which remain unchanged for the most part.

Thus, the commitments and offers clearly indicate that there is some variation in the liberalization stance and how it has changed over time among the SAARC member countries. A comparison of these commitments and offers with the unilateral liberalization and regulatory reforms undertaken in these countries suggests that the countries have by and large not been prepared to bind in their existing policies and reforms in the WTO. For instance, although FDI participation is permitted up to 74 per cent in basic services in India, this has been offered only up to 49 per cent. There are two possible interpretations of such differences between the WTO commitments and the countries' current policies in this sector.

Either it implies that the SAARC countries would like to retain policy space to roll back their unilateral liberalization so as not to violate their multilateral obligations, or they would like to sequence their liberalization from unilateral to multilateral opening up, so that they can understand the consequences of liberalization and commit when they are prepared domestically and with appropriate conditions. It is also worth noting that the South Asian countries have not accepted the Telecom Reference Paper on regulatory principles in its entirety, although many of the pro-competitive provisions have been accepted under their national telecommunications policies. Hence, again the countries have not been prepared to lock in their regulatory reforms.

Telecom services do not feature importantly in most of the other agreements that have been entered into by the SAARC countries. However, whenever the telecom sector has been negotiated in these other agreements, such as in the Pakistan–China FTA, the Pakistan–Malaysia FTA, or the India–Singapore Comprehensive Economic Cooperation Agreement (CECA), the commitment is more liberal than it is under the GATS. Shareholding restrictions have been relaxed compared to the GATS offer and additional sub-sectors have been scheduled in the bilateral agreements. Hence, willingness to commit to liberalization is greater in the bilateral context than it is multilaterally under the WTO in telecom services. This might suggest that the South Asian countries may be willing to commit more liberally in the context of SAFTA than they have under the GATS.

Looking Ahead

In view of the preceding discussion on policy trends and outcomes and the status of intra-regional cooperation, what are the likely prospects for integration of telecom services within South Asia and what are the main issues and challenges that would need to be addressed for this purpose? The evidence presents a mixed picture of both opportunities and practical difficulties.

It is quite evident that the telecom sector shows promising prospects for growth, and given demographic and economic trends, there remains considerable untapped potential in this sector in South Asia. From a development perspective, there is also a common interest in this sector among all the countries in the region. Improved telecom services can help the South Asian countries overcome challenges of geography, reach out to remote areas, improve government efficiency through e-governance related initiatives, improve delivery of services such as healthcare and education, and create opportunities in other sectors such as IT. Improved telecom services and greater cooperation in this sector within the region provide an opportunity to overcome the challenges of poor land and air connectivity. There are several large operators, particularly in India, who have a strategic interest in investing in the other countries of South Asia in view of the expanding subscriber base, particularly in the mobile telephony segment. There is also strategic interest among some Indian operators to enter into infrastructure sharing arrangements with other South Asian countries to overcome geographic constraints. The opening up of telecom services to FDI creates opportunities for such intra-regional investment and partnerships among the players in the region. There are also common areas of concern, such as roaming tariffs and harmonization of certain services within the region. The fact that the commitment schedules under the GATS already make room for preferential accounting rates for operators within the region indicates that such initiatives may be feasible under a regional agreement.

Why then have the initiatives in telecom shown such limited progress? Going beyond the general problems of lack of political will, the absence of friendly relations among some of the key member countries, and limited intra-regional trade which limits their interest in regional cooperation, there are certain other challenges which the preceding discussion has highlighted. Although the sector has been liberalized to some extent in all the countries, there is still an anti-competitive policy stance which affects investment attractiveness of certain markets. This is highlighted by the case of Bharti Airtel in Sri Lanka and the TRE survey results for the various countries in the region. There are issues of institutional transparency, regulatory independence, investment climate, and governance which need to be addressed if regional investment is to be spurred in this sector. This lack of a pro-competitive policy orientation is reflected in the nature of the GATS commitments by the South Asian countries, the fact that all the GATS reference paper principles have not been adopted. Such a policy stance potentially poses a challenge for regional cooperation in this sector. Moreover, regional investment in telecom remains constrained by the fact that some segments still remain closed to private participation. There is also the challenge of security concerns with regard to cross-border investments, associated movement of persons, and sharing of telecom infrastructure among some of the member countries.

In light of these challenges, it may be optimistic to expect very rapid progress in any regional efforts on telecom services. What can spur progress is action at both the regional and national levels. There are three main issues to address. First and foremost it would be important to accelerate the pace of discussions on regulatory cooperation and to deliver something concrete with regard to the initiatives on harmonization of numbers for identified services. This would be a concrete deliverable and would lend credibility to the various regional discussion forums that have been in place in this sector for several years. Second, the countries need to focus on bringing down intra-regional call rates given the potential wider benefits in many other sectors, including tourism, business travel, investment, and potential outsourcing and ICT services within the region. However, this would require a more pro-competitive stance within the countries to lower termination charges for calls originating in other SAARC countries and also passing on these benefits to consumers in these countries. The third issue to address is not specific to telecom. It pertains to improving the investment climate and the institutional streamlining of investment approvals and clearances within the region. In several investment projects, even where the benefits are evident, there have been delays in approvals, resulting in uncertainties for investors and changes in investment plans. In general, the South Asian region does not perform well on investment related parameters, such as setting up of businesses or governance structures. As increased intra-regional penetration and collaboration in telecom will largely depend on investment opportunities, improving the investment climate operationally and not just on paper, would be a must.

Appendix 3A

Table 3A.1 Indices of Restrictiveness in Fixed Line Telecom Services in Selected South Asian Countries

Restriction	Criteria	Score	Weights	Bangladesh 2000	Bangladesh 2009	India 2000	India 2009	Pakistan 2000	Pakistan 2009	Sri Lanka 2000	Sri Lanka 2009
Foreign equity limits	Foreign ownership not permitted	1	0.13	0	0	0.51	0.26	0	0	1	0
	Foreign ownership permitted	0									
Min. investment requirement	Min. investment requirement condition is attached with FDI approval	1	0.05	0	0	0	0	1	1	1	1
	No Min. investment requirement condition is attached with FDI approval	0									
Joint venture arrangements	Foreign company entry is allowed only through joint ventures with domestic company	1	0.11	1	0	1	0	0	0	1	0
	No requirement for a foreign company to enter through a joint venture with a domestic company	0									
Level of competition	Monopoly	1	0.13	1	0	0	0	1	0	1	0.5
	Partial competition	0.5									
	Full competition	0									
Regulatory body	There does not exist an independent regulatory body	1	0.05	1	0	0	0	0	0	0	0
	There exists an independent regulatory body	0									
Licensing—separate for domestic and foreign subsidiaries to determine the NT restrictions	Issues no new licenses	1	0.12	0.5	0.5	0.75	0.25	0.5	0.5	0.75	0.5
	Licenses are issued through complicated and costly procedures	0.75									
	Licenses are issued with application fee and several requirements	0.5									
	Licenses are generally issued with application fees	0.25									
	Licenses are automatically issued upon application without any cost	0									

Category	Criteria	Score	Index						
Restrictions on some types of services	Restrictions on providing some types of telephone services (value added services)	1	0.06	0	0	0	0	0	0
	No restriction on providing any type of telephone services	0							
Screening and approval—separate for domestic and foreign companies to determine NT restrictions	Investors must show economic benefits/ viability	1	0.13	0	0	1	0.66	0.33	0.33	0.33
	Approval unless contrary to national interest	0.66							
	Notification (pre- or post-) requirements	0.33							
	No screening or approval requirements	0							
Acquisition of immovable property	Acquisition of immovable property is not permitted	1	0.12	0.5	0.5	0.5	0.5	0.5	0.5
	Acquisition of immovable property is permitted but with certain conditions/ extra fees	0.5							
	Acquisition of immovable property is permitted without any restriction	0							
Corporate tax laws	Tax rates are very high than the average	1	0.05	0.75	0.75	1	0.5	0.75	0.75
	Tax rates are moderately higher than the average	0.75							
	Tax rates are average of Asia level	0.5							
	Tax rates are moderately lower than the average,	0.25							
	Tax rates are very low than the average	0							

(Contd. . . .)

(Table 3A.1 contd . . .)

Restriction	Criteria	Score	Weights	Bangladesh		India		Pakistan		Sri Lanka	
				2000	2009	2000	2009	2000	2009	2000	2009
Discriminatory tax treatment	Tax rates for foreign firms are more than 15 per cent higher than the rates for domestic firms	1									
	Tax rates for foreign firms are more than 11–15 per cent higher than the rates for domestic firms	0.75									
	Tax rates for foreign firms are more than 6–10 per cent higher than the rates for domestic firms	0.5	0.05	0.25	0	0.75	0.5	0	0	0	0
	Tax rates for foreign firms are more than 1–5 per cent higher than the rates for domestic firms	0.25									
	Tax rates are equal for foreign and domestic firms	0									
	Mode 3 trade restrictiveness index		1	0.46	0.158	0.604	0.26	0.38	0.25	0.65	0.315

Source: Author's compilation based on Dihel and Shepherd (2007) and various web sources.

Notes: The creation of telecom restrictiveness indices is inspired by an OECD study done by Dihel and Shepherd (2007). However, some more regulations appropriate for the telecom sector have been added to their templates to better reflect the regulatory environment prevailing in these countries. The weights are based on the OECD study by Dihel and Shepherd (2007), but with the weights adjusted to account for the additional regulations. There is a problem with the availability of information for some of the parameters used in this table. In such cases, inferences have been drawn from available information and so some degree of subjectivity cannot be ruled out.

Table 3A.2 Roaming Rates for Incoming and Outgoing Calls within SAARC

Incoming Call while Roaming—February 2009							
	Afghanistan	Bangladesh	Bhutan	India	Maldives	Nepal	Pakistan	Sri Lanka
Visiting Afghanistan		0.84	–	0.97	–	0.48	0.38	1.37
Visiting Bangladesh	0.96		0.44	0.84	0.69	0.39	0.38	0.81
Visiting Bhutan	–	1.55		1.68	2.43	1.22	–	2.1
Visiting India	1.44	1.83	1.72		2.62	1.51	–	2.09
Visiting Maldives	0.96	0.43	–	0.77		0.29	0.38	0.59
Visiting Nepal	1.44	0.67	0.48	0.96	–		0.38	0.9
Visiting Pakistan	0.96	0.49	0.21		–	0.22		0.61
Visiting Sri Lanka	1.92 Roshan	0.58 Grameen Phone	0.32 Bhutan Telecom	0.8 Bharti Airtel	0.73 Bhirragu	0.31 Spice Nepal	0.38 Mobilink	Dialog

Outgoing Call to the Visiting Country while Roaming—February 2009							
	Afghanistan	Bangladesh	Bhutan	India	Maldives	Nepal	Pakistan	Sri Lanka
Visiting Afghanistan		0.6	–	0.59	–	0.58	0.9	0.69
Visiting Bangladesh	1.44		0.5	0.44	0.61	0.42	0.9	0.46
Visiting Bhutan	–	1.29		1.2	1.89	1.22	–	1.51
Visiting India	2.4	1.07	1.12		1.61	0.99	–	1.3
Visiting Maldives	1.44	0.17	–	0.29		0.29	0.9	0.34
Visiting Nepal	2.4	0.41	0.48	0.48	–		0.9	0.66
Visiting Pakistan	1.44	0.41	0.46	–	–	0.39		0.45
Visiting Sri Lanka	2.88 Roshan	0.32 Grameen Phone	0.32 Bhutan Telecom	0.31 Bharti Airtel	0.43 Bhirragu	0.31 Spice Nepal	1.49 Mobilink	Dialog

Calling Home Country while Raoming—February 2009							
	Afghanistan	Bangladesh	Bhutan	India	Maldives	Nepal	Pakistan	Sri Lanka
Visiting Afghanistan		2.2	–	1.56		2.12	0.9	3.63
Visiting Bangladesh	1.92		0.71	0.26	0.92	0.69	0.9	0.81
Visiting Bhutan	–	2.13		1.5	3.12	2.02	–	3.01
Visiting India	3.84	2.12	2.27		3.25	1.99	–	2.63
Visiting Maldives	1.92	1.58		2.3		1.96	0.9	2.24
Visiting Nepal	3.84	1.02	1.19	1.07	–		0.9	1.38
Visiting Pakistan	1.92	0.27	0.46		–	0.31		0.8
Visiting Sri Lanka	5.75 Roshan	2.11 Grameen Phone	2.13 Bhutan Telecom	1.75 Bharti Airtel	0.73 Bhirragu	2.03 Spice Nepal	1.49 Mobilink	Dialog

Source: Reproduced from Samarajiva (2009), Table 3. See http://www. lanka businessonline.com/fullstory.php?nid=2109193520, accessed on 13 October 2009.

4

Energy Services

Deepening Integration through Political and Economic Cooperation

The importance of an efficient and well regulated energy service sector is recognized the world over. For developing countries, access to secure, sustainable, and reliable energy sources is critical to realizing their long term growth, equity, and development objectives. The energy sector has thus been witness to significant reforms in many countries aimed at improving competitiveness and efficiency in energy supply and delivery. These reforms have ranged from the entry of private participants (domestic and foreign), the unbundling of different services, restructuring of state utilities, and the establishment of regulatory bodies. The reform process has, however, been a complex one in many countries, given the bearing of this sector on a wide range of potentially conflicting commercial, social, regulatory, infrastructural, geo-political, national security, and strategic objectives. In recent years, an important issue that has emerged in energy services is the scope and need for cross-country cooperation and regional integration with the objective of pooling energy resources and exploiting opportunities in energy trade. There are regional power organizations, and regional and sub-regional initiatives that aim at harnessing complementarities in resource endowments and integrating power systems across countries.

In the context of South Asia, growing demand for energy, which has consistently outpaced growth in energy production makes energy security and improved competitiveness and efficiency in the sector a priority for all governments. The region's demand for energy has been growing at a rate of 9 per cent per year and the region's deficit in energy production has doubled in the last decade and costly, frequent, and widespread power outages are a common phenomenon.[1] Such constraints pertaining to the supply and provision of energy hamper the region's growth prospects and make most economies in South Asia highly dependent on energy imports and vulnerable to external shocks in energy prices. In the past decade or more, almost all the South Asian countries have embarked on power sector reforms, involving liberalization and promotion of private participation, promoting foreign investment for energy infrastructure development, investments in renewable energy and energy efficient technologies, expanding the use of indigenous resources and diversifying energy supply sources, and establishing regulatory frameworks. There has also been considerable discussion about the need to cooperate in the energy sector at a regional level, both under the auspices of SAARC and under bilateral and other sub-regional initiatives. Many studies have highlighted the potential for energy trade in South Asia given the contiguous landmass and complementary energy resource endowments. Governments in this region have become increasingly aware of the win-win possibilities in energy trade within South Asia. However, numerous political and institutional challenges have constrained this process and cooperation and commercial efforts have thus far remained confined to limited bilateral initiatives between certain SAARC member countries.

This chapter assesses the scope for regional energy cooperation in South Asia and the opportunities and challenges in this regard. To begin with the chapter highlights the energy status of this region vis-à-vis other regions to present South Asia in a comparative perspective. The energy status of individual countries in this region is also discussed in order to highlight the importance of energy services for the region, and to identify where the region's needs lie in this sector. The chapter then outlines the regulatory reforms and liberalization undertaken in the energy sector and the related outcomes. It then moves on to discussing the existing and proposed intra-regional cooperation initiatives and regional projects at the governmental, multilateral, and private sector levels, and in the SAARC context and the progress that has been made. Following this, the chapter outlines the main challenges to realizing energy cooperation and commercialization at a regional level and then discusses the status of multilateral and other commitments made by the South Asian countries in the energy sector and what this indicates regarding their preparedness to negotiate commercial opportunities in energy services with other countries. Finally, the chapter outlines

---

[1] See 'Energy Cooperation in South Asia'. Available at http://www.southasianmedia. net/Magazine/Journal/9_energy_cooperation.htm, accessed on 30 September 2008.

some policy measures and specific steps that could be taken to translate much of the understanding that already exists regarding the value and possibilities for energy cooperation at the regional level, into a reality.

Energy Status and Performance

The South Asian countries are characterized by their reliance on a mix of commercial energy sources, which include natural gas, oil, hydropower, and coal. They are also highly dependent on energy imports, mainly in the form of oil imports. With electricity production unable to keep pace with growing demand, combined with high transmission and distribution losses and high energy intensity, energy security has become a major area of concern for all governments in this region. The following tables and figures highlight recent trends in energy use, production, and trade for South Asia as a whole vis-à-vis other regions, as well as trends in key energy status indicators for individual South Asian countries and other comparable developing countries. These summary indicators highlight the most salient features of South Asia's energy market.

Several interesting facts emerge from the statistics shown in Table 4.1. The SAARC region (which here includes Afghanistan) has the lowest energy consumption per capita among all the geographic regions. Its per capita energy consumption is half that of ASEAN, around 60 per cent that of Africa, and roughly one-fourth of the world average. This low ranking reflects the low levels of income, the poor state of energy infrastructure, and lack of basic access to energy facilities for a significant part of the population in all the South Asian countries. However, the region's average annual growth rate of per capita energy consumption is broadly comparable to that in other regions. It exceeds the world average and has shown an upward trend in recent years. The region also shows very high energy intensity. Its energy consumption per dollar of GDP is among the highest in the world, reflecting inefficient utilization of energy. The SAARC region, however, has experienced one of the largest declines in the energy use to GDP ratio, greater than the average decline for the world, reflecting measures to improve energy efficiency in these countries. While all countries within the SAARC region exhibit improvements in energy efficiency, India has experienced the largest decline in the energy consumption per unit of GDP during the past decade. Thus, the picture that emerges is of a region that is confronted with infrastructural and accessibility challenges in the energy sector, combined with growing energy requirements due to economic growth and rising incomes, along with steps in some countries to improve efficiency in energy utilization and lower energy intensity.

Table 4.1 Energy Use in Different Regions of the World

Country/Region	Energy Consumption per Capita (Kg of oil equivalent)				Growth Rate (% per annum)		Energy Supply, Apparent Consumption per Unit of GDP (Kg of oil equivalent per 1,000 [2005 PPP dollars])				Growth Rate (% per annum)	
	1990	1995	2000	2006	1990–2006	2000–6	1990	1995	2000	2006	1990–2006	2000–6
Asia and the Pacific	773	749	731	853	0.6	2.6	312	287	257	241	−1.6	−1.1
LLDC	1,834	1,199	1,047	1,129	−3	1.3	712	790	647	451	−2.8	−5.8
LDC	159	168	172	191	1.1	1.7	277	267	233	176	−2.8	−4.5
ASEAN	417	498	557	633	2.6	2.2	241	230	237	218	−0.6	−1.4
ECO	937	850	849	1,010	0.5	2.9	306	286	270	249	−1.3	−1.3
SAARC	278	287	294	318	0.8	1.4	292	278	253	209	−2.1	−3.1
Central Asia	2,284	1,435	1,270	1,400	−3	1.6	693	823	661	447	−2.7	−6.3
Pacific Island Dev. Economy												
Low-income	395	357	362	295	0	1.4	377	339	317	264	−2.2	−3
Middle-income	717	676	648	797	0.7	3.5	425	374	312	282	−2.5	−1.7
High-income	2,312	2,667	2,837	2,900	1.4	0.4	153	160	161	148	−0.2	−1.4
Other world regions												
Africa	487	470	481	505	0.2	0.8	298	314	296	272	−0.6	−1.4
Europe	2,459	2,281	2,342	2,488	0.1	1	192	175	155	144	−1.8	−1.3
Latin America and Caribbean	792	835	873	930	1	1.1	152	148	148	143	−0.4	−0.5
North America	5,163	5,231	5,561	5,288	0.1	−0.8	245	237	213	186	−1.7	−2.2
Other countries/areas	1,446	1,549	1,583	1,751	1.2	1.7	218	240	249		0.5	−1
World	1,187	1,146	1,151	1,226	0.2	1.1	248	234	213	200	−1.3	−1
South and South-West Asia	328	353	368	417	1.5	2.1	256	254	239	209	−1.3	−2.2
Afghanistan												
Bangladesh	98	108	110	129	1.7	2.6	163	164	149	143	−0.8	−0.6

(*Contd . . . .*)

(*Table 4.1 contd . . .*)

Country/Region	Energy Consumption per Capita (Kg of oil equivalent)				Growth Rate (% per annum)		Energy Supply, Apparent Consumption per Unit of GDP (Kg of oil equivalent per 1,000 [2005 PPP dollars])				Growth Rate (% per annum)	
	1990	1995	2000	2006	1990–2006	2000–6	1990	1995	2000	2006	1990–2006	2000–6
Bhutan												
India	294	301	306	329	0.7	1.2	313	296	265	213	−2.4	−3.5
Iran (Islamic Republic of)	950	1,247	1,410	1,945	4.6	5.5	202	235	242	254	1.4	0.8
Maldives												
Nepal	302	309	332	337	0.7	0.3	433	390	372	352	−1.3	−1
Pakistan	326	354	359	407	1.4	2.1	240	239	240	218	−0.6	−1.6
Sri Lanka	310	315	391	451	2.4	2.4	165	137	146	130	−1.5	−1.9
Turkey	702	763	856	994	2.2	2.5	166	165	169	158	−0.3	−1.2
Southeast Asia	**417**	**498**	**557**	**633**	**2.6**	**2.2**	**241**	**230**	**237**	**218**	**−0.6**	**−1.4**
Brunei Darussalam	1,654	2,268	2,139	2,076	1.4	−0.5	142	161	159	152	0.4	−0.8
Cambodia		278	288	319	0.9	1.7		374	310	224	−3.2	−5.3
Indonesia	433	479	560	587	1.9	0.8	277	243	269	240	−0.9	−1.9
Lao PDR												
Malaysia	803	1,130	1,325	1,582	4.3	3	192	206	212	215	0.7	0.3
Myanmar	234	245	244	268	0.8	1.5	786	654	479		−4.8	−4.9
Philippines	249	318	330	304	1.3	−1.3	176	205	211	163	−0.5	−4.2
Singapore	2,273	2,465	2,581	3,736	3.2	6.4	187	197	150	158	−1.1	0.8
Thailand	567	804	858	1117	4.3	4.5	195	191	216	221	0.8	0.4
Timor-Leste												
Vietnam	340	384	424	535	2.9	4	407	340	300	271	−2.5	−1.6

Source: Reproduced from UNESCAP (2009b: 203, Table 29).

The SAARC region has also experienced a growing dependence on energy imports as shown in Table 4.2. Energy imports as a share of total energy supply increased from around 12 per cent in 1990 to close to 30 per cent in 2006, while the comparable figures for the world declined over this period from 11 per cent to around 9 per cent, and likewise in other regions. This suggests that growth in energy consumption in the South Asian region has not been matched by commensurate increases in energy supply, thereby increasing the region's overall dependence on energy imports. This dependence in part also reflects the lack of diversification and lack of indigenization of energy supply sources in the SAARC countries, with continued dominance of coal and oil in their commercial energy mix. It is also interesting to note that energy exports rose for the SAARC region between 1990 and 2006, which indicates the potential for leveraging supply and demand complementarities and for energy trade within the region.

Energy Sector Trends in Individual Countries

South Asia accounts for about 5.9 per cent of the world's commercial energy consumption. The countries in this region are endowed with a mix of energy resources, including hydropower, coal, natural gas, and oil. Bangladesh and Pakistan are well endowed in natural gas reserves, India in coal reserves, and Bhutan and Nepal in hydropower resources. None of the countries is well endowed in oil reserves. This endowment mix in a large part determines the pattern of commercial energy consumption in the region and the countries' overall dependence on energy imports.

Table 4.3 shows the energy resource endowments as well as energy production patterns for each of the South Asian countries. Two important features are highlighted in this table. First is the large unexploited potential in most forms of energy resources, in particular, natural gas and hydropower resources. Less than 5 per cent of the hydropower potential in Nepal and Bhutan has been exploited and only a mere fraction of Bangladesh's natural gas reserves have been tapped thus far. The latter clearly reflects the need for huge investments in this sector if these countries are to become more self-reliant on indigenous resources. A second important feature is the complementarity in resource endowments across the countries in the region, which in turn indicates the scope for regional cooperation and trade so as to pool and harness each other's resources.

The energy usage mix also varies across countries in the region, in line with the varied endowment mix within the region. For instance, India's energy basket is dominated by coal, which is indigenously available in a large supply. Hydropower is abundantly available in Bhutan and Nepal: it is the main constituent

Table 4.2 Energy Balances in South Asia and Other Regions

Country / Region	Primary Production			Imports			Exports			Energy Supply		
	1990	2000	2006	1990	2000	2006	1990	2000	2006	1990	2000	2006
						(Million tonnes of oil equivalent)						
Asia and the Pacific	3,267.3	3,412	4,734.9	412.8	496.8	776.7	−990.4	−923.1	−1,345.5	3,382.9	3,885.1	5,087.9
LLDC	238.2	212.2	304	84.6	17.4	32.2	−126.8	−93.5	−173.7	196	136.5	162.5
LDC										29.3	43.4	53.7
ASEAN	311.5	467.1	606	115.6	196.3	266.1	−168	−243.6	−348.7	246.4	398.6	498.8
ECO	444	490.6	662.5	92.6	37.2	63.8	−244.8	−220.5	−327.7	344.1	383.6	491.9
SAARC	345.9	438.3	531.2	48.5	126.8	198.1	−3.5	−9.8	−35.4	387.5	558.7	689
Central Asia	231.8	204.5	293.9	95.2	17.6	32.7	−128	−93.6	−172.8	199.1	128.9	153.6
Pacific Island Dev. Economy												
Low-income	158.1	212.6	271.1	43.1	40.6	46.9	−11	−31.8	−55.2	189.8	220	261.9
Middle-income	3,093.5	3,179.7	4,442	294.3	352.3	585.3	−926.6	−830.4	−1,205.2	2,528.5	2,779.7	3,890.3
High-income	15.7	19.7	21.8	75.5	103.9	144.5	−52.8	−60.9	−85.1	664.6	885.4	935.7
Other world regions												
Africa	688.4	890.8	1,110.5	47	81.1	102.6	−341.4	−461.7	−591.3	392.7	507.4	614.3
Europe	230.7	149.6	159.4	336.5	148.8	185.2	−85.3	−27.8	−48.7	2,049.8	1,968.5	2,084.5
Latin America and Caribbean	427.5	621	704/3	103.4	151.8	163.8	−172.9	−305.3	−333	469.3	610.3	708
North America	765.5	1090.6	1,244.3							2,135.8	2,554.6	2,590.4
Other countries/areas				84.2	138.5	190.2	−622.1	−848.4	−942.6	−215.6	362.4	471.8
World	5,379.4	6,164	7,953.4	983.9	1,017	1,418.5	−2,212	−2,566.3	−3,261	8,646	9,888.3	11,557
South and South-West Asia	525.7	679.2	840.5	55.9	131.5	213.7	−121.4	−136.1	−189	509.3	754.4	953.8
Afghanistan												

Bangladesh	10.8	15.2	20.3	2.3	3.5	4.8	−0.1	−0.1	−0.1	12.8	18.7	25
Bhutan												
India	291.1	364.3	435.6	34.5	100.3	168.6	−2.8	−8.8	−33.8	319.9	459.8	565.8
Iran (Islamic Republic of)	179.8	240.9	309.3	7.4	4.8	15.6	−117.9	−126.3	−153.6	68.8	118.8	170.9
Maldives												
Nepal	5.5	7.1	8.3	0.3	1	1.1	0	0	0	5.8	8.2	9.4
Pakistan	34.4	47.1	61.3	9.5	18	19.5	−0.3	−0.8	−1.4	43.4	64	79.3
Sri Lanka	4.2	4.5	5.5	1.9	3.9	4.2	−0.2	−0.1	0	5.5	8.1	9.4
Turkey										52.9	76.9	94
Southeast Asia	**311.5**	**467.1**	**606**	**115.6**	**196.3**	**266.1**	**−168**	**−243.6**	**−348.7**	**246.4**	**398.6**	**498.8**
Brunei Darussalam	15.6	19.7	21.8	0	0	0	−13.8	−17.3	−19.1	1.8	2.5	2.8
Cambodia		3.2	3.6		0.8	1.4					4	5
Indonesia	170	235.6	307.7	9.7	24	33.4	−76.3	−108	−161.2	102.8	151.4	179.1
Lao PDR												
Malaysia	50.3	80.4	97.9	9.5	16.2	23.7	−36.4	−44.9	−52.8	23.3	51.3	68.3
Myanmar	10.7	15.4	22.1	0	1.4	0.9	0	−4.4	−8.7	10.7	12.6	14.3
Philippines	13.7	20.9	24.7	13.3	23.5	20.4	−0.7	−1.9	−1.9	26.2	42.4	43
Singapore										13.4	22.2	30.7
Thailand	26.5	43.9	56.2	18.8	38.9	57.2	−0.8	−6.9	−10.3	43.9	75	103.4
Timor-Leste												
Vietnam	24.7	48.1	71.9	3	8.9	12.2	−3.1	−18.6	−31.1	24.3	37.2	52.3

Source: Reproduced from UNESCAP (2009b: 204, Table 28.2).

Table 4.3 Energy Resource Endowments in South Asian Countries (units varying with energy resource)

Resource		Bangladesh	Bhutan	India	Maldives	Nepal	Pakistan	Sri Lanka
Oil	Oil reserves (Mt)	7.8	0	786	–	0	105	14–18
	Oil production (Mt/year)	0.34	0	33.00	–	0	3.10	0
Gas	Proven gas reserves (bcm)	580/810	–	948	–	0	1300/5700	0
	Gas production (bcm/day)	13.8	–	32.68	–	0	28.00	0
Coal	Coal reserves (Gt)	2.2	0	25/285	–	modest	185	0
	Coal production (Mt/year)	–	0	409.00	–	0	3.30	0
Hydropower	Hydropower potential (MW)	775	23,760/30,000	84,000/150,000	–	43,000/83,000	54,000	9,100
	Developed (MW)	230	468	32,300	–	600	6,500	1,250
	Percentage harnessed (%)	30.5	1.9/1.6	38.5/21.5	–	1.4/0.72	12.0	13.7

Source: Based on Malla (2008), Table 5, p. 5.

Note: Mt=million tonnes, Gt=giga tonnes, MW=mega watts, bcf=billion cubic feet, bb=billion barrels, bcm=billion cubic metre.

constituent of Bhutan's energy basket and to some extent of Nepal. Bangladesh relies heavily on natural gas in which it is abundant. Figure 4.1 shows the composition of the energy basket in each of the South Asian countries. It reflects the varied mix of energy sources that are relied upon by the countries in this region, and its close alignment with existing country endowments. The data also reflect the general lack of diversification of energy sources, with all the countries relying on one single source of energy for half or more of their energy requirements. Alternative and renewable energy sources account for only a negligible portion of the energy basket and are evident only in the case of India.

An examination of the data on electricity production and sources of electricity over 1990–2004, as shown in Table 4.4, indicates that there has been some shift in the pattern of resource use in the larger countries of this region. There is increased reliance on natural gas for electricity production accompanied by reduced dependence on hydropower resources in India, Bangladesh, and Pakistan while in Sri Lanka, there is increased dependence on oil. The region as a whole is broadly comparable with the rest of the world in its use of gas, oil, and hydropower as sources of electricity, but it is more dependent on coal based electricity production than the rest of the world and lags behind the world in nuclear based electricity production. Thus, what emerges is that the countries are largely dependent on traditional sources of energy for electricity production though there seems to be a clear focus on moving

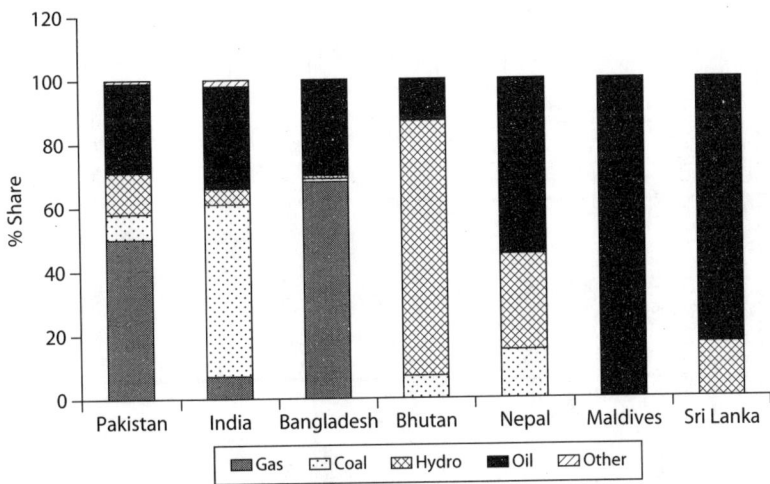

Figure 4.1 Commercial Energy Mix in South Asian Countries

Source: USAID SARI/Energy Programme (2006: 2-3, Figure 2-1). Available at http://www.sari-energy.org/ProjectReports/RegionalEnergySecurity_RegionalReport_Complete.pdf, accessed on 12 March 2009.

Table 4.4 Electricity Production and Sources of Electricity

Country/Region	Electricity Production (billion KWH) 1990	2004	Per Capita Electricity Production (KWH) 1990	2004	Source of Electricity (percentage of total) Coal 1990	2004	Gas 1990	2004	Oil 1990	2004	Hydropower 1990	2004	Nuclear 1990	2004
Bangladesh	7.7	21.5	–	149.3	–	–	84.3	87.5	4.3	6.7	11.4	5.7	–	–
Bhutan	–	–	–	–	–	–	–	–	–	–	–	–	–	–
India	289.4	667.8	–	618.9	65.5	69.1	3.4	9.5	4.3	5.4	24.8	12.7	2.1	2.5
Maldives	0.9	2.3	–	86.1	–	–	–	–	0.1	0.2	99.9	99.8	–	–
Nepal	–	–	–	–	–	–	–	–	–	–	–	–	–	–
Pakistan	37.7	85.7	–	563.4	0.1	0.2	33.6	50.7	20.6	15.9	44.9	30	0.8	3.3
Sri Lanka	3.2	8	–	412.3	–	–	–	–	0.2	63.2	99.8	36.8	–	–
South Asia	338.9	785.3	–	549.7	55.8	58.7	8.6	16	6.1	7.1	27.6	14.9	1.9	2.5
World	11,787.7	17,372.6	–	28,250	38.1	39.8	13.8	19.7	10.3	6.4	18.1	16	17.1	15.8
South Asia as a per cent of World	2.8	4.5	–	19.4	–	–	–	–	–	–	–	–	–	–

Source: Reproduced from Malla (2008: 10, Table 5).

towards natural gas in the future. The latter in turn has its own implications for regional cooperation and integration prospects given the complementary pattern of resource endowments and energy demand across the countries.

The South Asian countries are dependent on energy imports to meet their commercial energy requirements. Figure 4.2 shows that in 2004, energy imports constituted between 9 and 59 per cent of the total (commercial and non-commercial) energy requirements in the South Asian countries, with an average import dependence of around 25 per cent. However, if one excludes non-commercial energy sources, such as wood, animal waste, and biomass, which constitute around half of the region's total energy consumption, then the reliance on energy imports for meeting commercial energy requirements was very high, averaging around 53 per cent and ranging from 24 to 87 per cent.

If one examines import dependence over time, the data reveal that the share of imports in total energy supply increased for the SAARC region as a whole, and also for each of the countries over the 1990 to 2006 period. In particular, India experienced a secular upward trend in its dependence on energy imports, with this share rising from 10 per cent in 1990 to nearly 30 per cent in 2006 (although this rise is broadly comparable with that

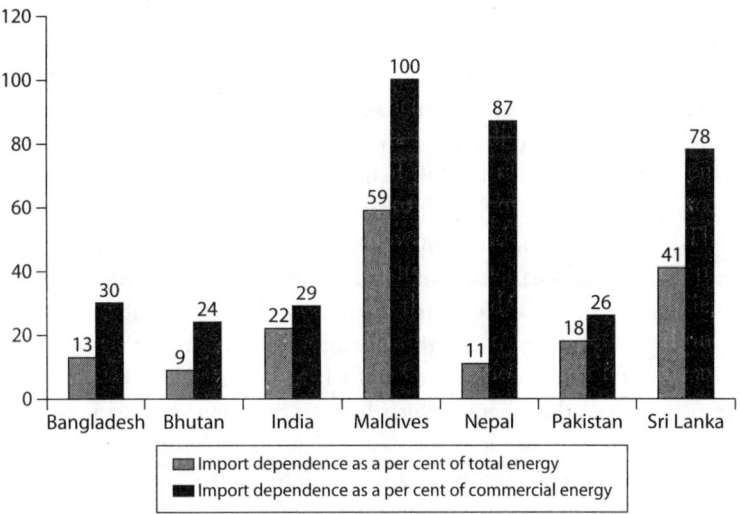

Figure 4.2   Dependence on Energy Imports

Source: USAID (2006: 2-5, Tables 2-4). Available at http://www.sari-energy.org/ ProjectReports/RegionalEnergySecurity_RegionalReport_Complete.pdf, accessed on 12 March 2009.

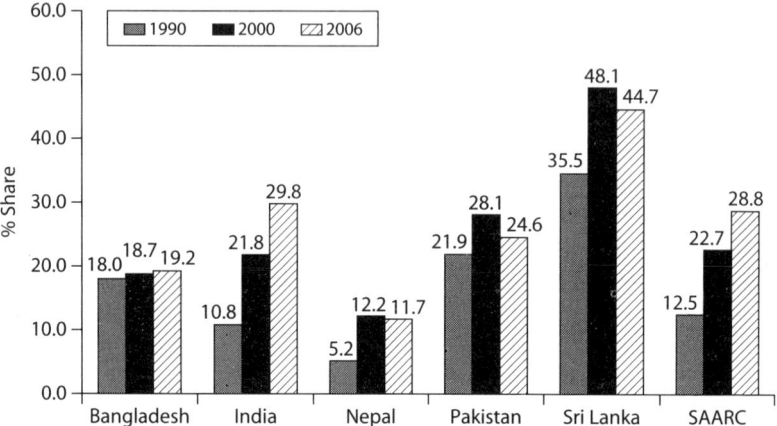

Figure 4.3   Energy Imports as a Share of Total Energy Supply in Individual South Asian Countries and in SAARC

Source: Based on UNESCAP (2009b: 204, Table 28.2).

witnessed in other high growth economies in Southeast Asia). India's energy imports increased 70 per cent in volume terms over this period. Figure 4.3 illustrates the growing energy import dependence of individual South Asian countries. It also highlights the importance of trends in the Indian energy market in determining trends in the overall regional energy market.

According to a USAID study (2006), India and Pakistan can be characterized as energy crisis countries given their high energy intensity (high share of energy use per unit of output reflecting their inefficiencies in energy usage) combined with their high dependence on energy imports as well as the high share of these imports in their total exports (a reflection of the proportion of export earnings absorbed by energy imports). Figure 4.4 places the South Asian countries against other developed and developing countries in terms of their energy intensity and import share indicators.

The growing import dependence of the South Asian countries is a reflection of growing consumption of all major forms of energy sources in the countries of this region, which has not been matched with commensurate growth in indigenous sources of energy supply or diversification to other forms of energy. Tables 4.5 and 4.6 highlight the growth in consumption of oil, coal, and natural gas and the significance of each of these energy sources in the countries' energy imports.

It is evident from Table 4.5 that there has been considerable growth in energy consumption in the SAARC member countries in recent years, obviously reflecting the impact of industrial growth and rising incomes. This

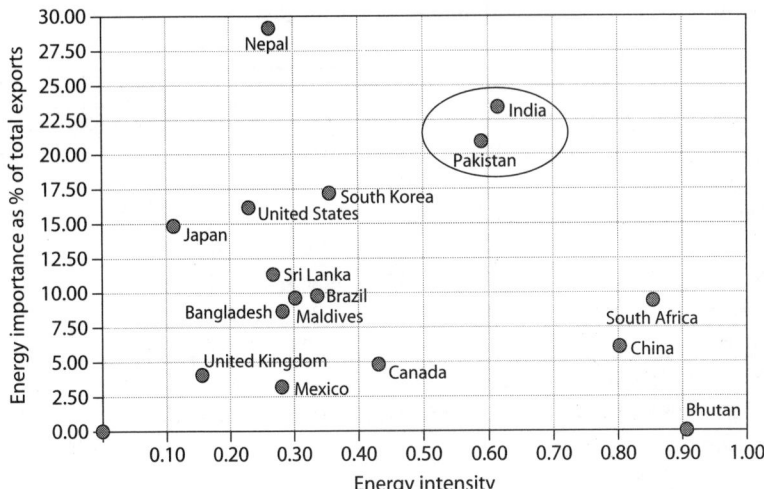

Figure 4.4 Energy Imports and Intensity in South Asian and Other Countries

Source: Reproduced from Jetley and Lodhi (2009). Available at http://www.isasnus.org/events/activities/20090730%20-%20Dr%20Rajshree%20Jetly.pdf, accessed on 16 September 2009.

growth is dominated by certain energy sources in each country. It is also interesting to note the high growth in natural gas consumption compared to other sources in the case of Bangladesh and India. The emergence of natural gas as an important contributor to the energy basket is also reflected in Table 4.6. While the greatest increase over the 1990–2004 period has been in petroleum and coal imports, there is a perceptible shift towards natural gas imports in the case of India, a fact also highlighted earlier in the context of electricity production. Such a shift is indicative of the prospects for trade in natural gas within the region, given India's growing demand for

Table 4.5 Average Growth in Consumption of Different Energy Sources, 2001–7 (per cent growth)

Country	Petroleum	Natural Gas	Coal
Bangladesh	4.29	7.14	2.04
India	3.79	9.28	5.65
Maldives	15.52		
Nepal	2.15		6.67
Pakistan	−0.2	3.74	10.27
Sri Lanka	2.17		

Source: EIA web sources for each country.

Table 4.6 Net Exports and Imports of Energy Resources in South Asian Countries

	1990		2000		2007		
	Petroleum	Coal	Petroleum	Coal	Petroleum	Natural Gas	Coal
Bangladesh	−35	−15.8	−66	−13.7	−84	0	−14.6
Bhutan	−1	−0.5	−1	−0.4	−1	0	−0.4
India	−487	−112.4	−1,357	−575.9	−1,919	−282.2	−1,494
Maldives	−1	0	−3	0	−6	0	0
Nepal	−4	−0.3	−15	−10.3	−17	0	−12.5
Pakistan	−158	−21.1	−308	−26	−322	0	−75.5
Sri Lanka	−35	0	−75	−0.1	−87	0	−2.9

Source: EIA web sources for each country.
Note: Petroleum—1,000 barrels per day, natural gas—billion cubic feet, coal—trillion btu.

natural gas, and Bangladesh's sizeable natural gas endowment and thus the scope for leveraging complementarities in this resource. Figure 4.5 shows the natural gas deficit projected for India and Pakistan in 2010–20. Clearly, access to natural gas resources and exploitation of domestic availability will be important for both these countries in the medium and long term.

Trends in electricity production and consumption highlight the growing power shortages in this region, in particular in the larger countries, and indicate the potential for electricity trade through integration of power

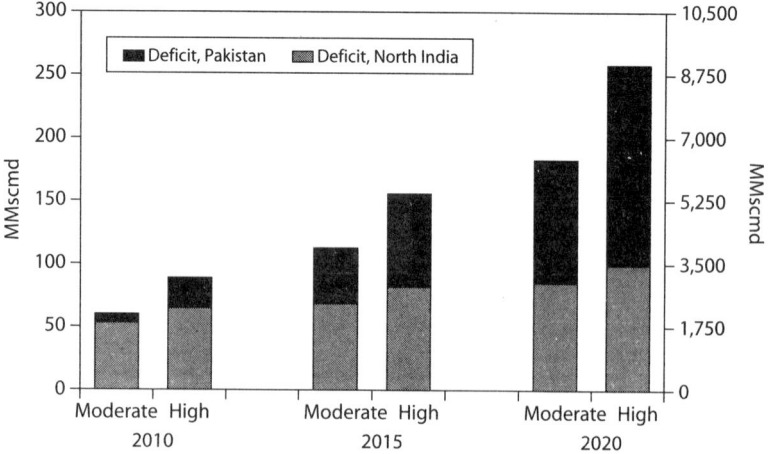

Figure 4.5 Projected Deficits in Natural Gas in India and Pakistan
Source: Reproduced from World Bank (2008a: 42, Figure 5.3).

Table 4.7 Average Growth in Electricity Production and Consumption (%) and Net Electricity Imports (bn KW hours)

Country	Consumption (%) 1996–2000	2001–6	Production* (%) 1996–2000	2001–6	Net electricity imports (bn KW hours) 2000	2005
Bangladesh	7.8	9.39	7.5	7.44	0	0
Bhutan	28.33	22.22	1.3	6.58	−1.44	−1.542
India	3.37	5.5	5.97	4.86	1.345	1.554
Maldives	0	16.67	0	16.67	0	0
Nepal	8.45	9.19	7.82	8.05	0.101	0.108
Pakistan	4.05	6.59	4.18	6.18	0	0
Sri Lanka	6.63	4.64	6.6	4.55	0	0

Source: EIA web sources for each country.

Note: *Electricity production refers to production of conventional thermal electricity, hydroelectric power, nuclear electric power, geothermal solar, wind, and wood, and waste electricity power generation.

systems within the region. Electricity production has grown more slowly than electricity consumption in all the countries in South Asia (Table 4.7). The equivalent data for electricity exports and imports for Bhutan and India, respectively, reflect bilateral trade in electricity (and associated cross-border investment flows) between these two countries and thus the sub-regional prospects for electricity trade in South Asia.

The medium and long term projections for growth in energy demand across various segments are provided in Table 4.8. The projections indicate

Table 4.8 Medium-term and Long-term Commercial Energy Demand Projections, 2002–10 and 2010–20

Growth Rate (% year)		Bangladesh	Bhutan	India	Maldives	Nepal	Pakistan	Sri Lanka
Electricity demand	Medium term	7.4	15.0	7.2	16.0	8.3	8.2	6.7
	Long term	8.8	15.0	7.0	16.0	7.8	6.8	7.9
Oil Demand	Medium term	7.4	16.0	4.4	12.0	6.5	4.4	8.2
	Long term	7.4	16.0	5.1	12.0	3.7	4.4	4.1
Gas demand	Medium term	9.4	0.0	6.8	0.0	0.0	6.2	0.0
	Long term	11.0	Nil	8.0	0.0	0.0	6.4	0.0
Coal demand	Medium term	0.0	5.0	6.6	0.0	8.0	9.0	0.0
	Long term	5.8	5.0	6.1	0.0	11.2	11.2	24.0

Source: USAID SARI/Energy Programme (2006). Available at http://www.sari-energy.org/ProjectReports/RegionalEnergySecurity_RegionalReport_Complete.pdf, accessed on 12 March 2009.

that all the South Asian countries will experience very high rates of growth in electricity demand and for various energy sources, in the medium and long term.

If one juxtaposes these demand projections and patterns against the growing import dependence, relatively high energy intensity, capacity shortages, and the nature of energy resource endowments in this region, it is evident that energy security is a critical issue for South Asian countries. The main challenge confronting these countries is getting increased access to diversified sources of energy, as well as improving energy efficiency, particularly in the case of India and Pakistan. For the smaller countries, as well as Bangladesh, the most critical issue is the exploitation of domestic energy resources and leveraging this endowment to tap regional export opportunities.

Policy and Regulatory Reforms

The energy sector faces various infrastructural, institutional, operational, and financial challenges in South Asia. As discussed earlier, rapidly growing power demand combined with supply shortages has been a major constraint to growth in the region. Energy utilities in South Asia have been, and remain commercially unviable, with poor quality of service delivery. Universal service provision has not been achieved with only a minority of the population in the region having access to energy sources. Transmission and distribution losses for electricity are very high due to leakages, weak networks, and poor monitoring. In addition, energy related environmental challenges also plague the region, thus requiring a push towards alternative and renewable energy and improving energy efficiency. Hence, there has been a clear need for power sector reforms and associated institutional restructuring and privatization. This need has been recognized in all the countries in this region.

Status of Reforms

The energy services sector has undergone reforms in all the South Asian countries, though it is under different stages of implementation in the different countries. The main feature of these reforms has been the increased role of the private sector and liberalization of foreign direct investment in several important segments. Private participation in power generation is now allowed in all the countries in the region, which in turn has attracted domestic and international investments in energy exploration and generation in many of the countries. The main form of private participation has been by independent power producers (IPPs) under long-term power purchase agreements with the buyer normally being the incumbent power company or the state electricity board. Bangladesh, Sri Lanka, and

India have encouraged private companies to enter into the exploration and production of oil and gas. In their drive for energy security, some of the countries have encouraged the acquisition of overseas energy assets by their public and private sector companies.[2] Liberalization has led to the emergence of corporate players, especially in India, who are interested in investing in other markets in the region.

There have also been complementary structural reforms, including disinvestment, restructuring, and corporatization of public sector companies, and steps to move towards more reasonable and competitive tariffs. The existing state owned utilities have been unbundled into separate functional companies to improve their financial position and operational efficiency. Regulatory agencies have also been established. The structural reforms have been driven by explicit policies to improve access to electricity in all the countries of this region. Among all the countries, India has undertaken the most liberalization and has opened up most of its energy segments.

Tables A.2 to A.8 (see Annexure) summarize the main policy and regulatory changes that have occurred in selected segments of the energy services sector for each of the South Asian countries. They highlight the fact that the main thrust has been on encouraging private participation, particularly in energy generation and the corporatization of this sector.

However, as pointed out in many studies, reforms need to go further in South Asia. Although private contribution to the national generation capacity has increased to about 20–30 per cent, the public sector continues to dominate. The high tariffs charged by the independent power producers due to perceived risks and high cost of debt finance, have in turn caused financial distress to the state electricity boards which are faced with high cost of power purchase agreements coupled with low revenues from retail electricity due to commercially unviable tariffs. Electricity pricing has remained subject to political interference. Reforms have also not taken place in the distribution sector. Commercial distribution at viable tariff rates is required to attract private investment into generation. Overall, the power industry continues to be plagued by poor governance, inefficiencies, lack of transparency and accountability, anti-competitive cross subsidization policies, reversals on tariff increases, and populist resistance to pro-competitive and commercially justified measures.

---

[2] ONGC Videsh, which is a wholly owned subsidiary of India's largest oil and gas producer has the task of acquiring productive assets abroad and has acquired oil and gas fields overseas. India's overseas investment in oil fields is expected to amount to US$3 billion in the near future.

Multilateral and Other Commitments in Energy Services

None of the WTO member countries of South Asia has scheduled energy services under the WTO. This obviously reflects their unwillingness and unpreparedness to negotiate this sector multilaterally, despite having undertaken reforms to encourage private participation, both domestic and foreign. This conservative multilateral stance in energy services is due to the sensitive nature of this sector, given its geo-political and strategic nature. It is also due to the fact that the sector still remains largely state-dominated despite the entry of private players. It is mainly energy exploration that has been opened up to private participation. Other segments, such as transmission, distribution, and issues related to pricing are still under the control of electricity boards and state owned power utilities given the various social and infrastructural objectives that this sector is meant to serve. Thus, the regulatory environment is still not conducive to private investment and the playing field is still not level for public and private players despite the sectoral reforms in most countries in this region. This is thus a sector where unilateral liberalization exceeds multilateral liberalization, indicating the fact that countries would rather leave themselves space to reverse policies if so required and to learn from their autonomous liberalization before committing multilaterally.

It is, however, interesting to note that the energy sector does figure in some of the bilateral and extra-regional agreements signed by the SAARC member countries. For instance, the Pakistan–China FTA includes energy among the five identified major sectors for cooperation between the two countries. Likewise, the proposed Pakistan–Afghanistan Economic Cooperation Agreement does include energy and the specific issue of gas pipelines as an item for discussion. The India–Singapore CECA covers services incidental to electricity distribution. The proposed Bangladesh–US Trade and Investment Framework Agreement and the proposed Bangladesh–Russia FTA both cover the power sector. Under the BIMSTEC sub-regional agreement, in which several of the SAARC countries are also members, the energy sector has received focus with stated objectives of establishing power exchange and grid connections among the BIMSTEC member countries, establishing a common regulatory framework, a trans-BIMSTEC gas pipeline, promoting hydropower projects, promoting the use of non-conventional sources of energy, and technical cooperation in the sub-region. Given the commonality of member countries between SAARC and BIMSTEC, it is not surprising that many of the areas identified for cooperation are quite similar across the two regional blocs.

Overall, there have been significant reforms and changes in the operating and regulatory structure in energy services in most of the South Asian countries. However, the basic structure of state owned utilities remains, combined with private players in some selected segments. Non-commercial considerations still dominate the functioning of this sector. The focus of deregulation has been to facilitate investment in infrastructure, investment in discovery of energy resources, and to improve efficiency in energy utilization.

Status of Intra-regional Cooperation and Initiatives

There has been a general recognition among member governments both in the context of SAARC discussions as well as in bilateral discussions, that energy cooperation and trade in South Asia can play an important role in addressing the energy security interests of the countries in this region. Many studies have highlighted the scope for mutual benefit from exports of generation surpluses from Bangladesh, Bhutan, and Nepal to meet the huge power deficits in India, and the scope to structure this generation mix in a way that can meet the region's demand pattern and also make possible lower electricity prices for all countries concerned. For instance, effective development of Nepal and Bhutan's huge hydropower potential could serve regional electricity needs while also addressing those countries' trade deficits with partner countries like India. Tables 4.9 and 4.10 highlight the potential for cross-border energy trade in the eastern and western parts of SAARC as documented in earlier studies.

The estimated direct benefits from energy cooperation in the region are considerable. These benefits relate to investments in energy supply and demand technologies, as well as environment related outcomes. According to one source, this benefit is projected to be as large as $359 billion for the 2010–30 period, or 0.98 per cent of the region's GDP, as shown in Table 4.11.

There are also indirect benefits from such regional cooperation, for instance due to the development of water markets, infrastructure development, and increased agricultural productivity due to better irrigation. Hence, the cost of not cooperating in the energy sector is quite high.

Bilateral and Sub-regional Cooperation: Successes and Failures

Energy cooperation within SAARC has progressed mainly at the bilateral level, between India and Nepal, and between India and Bhutan. It has taken the form of energy exchanges and is mainly limited to hydroelectric power though there have been some discussions regarding natural gas and

Table 4.9 Overview of Trade Prospects in the Eastern and Northern SAARC Region

Exporting Countries	Importing Countries				
	Bangladesh	Bhutan	India	Nepal	Sri Lanka
Bangladesh		Small amounts of thermal power and gas connection possible via India***	Natural gas and power exports possible*	Small amounts of thermal power and gas connection possible via India***	Not likely due to distance****
Bhutan	Some hydropower potential via India***		Large quantities of hydropower exports possible*	Unlikely due to similar resources and seasonal shortages****	Not likely due to distance****
India	Sharing reserves, electricity swaps**	Dry season support*		Dry season and thermal power support*	Dry season and thermal power support**
Nepal	Some hydropower potential via India***	Unlikely due to similar resources and seasonal shortages****	Large quantities of hydropower exports possible*		Not likely due to distance****
Sri Lanka	No scope****	No scope****	Could provide peak power support**	No scope****	

Source: Based on World Bank (2008a: xxvi, Table ES2).

Note: * denotes that trade prospects are significant and are being exploited or could be exploited in the short to medium term. ** denotes trade prospects could materialize in the medium term. *** denotes prospects may be limited and may materialize only in the medium to long term. **** denotes that prospects are weak or unlikely.

Table 4.10   Overview of Trade Prospects in the Western SAARC Region

Exporting Countries Inside and Outside SAARC	Importing Countries in SAARC	
	India	Pakistan
Afghanistan	Possibility of transit of gas***	Possibility of transit of gas***
India		Short-term trading in power and mutual support possible**
Iran	Significant potential for gas exports and transit via Pakistan*	Significant potential for gas export, cross-border electricity trade could grow*
Pakistan	Short-term trading in power and mutual support possible**	

Source: Based on World Bank (2008a: xxiii, Table ESI).

Note: * denotes trade prospects are significant. ** denotes possibilities in the medium to long term. *** denotes prospects related to developments in other countries.

Table 4.11   Cumulative Benefits from South Asia Regional Cooperation, 2010–30

Benefits (Saving)		$ Billion	% of Region's GDP
Energy (Direct Benefits)			
Energy	60 Exa Joule	180	0.49
Investment in Energy Supply Technologies		72	0.19
Investment in Energy Demand Technologies		69	0.18
Environment (Indirect Benefits)			
Carbon	1.4 Billion Tonne	28	0.08
Sulfur Dioxide (SO_2)	50 Million Tonne	10	0.03
Total Direct and Indirect Benefits		359	0.98
Spillover Benefits			
Water	16 GW additional Hydro capacity		
Flood control	From additional dams		
Competitiveness	Reduced unit energy/electricity cost		

Source: Reproduced from IIM Ahmedabad (2000: 114, Table 8.2).

renewable energy. There are also some sub-regional initiatives though these remain at a conceptual stage and nothing has materialized on the ground.

A few cases of bilateral cooperation highlight the potential that exists in the region. The most successful case is that of electricity trade between Bhutan and India. From being an importer of electricity from India, today Bhutan is an exporter of electricity to India. India absorbs around 75 per cent of the electric power generated in Bhutan while Bhutan in turn imports all its petrol requirements from India. The export of electricity is the single largest source of export earnings for Bhutan.

The history of India–Bhutan cooperation in the energy sector goes back to the 1960s when the first bilateral agreement was signed between the two countries, enabling construction of a barrage in Bhutan and a power plant in West Bengal at an agreed rate on royalty payment by India to Bhutan, and agreement on availability of free power, and on the import of power to parts of Bhutan from India.[3] The Bhutanese government has received technical and financial assistance from the Indian government for the development of its hydropower resources. Bhutan's first hydroelectric plant at Joshina received grant assistance from the Government of India.

Today, there are several hydropower projects under which Bhutan exports energy to India. For example, 84 per cent of the energy generated from the Chukha plant, which was developed as a joint venture project between the Government of India and the Royal Government of Bhutan, is exported to India. The Power Trading Corporation (PTC) is responsible for this trade. During 1992–2000, India purchased power at an average rate of 1,000 GWh per year. Another such joint project is the 60 MW Kurichhu Hydroelectric Power Project in eastern Bhutan for domestic energy use and where the PTC is again the agency responsible for power trade. The surplus power from this project is sold to Damodar Valley Corporation and the West Bengal Electricity Board, and the generating units have been connected to the Indian grid.

Another successful case is that of the 1,020 MW Tala Hydropower Project which exports a majority of its output to north India. This was also the first successful public–private partnership of its type.

In 2006, the two governments signed a framework agreement on hydropower development and trade through public and private participation. The agreement also covers issues of renewable energy and for accelerated hydropower development. There are plans to jointly develop three more projects in Bhutan, in addition to upgrading the existing transmission link to enable 5,000 MW of electricity imports into India by 2020. Apart from the revenue and energy supply related benefits, energy cooperation between India and Bhutan has yielded wider benefits in the form of increased merchandise trade, employment opportunities, construction, and socio-economic developments. Revenue inflows from the Tala Project are being used by the Bhutanese government to expand the social services network. The successful bilateral relationship between India and Bhutan has been made possible by political will, the presence of favourable terms of bilateral financing, political stability, and good relations between the two countries.

---

[3] Under the Jaldhaka Hydroelectric Project, India supplied electricity to border towns of Bhutan.

Indo-Nepalese cooperation in energy has not been as successful as in the case of Bhutan due to political and infrastructural challenges, but there are again some cases worth highlighting. Cooperation in this sector has mainly involved assistance by India to Nepal for the development of its hydropower potential. The Indian government has provided financial and technical assistance to four hydroelectric schemes in Nepal. The Power Trade Agreement signed between India and Nepal in 1996 has created opportunities for power trading between the two countries at the governmental and private sector levels. This agreement allows contracting parties to enter into a separate agreement and to decide terms and conditions regarding power supply and tariffs, thus creating opportunities for domestic and foreign private investors to invest in hydropower development in Nepal for sale of power in India. The Government of India nominated the PTC to take charge of issues pertaining to power exchange with Nepal in 2001 and to finalize commercial and technical arrangements with the Nepal Electricity Authority (NEA). The PTC and NEA are responsible for sale of surplus power between the countries. There are 22 interconnection points between the two countries enabling power exchange. In 2004, Nepal supplied 110.7 GWh of electricity to India with revenues of Rs 573 million to the country. In turn, Nepal has received energy from India under the Koshi and Tanakpur treaties. These arrangements have also enabled a greater degree of cooperation between the two countries on water resources.

In view of growing demand in India and Nepal's large untapped hydropower potential, there is an understanding between the two governments to increase the exchange of electricity by extending transmission lines at selected border points. Studies show that projects of about 42,000 MW are economically feasible in Nepal while the country's current installed capacity is only 600 MW. For increased transfer of power, transmission facilities need to be expanded. Developments in the transmission network could potentially enable Nepal to export power to India during the wet season and import power from India during the dry season. Towards this end, several other projects have been identified for cooperation. Some of these include the Pancheswar Multipurpose Project, the Sapta Kosi High Dam Multipurpose Project, the West Seti, Karnali, and Burhi Gandaki projects. Some of these projects have the potential to generate huge amounts of peaking power and to generate huge revenues for Nepal. Joint technical expert groups have been formed to prepare feasibility studies for some of these projects.

Tables 4.12 and 4.13, highlight the revenues generated from Bhutan and Nepal's electricity sales to India and the importance of the Indian

Table 4.12   Power Sales from Bhutan to India (mn Ngultrum)

Year	Export of Power to India	Total Export of Principal Commodities	Proportion of Power in Exports to Total Exports (%)
2000	2,189.5	3,174.2	68.98
2001	2,072.0	3,271.5	63.33
2002	2,344.2	3,307.9	70.87
2003	2,603.5	3,629.8	71.73

Source: Reproduced from Srivastava and Mishra (2007: 3363, Table 2).

Table 4.13   Revenues from Nepal's Electricity Sales to India

Year	Bulk Supply to India (GWh)	Revenue (in mn Rs)
2000	95.00	327.80
2001	126.00	396.06
2002	133.86	514.12
2003	192.2	809.0
2004	141.2	673.7
2005*	110.7	573.4

Source: Reproduced from Srivastava and Mishra (2007: 3364, Table 3).

market as a source of demand for their energy resources, respectively. The benefits accruing to these countries from power trade with India are evident. Energy exports can clearly serve as a means to address the trade imbalance between these two countries and India. The ADB projects that Bhutan's current account deficit could move into surplus as a result of hydropower exports.

The Indian government has been working on a power import policy that aids hydropower development in Nepal and Bhutan to facilitate electricity inflows into India and also provides a greater role to private sector firms in this process. The intent is to broad base India's energy security by getting access to hydropower resources in these two neighbouring countries and wheeling back most of the power that is generated to address peak period shortages in India. The key issues in taking forward these initiatives are those of tariff fixation and mechanisms for tariff review, extent of free power to be offered to the host country, the nature of the financial and technical assistance to be given by the Indian Government, and the terms and conditions for the developers and lenders.

There is discussion between India and Sri Lanka for laying a transmission line between the two countries. This line would connect Madurai and New Anuradhapura sub-stations and would be 385km long including a

30km submarine cable. This cable would carry power from India to Sri Lanka, but could potentially carry power the reverse way depending on seasonal variations and load profiles. The line would have an initial capacity of 500 MW, and later another 500 MW.

Although much of the bilateral cooperation efforts in the energy sector are driven by inter-governmental agreements and initiatives, increasingly, bilateral energy cooperation is being facilitated by the liberalization of the energy market in South Asia, particularly in India. This has not only led to growing private sector participation and presence of multinational energy companies in the region in a wide range of activities, including generation, transmission, and distribution (excluding nuclear power) in these countries, but there has also been growing interest among private players to penetrate other markets in the region. Indian companies have submitted proposals for investments in other countries in South Asia. The Government of Nepal awarded the 200MW Upper Karnali Hydroelectric Project to the GMR Group of Companies in India.[4] The fact that the energy sector has been opened up to international competitive bidding has made such cross-border private participation within the region possible. India's National Thermal Power Corporation has an agreement with Sri Lanka's Ceylon Electricity Board to develop a coal-based power plant in that country. Indian Oil is one of the largest retailers of petroleum products in Sri Lanka. The Tata Group recently submitted a proposal to develop an integrated steel and power facility in Bangladesh, which would use local gas and coal resources for generating electricity intended for export to India (although this proposal has since been withdrawn).

Many Indian companies submitted bids for Nepal's hydropower sites when these were opened for bidding. Two Indian firms, the GMR Group and the state owned Satluj Jai Vidyut Nigam are setting up hydroelectric stations in Nepal. Several Indian civil engineering firms, such as Nagarjuna Construction Limited and Continental Construction Limited are in the running for contracts for hydroelectric power projects in Nepal. TPTCL, a wholly owned subsidiary of the Tata Power Company Limited (TPC) is part owner of the transmission line between the Tala Project in Bhutan and Delhi. It is entering into joint projects with SN Power, the largest independent power producer in Nepal, for the development of hydropower

---

[4] This is a joint venture arrangement between GMR as a majority partner and lead developer with an Italian-Thai company. According to the MoU between the parties and the Government of Nepal, the developers will provide 12 per cent free energy to the Government of Nepal and 27 per cent free equity to the NEA and the project is on a BOOT basis.

resources in Nepal, Bhutan, and the border between India and Nepal. The Indian Government is increasingly looking at ways to help its private sector companies to get projects in Bhutan and Nepal, marking a shift from its traditional approach of using state-owned companies in the area of energy diplomacy in the region.

Foreign investment is also playing a role in furthering regional cooperation in energy. As highlighted earlier, the opening up of this sector to foreign direct investment and its unbundling has created opportunities for cross-border investment from companies within the region, as well as by multinationals. There is interest from multinational energy companies which are present in India and other countries in South Asia to do business in other countries in the region. The Government of Bhutan is working on the possibility of allowing 100 per cent foreign equity investment by Indian companies in several sectors, including hydropower. Thus, growing corporate interest in exploiting regional opportunities in energy trade, which has been made possible by deregulation of the energy sector in South Asia, is emerging as an important driver of energy relations in the region.

In contrast to these cases of India–Nepal and India–Bhutan cooperation, bilateral cooperation between India and Pakistan, and between India and Bangladesh, has been fraught with challenges and has not materialized. For instance, there is interest on the part of India to access Bangladesh's natural gas reserves. There have been discussions about a natural gas export pipeline from northeastern Bangladesh to the markets in West Bengal and north India. Players such as Petrobangla in Bangladesh have shown interest in such export possibilities. However, due to concerns about domestic availability and growing demand within Bangladesh, such plans have not taken off.

Extra-regional issues extending beyond SAARC to Myanmar in the east and to Iran in the west have also complicated India's bilateral dynamic with Bangladesh and Pakistan, respectively. India has been keen to import gas from certain gas fields in Myanmar. Oil and Natural Gas Corporation (ONGC) and Gas Authority of India (GAIL) have 20 and 10 per cent shares, respectively, in one of Myanmar's gas fields and have been interested in exporting via a gas pipeline that links the Myanmar gas field to India via Bangladesh. This proposed project was seen as a win-win case, wherein Bangladesh would have had an investment of $350 million, earned $100 million in transmission fees, $100 million as one-off right of way charges, and $25 million each year for sharing management expertise, while India would have been able to import gas to its northeastern state of Tripura, and through Bangladesh to West Bengal. However, this pipeline project has failed due to counter demands by Bangladesh which were not met by India for reasons of internal security and strategic interests. In return for transit rights, Bangladesh had insisted on reduction of non-tariff barriers in India to reduce its trade imbalance with India, a corridor via India for Nepalese goods to reach Bangladeshi ports, and access to Nepal and Bhutan through India for imports of hydroelectricity from those countries. As the discussions between India and Bangladesh failed, the pipeline project had to be shelved forcing India to consider a longer route for bringing the gas from Myanmar bypassing Bangladesh, thus also raising costs by an estimated $3 billion. In turn, Bangladesh also lost a good opportunity to earn revenue and get energy infrastructure.

Likewise, India's plans to access Iran's natural gas reserves through a gas pipeline from Iran's South Pars natural gas field in the Persian Gulf via Afghanistan and Pakistan have not materialized. Pakistan was close to signing a pricing formula with India and Iran for building this much delayed $7 billion pipeline. But the project could not take off due in part to India and Pakistan's failure to reach an agreement on account of security concerns and political differences, as well as other geo-political issues involving the US and Russia. Again, potential benefits to Pakistan in the form of infrastructure development, energy security, and transit fees, and to India in the form of increased energy security have been foregone.

Within SAARC, the sub-region consisting of Bangladesh, Nepal, India, and Bhutan has been identified as having considerable potential for energy trade, but there has been no progress at the sub-regional level. For instance, there has been interest on Bangladesh's part to import electricity from Bhutan and Nepal and related discussions about connecting Bangladesh's electricity grid to the grids in Nepal, India, and Bhutan. Two direct interconnections have been under consideration between the northeastern region of India and the eastern zone of Bangladesh, with the potential to transfer power of about 150 MW. There has also been some discussion about cooperative arrangements with India, including joint development of hydropower projects and swap deals for exchange of power with the eastern and northeastern Indian states. However, till date, these possibilities remain unrealized. No concrete projects have been implemented between Bangladesh and the other SAARC countries, and no link has been established yet between India and Bangladesh.[5] Regional interconnection of transmission systems of these four countries has also been an area of focus under the USAID's South

---

[5] Recently, however, the Government of Bangladesh decided to discuss the possibility of interconnecting the country's national power grid with the northeastern power grid in India, wherein it would buy 200 MW of electricity from Tripura or Assam where India has hydroelectric plants.

Asia Regional Initiative/Energy (SARI/Energy) programme. The Four Borders Region project under this programme aims at tapping regional power transfer opportunities in order to improve power system reliability in the region, diversify sources of energy supply, increase energy security, improve efficiency, and lower costs to consumers. However, to date, there has been no success in effecting power exchange between Bangladesh and the other countries under this project.

Overall, South Asia remains much less integrated in the energy sector, than many other regions. Only the most minimal form of cooperation, which is bilateral cooperation, has been achieved. This too has been limited to a handful of countries within the region. Bilateral prospects between other sets of countries and sub-regional prospects across a wider group of countries still remain to be exploited. Most of the discussion has either remained at a conceptual level or has at most made it only to the drawing board and not to the ground.

Regional Forums and Initiatives

There are some regional and sub-regional forums where cross-border trade, investment, and cooperation in the energy sector and possible synergies have been discussed. At the SAARC level, there have been efforts to facilitate dialogue on regional cooperation and to promote capacity building and information dissemination in the energy sector. The real push came at the 12th SAARC Summit in 2004 where it was decided to undertake a study on South Asian Energy Cooperation including the concept of an Energy Ring, that is, a regional transmission link in the region which would consist of transnational lines for trade in electricity, gas, and oil.[6] The joint statement by SAARC Energy Ministers clearly recognizes the importance of regional cooperation for promoting trade and investment in the energy sector and its bearing on accelerated social, economic, industrial, and technological development in the region. The SAARC working group on energy has also identified a number of areas for regional cooperation. The SAARC Energy Centre (SEC) was established in March 2006 in Islamabad. The role of this Centre is to initiate, coordinate, and facilitate regional, joint, and collective activities on energy, and to provide technical inputs to the SAARC working group meetings on energy. Its goals are to promote the development of energy resources in the region, to

---

[6] In 2002, a SAARC Technical Committee on Energy and Power recommended a power grid that would run through Bangladesh, Nepal, India, and Bhutan, which would provide 100,000 MW of power for common use across these countries.

develop renewable and alternative energy resources, and to promote energy efficiency and conservation in the region.

The work under SAARC, and specifically the SEC, has thus far focused on matters, such as renewable energy projects in South Asia, developing a regional energy database, training workshops for sharing of experiences and learning of best practices, interdependence of policies in the energy sector and in other sectors, and exchange of experts and officials among energy research institutes in the region. An agreement has been signed between the SAARC Secretariat and the ADB for technical assistance to SAARC for the energy sector dialogue and the SEC's capacity development project, which mainly consists of a SAARC regional energy trade study. A regional committee has prepared a survey report on the availability of surplus power and electricity demand, as well as load forecast over the medium term, which is to form the basis for discussing energy trade in the region. However, most of the discussion under SAARC remains in the form of proposals and vision statements rather than concrete outcomes on the ground.

There has also been considerable interest in regional energy cooperation in South Asia from various multilateral and other funding agencies. One of these regional initiatives is the SARI/Energy programme mentioned earlier that has been undertaken by the USAID to create awareness and to facilitate energy security in the region. The aim of this programme is to promote energy security through three activities: cross-border energy trade, creation of energy markets, and partnerships to facilitate access to clean energy so as to enable more efficient regional energy resource utilization, increase the region's access to energy sources, and to also mitigate the environmental impacts of energy production. In the context of cross-border trade, the main focus of this regional initiative is to identify potential energy projects and to provide technical assistance for the development of projects. Some such efforts include pre-feasibility studies of projects, such as the Nepal-India petroleum pipeline, a power exchange tracker which would provide a profile of cross-border exchange of electricity, investment infrastructure, and potential for additional cross-border exchange among SARI/ Energy participating countries, and the regional clean coal partnership. With regard to the fostering of regional energy markets, SARI's activities have focused on information dissemination and capacity building. On the clean energy access front, there have been some activities to support private sector financial institutions to set up equity and venture funds for investments in clean energy projects and activities to engage the private sector from across countries in the region in various clean energy projects, such as in hydropower and energy efficiency programmes. But as with SAARC, the bulk of the work has been in capacity building, sharing best practices, and identification of possibilities rather than the actual implementation of concrete projects with outcomes.

Other multilateral agencies such as the World Bank and the ADB have also been involved in country level as well as cross-country projects at a bilateral level, mainly in the form of technical and financial assistance. Hence, this has clearly been a sector that has attracted considerable attention from various funding agencies in the context of infrastructure financing, investment, public private partnerships, electricity reforms, and technical assistance related issues that are important in this sector.

Constraints to a Regional Energy Market

Although there has been some progress at energy cooperation and trade at the bilateral level, by and large, these remain isolated projects. There has been limited attempt to systematically tap the region's energy potential. For instance, there is still no transmission grid with sufficient capacity to bring hydropower from Nepal and Bhutan to India. There is still no regional transmission grid. Sub-regional cooperation has failed and energy cooperation between some partner countries has not taken off at all. South Asia thus remains one of the least integrated regions in the energy sector.

A variety of political, institutional, infrastructural, and geographic factors have constrained regional cooperation and trade in the energy sector. Perhaps the most important challenge is the political and security situation in the region. Political instability in Nepal, Sri Lanka, and Bangladesh has deterred investments in the energy sector in these countries, thus inhibiting the scope for energy trade. Poor political relations and misgivings between several countries in SAARC have also been a major deterrent. Implementation of important treaties has been held up due to political misgivings between governments, as in the case of India and Nepal. The possible export of surplus power from independent power producers in Pakistan to India failed due to political uncertainties and misgivings about possible supply disruptions. Likewise, political misgivings led to the failure of a proposal for gas and power export from Bangladesh to India by Indian and international investors. The absence of good political relations between key players in the region and the lack of political stability in several of the countries has made the climate unattractive for bilateral and intra-regional cooperation in the energy sector.

A related constraint is the prevailing ideology of self-sufficiency that underlies the move towards energy security. Energy exports are seen as cutting into domestic supply of energy resources and creating future uncertainties rather than as a means to achieving greater energy security and improved efficiency and the larger implications for economic growth. Such a mindset, which perceives power trade as nothing more than trade and does not recognize its longer term benefits, is a major deterrent to regional energy cooperation.

Another constraining factor is the lack of institutional arrangements and lead institutions responsible for energy cooperation arrangements. There is also inadequate institutional capacity for power development, planning, and implementation in the region. Joint development and utilization of power is impeded by the absence of a regional network of institutions and the identification of focal institutions in each country to work out power purchase agreements and the procedural and legal issues involved. There is also an absence of regional power trading frameworks, which establish basic principles of power trading and the rights and obligations of participants, which define the procedures for full cost recovery and outline the elements for equitable sharing of benefits. One of the problems in this regard has been the lack of clarity on how to integrate and expand the electricity grids in the region. Absence of such frameworks constrains the drafting of inter-governmental agreements in the energy sector. There is inadequate technical and planning capability in several South Asian countries and there has also been a failure to cooperate with countries, such as India, which have this technical capacity.[7]

There are also infrastructural and resource-specific challenges. Cross-border electricity trading is constrained by the absence of a transmission grid with enough capacity to bring hydropower from Nepal and Bhutan to India. According to some studies, given the dynamics of energy demand in India and the unpredictability of river flows and high costs of hydropower development, regional transmission lines may be difficult to build, and large-scale development to serve regional demand remains unlikely at this time. Hence, given infrastructural requirements and resource dynamics, the likely scenario according to these studies is isolated projects with dedicated plants to load centres in India rather than a regional transmission grid.

The ownership and financing structure in the energy sector is another constraint. It is not mature enough to support regional cooperation. Although reforms have made possible an increased role for the private sector, created multiple buyers and sellers, and led to the establishment of regulatory bodies, public players still predominate and the role of private

---

[7] A wider integration of energy, environment, and transport systems in the region has similarly been wanting.

players is still limited. The poor operational and financial performance of electricity utilities in the South Asian countries constrains energy trade and investment in the region. The utilities suffer from problems of low quality and unreliable power systems, large losses due to uneconomic pricing and misuse of power, and huge supply constraints, which result in load shedding and power shortages during peak hours. For instance, the total financial losses of all state electricity boards in India stood at $4.9 billion or 1.2 per cent of GDP in 2005. Nepal's system loss was as high as 25 per cent in 2005. Likewise, the financial loss of the Bangladesh Power Development Board exceeded $100 million in 2006. Financing constraints in turn pose a serious constraint to energy development in the region. Given such operational and financial circumstances, it is difficult for the region's power utilities to fulfil contractual obligations with independent power producers and to engage in power trade arrangements.

Another major constraint to regional energy cooperation is the lack of commercial considerations in the pricing of power and the lack of transparency and accountability in the region's power systems. Without economic rationalization of power tariffs and harmonization of the pricing policy among the countries in South Asia, public undertakings face a problem in paying IPPs their asking price for power while at the same time having to provide low electricity rates to customers. Regional electricity trade would require that the power that is generated be made available at competitive prices for export to neighbouring countries, which in turn would require regulatory cooperation among the concerned countries.

Thus, the unstable political environment, lack of infrastructure, inadequate institutional and legal frameworks, lack of political commitment, and economic barriers create challenges for regional energy cooperation. Such factors have made it difficult to harmonize regulations, to agree on common policies and standards, and to develop trading mechanisms.

Steps to Deepen Energy Integration

It is evident from the preceding discussion that regional energy trade remains an untapped area in South Asia. Although there are complementarities in energy resource endowments and energy consumption needs, which could be used to meet the larger objective of energy security, these complementarities remain unexploited. However, governments in this region are increasingly becoming aware of the win-win opportunities in regional energy trade, particularly in electricity and natural gas trade. They are also looking at extended commercial relations beyond the South Asian region to countries in the East such as Myanmar and countries in West and Central Asia, such as Iran and Turkmenistan.

As outlined in studies by the World Bank, USAID, ADB, SANEI, and SAARC, energy integration in the region would require political will and agreement on some basic principles and mutually beneficial sustainable solutions. This agreement would need to be forged based on an evaluation of existing studies on energy cooperation in the region and an understanding of the implications of the current regulatory and policy environment for regional energy cooperation. It would also require an evaluation of the trade-offs between energy trade versus self-sufficiency in energy, an assessment of the technical and economic feasibility of an integrated electricity network in the region, and an examination of contractual obligations and terms of agreement for energy trade. Without an agreement and understanding of these issues, it would not be possible to undertake any sustainable initiatives. Moreover, given the complexities of energy sector cooperation, it would also be best to take a gradual approach, selecting pilot projects, starting on a smaller scale, and building up confidence to move to larger initiatives.

To reach such an agreement on principles and mutually sustainable solutions, regional cooperation initiatives will be needed at the institutional, infrastructural, informational, and regulatory levels. There is first and foremost the need for institutional cooperation. One possibility is to set up an apex regional body which consists of state owned and leading private sector companies which are engaged in energy exploration, production, and sales in the region. So far, institutional cooperation in the region has mainly occurred among government officials at various SAARC summits and under the aegis of the SAARC Energy Centre. However, there is need for dialogue among energy sector companies, both public and private, that are operating in the region as regional cooperation in energy will involve joint ventures, build, own, operate, and transfer (BOOT) arrangements, and public–private partnership arrangements. Given the growing role of private players in the energy sector, an apex body consisting of private companies would be important. Companies such as ONGC, Petrobangla, GAIL, Sui Gas of Pakistan, and Ceylon Petroleum Corporation could be part of this apex body. They could jointly undertake an assessment of material and other resources pertinent to the energy sector in this region, take up joint research and development, collective action on renewable energy sources and improving energy efficiency, sharing of information and experiences to evaluate the benefits of cooperation, and capacity building through seminars and training programmes. Such joint initiatives would also help develop a common understanding of the issues involved in regional energy cooperation, bring together technical knowledge and expertise available in the region, and complement the work of other regional bodies such as the SAARC Energy Centre.

Dialogue is also required under a broad-based regional forum that covers a wide range of stakeholders in this sector, including private and public institutions, industries, regulatory authorities, civil society, experts, government officials, industry associations, academics, and multilateral agencies. A broad-based forum will be needed given the cross-cutting nature of issues associated with energy sector development and trade. These discussions would have to cover subjects, such as the establishment of a SAARC grid, the social and environmental impact of developing energy resources, financing of energy projects, technical specifications and standards, contractual arrangements, and alternative energy resources.

Discussions among the apex body members as well as a multi-stakeholder dialogue in the region would need to be complemented by information gathering and dissemination in this sector. An information databank on issues, such as renewable energy, trends in energy supply and demand, and a regulatory and policy environment not only in energy services but also in related areas, such as energy products and equipment, investment opportunities, energy conservation and efficiency efforts, and research and development activities, could provide a boost to regional cooperation. Sharing of information and technology on electric power and gas in particular would be useful given the two main focus areas of establishing a regional electricity grid and natural gas trade in the region.

The Energy Ring concept has to be discussed further and brought to fruition. There are already grid interconnections between India and Nepal, between India and Bhutan and technical studies have been done to assess the feasibility of similar transmission links with Sri Lanka and Bangladesh. This will need agreement to move beyond bilateral arrangements to a plurilateral approach, which in the past has not been accepted by some member countries.[8] The way forward would be to build on the bilateral treaties on power exports for helping build a SAARC grid and a step-by-step approach to interconnection.

---

[8] In 1998, the SARI had proposed the creation of an 80,000 MW power reserve to supply electricity to Bangladesh, Bhutan, India, and Nepal. However, it could not be implemented as India wanted a bilateral agreement with the countries.

First, power cooperation can be promoted based on a common understanding of spare capacity, that is, national networks will be interconnected and operated but power exchange would take place only when there is a system problem, thus enabling the countries to share in time of need, reducing spare capacity, and making better use of existing generation. This would also lead to coordination of their generation systems, which would be required as a first step in establishing a power grid. This can be followed by short and long-term power exchange using these interconnections, based on an evaluation of the supply and demand characteristics of the various networks. The latter will again move the participating countries closer to a coordinated approach by increasing the interdependence of their operations. This can be followed by joint planning, design, funding, construction, and operation of transmission lines, finally followed by joint construction of power stations with associated power trade on a plurilateral basis.

It has been suggested that some of these joint projects could start with promising sub-regional electric power and natural gas projects, which could be undertaken on a priority basis. Success in these projects could be used to build mutual trust, confidence, and develop larger regional projects. The possibility of lagged cooperation has also been proposed, whereby one country would provide the energy resource to the other country in the region for a defined period while the latter would be required to provide the former country with the contracted amount of energy in the future. Such an arrangement could address concerns over future shortages and uncertainties about future demand in exporting countries and take into account the possibilities of future resource finds in the importing countries. But studies are required to assess the costs and benefits of such lagged cooperation arrangements.

However, cooperation in electricity trading would require further reforms of the state electricity boards, in terms of more competitive retail pricing of electricity, more commercial discipline, and less political interference in the functioning of these boards if regional investments and cross-border sales of electricity are to be viable. Without such reforms, cross-border investment in the region will remain hampered by inefficient public sector utilities and electricity boards. Sale of power by IPPs under power purchase agreements (PPAs) to unreformed state electricity boards will not result in increased private investment, for the reasons outlined earlier. The power that is generated needs to be available at prices that are competitive for export to neighbouring countries. Such reforms would also help make the investment climate more conducive to attracting and retaining private investors, both foreign and domestic, as this would be essential for overcoming the financial resource constraints faced by governments in developing this sector.

Another area that would need focus is natural gas trade in the context of India–Pakistan–Iran and India–Bangladesh–Myanmar and associated issues of transit, security, and geo-politics. This can only be addressed through political dialogue between governments, dialogue which is also complemented by a push from private sector entities interested in such trade. Some of the concerns could be allayed through such discussions (though there are additional complexities in the western energy grid due to US sensitivities). In the case of the India–Pakistan natural gas transit, the main concern has been the possibility of disruptions in supply and threats of stoppage. What is required here is to highlight through regular discussions the fact that as a transit and consumer country and given private sector investment by Pakistani companies in the pipeline, it would not be in Pakistan's interest to disrupt supply even if this is a means of putting political pressure on India. Regular discussions can help provide an understanding of the costs of not cooperating. The ultimate requirement, of course, is political will, which unfortunately seems unlikely in the near term given the current political climate and instability in Pakistan which have soured relations with India. (In addition, the US' opposition to trade with Iran will remain a major impediment to progress on the India–Pakistan–Iran pipeline). In the case of India-Bangladesh natural gas trade, the prospects are more promising, as political will is more likely under the new government in Bangladesh. However, companies such as Petrobangla and GAIL, which have a stake in such trade, will need to push their governments in these efforts.

It is also important to recognize that given the geo-political complexities involved in natural gas trade, it may not be advisable to link up third country and plurilateral issues as this would only delay progress. It may be better to use other fora in parallel to discuss other issues, such as those of non-tariff barriers affecting Bangladesh's exports to India and access to Nepal and Bhutan via India, which have been raised by Bangladesh in the past. Progress can be made on these other issues in the context of discussions on trade facilitation and goods trade and need not be linked as a precondition to energy trade as this would only make energy cooperation discussions more complicated.

Clean and alternative energy is another area that provides scope for regional cooperation, given the growing energy requirements in the region and the region's environmental concerns in light of its high dependence on fossil fuels. Given the growing focus on development of renewable energy sources, this is an area of common interest and there are possibilities of initiating cross-country joint projects. For instance, the potential for wind energy in South Asia remains unexplored. Modern and cost-effective wind power technologies are indigenously available in India, but as Pakistan does not permit the payment of technology fees to India, it imports higher cost technologies from the West. This creates scope for launching a bilateral wind energy technology sharing project. Likewise, joint bio-fuel projects could also be initiated in the region given growing interest in some of the countries, such as Sri Lanka and India to promote bio-diesel production. Joint feasibility studies, joint development projects, and analyses of the environmental and socio-economic consequences of alternative and renewable energy sources could be carried out within the region. There are existing institutional frameworks, such as the Regional Secretariat on Renewable Energy and Energy Efficiency Programme (REEEP) and the USAID's South Asia Regional Initiative on Energy which have already identified regional cooperation in the area of clean energy among their main objectives in the region. Such institutional mechanisms can be leveraged to initiate regional projects on clean and renewable energy. Attempts should also be made to leverage financial resources for private sector companies engaged in renewable and clean energy projects from private sources such as the South Asia Clean Energy Fund (a private equity fund) which is dedicated to the clean energy sector in South Asia.[9]

As energy trade requires costly infrastructure, if regional cooperation in energy is to succeed, there is need for a legally binding instrument, such as a charter or treaty, which covers issues of investment, trade, transit, safeguards for investors, and dispute resolution. The energy charter treaty in South Asia provides such a framework of rules governing energy cooperation and aims to create a level playing field among all member governments so as to reduce the risks associated with energy cooperation, trade, and investment. It is thus important to get all the countries of this region to become members of this treaty.

Underlying this agreement on a regional charter on energy would be cooperation on the legal and regulatory framework and harmonization of energy policies. Given the varying stages of reforms in this sector among the South Asian countries, there is need to review the legal and regulatory frameworks in the region, the approaches taken to private investment by

[9] See http://www.greeneconomyinitiative.com/news/183/ARTICLE/1675/2009-08-22. html, accessed on 22 February 2010.

the different countries, their tariff setting principles, and issues of standards and specifications.

Institutional frameworks would also need to be developed to effect energy trade. Past arrangements have been ad hoc, mostly driven by bilateral negotiations and goodwill. But extending such trade to a sub-regional or regional level with substantial amounts of power trade will require detailed frameworks for contractual arrangements and operating procedures. In this regard the idea of a SAARC Regional Power Trading Corporation has been proposed to provide a market mechanism for energy trade. This institution would maintain and provide information on plant structures, production costs, sales prices, utilization rates, profitability, market conditions, consumer demand, and investments, thus gathering and analysing information on generation, demand, transmission, payment, and operation of markets. Such a mechanism could help in the development of a bidding system for power generation projects in the region.

In sum, a combination of political, institutional, technical, and commercial efforts will be needed to push the process of energy integration in South Asia. The various elements of cooperation and the approach that have been suggested here are not new. They have been highlighted in some earlier studies. The importance of political will, improved political relations, and a better political climate in the region has also been emphasized in these studies. However, it may be worth considering the reverse, that is, the possibility of economic integration in a sector, such as energy, where there are substantial benefits to be derived, driving political relations and helping to build mutual trust and confidence.

5

Tourism Trade

Realizing the Potential in South Asia

Tourism is the world's largest and fastest growing service industry. Within the South Asia region too, the sector has grown considerably in recent years and presents significant opportunities for further development. Tourism is usually one of the easiest sectors to negotiate in bilateral and regional talks given its non-controversial and largely commercial nature. It thus comes as no surprise that in South Asia too, negotiations and cooperation on tourism issues have seen much more movement than in the other sectors, whether it be at the SAARC, SASEC, or BIMSTEC levels. The South Asian countries recognize tourism services as an area where there is considerable intra-regional growth potential and thus there is broad agreement among them regarding the need for further integration in this sector. However, to date, little has been achieved in concrete terms despite many discussions and joint declarations on this sector.

This chapter examines the status of tourism cooperation and trade in South Asia, the associated constraints, and how regional integration can be promoted in this sector. It begins by outlining recent growth, employment, and investment trends in tourism services, and also highlights where South Asia stands when compared to other regions. This is followed by a summary of the regulatory and policy environment and recent developments with regard to foreign direct investment, domestic private sector participation, and other institutional issues. The chapter then discusses the extent and nature of intra-regional tourism trade and cooperation in South Asia at the inter-governmental, private sector, sub-regional, and multilateral levels. It also highlights industry initiatives with regard to cross-border investments in the tourism industry. The next section outlines the main constraints affecting intra-regional cooperation in tourism services, focusing in particular on issues of connectivity, people mobility, and investment. The chapter then moves on to discussing the status of multilateral and other commitments by the South Asian countries in tourism services to highlight their preparedness to negotiate and liberalize under a regional agreement. The last section discusses the way forward.

Tourism Trends

South Asia compares quite poorly with the rest of the world in the tourism sector. It accounts for a negligible share of international tourist arrivals and receipts. According to the United Nations World Tourism Organization (UNWTO), South Asia currently accounts for only 1.2 per cent of world tourist arrivals compared to destinations such as Europe, North America, and emerging destinations in East Asia, which account for 52.9 per cent, 10.6 per cent, and 11.3 per cent of international tourist arrivals, respectively. However, it is encouraging to note that South Asia has recorded a robust average annual growth rate of 7.1 per cent in the past decade. The only other regions with higher growth rates are the Middle East, Central America, and Northeast Asia.[1] This points to the growing popularity of the region among international travelers and, consequently, to the potential for developing tourism further in the region, though this growth has mainly been accounted for by increased tourist arrivals into India.

In terms of tourism receipts, South Asia received US$ 13.4 billion in 2007, which accounts for a meagre 1.6 per cent of the total world receipts from tourism. While this is in itself a negligible share, it is important to note that the region's market share in world tourism receipts is higher than its market share in world tourist arrivals, implying a relatively higher spending per capita by tourists in this region than in other parts of the world. In 2007, South Asia had the highest per arrival tourist receipts of US$ 1,367.35, far higher than the world average of US$ 947.95 per arrival. Although this higher spending per capita could be due to a number of reasons, and it is also unclear as to what proportion of these receipts stays back within the region, this does indicate the potential capacity of this region to attract high-spending tourists and thereby garnering greater economic gains from tourism. Table 5.1 provides South Asia in a comparative perspective with other regions in terms of international tourist arrivals, tourism receipts, and per capita tourist spending.

The tourism sector is an important contributor to GDP and employment in the South Asia region. According to data from the World Travel and Tourism Council's (WTTC) Economic Impact Analysis for 2009,

[1] Based on data available at http://www.unwto.org, accessed on 19 May 2009.

Table 5.1   Trends in International Tourist Arrivals and Tourism Receipts
(by sub-region)

					International Tourism Receipts		Receipts
	International Tourist Arrivals						per
			Market share	Avg. annual growth rate of arrivals (%)	Receipts in billion US$	Market share (%)	Arrival in 2007* US$
	Numbers in million		(%)				
	1990	2000	2008	2008	2000–07	2007	2007	
World	436	683	924	100	4.1	856	100	947.95
Europe	262.6	393.5	488.5	52.9	3.0	433.4	50.6	894.72
North America	71.7	91.5	98.4	10.6	0.6	125.1	14.6	1312.70
Caribbean	11.4	17.1	19.7	2.1	1.9	22.6	2.6	1158.97
Central America	1.9	4.3	8.4	0.9	8.6	6.3	0.7	818.18
Africa	15.2	27.9	46.9	5.1	6.9	28.3	3.3	637.39
Middle East	9.6	24.4	52.9	5.7	10.0	34.2	4.0	718.49
Northeast Asia	26.4	58.3	104.7	11.3	8.6	89.2	10.4	856.05
Southeast Asia	21.1	35.6	61.8	6.7	7.6	54.0	6.3	906.04
South Asia	**3.2**	**6.1**	**11.3**	**1.2**	**7.1**	**13.4**	**1.6**	**1367.35**

Source: World Tourism Organization (January 2009), online statistics.
Note: *Calculated by dividing receipts (after converting into million) by arrivals
for every region in 2007.

South Asia is expected to generate US$ 84 billion from the travel and
tourism sector of which the direct impact would constitute US$ 34 bil-
lion and the rest would be in the form of indirect and extended benefits
to other sections of the economy (like transportation).[2] The travel and
tourism sector accounts for 5.5 per cent of the region's GDP, 5.8 per cent
of its employment, 6.1 per cent of its total exports, and 7.7 per cent of
its capital investment. As shown in Figure 5.1, over the last decade, South
Asia has registered the highest average annual growth rate in tourism
GDP, at 9 per cent, which is far higher than the growth in tourism GDP
recorded in other developing regions such as the Middle East or Southeast
Asia, which have shown higher growth rate of arrivals. This in part also
reflects the relatively lower base for this region and the unrealized potential. There has also been significant growth in tourism employment, with a
CAGR of 4 per cent over the 2001–8 period, for the South Asia region as
a whole, exceeded only by one other region, the Middle East, as shown in
Figure 5.1. However, employment growth in tourism has not been commensurate with GDP growth, which raises issues regarding the long-term

[2] See http://www.wttc.org/bin/pdf/temp/southasia.html, accessed on 12 December
2008.

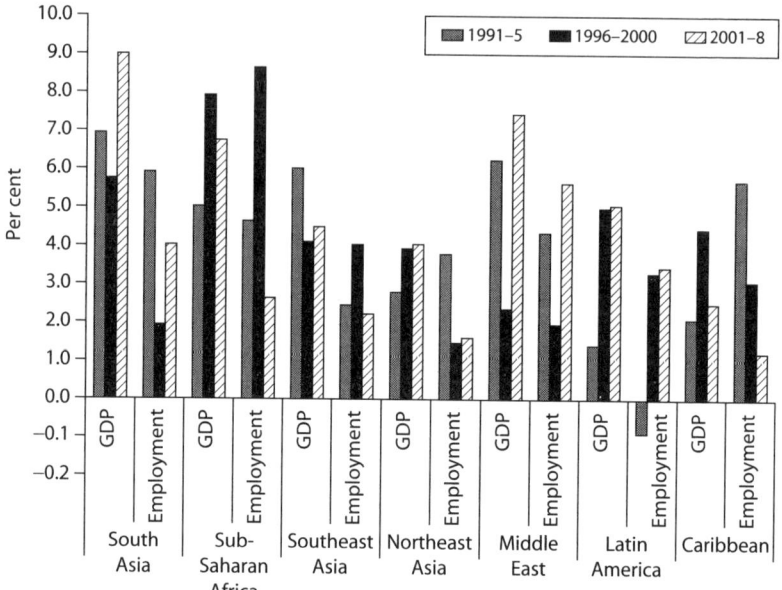

Figure 5.1   CAGR of GDP and Employment in Tourism for Different Developing Regions

Source: Based on data from WTTC's Tourism Impact Data Forecasting Tool (online version).

developmental and sustainability implications of growth and the required pattern of development in this sector.

There has also been very high growth in capital investment and government expenditures in the tourism sector. South Asia has again registered higher growth rates than other developing regions, with an average annual growth rate of above 12 per cent, and 6 per cent for capital investment and government expenditure, respectively, over the past decade (Figure 5.2). These numbers highlight two important facts regarding the tourism sector and its importance in South Asia. Firstly, the region has become increasingly attractive as a tourism destination and has also been attracting increased investment (although the extent of intra-regional investment is not clear). Secondly, growing government expenditure in tourism indicates that this is a sector which is receiving attention from the governments in this region, given its potential for generating employment and creating economy-wide gains.

Given such promising growth trends, international agencies like the UNWTO and WTTC have made highly optimistic forecasts for tourism in South Asia. The WTTC projects that the tourism sector will register

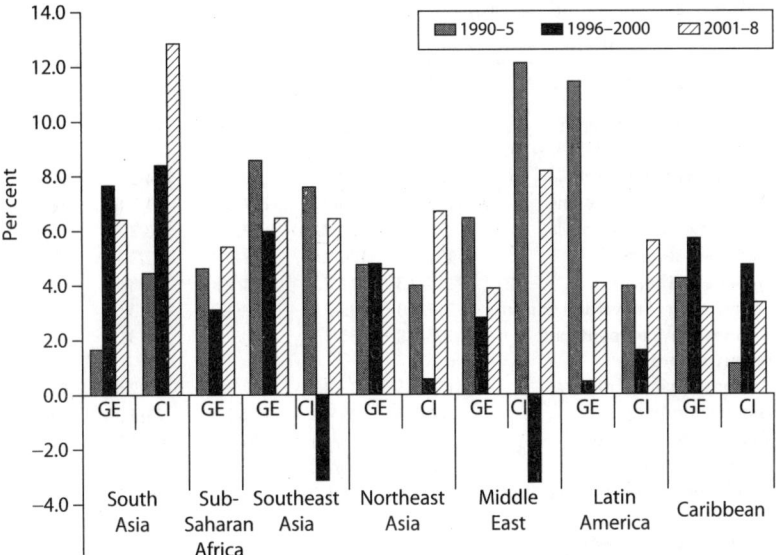

Figure 5.2 Average Annual Growth Rate of Capital Investment and Government Expenditure in Tourism across Different Developing Regions

Source: Based on data from WTTC's Tourism Impact Data Forecasting Tool (online version).

growth of 6.3 per cent per year in output, 2.2 per cent in employment, and 8 per cent in capital investment between 2009 and 2019, and that the region's tourism economy will touch US$ 224.9 billion in a decade. The UNWTO, in its 'Tourism 2020 Vision Document' estimates that South Asia will have 19 million international arrivals by 2020, at an annual growth rate of 6.2 per cent in tourist arrivals. This increase will, however, largely be due to an increase in international long-haul visitors rather than intra-regional tourism, a point worth noting from the point of view of promoting intra-regional trade in tourism services. Individual country-level forecasts predict that this growth will be led by arrivals into India with an estimated 8.9 million arrivals by 2020, followed by Nepal, Sri Lanka, and the Maldives. Outbound tourism from the region will also show impressive growth, reflecting rising affluence in the region, again led by India.

The South Asian region, however, presents a mixed picture in terms of its global ranking on competitiveness indicators in the tourism sector. According to the Travel and Tourism Competitiveness Indicators developed by the World Economic Forum, which provide ranks for a total of 132 countries

Table 5.2   Travel and Tourism Competitiveness Indicators—2009: Ranks and
Scores of South Asian Countries

Indicator (Rank/Score)	Bangladesh	India	Nepal	Pakistan	Sri Lanka
Overall Travel and Tourism Competitiveness Rank/Score (2009)	129/3.0	62/4.1	118/3.3	113/3.3	78/3.8
Regulatory Framework	130/3.2	107/3.9	119/3.7	124/3.6	86/4.3
Policy rules and regulations	117/3.5	108/3.7	127/3.1	81/3.6	86/4.3
Environmental sustainability	125/3.6	74/4.4	87/4.2	118/3.9	112/3.9
Safety and security	131/3.1	120/3.9	123/3.8	132/3.1	107/4.4
Hygiene and health	115/2.3	111/2.6	114/2.3	98/3.4	90/3.9
Prioritization of travel and tourism	117/3.3	42/4.8	39/4.9	113/3.5	47/4.7
Business Environment and Infrastructure	103/2.8	63/3.7	120/2.5	94/3.0	73/3.3
Air transport infrastructure	111/2.3	37/4.2	109/2.3	99/2.5	87/2.7
Ground transport	60/3.7	49/4.1	123/2.3	73/3.3	32/4.5
Tourism infrastructure	132/1.0	73/3.1	130/1.1	102/1.8	92/2.0
ICT infrastructure	125/1.6	104/2.0	130/1.5	101/2.1	90/2.3
Price competitiveness in the T&T industry	18/5.4	46/5.0	10/5.5	35/5.1	28/5.2
Human, Cultural, and Natural	130/3.1	18/4.7	97/3.6	108/3.5	71/3.9
Human resources	110/4.3	90/4.8	118/4.0	115/4.1	49/5.2
Affinity for travel and tourism	126/4.1	96/4.5	61/4.8	129/4.0	65/4.8
Natural resources	102/2.6	14/4.9	37/4.1	83/2.9	59/3.4
Cultural resources	110/1.5	18/4.7	119/1.4	44/2.9	75/2.0

Source: World Economic Forum (2009); Travel and Tourism Competitiveness
Reports (online version).

across a variety of parameters concerning tourism, the five South Asian countries that are included in this list, fare well on intrinsic factors but fare poorly
on policy related parameters.[3] Table 5.2 provides these rankings for these five
South Asian countries.

The rankings indicate that the South Asian countries perform well on
their natural, cultural, and historical advantages, and on price competitiveness, with India performing the best among these countries, followed by
Sri Lanka. But they lag far behind others when it comes to the policy and
regulatory environment and availability of tourism infrastructure. There
are, however, some differences across the countries. For instance, India
and Sri Lanka perform reasonably well on indicators like environmental
sustainability compared to the other countries, and India performs better

[3] The indicators provide ranks for each country and scores from a high of 7 to a
low of 0, for important parameters concerning the regulatory and policy framework,
infrastructural support, willingness and ease of tourism operation, attractiveness and
sustainability of the sector. The five South Asian countries that are included in this list
are: Bangladesh, India, Nepal, Pakistan, and Sri Lanka.

on air transport infrastructure. These latter differences for certain parameters are a reflection of variations across the countries in terms of the degree of liberalization and pro-competitive policies that have been introduced in related areas, such as civil aviation, as well as differences across the countries in their policy thrust and orientation within the tourism sector.

Overall, at the regional level, the tourism sector has shown impressive growth, especially post-2000. If these trends continue, the outlook is promising.[4] It is evident, however, that the governments in this region need to focus on tourism infrastructure development and on the regulatory and policy framework governing tourism.

Tourism Trends in Individual South Asian Countries

Although South Asia as a whole has registered remarkable growth in tourism in recent years, this growth has been far from uniform across the various countries in the region. Several factors account for the differences in individual country performances. These include factors, such as the level of overall economic development of the country, the history and stage of tourism development, the forms of tourism that are promoted, cultural and ecological resources, and local attitudes and affinity towards tourism, to name a few. The differences in tourism performance within the region also reflect the considerable variation across countries in terms of their thrust on tourism development and the objectives they wish to address through the development of this sector.

As shown in Table 5.3, all the countries in this region have experienced an increase in tourist arrivals, with India receiving the highest number of tourists in the region. There is, however, wide variation in growth rates

Table 5.3 Tourist Arrivals into South Asia Countries from 1990–2006 (in thousand)

Country	1990	1995	2000	2006
Bangladesh	115	156	199	200
Bhutan	2	4.8	7.6	17.3
India	1,707	2,143	2,677	4,626
Maldives	195	315	467	602
Nepal	255	363	464	384
Pakistan	424	378	557	898
Sri Lanka	298	414	445	689
South Asia	2,996	3,773.8	4,817	7,416

Source: UNCTAD, *Handbook of Statistics* (online version).

[4] Although the discussion focuses only on international tourism, it is important to note that domestic tourism is an important contributor to overall tourism in South Asia, particularly in the larger economies.

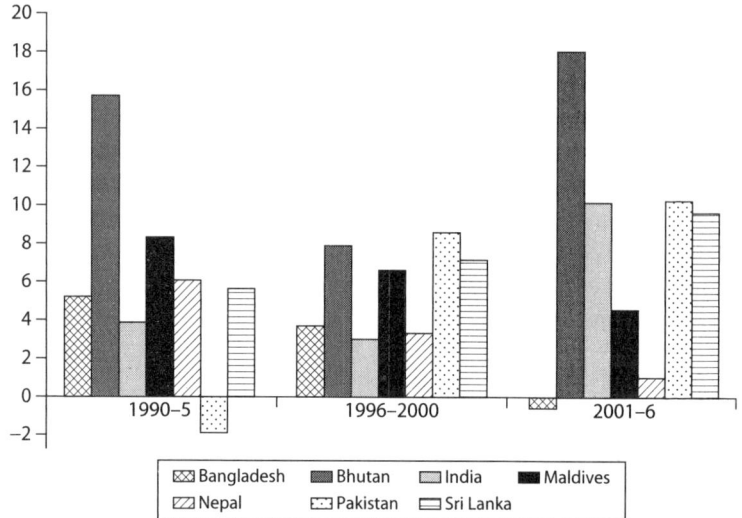

Figure 5.3   CAGR of Tourist Arrivals in South Asian Countries

Source: Based on World Tourism Organization, Tourism Barometer (October 2008).

across countries as shown in Figure 5.3. Both the Maldives and Nepal have experienced a decline in international tourist arrivals in the post-2000 period. Nepal, in particular, has witnessed a sharp decline, from over 6 per cent in the 1990s to less than 1 per cent in the current decade. In contrast, India, Sri Lanka, and Pakistan have experienced higher growth rates for international tourist arrivals in recent years, with all three recording a CAGR of nearly 10 per cent in the past decade.

There has also been considerable volatility in tourist arrivals on an annual basis (Figure 5.4). In part this reflects the base effect in some of the smaller countries which receive small numbers of tourists. But it also reflects the impact of external factors and dependence on economic conditions in source markets for tourists, a feature that commonly characterizes the tourism sector. For instance, all countries in the region, except Bhutan and Pakistan, show a significant drop in arrivals in 2005 on account of the Indian Ocean tsunami of December 2004. Similarly, all countries experienced a decline in tourist arrivals around 2000–1 corresponding with the global recession at the time. But one could argue that to some extent the large fluctuations in tourist arrivals also reflect the region's failure to create a competitive and sustained high growth tourism sector and thus the sector's susceptibility to external market conditions.

The countries in South Asia also exhibit considerable differences in terms of the trends in international tourism receipts. As shown in Figure 5.5, the

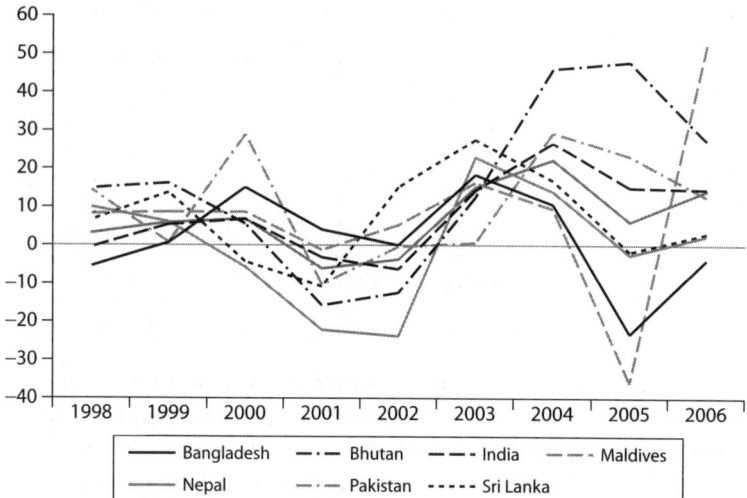

Figure 5.4 Annual Growth Rate of Tourist Arrivals into South Asian Countries, 1998–2006

Source: Based on UNCTAD, *Handbook of Statistics 2008* (online version).

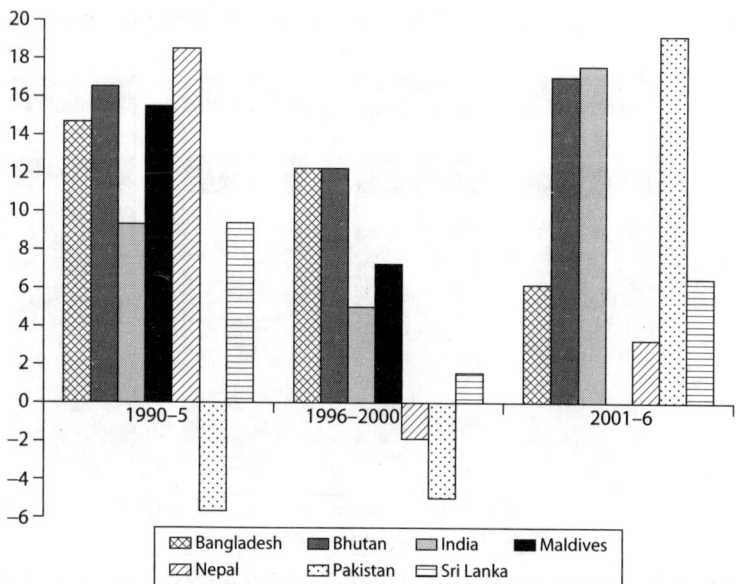

Figure 5.5 CAGR of Tourism Receipts into South Asian Countries, 1990–2006

Source: Based on UN World Tourism Organization, Tourism Barometer (October 2008).

Table 5.4   Tourism Receipts into South Asian Countries (US$ mn)

	1990	1995	2000	2006	Receipts per Arrival
Bangladesh	11	25	50	76	380.00
Bhutan	2	5	10	30	1,734.10
India	1,513	2,581	3,460	10,729	2,319.28
Maldives	89	211	321	n/a	0.00
Nepal	64	177	158	198	515.63
Pakistan	156	110	81	276	307.35
Sri Lanka	132	226	248	385	558.78
South Asia	**2,029**	**3,404**	**4,797**	**9,816**	**1,323.62**

Source: UN World Tourism Organization, Tourism Barometer (October 2008).

Maldives and Nepal again exhibit a sharp decrease in tourism receipts over the 1990–2006 period, while India and Bhutan consistently performed well throughout this period. India had the highest receipts per arrival in the region, at US$ 2,319 followed by Bhutan at US$ 1,734 per arrival in 2006 (Table 5.4).

India dominates the region in terms of absolute number of arrivals. It accounted for 62 per cent of all tourist arrivals into South Asia in 2006, up from 56 per cent in 1990 (Figure 5.6). While most other countries maintained their shares within the region, Nepal experienced a decline, which is also consistent with its poor performance in tourism arrivals and receipts in recent years.

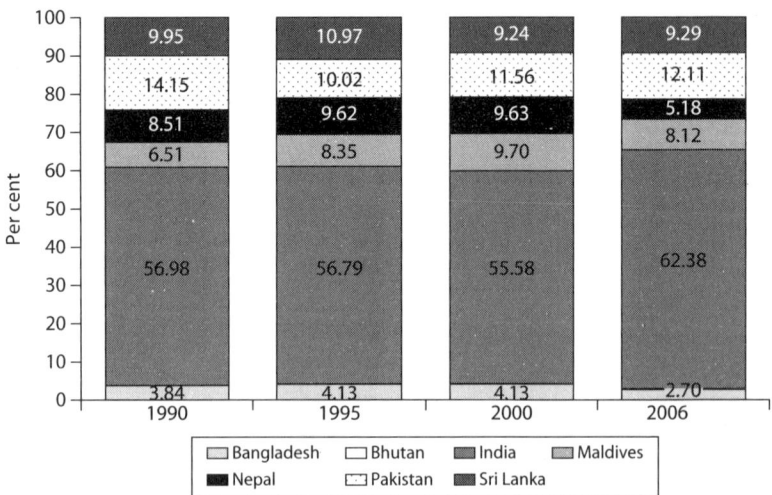

Figure 5.6   International Tourist Arrivals in South Asia: Share of Individual Countries

Source: Based on UN World Tourism Organization, Tourism Barometer (October 2008).

Thus, tourism trends in the region reveal South Asia's rising popularity as an international tourism destination, especially in the case of emerging economies like India and unique cultural and natural destinations like Bhutan. There is also a clear correlation between tourism performance and economic and political stability in the region, with emerging markets such as India and politically stable markets such as Bhutan generally outperforming the other countries.

The main source countries for tourists in South Asia are mostly outside the region. Table 5.5 shows the top five tourist-generating markets for the countries in South Asia in recent years. A few developed countries such as the US and the UK dominate, though India also features among the top five source markets for several of the South Asian countries.

Although Table 5.5 reveals the dependence of the South Asian countries on a few source markets for tourists, and thus the region's high degree of susceptibility to fluctuations in external demand, the statistics also reveal the potential for intra-regional tourism trade. India accounts for over half of all tourist arrivals in Bangladesh, and for around 18–20 per cent of all tourist arrivals in the case of Nepal and Sri Lanka. Likewise, Sri Lanka features as an important source country for tourists in the case of India and Nepal. The presence of such intra-regional tourist flows, as well as the recent growth in outbound tourism from the region, and in particular from India (which according to WTO estimates is expected to reach 20 million by 2020 at an annual growth rate of 5.7 per cent), clearly highlights the prospects for promoting tourism trade within South Asia and for diversification of source markets. One must, however, note that it is difficult to

Table 5.5 Top Five Tourist-generating Markets for Countries in South Asia (per cent)

Country/Rank	Bangladesh	Bhutan	India	Maldives	Nepal	Pakistan	Sri Lanka
1	India (53)	n/a	USA (15.4)	UK (18.5)	India (18.2)	UK (32.8)	India (19.4)
2	UK (15)	n/a	UK (14.6)	Italy (17.3)	Sri Lanka (7.6)	USA (14.5)	UK (18.5)
3	USA (8)	n/a	Bangladesh (10)	Germany (10.7)	UK (6.7)	Afghanistan (9.6)	Germany (7.2)
4	China (4.3)	n/a	Sri Lanka (4.2)	France (6.7)	USA (6)	India (5.7)	Maldives (7)
5	Japan (3.9)	n/a	Canada (4.1)	Japan (6.1)	Japan (4.7)	Canada (4.3)	Australia (4.5)

Source: Compiled from National Tourism Statistics and Annual Reports of all the countries (latest year available).

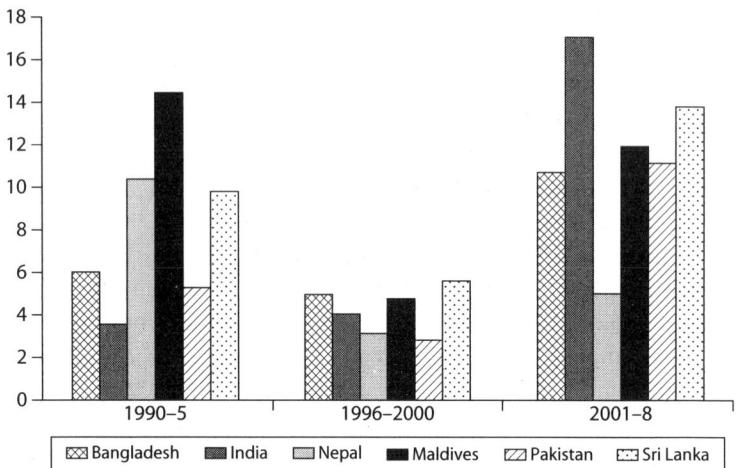

Figure 5.7 Average Annual Growth Rate of the Tourism Economy in South Asian Countries

Source: Based on WTTC's Tourism Economic Impact Data Tools (online version).

determine to what extent such arrivals are for tourism purposes as opposed to other motivations, such as visiting family or business given the way in which tourism data are collected.

Contribution of Tourism Services

Just as tourism has contributed significantly at the regional level, it has also played an important role in the economies of this region as measured by the contribution of the travel and tourism economy to national GDP.[5] Data from the WTTC's Economic Impact database as shown in Figure 5.7 reveal that there has been considerable growth in the sector's contribution to GDP, especially in the post-2000 period. For instance, travel and tourism's contribution to India's GDP has grown at an average annual growth rate of 17 per cent during 2001–8, compared to an average growth rate of 3–4 per cent during 1990–2000. In general, those countries which have experienced high growth in tourism arrivals and receipts have also experienced a greater contribution of the travel and tourism sector to their economies, indicating that international tourism has had a beneficial effect in the region through its contribution to national GDP.

[5] The term 'economy' signifies a combination of direct and indirect effects of tourism activities across all sectors of the economy.

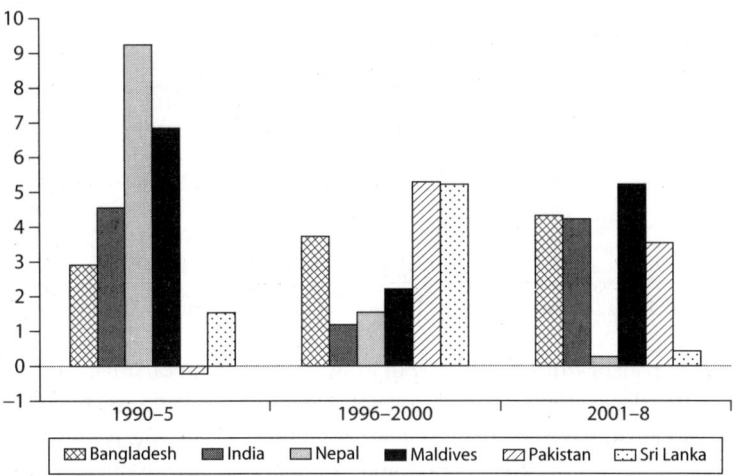

Figure 5.8   Annual Average Growth Rate of Tourism Employment in South
Asian Countries

Source: Based on WTTC's Tourism Economic Impact Data Tools (online version).

However, growth in tourism employment has not been commensurate
with the sector's growing contribution to output, a feature also highlighted
earlier at the regional level, and which is in contrast with the experience
of other developing regions in the tourism sector. It mirrors the overall
discrepancy discussed earlier between services growth and services employment trends in South Asia. Figure 5.8 indicates that growth in employment
has remained largely stagnant in the tourism sector. In India, for example,
tourism employment has been stagnant at around 5 per cent, while in the
case of the Maldives, employment growth in tourism actually declined in
recent years (Figure 5.8). As employment is one of the main indicators of
the extent of socio-economic benefits derived by local communities from
tourism, the weaker performance of the tourism sector in this regard is a
matter of concern and certainly an issue that would need to be kept in
mind when exploring intra-regional trade prospects in this sector.

Along with the increase in tourist arrivals and in the sector's contribution
to GDP in recent years, capital investment in the travel and tourism sector
has also been increasing in all the South Asian countries. Table 5.6 provides
data on capital investment in the travel and tourism industry at the country
level. Asymmetries in size are once again reflected in the large differences in
the quantum of capital investment across the countries, with India registering
investment of over US$ 20 billion in 1990, up from US$ 5 billion in 1990.

Table 5.6   Capital Investment in the Travel and Tourism Industry in South
Asian Countries (US$ bn)

Capital Investment	1990	1995	2000	2005	2008
Bangladesh	0.203837	0.324609	0.461422	0.597081	0.727893
India	4.42075	5.40344	7.51434	16.704	21.4247
Maldives	0.03	0.03	0.05	0.122265	0.191232
Nepal	0.04	0.105196	0.151888	0.121277	0.169174
Pakistan	0.749844	0.840221	1.37344	2.15201	3.06862
Sri Lanka	0.265976	0.366982	0.790199	0.571108	0.740571

Source: WTTC Tourism Economic Impact and Data Analysis Tool (online version).

But as is evident from Figure 5.9, in growth terms it appears that countries which have been affected by political and economic instability, such as Nepal and Sri Lanka, have experienced a sharp decline in capital expenditures in this sector in the post-2000 period, indicating problems with investor confidence and the general investment climate in those countries in recent years. As the data do not provide a breakdown between foreign versus domestic investment or for that matter investment sourced from within the region, it is difficult to infer about the dependence of these countries on external versus internal resources and the potential role of intra-regional investment in developing the tourism sector in these countries.

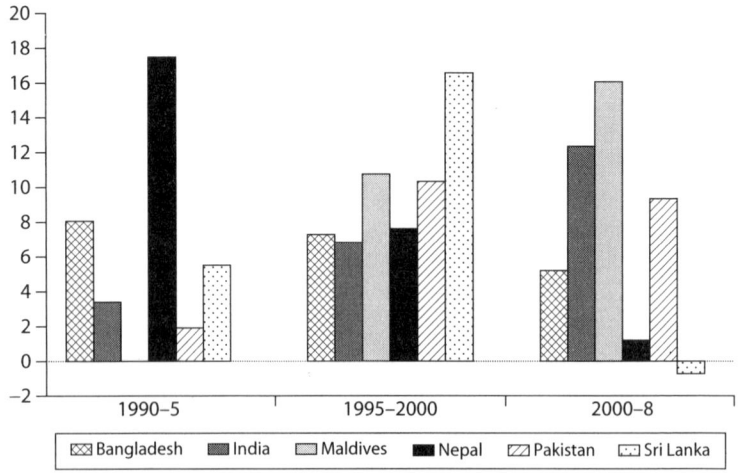

Figure 5.9   CAGR of Capital Investment in the Travel and Tourism
Industry in South Asian Countries

Source: Based on WTTC Tourism Economic Impact and Data Analysis Tool (online version).

Policy and Regulatory Environment

Tourism is a sector which has been receiving growing attention from the governments in South Asia. All the countries in this region have enacted tourism policies which broadly focus on ways to increase tourist arrivals, relieve infrastructure and transport related bottlenecks, and to varying degrees ensure environmental protection and cultural promotion through tourism. There are, however, also differences in approach and objectives across the countries and in the models of tourism development that are being pursued.

In the case of Bhutan, where tourism is relatively new, the industry 'is founded on the principle of sustainability, meaning that tourism must be environmentally and ecologically friendly, socially and culturally acceptable, and economically viable',[6] whereas in Nepal, the national goal of tourism development is 'to improve the living standards of the people through tourism activities with a substantial contribution towards national income'.[7] For the Maldives, the objective of tourism is to 'improve the quality of life of the Maldivian people by optimizing and balancing the economic, environmental, and socio-cultural benefits of tourism'[8] while in India the main objectives of the 2002 national tourism policy are to 'position tourism as a national priority'[9] and to work toward improving competitiveness and infrastructure. Different models of tourism are followed across the countries, from the 'low volume-high value' model in Bhutan where there is a restriction on the number of tourists, to the investor-driven model in Sri Lanka and the Maldives and the community-based tourism model in Nepal. The niches focused on within tourism also vary across the countries. Nepal has focused on promoting mountain trekking as a specialized tourist activity and marketing of the same, while India launched an 'Incredible India' promotional campaign, and Sri Lanka and the Maldives have targeted eco tourism and aesthetically appealing tourism products and destinations that cater to international tourists.

Tourism is among the most liberalized service sectors in South Asia. Private participation from foreign and domestic investors is permitted in all

[6] Tourism Authority of Bhutan, available at http://www.tourism.gov.bt/about-tcb, accessed on 3 December 2008.

[7] Nepal Tourism Board, available at http://www.welcomenepal.com/corporate/473182689482-574861922369, accessed on 2 December 2008.

[8] Maldives Ministry of Tourism and Civil Aviation, available at http://www.tourism.gov.mv/article.php?aId=3, accessed on 2 December 2008.

[9] National Tourism Policy 2002, Government of India, available at http://www.tourism.gov.in/, accessed on 3 December 2008.

the countries, though the extent of entry and associated conditions differ. The relatively high growth in capital investment in tourism in most of the South Asian countries in large part reflects increased private sector participation in this sector. An examination of the policy and regulatory environment affecting the two main segments of the tourism sector—hotels and travel tour and operators—indicates several commonalities as well as differences in objectives and concerns across the South Asian countries in this sector.

The foreign investment regime is very liberal for hotels across all the countries. FDI is permitted up to 100 per cent in the hotel segment in all the countries, excepting Bhutan where foreign equity participation is capped at 70 per cent. Barring Nepal and Bhutan, which require foreign investors to be approved by investment authorities and the concerned department, all the other countries permit foreign investment under the automatic route. There are, however, several conditions attached to foreign investment in hotels across all the countries. These include minimum capital requirements, requirements to form joint ventures with local investors, and various licensing and registration requirements. An examination of these conditions indicates that one of the primary objectives in attracting foreign investment is to encourage technology transfer, learning and transfer of management and other practices in the sector, ensuring a minimum degree of involvement and contribution by foreign investors to the economy, and accountability of foreign investors with regard to social and environmental norms and specifications set by authorities.

Regulations concerning investment in hotels in several of the countries reflect the fact that environmental sustainability is an area of concern. In Bhutan, sector-specific policies have to be followed for construction of hotels in addition to imposing restrictions on the number of tourist arrivals into the country to make tourism environmentally sustainable and eco-friendly. In the Maldives, private investment is governed by zonal and other regulations aimed at preserving the marine ecology and minimizing environmental damage.

The norms are applied uniformly across foreign and domestic investors, though in some countries domestic investors are granted special infrastructure related incentives which may not be available to foreign investors. Overall, the policy framework reflects an emphasis on infrastructure development along with an attempt to balance commercial considerations against social and environmental concerns.

The policy environment in tourism services is characterized by multiplicity of taxes, ranging from value added taxes, luxury taxes, expenditure taxes, hotel taxes, and service taxes to taxes on capital goods and high import duties on liquor. The tax rates are quite high in some of the countries. In countries, such as India, they are applicable at various levels, for instance at the central and state government levels. In some countries like Bangladesh, the taxes are multi-layered and complex, with their applicability depending on turnover and varying with different scales of operations. Thus, the overall incidence as well as structure of taxation is burdensome in this sector, a point also highlighted in earlier studies as a constraint to infrastructure development and growth of the tourism industry in South Asia.

The policies affecting the other important segment of the tourism sector, the travel and tour operators segment, tend to be more restrictive than in the case of hotels. Although foreign operators are allowed in some of the countries, operations are restricted by conditions pertaining to training at specified agencies/institutes in the countries, authorization and licensing by specified agencies, minimum capital requirements, and local commercial presence requirements. In some countries like Nepal, certain kinds of activities are not open to foreign travel operators and tour guides. The restrictions reflect employment and quality related considerations in this segment, which result in a more conservative policy stance in this area than in the case of the hotel segment, which is seen as benefiting infrastructure development in the sector.

Tables A.9–A.15 in the Annexure summarize the policy and regulatory environment in the hotel and travel and tour operator segments in the SAARC countries. They highlight the thrust on tourism infrastructure development, the focus on niche segments, such as eco-tourism in some countries, and the burden imposed by taxes and levies in this sector.

Appendix Table 5A.8 supplements the information in the preceding tables by providing estimated indices of FDI restrictions in tourism services in the Bangladesh, India, Pakistan, and Sri Lanka. Notwithstanding the subjectivity involved, it is evident from the estimates that the extent and nature of liberalization in tourism services has been broadly similar across all four countries. Taxes constitute one of the main impediments to provision of tourism services in these countries. However, as is evident from Tables A.9–A.15 (see Annexure) and Appendix Table 5A.8, the overall policy environment is quite liberal in this sector. The latter has in turn led to growing private-sector participation in South Asia's tourism industry. Several well-known corporate players have emerged in this sector, who are investing globally and within the region, as discussed in the next section.

Status of Intra-regional Cooperation and Initiatives

In light of the region's focus on infrastructure development and on attracting investment in the tourism sector, coupled with the relatively liberal policy environment as well as the commonalities across the countries in terms of language, culture, history, religion, and geography, tourism services are perhaps one of the most promising areas for regional integration in South Asia. It is thus no surprise that tourism has been identified as a priority sector under SAARC for promoting inter-governmental cooperation and deepening regional integration. The following discussion highlights the current status of intra-SAARC travel and then outlines the cooperation efforts undertaken in this sector at various levels and under various forums as well as the challenges confronting this process.

Status of Intra-SAARC Travel

Growth in outbound tourism from the SAARC region, and the significance of some SAARC countries as source markets for tourists for other countries in the region makes the outlook for intra-regional tourism promising. On average, intra-SAARC travel (for tourism and other reasons) accounted for about 20 per cent of all international arrivals in the SAARC countries in recent years, although there is considerable variation across countries. Table 5.7 shows the extent of tourism accounted for by intra-SAARC movement in the various South Asian countries.

As Table 5.7 indicates, there is considerable variation in the degree of dependence on other SAARC countries for international tourist arrivals. While intra-SAARC travel accounts for close to 50 per cent of all international arrivals in the case of Bangladesh, it is less than 5 per cent in the case of the Maldives. The data suggest that intra-regional travel is strongest among Sri Lanka, Nepal, and India, where the share of intra-SAARC

Table 5.7   Share of Tourists from South Asia in Individual SAARC Countries

Tourists from SA as a % of All International Arrivals	2000	2001	2002	2003	2004	2005 %	2005 No.	2006
Bangladesh	46.69	45.27	46.90	41.75	36.64	47.68	99,010	
India		25.98	25.70	23.45	21.79	20.40	799,253	19.35
Nepal	23.80	30.85	31.81	32.52	37.55	23.80	18,633	
Maldives	4.37	3.63	4.10	3.74	3.49	4.71	140,965	3.69
Pakistan	13.47	14.11	2.33	3.73	20.76	9.01	71,900	9.56
Sri Lanka	12.88	15.94	22.61	22.91	23.29	27.65	151,877	29.99

Source: Based on tourist arrival data from official sources in all six countries.

travel is in the range of 20–30 per cent. Pakistan and the Maldives are exceptions. Both have a very small share of intra-SAARC travel within total tourist arrivals. Most interesting though is the case of the Maldives, one of the more advanced tourism destinations in the region, where South Asians account for less than 5 per cent of all international arrivals. A majority of the visitors to this island nation come from outside the region (mainly Europe and the US). Appendix Tables 5A.1 to 5A.7 provide data on intra-SAARC tourist arrivals for individual SAARC member countries.

A few countries feature significantly in intra-SAARC travel. India accounts for the bulk of intra-SAARC travel. In the case of Bangladesh, India accounts for 87 per cent of all tourists from within SAARC while in the case of Sri Lanka and Nepal, Indian visitors account for 76 and 68 per cent of total intra-SAARC arrivals into those countries, respectively. Bangladesh is also an important source country for some SAARC nations, accounting for 54 per cent of all South Asian visitors entering India. Although country-wise arrival data are not available for Bhutan, one would expect India to dominate as the main source country for tourists into Bhutan.

It is important to note, however, that the data do not distinguish between a 'traveller' and a 'tourist'. Given the strong historical, social, and cultural ties, as well as the high degree of informal trade that occurs among some of the countries in this region, it is highly probable that a large proportion of the visitors from other South Asian countries come to visit family, or for business deals, and are a part of the formal/informal migration network. This most likely explains the high share of Bangladeshis and Indians in each other's markets. Hence, even though intra-SAARC travel may account for a significant share of total inbound tourism, this data may overstate the actual contribution of intra-regional travel to these countries in terms of expenditures on accommodation, restaurants, shopping, or recreation facilities.

The figures also indicate the presence of a sub-regional tourism circuit consisting of India, Sri Lanka, and Nepal. The number of Sri Lankans traveling to Nepal has increased steadily in recent years, with the country's share rising from 11 to 13 per cent in the last five years. Given that the two countries do not share borders, thereby reducing the possibility of travel for migration or trade purposes, one can infer that this increase represents an increase in pure tourism between the two countries, possibly on account of the two countries' links to Buddhism and consequent pilgrim tourism. Overall, the data indicate that there is a significant and in some cases growing proportion of intra-regional travel, especially between specific countries or groups of countries.

Some Segments of Interest

There are several segments where the scope for intra-regional tourism is well-recognized. These include, among others, sports and recreational tourism, adventure and eco-tourism, religious and cultural tourism, and medical value travel.[10] All these segments present excellent opportunities for expanding conventional forms of tourism and for infrastructure development and employment creation within the region with all the related positive externalities.

One of the most promising segments is sports tourism. Events such as the Indian Premier League cricket, the Triangular Series involving multiple countries in South Asia, or regional events such as the South Asian Federation Games bring in many spectators from within the region. The 11th South Asian Federation Games held in 2010 were a major sports event involving around 1,800 athletes from the eight SAARC member countries, competing in over 20 different sports.[11] The South Asian Games, which are held once in two years promote cultural exchange between the member countries. There are also lesser known events, such as the SAARC Countries Carom Championship, or hockey and badminton meets. The large number of regional spectators, officials, and athletes who come to such events present a good opportunity to promote cultural and historical sightseeing visits in the host countries, with all their related positive externalities. Table 5.8 provides an illustrative set of sporting events involving countries in the region.

It is difficult to obtain information on the number of spectators who attended these kinds of sports meets within the region and the resulting tourism. However, from the extent of interest that sports like cricket elicit and traditional rivalries in areas like cricket, these are potentially large crowd pullers within the region. As pointed out by an Indian journalist, while regional sports events may not resolve the political problems in South Asia, they can serve as a confidence building measure, improve people to people interaction, and help put local pressure on leaders to improve political relations in the region.[12]

[10] Medical value travel is discussed in Chapter 6 on health services.

[11] Online news articles.

[12] The motto of the South Asian Federation Games is peace, perseverance, and progress and its hymn states that 'Sports is our life, Unity our strength. Our skills shine through perseverance. SAF will prosper through peace and stability.' Sport is seen as way to bring the nations closer together. See http://www/nsc.gov.np/report.php, accessed on 10 February 2010.

Table 5.8 Representative List of Sports Events in SAARC Region

Sport, Event and Year	Venue	Frequency	Brief Description	Issues
South Asian Federation Games, played 10 times before 2009	Various South Asian capitals or important cities	Twice in Kathmandu, twice in Islamabad, thrice in Dhaka, twice in Colombo, and once in Calcutta Scheduled to be held in Dhaka in 2010, in New Delhi in 2012	The 2006 South Asian Games were held in Colombo, Sri Lanka from 18 to 28 August 2006 in the Sugathadasa Stadium with more than 2,000 sportspersons competing in the record 20 sports disciplines.	Unprecedented high levels of security for officials and players amid violent clashes between Sri Lankan Government troops and Liberation Tigers of Tamil Eelam. The games originally scheduled to be held in 2005 had been postponed after a tsunami wave devastated the region.
			Bi-annual multi sports events held among the athletes of South Asia including athletics, boxing, football, swimming, and weightlifting The objective was promotion of cultural exchange between the member countries	Lack of sporting competition among the nations—cannot match up to world standards
Asia Cup Hockey, 2007	Chennai	First Asia Cup Hockey played in 1982 in Karachi, 1985 in Dhaka, 1989 in New Delhi, and 2007 in Chennai		
Asia Cup Cricket, 2008	Karachi	Played 9 times before 2008, starting from 1984 (twice in Bangladesh, twice in UAE, twice in Pakistan, thrice in Sri Lanka, and once in India) To be held biennially from 2008 onwards as decided by the Asian Cricket Council		
World Badminton Championship, 2009	Hyderabad		Hosted by the Badminton Association of India, held for the first time in India	India creates history by holding a world championship of an all Olympic sport for the first time ever

Source: Miscellaneous online news articles.

Beyond traditional sporting events, the South Asian countries have promising prospects in recreational sports such as mountaineering, trekking, mountain sports, white water rafting, and various beach and water sports. But again, getting an idea of the extent of intra-regional tourism in these segments is difficult, though clearly some of the tourism traffic within the region reflects movement for such recreational purposes. There are also recreational tourism opportunities, such as spas, resorts, wellness tourism resorts, cruises, and ample scope for coordinated holiday packages combining locations across different countries in the region. Eco-tourism based on nature and culture has been identified as one of the product-specific programmes for promoting South Asia as a tourist destination. Religious tourism also holds much promise within the region, in particular the sub-regional Buddhist circuit.

Inter-governmental Cooperation Efforts

Tourism is one of the sectors where there is most visible progress under SAARC, most likely on account of its uncontroversial nature. Tourism has been an area of cooperative interest in SAARC since the 1980s. In 1986, the Scheme for Promotion of Organized Tourism was initiated. Within this scheme, member states agreed to work together to promote tourism abroad and develop it at home. Members also agreed on a travel voucher system that would promote intra-SAARC tourism without the outflow of foreign exchange.[13] The Technical Committee on Tourism was organized in 1991 within the framework of SAARC. The most significant institutional development since then has been the formation of the SAARC Working Group on Tourism, which was established by the Council of Ministers during its 24th session in Islamabad in January 2004.

To date, the Working Group has met four times, but with little to show in terms of concrete progress. The first and the second meetings that were held in Colombo, in 2004 and 2005 merely re-emphasized the need to promote tourism within the region, bring in the private sector as a participant in the process, and to observe 2006 as the South Asia Tourism Year. Regional tourism plans were more like vision statements rather than concrete action plans. It was only in 1996, with the SAARC Cox's Bazaar Action Plan on Tourism that for the first time, concrete suggestions were made on how to promote tourism within the region. Some of the key suggestions made to enhance intra-SAARC travel in the action plan were:

[13] See Ahsan (1988) and Hussain (1999).

- Promoting direct air links among member states
- Expeditious development of road and rail links among member states
- Separate counters for SAARC nationals at international airports in the region
- Possible recognition of national driving license by SAARC member states on a reciprocal basis
- Rationalization or reduction of entrance fees for SAARC nationals for entry into archaeological sites and other public tourist attractions
- Further simplification of visa formalities for SAARC citizens

However, there has been no progress under SAARC in implementing these recommendations. Although the action plan accurately identified some of the key constraints in intra-regional travel and tourism, it did not detail how these constraints would be overcome and till date, these constraints have not been addressed in a comprehensive manner by SAARC authorities. Instead, the thrust of SAARC discussions has been on promoting the region as a 'single destination' and thereby promoting 'South Asia-*ness*', with recommendations such as observing the South Asia Tourism Year, publishing joint promotional material, and using SAARC as a platform for greater visibility and marketing support to the countries within the region. But in this regard, there has been no identification of such joint projects, no initiatives to date on a joint basis, and the focus of policies in each of the countries has remained on tourism promotion at the country level rather than for the region as a whole with no coordination across countries in their national tourism policies and plans of action.

The importance of regional cooperation in the areas of culture, sports, and arts has also been emphasized at various SAARC summits as a basis for improving relations among the people in the region and for promoting cultural and heritage tourism. Common ethnicity, history, tastes, and habits among the peoples of South Asia provide a good basis for cultural cooperation and related tourism in the region. SAARC cultural festivals are held regularly and film festivals have also been organized in the region. There have been several meetings of SAARC cultural affairs ministers and there have been discussions regarding the establishment of a regional cultural centre, the promotion and preservation of traditional arts and crafts, youth exchange in sports and culture, and broadening regional cooperation on cultural and heritage tourism. Cooperation with international organizations has also been proposed for promoting the region's cultural agenda.[14]

[14] See http://www.saarc-sec.org/main.php?t=2.9.1, accessed on 13 March 2010.

Tourism has also been a focus area for other regional forums such as South Asia Sub-regional Economic Cooperation (SASEC) set up by the Asian Development Bank (ADB) and BIMSTEC.[15] There has been little more progress in these forums than in the context of SAARC in terms of developing concrete plans for regional tourism. SASEC, which consists of Bangladesh, Bhutan, Nepal, and India's northeastern states, has identified tourism as a priority sector. Sri Lanka has been invited as a member of the Tourism Working Group given its close links to some of the SASEC countries. The SASEC Tourism Development Plan (TDP) of 2004 identified 23 cross-border tourism projects to be developed within seven key areas, largely covering the themes of eco-tourism and the Buddhist circuit. For instance, the TDP identified a priority product named 'Footsteps of Lord Buddha' circuit, including destinations in India and Nepal (including some world heritage sites) to capitalize on the already large number of visitors to these locations and to further attract Buddhist pilgrims and spiritual tourists from the rest of the world. Another product identified under the TDP builds on the concept of the 'Great Himalayan Trail' to promote the integrated development of trekking and linking established treks in Bhutan, India, and Nepal.[16] A major focus area under the TDP is the facilitation of intra-regional travel, with proposed measures to improves highways (for example, links to the Asian Highway project), develop new airports (for example making Bagdogra in northeast India a hub), and easing border restrictions. The SASEC TDP has received financial support from the ADB and has taken the form of a loan project to the tune of US$ 950,000.

However, although the SASEC TDP does address several important issues that are critical to any regional tourism efforts, it has been subject to a lot of debate. Several aspects of the plan have been criticized. These include aspects, such as the absence of genuine community participation in the planning process, the potential impact of the planned eco-tourism projects on the region's ecology and socio-cultural milieu, the non-recognition of sustainability parameters for the TDP, and the extent to which the planned projects would actually benefit local communities (Equations 2006). The status of implementation of the TDP is as yet unclear. Moreover, although it has been claimed that there is broad convergence between the TDP and SAARC, there is little evidence on the ground to suggest that the SASEC TDP and SAARC's tourism plans are indeed coordinated.

[15] SASEC was set up under the auspices of the South Asia Growth Quadrangle, with financial assistance and support from the ADB.

[16] See ADB (December 2006a).

In the context of another regional grouping, BIMSTEC, which consists of Bangladesh, Bhutan, India, Nepal, Sri Lanka, Thailand, and Myanmar, the approach has been along the same lines as under SAARC. India has taken the lead in this grouping. At the 2nd Roundtable and Workshop of BIMSTEC tourism ministers held in August 2006, the Kathmandu Declaration on Tourism Cooperation and Plan of Action were adopted. The main points of this plan of action are quite similar to those outlined by the SAARC Working Council, such as joint promotion of heritage, cultural, adventure, and MICE (Meetings, Inventions, Conventions, and Exhibitions) tourism and development of joint packages, setting up of an information centre in India to disseminate tourism information about BIMSTEC member countries, setting up a tourism fund, meeting on an annual basis, and exploring synergies with SASEC. There has also been discussion on related issues of transport infrastructure and improving rail, land, water, and air transport connectivity. However, nothing substantial has been achieved by BIMSTEC towards any of these objectives. At best, BIMSTEC's tourism efforts are a political agreement to cooperate on regional tourism, as is also true of other regional inter-governmental efforts in promoting intra-SAARC tourism.

There are some bilateral agreements among the SAARC governments to promote hospitality and tourism. India and the Maldives have, for example, signed a MoU to promote bilateral tourism, mainly through hospitality projects. This MoU aims to build on the recent growth in tourism between these two countries by addressing issues, such as increased flight frequency between the two countries, cross-border cooperation between travel agents, and joint development of hospitality projects in each other's countries.

Private Sector Initiatives

Several well-known companies in the region have established their presence in the tourism sector, particularly in the hotels segment. Importantly, these companies involve not only Indian majors but also companies from other South Asian countries like Sri Lanka, indicating that this is one sector where investment sources are not limited to India. Similarly, the investment destinations include a wider set of countries within the region, including all the smaller countries of the region. The greater variety in source and destination countries for private investments in the tourism sector suggests that there is scope for mutual benefit in developing tourism services in the region. A few examples of hospitality groups in the region highlight this potential.

Among the most widely present private sector companies in the region is the Taj Hotels and Resorts Group. This has hotels in several of the South Asian countries, including the Taj Samudra in Colombo, Taj Exotica in

Bentota, Sri Lanka, Taj Tashi in Thimphu, Taj Coral Reef Resorts and Taj Exotica Resort and Spa in the Maldives. The Taj Group has recently opened its first property in Bhutan, the Taj Tashi, at an investment of Rs 50 crores. This hotel has been launched by the Taj Leisure Hotels, the strategic business unit of Taj Hotels Resorts and Palaces and has been developed by the Tashi Group of Companies, one of the large industrial houses in Bhutan. This hotel is being developed as a high value hotel that leverages Bhutan's rich cultural heritage and natural landscape. The Taj Group has entered into a management contract with the Tashi Group. The Taj Group also owns the Druk Group of Hotels in Bhutan. In Nepal, the Taj Group own 33 per cent of Hotel Annapurna in Kathmandu and has also invested Rs 30 crores to upgrade this property. The Taj Group has also entered into new business segments in tourism, such as eco-tourism and wilderness travel, given the rising international demand for these segments. It has entered into a tripartite joint venture along with Conservation Corporation Africa and the Chaudhury Group of Nepal to develop its business in these areas.

The hospitality major, Leela Group has entered into an overseas alliance with Kempinski to jointly manage luxury projects in the Maldives (and Mauritius). It was offered land by the Maldives government some time back and has now decided to enter into project development in that market. The Oberoi Group of Hotels, which is an Indian luxury hotel chain, has plans to invest in Bhutan. It plans to build two luxury hotels in Bhutan under a joint venture arrangement with local partner Chhundu Travels, at a cost of around US$ 25 million. Although this project was supposed to begin in 2001, the decision was delayed until 2007. Construction of both the hotels began in 2008 and is expected to end by early 2011. These are luxury resorts, primarily aimed at the high-end market, in keeping with Bhutan's low-volume, high-value model of tourism. The local partner would hold 30 per cent and the Oberoi Group would control 50 per cent, with the remaining 20 per cent of the shares being floated to the public. The group will primarily hire local employees and send those in management positions for training at its school of management in Delhi.

There are also companies from other countries which have entered other markets in the region. Two of Sri Lanka's top conglomerates, Aitken Spence Hotel Holdings and John Keells Hotels, have resorts in the Maldives. Both companies have significant hotel portfolios in that country, as part of their diversification strategy to reduce their dependence on earnings from Sri Lankan hotels which were adversely affected by the political turmoil. Both companies are looking at further diversifying their hotel business by investing in India and elsewhere in South Asia. There are also companies from some of the smaller countries, such as the Maldives, which have established themselves in the tourism sector to invest in the larger markets in the region. For example, many Maldivian hotel companies, such as the Villa Hotels Group are interested in investing in hotel projects in India. There are some Maldivian companies which are likely to set up hotel projects in certain Indian states. The government has supported these private sector expansion plans.

Challenges to Tourism Development

As highlighted earlier, although there has been much talk about prioritizing tourism as a sector for regional cooperation and various action plans and discussion forums that have focused on this sector, little concrete has been realized on the ground. One of the main reasons is that key challenges have not been addressed. In particular, practical issues, such as improving air connectivity, streamlining visa formalities, and identification of specific joint tourism promotion projects and programmes have received little attention at the regional level.

Transport and Connectivity

Lack of integrated transport infrastructure in South Asia has been one of the main challenges to promoting regional cooperation in various spheres, be it in tourism, trade in goods, or investment flows and associated mobility of factors of production across a variety of sectors. Many experts and agencies have pointed out that integration of South Asia's transport network is critical to reducing the cost of travel and trade in the region. The existing transport networks and infrastructure are in disuse and badly need upgrading in many parts of mainland South Asia. India's northeastern region is connected to the rest of India by a narrow congested land corridor between Bangladesh and Nepal thus affecting not only transport of goods (which has been much discussed in the context of trade facilitation issues in South Asia), but also movement of people in this region. The absence of extensive cross-border road and rail links is a major constraint to subregional tourism in South Asia, although there is some discussion under SASEC to operationalize agreements in these areas.[17]

[17] Some of the key transport infrastructure related proposals under SASEC are to develop a road corridor component and a rail link component between Agartala and places in northeastern India and Dhaka and Chittagong in Bangladesh, as well as to modernize cross-border regimes with regard to transit agreements and border crossings. Economic and technical feasibility analyses, environmental impact assessment, and social issues of displacement, land acquisition, and developmental impact will be undertaken as part of this initiative. See ADB (December 2007b).

In the context of leisure or business travel, air connectivity is one of the most important driving forces. An examination of the statistics on air connectivity highlights the logistical difficulties in promoting intra-regional tourism in South Asia. Some countries in the region are not even directly connected between their capital cities or between capital and non-capital or between two non-capital cities. Weekly flight frequencies are in the range of two to six for some of the countries. Bhutan has the lowest flight connectivity with the rest of the countries, accounting for only 11 of the 562 weekly flights operating within the region, followed by Pakistan which accounts for a mere 17 flights per week, and the Maldives which accounts for 37 weekly flights in the region. India is the best connected, accounting for around half of all weekly flights operating in the region, with almost all the countries, barring Pakistan, having a sizeable number of direct flights with capital and/or non-capital cities in India. Tables 5.9 and 5.10 provide

Table 5.9 Number of Direct Flights per Week between Individual Countries in the South Asia Region

	India	Bangladesh	Nepal	Pakistan	Sri Lanka	Maldives	Bhutan	**Total**
India	–	82	72	5	52	31	5	**247**
Bangladesh	82	–	10	6	–	–	2	**100**
Nepal	72	10	–	4	–	–	4	**90**
Pakistan	5	6	4	–	2	–	–	**17**
Sri Lanka	52	–	–	2	–	6	–	**60**
Maldives	31	–	–	–	6	–	–	**37**
Bhutan	5	2	4	–	–	–	–	**11**
Total	**247**	**100**	**90**	**17**	**60**	**37**	**11**	**562**

Source: Based on websites of all airlines in the South Asia region, websites of airlines of neighbouring countries flying in the region, and other web sources.

Table 5.10 Number of Capital–Capital City Flights per Week in the South Asia Region

	Dhaka	Kathmandu	Delhi	Bhutan	Islamabad	Colombo	Male
Dhaka	–	10	7	2	–	–	–
Kathmandu	10	–	64	4	1	–	–
Delhi	7	64	–	–	–	7	–
Bhutan	2	4	–	–	–	–	–
Islamabad	–	1	–	–	–	–	–
Colombo	–	–	7	–	–	–	6
Male	–	–	–	–	–	6	–

Source: Based on websites of all airlines in the South Asia region, websites of airlines of neighbouring countries flying in the region, and other web sources.

the number of direct flights between countries and between capital cities, respectively, in the region.

A few examples of poor connectivity between certain countries based on these tables highlight how air transport logistics constrain growth in regional tourism. The very poor connectivity between Pakistan, a potentially important source country for tourists to other markets in the region is worth noting. For instance, there are no direct flights between the Maldives and Pakistan or between the Maldives and Bangladesh. Given that the Maldives is a well-established island tourism economy, lack of direct connectivity to other larger source countries for tourists in the region, such as Pakistan and Bangladesh, is certainly a constraint to promoting tourism between the two countries. In addition, regional tourism to that country is also constrained by the low frequency of travel between larger source countries like Pakistan and potential transit markets, such as Sri Lanka or India. Similarly, Bhutan, an important destination market within SAARC is not directly connected to potential source countries, such as Pakistan and Sri Lanka. Again, the prospects for using transit routes through other SAARC countries, such as from Pakistan to Bhutan via India or via Nepal, are limited due to the poor connectivity between Pakistan and these other potential transit countries. Thus, both in terms of direct access to other markets within SAARC, as well as indirect access through transit countries in SAARC, connectivity is poor. The potential for transit tourism is thus also limited.

It goes without saying that faster, efficient, and affordable air connectivity is an absolute necessity for promoting intra-SAARC tourism. Statistics from all countries in the region underline the fact that air is the preferred mode of transport used by a majority (above 90 per cent) of international tourists visiting the region. The current status of air connectivity, direct and indirect, is clearly inadequate for boosting either leisure or business travel in the region.

Visa Regimes

Visa requirements are not per se a constraint to intra-SAARC travel except in the case of certain countries. Visa on arrival and gratis visas with minimal conditions are available in some of the countries for tourists. However, visa requirements for business travel, employment, and for other purposes such as medical and educational, are cumbersome. Multiple entry visas are typically not provided. Visas are also typically given for very short duration, only 15–30 days on a single entry basis. The documentation requirements between India and Pakistan are particularly onerous. There are reporting requirements at the local police station or registration authorities for Indians and Pakistanis traveling to each other's countries and when moving to different parts of those countries, due to internal security reasons. Even for major sports events involving movement of athletes and sports teams, security concerns have posed a major challenge in the issuance of visas, jeopardizing the prospects for sports related tourism in the region. The problems experienced recently by Pakistani cricket players in getting visas for the Indian Premier League in India, are a case in point.

Visa fees are also quite steep in many of the countries. Some of the countries do not have provision for transit visas. There are no separate counters for SAARC travelers to facilitate intra-regional movement, for business or leisure. The status of the visa regimes in the region is in contrast to that found among ASEAN countries, where there are facilitation counters for ASEAN travelers, where gratis visas on arrival are the norm for partner countries, and there is provision of an ASEAN Air Pass where travel to one ASEAN country qualifies a traveler to visit other countries at a concessionary airfare.

Domestic Challenges

In addition to issues of air transport connectivity and cumbersome visa regimes, there are policies and market conditions at the national level which pose a challenge to promoting intra-regional tourism. Chief among these constraints are inadequate domestic infrastructure, lack of integrated tourism policies, and high transactions costs arising from multiple taxes and regulations. There are also broader issues which go beyond the tourism sector, such as the investment climate, political instability, and uncertainties regarding the economic and regulatory environment, which affect cross-border investments in the tourism sector. The latter is evident from the delays in implementing several private sector hotel projects several years after receiving approvals from host country authorities. Manpower and hospitality training issues are another challenge facing individual countries and are also likely to affect regional tourism prospects. Thus, domestic infrastructural, resource, institutional, and manpower related constraints which affect the development of the tourism industry in the individual South Asian countries and consequently the sector's global competitiveness, also affect the region's ability to leverage the intra-SAARC market.

Multilateral and Other Commitments in Tourism and Travel Services

In line with the prevailing liberal policy environment in tourism and travel services, excepting the Maldives, all the South Asian member countries of the WTO have scheduled this sector under the GATS. This is the one sector, other than telecommunication services, which is common across most of the countries, indicating their general willingness to negotiate multilaterally in tourism services. The two main segments that have been scheduled are hotel and lodging services and travel agency and tour operator services. Modes 1 and 2 are largely unbound while mode 3 commitments are mostly fully or partially open, though there are conditions in the form of approvals and local incorporation requirements. As in the case of all sectors, mode 4 is unbound, though sensitivities in terms of the potential impact on local less skilled labour is evident in some commitments. Table 5.11 shows the Uruguay Round commitments and subsequent initial and revised offers in this sector by the South Asian countries.

By and large, countries have bound their unilateral policies in mode 3. However, some such as India have been more conservative in their GATS commitments and offers when compared to their actual policies in this sector. India, for instance has made investment in hotels subject to FIPB approval although this is permitted under the automatic route in practice. It is also interesting to note that many of the countries have left mode 2 unbound, although there are no restrictions in practice on outbound travel from these countries. There is little or no change in the offers even in modes where no restrictions apply. Hence, an examination of the commitments and offers in tourism services suggests that although the countries may be willing and prepared to negotiate multilaterally in this sector, they would still like to retain some policy flexibility. Nor has there been much signaling value attached to this sector in terms of improving their offers, perhaps because the regimes are already open and tourism is not a sensitive or high profile sector when it comes to multilateral negotiations.

Tourism services are also a commonly identified sector in most of the bilateral FTAs and trade and investment agreements that have been signed by the South Asian countries with countries outside SAARC. The Pakistan–Malaysia and Pakistan–China FTAs, the India–ASEAN and India–Singapore CECA, and the Pakistan–Mauritius PTA all cover tourism services. Some of the agreements also cover issues of rail and road links, services auxiliary to transport services, improving air connectivity through open skies agreements, and general trade facilitation issues. BIMSTEC, as already discussed, has focused on tourism promotion in the sub-region through increased cooperation in many areas. Thus, there is clearly a common recognition of the importance of tourism services for regional and sub-regional cooperation and the associated issues of transport infrastructure and connectivity that have a bearing on tourism prospects. However, none of these extra-regional agreements deal with visa issues or mechanisms

Table 5.11 Commitments and Offers in Tourism and Travel Related Services by South Asian Countries

Sector/ Sub-sector	Uruguay Round Commitments	Conditional Initial Offer	Revised Offer
Bangladesh Five star hotel and lodging services	**April 1995** 1. Unbound 2. Unbound 3. Commercial 　establishment in 　accordance with all local 　laws and regulations; 100 　per cent foreign equity 　participation permitted 4. Employment of 　foreign nationals 　to be approved by 　government and such 　personnel shall be 　employed in higher 　management and 　specialized jobs only		
India Hotels and lodging services	**April 1995** 1. Unbound 2. Unbound 3. Only through 　incorporation 4. Unbound	**12 January 2004** 1. No change 2. None 3. FIPB approval 　requirement added 4. No change	**24 August 2005** 1. None 2. No change 3. No change 4. No change
Travel agency and tour operator services	1. Unbound 2. Unbound 3. Only through 　incorporation 4. Unbound	1. No change 2. None 3. FIPB approval 　requirement added 4. No change	1. None 2. No change 3. No change 4. No change
Tour guide services	Sector not scheduled	Sector not scheduled	1. Unbound 2. None 3. Limitations: 　- Only through 　　incorporation 　- Total ceiling of 　　500 tour guides 　　conversant in 　　Chinese, Japanese, 　　French, Spanish, and 　　Portuguese 　- FIPB approval 　　required 4. None for tour 　guides conversant in 　Chinese, Japanese, 　French, Spanish, 　and Portuguese up 　to a ceiling of 500; 　Unbound for others

(Table 5.11 contd . . .)

Sector/ Sub-sector	Uruguay Round Commitments	Conditional Initial Offer	Revised Offer
Maldives	**April 1995**		
Nepal	**(Date of submission: 30 August 2004)**		
Hotels and restaurants, travel agency, and tour operator services	1. None 2. None 3. None, except only through incorporation in Nepal and with maximum foreign equity capital of 51 per cent for travel agency and tour operator (CPC 7471) and 80 per cent for hotel, lodging services (CPC 6411) (star hotels only), and graded restaurants (CPC 6421–6423)** 4. Unbound, except as indicated in the horizontal section		
Pakistan	**April 1995**	**30 May 2005**	
Hotels and restaurants	1. Unbound 2. Unbound 3. None 4. Unbound	1. None 2. None 3. No change 4. No change	
Travel agencies and tour operator services	1. Unbound 2. Unbound 3. None 4. Unbound	1. None 2. None 3. No change 4. No change	
Sri Lanka	**April 1995**	**September 2003**	
Hotel and lodging services	1. Unbound 2. Unbound 3. None except as mentioned in horizontal services 4. Provision of labour, immigration, and custom laws	1. No change 2. No change 3. None 4. Unbound except as indicated in horizontal section	
Travel agency and tour operator services	1. None 2. Unbound 3. None except as mentioned in horizontal services 4. Provision of labour, immigration and custom laws	1. No change 2. No change 3. None 4. Unbound except as indicated in horizontal section	

Source: Based on WTO member countries' GATS Commitment and Offer Schedules.
Note: ** Unbound for reasons of technical infeasibility.

to facilitate cross-border movement of travellers, indicating the sensitive nature of this issue not only in SAARC but also more generally.

Steps to Promote Regional Tourism

The preceding discussion indicates the unrealized potential for regional tourism in South Asia. It also highlights the need to focus on tourism services as a high priority sector for regional cooperation, given the many commonalities across the countries in this sector and the ready existence of various forums to promote cooperation in this sector. This is a sector where successful and mutually beneficial outcomes are possible which can be used to build confidence in the overall regional integration process in South Asia. Thus tourism could potentially serve as pilot sector for services integration in South Asia with positive learning and demonstration effects for integration efforts in other services.

Some of the main issues that would need to be addressed regionally and nationally would be to lower travel costs between the countries, improve transport connectivity especially air links, streamline visa procedures along with longer duration and more flexible visa arrangements for intra-regional travel, streamline the tax structure in the tourism industry, joint marketing and development of tourism projects around selected themes such as religion, heritage, nature, and geography, and sharing of best practices within the region. Thus both sector-specific and cross-cutting issues of investment, transport logistics, visa facilitation, environment and ecology have to be addressed. There are three broad areas where initial efforts could be pitched.

The first is at the sub-regional level. The data on flight frequencies presented earlier reveals that in addition to certain pairs of countries, such as India–Nepal, India–Sri Lanka, and India–Bangladesh, where connectivity is good, there are also sub-groups of countries, such as India–Nepal–Sri Lanka, or India–Sri Lanka–Maldives, where there is potential for developing sub-regional tourist circuits and for promoting transit tourism around those circuits. Some promising sub-regional tourism themes would be nature and adventure tourism involving India, Nepal, Bhutan, and linking Bangladesh with the two Himalayan countries via India, beach and coastal resort tourism involving southern India, the Maldives, and Sri Lanka, and religious tourism involving India, Nepal, and Sri Lanka for the Buddhist pilgrimage circuit and India, Pakistan, and the Maldives for the Muslim circuit. In addition, sports tourism centred around specific events and sports and sub-sets of countries could be a focus segment. Regional cooperation in tourism could take the form of joint documentation, joint marketing campaigns at a regional level, better transport connections, and special airfares and tour packages for travel among the countries. India would clearly have to be a common thread in developing regional tourism, given its better connectivity with the other countries in South Asia, and better developed transport infrastructure, and thus its potential as a source, destination, and transit country. This sub-regional approach would of course need to be supported by efforts on transport links, visa facilitation, and coordination across national ministries for developing local infrastructure in each of the countries.

The second area for cooperation is investments. As seen earlier, there is considerable interest among regional hospitality groups to invest in other SAARC countries. Initiatives can be taken to provide preferential investment incentives to investors from within SAARC, in terms of land acquisition or speedier clearances and approvals for projects. Joint ventures with local private sector players or with the host country government could be encouraged to ensure that local interests are kept in mind and for technology and knowledge transfer to the host country. Cross-border investment facilitation and cooperation would not only help in the development of tourism infrastructure and cross-country learning, but if targeted properly could also complement efforts at developing sub-regional tourism circuits.

The third broad area that needs to be pursued is institutional collaboration. This would require not only inter-governmental cooperation across government ministries and concerned agencies, but also discussions among hospitality groups in the region, among industry associations, hospitality management training institutions, tour agencies, and even civil society organizations working on tourism, sustainable development, and environmental issues. Such broad based multi-stakeholder forums as well as focused groups need to be formed so that considerations, such as environmental sustainability and ecology, soft skills and training, manpower development, regulations, standards, and local employment, can be taken into account when initiating tourism projects. Institutional cooperation would also be essential for cross-country learning of best practices and to learn about the success of different models of tourism adopted across the different countries in this region.

Needless to say, without a greater national thrust on tourism and development of related infrastructure and systems in each of the South Asian countries, none of these cooperation initiatives can materialize. Likewise, without political and economic stability, neither national nor regional level tourism initiatives can take shape.

Appendix 5A

Table 5A.1 Tourist Arrivals into the Maldives from Other SAARC Countries

	2000	2001	2002	2003	2004	2005	2006
Bangladesh	321	321	241	313	667	643	1050
India	10,616	8,511	11,377	11,502	10,999	10,260	12,071
Pakistan	1,049	1,017	1,329	1,942	1,529	565	1,119
Sri Lanka	8,413	6,902	6,909	7,296	8,351	7,165	7,954
Total tourists from SA	20,399	16,751	19,856	21,053	21,546	18,633	22,194
Total foreign tourists	467,154	460,984	484,680	563,593	616,716	395,320	601,923
% of tourists from South Asia in total tourists	**4.37**	**3.63**	**4.10**	**3.74**	**3.49**	**4.71**	**3.69**

Source: National Tourism Ministry reports and official statistics.

Table 5A.2 Tourist Arrivals into Sri Lanka from Other SAARC Countries

	2000	2001	2002	2003	2004	2005	2006
Bangladesh	1,218	1,738	1,518	1,851	1,760	2,325	2,466
Bhutan	n/a	n/a	n/a	n/a	n/a	n/a	n/a
India	31,851	33,932	69,996	90,639	104,390	113,023	128,520
Maldives	7,941	8,975	9,855	11,577	15,201	24,396	24,505
Nepal	528	512	786	977	890	1,077	1,152
Pakistan	10,017	8,522	6,726	9,674	9,629	11,056	11,165
Total from South Asia	51,555	53,679	88,881	114,718	131,870	151,877	167,808
Total foreign tourists	400,414	336,794	393,171	500,642	566,202	549,308	559,603
% of tourists from South Asia in total tourists	**12.88**	**15.94**	**22.61**	**22.91**	**23.29**	**27.65**	**29.99**

Source: National Tourism Ministry reports and official statistics.

Table 5A.3 Tourist Arrivals into India from Other SAARC Countries

	2001	2002	2003	2004	2005	2006
Bangladesh	431,312	435,867	454,611	477,446	456,371	484,401
Bhutan	3,571	4,123	4,082	7,054	6,934	8,502
Maldives	17,564	18,826	18,345	21,099	33,915	37,652
Nepal	41,135	43,056	42,771	51,534	77,024	91,552
Pakistan	52,762	2,946	10,364	67,416	88,609	83,426
Sri Lanka	112,813	108,008	109,098	128,711	136,400	154,813
Total from South Asia	659,157	612,826	639,271	753,260	799,253	860,346
Total foreign tourists	2,537,282	2,384,364	2,726,214	3,457,477	3,918,610	4,447,167
% of tourists from South Asia in total tourists	**25.98**	**25.70**	**23.45**	**21.79**	**20.40**	**19.35**

Source: National Tourism Ministry reports and official statistics.

Table 5A.4 Tourist Arrivals into Nepal from Other SAARC Countries

	2001	2002	2003	2004	2005
Bangladesh	7,742	5,507	5,031	14,607	20,201
Bhutan	1,523	1,426	1,307	2,057	3,498
India	64,320	66,777	86,363	90,326	96,434
Maldives	214	230	165	156	309
Pakistan	2,319	1,241	761	2,020	1,753
Sri Lanka	9,844	9,805	13,930	16,124	18,770
Total from South Asia	85,962	84,986	107,557	125,290	140,965
Total foreign tourists	361,237	275,468	338,132	385,297	375,398
% of tourists from South Asia in total tourists	**23.80**	**30.85**	**31.81**	**32.52**	**37.55**

Source: National Tourism Ministry reports and official statistics.

Table 5A.5 Tourist Arrivals into Pakistan from Other SAARC Countries

	2000	2001	2002	2003	2004	2005	2006	2007
India	66,100	58,400	2,600	7,100	119,700	59,600	70,200	48,200
Bangladesh	1,400	6,200	5,600	7,600	8,900	6,000	8,300	6,400
Sri Lanka	4,100	3,100	2,000	2,600	3,700	4,100	4,800	4,300
Others from South Asia	3,400	2,800	1,400	1,400	2,200	2,200	2,500	2,100
Total from South Asia	75,000	70,500	11,600	18,700	134,500	71,900	85,800	61,000
Total foreign tourists	556,800	499,700	498,100	500,900	648,000	798,300	897,600	839,500
% of tourists from South Asia in total tourists	**13.47**	**14.11**	**2.33**	**3.73**	**20.76**	**9.01**	**9.56**	**7.27**

Source: National Tourism Ministry reports and official statistics.

Table 5A.6 Tourist Arrivals into Bangladesh from Other SAARC Countries

Country	1996	1997	1998	1999	2000	2001	2002	2003	2004	2005
Bhutan	568	959	441	730	1,010	1,263	1,241	1,228	847	1187
India	53,007	61,606	57,937	62,935	74,268	78,090	80,415	84,704	80,469	86,232
Maldives	97	123	63	53	189	129	150	182	98	220
Nepal	3,628	5,296	4,799	4,733	4,481	4,280	4,159	3,904	3,144	3,378
Pakistan	7,070	11,481	12,087	7,894	10,637	7,010	8,703	9,238	11,997	5,671
Sri Lanka	1,522	1,686	1,653	1,839	2,427	3,026	2,524	2,831	2,826	2,322
Total from South Asia	65,892	81,151	76,980	78,184	93,012	93,798	97,192	102,087	99,381	99,010
Total foreign tourists	165,887	182,420	171,961	172,781	199,211	207,199	207,246	244,508	271,270	207,662
% of tourists from South Asia in total tourists	**39.72**	**44.49**	**44.77**	**45.25**	**46.69**	**45.27**	**46.90**	**41.75**	**36.64**	**47.68**

Source: National Tourism Ministry reports and official statistics.

Table 5A.7   Relative Importance of Intra-SAARC Travel to SAARC
Countries, 2005

	Total Tourist Arrivals from Other South Asian Countries	% of Total Foreign Tourists into the Country
Bangladesh	99,010	47.68
Bhutan	n/a	n/a
India	799,253	20.40
Maldives	18,633	4.71
Nepal	140,965	37.55
Pakistan	71,900	9.01
Sri Lanka	151,877	27.65

Source: Based on Tables 5A.1–5A.6.

Table 5A.8   Indices of Restrictions on FDI in Tourism Services in Selected
South Asian Countries, 2000 and 2009

Restriction	Criteria	Score	Weights	Bangladesh 2009	India 2009	Pakistan 2009	Sri Lanka 2009
Foreign equity limits in hotels	Foreign ownership not permitted	1					
	Foreign ownership permitted	0	0.23	0	0	0	0
Foreign equity limits in travel agencies	Foreign ownership not permitted	1					
	Foreign ownership permitted	0	0.23	0	0	0	0
Min. investment requirement	Min. investment requirement condition is attached with FDI approval	1					
	No min. investment requirement condition is attached with FDI approval	0	0.06	0	0	1	1

(*Contd* . . .)

(*Table 5A.8 contd . . .*)

Restriction	Criteria	Score	Weights	Bangladesh 2009	India 2009	Pakistan 2009	Sri Lanka 2009
Joint venture arrangements	Foreign service provider entry is allowed only through joint ventures with domestic providers	1	0.06	0	0	0	0
	No requirement for a foreign institution to enter through a joint venture with domestic provider	0					
Limitations on establishment of small scale hotels and restaurants	Foreigners are not allowed to establish small scale hotels and restaurants	1	0.06	0	0	0	0.5
	Foreigners are allowed to establish small scale hotels and restaurants but with conditions	0.5					
	Foreigners are allowed to establish small scale hotels and restaurants	0					
Minimum turnover required for tour and travel operators	There is a minimum turnover/ residency requirement for getting license for tour and travel operators	1	0.06	1	1	1	0
	No such requirement for getting license for tour and travel operators	0					

(*Contd . . .*)

(*Table 5A.8 contd . . .*)

Restriction	Criteria	Score	Weights	Bangladesh 2009	India 2009	Pakistan 2009	Sri Lanka 2009
Tax on hotel services	Multiplicity of taxes, such as expenditure tax and luxury tax	1	0.06	1	1	1	1
	No multiplicity of taxes	0					
Double taxation on items served in hotels	Double taxation on items, such as liquor exists	1	0.06	1	1	0	1
	No double taxation	0					
Acquisition of immovable property	Acquisition of immovable property is not permitted	1	0.06	0.5	0.5	0.5	0.5
	Acquisition of immovable property is permitted but with certain conditions/ extra fees	0.5					
	Acquisition of immovable property is permitted without any restriction	0					
Corporate tax laws	Tax rates are much higher than the average	1	0.06	0.75	0.5	0.75	0.75
	Tax rates are moderately higher than the average	0.75					
	Tax rates are average of Asia level	0.5					
	Tax rates are moderately lower than the average	0.25					
	Tax rates are much lower than the average	0					

(*Contd . . .*)

(*Table 5A.8 contd* ...)

Restriction	Criteria	Score	Weights	Bangladesh 2009	India 2009	Pakistan 2009	Sri Lanka 2009
Discriminatory tax treatment	Tax rates for foreign firms are more than 15 per cent higher than the rates for domestic firms	1					
	Tax rates for foreign firms are more than 11–15 per cent higher than the rates for domestic firms	0.75					
	Tax rates for foreign firms are more than 6–10 per cent higher than the rates for domestic firms	0.5	0.06	0	0.5	0	0
	Tax rates for foreign firms are more than 1–5 per cent higher than the rates for domestic firms	0.25					
	Tax rates are equal for foreign firms and domestic firms	0					
	Mode 3 Trade Restrictiveness Index		1	0.255	0.27	0.255	0.285

Source: Based on Ministry of Tourism documents and travel industry sources from individual SAARC member countries.

Notes: There are various ways of allocating weights to different parameters used in calculating restrictiveness indices, such as a researcher's judgment and factor analysis. The weights used in this table are based on the researcher's judgment method. A higher weight has been assigned to FDI limits and remaining parameters have been weighted equally. There is a problem with the availability of information for some of the parameters used in the table. In such cases, inferences have been drawn from the available information. Some degree of subjectivity cannot be ruled out.

6

Health Services
Exploring Commercial and Collaboration Opportunities

Regional Prospects in Health Services

Access to quality and affordable healthcare is a pre-requisite for development. Health services constitute an integral part of a country's social infrastructure and attainment of the Millennium Development Goals (MDGs). South Asia presents a paradox when it comes to social sectors such as healthcare. The countries in this region are among the lowest ranked countries for human development indicators, including healthcare indicators. Yet at the same time, some of the same countries are host to world class corporate hospitals and telemedicine establishments which have forayed into overseas markets, receive medical value travellers from developing and developed countries, and attract investments in medical technology. The region is host to both first world and third world standards of healthcare delivery, ailments, and services.

Health services have been noted as one of the most promising sectors for regional cooperation in South Asia. The large regional market provides commercial and collaboration opportunities for companies from within the region and outside in various segments of healthcare, including pharmaceuticals, clinical trials, telemedicine, hospitals, diagnostics, education and training, and medical devices. There are potentially large gains from intra-regional trade and investment in health services in terms of addressing basic health infrastructure requirements, improving quality of health services, and addressing basic objectives of equity and access to healthcare. This chapter highlights these opportunities and some of the associated challenges based on primary and secondary sources.

The chapter begins with an overview of the basic health indicators and status of healthcare in each of the South Asian countries. It highlights the infrastructure and human resource requirements in this sector and thus the potential opportunity segments for commercial and collaborative engagement. This is followed by policy trends and regulations in this sector to indicate the extent to which health services have been opened up to private participation and foreign investment. The chapter then discusses the status of intra-regional trade, investment, and collaboration initiatives in health services, followed by some of the challenges that constrain regional initiatives in health services in South Asia. It thus provides a reality check on what is feasible regionally in this sector. The next section discusses the multilateral and other commitments made by the South Asian countries in health services to highlight how important this sector is in their trade engagements with other countries, as well as their preparedness for liberalization. Finally, the chapter summarizes the possible steps to furthering cooperation in health services in South Asia.

Healthcare Status

The South Asian countries, for the most part, fare very poorly on key human development indicators. They are among the lowest ranked countries in terms of the availability of physical and social infrastructure in the health sector and also basic health indicators such as mortality rates. As shown in Table 6.1, the per capita availability of doctors and nurses is much lower than the global average for almost all the countries. It is particularly low for Bangladesh, Bhutan, and Nepal, and is comparable with the global average only in the case of the Maldives. There is also a huge gap in terms of hospital availability per capita for all the countries except the Maldives and Sri Lanka. None of the countries in South Asia meet the WHO recommended norms for these parameters. The huge deficit in physical and human resource availability in the health sector is well highlighted in a CII-McKinsey study on India's health sector. The study notes that there is an additional requirement of 750,000 beds to meet the growing demand for in-patient services by 2012, and to reach a hospital bed to population ratio of 1.9:1,000. An estimated investment of US$ 24–34 billion will be required to set up infrastructure on such a scale (CII-McKinsey 2002).

The health status of the population in most of the South Asian countries is very poor. The average life expectancy at birth in South Asia (including in Afghanistan) is 63 years, which is lower than the average of 70 years for East Asia. The health status indicator for mortality rates among different groups is also very poor for the South Asian countries, except for Sri Lanka and the Maldives. Mortality rates for all groups, especially women,

Table 6.1 Status of Human Resources in Healthcare in South Asia and Other Regions (numbers in '000 and density in number per 10,000 population)

	Health Workforce											
	Physicians		Nursing and Midwifery Personnel		Dentistry Personnel		Community Health Workers		Other Health Service Providers		Hospital Beds (per 10,000 persons)
	No.	Density	No.	Density	No.	Density	No.	Density	No.	Density	
	2000–7		2000–7		2000–7		2000–7		2000–7		2000–7
Global avg.	8,404,351	13	17,651,585	28	1,854,512	3	–	–	14,631,863	24	25
Global median	5,201	11	12,746	29	900	2	548	2	2,767	5	25
Southeast Asia Avg.	849,324	5	1,955,203	12	92,759	1	132,612	1	2,002,575	12	9
South Asia											
Bangladesh	42,881	3	39,471	3	2,344	<1	21,000	2	24,035	2	3
Bhutan	52	<1	545	3	65	<1	195	1	926	4	16
India	645,825	6	1,372,059	13	61,424	1	50,393	1	1,752,027	16	7
Maldives	302	9	886	27	14	<1	515	16	827	25	23
Nepal	5,384	2	11,825	5	359	<1	16,206	6	5,631	2	2
Pakistan	126,350	8	47,380	5	15,790	1	65,999	4	37,034	2	10
Sri Lanka	10,479	6	33,431	17	1,245	1	–	–	5,405	3	29
Other countries											
Brazil	198,153	12	659,111	38	190,448	11	–	–	499,592	29	24
China	1,862,630	14	1,259,240	10	136,520	1	–	–	1,724,620	13	22
Malaysia	17,020	7	43,380	18	2,160	1	–	–	2,880	1	18
Singapore	6,380	15	18,710	44	1,190	3	–	–	1,280	3	32
South Africa	34,829	8	184,459	41	5,995	1	–	–	71,850	16	28
Thailand	22,435	4	172,477	28	10,459	2	–	–	71,528	12	22

Source: http://www.who.int/whosis/en/, accessed on 14 October 2009.

Table 6.2 Mortality Rates for Different Groups in South Asian and Other Countries

Member State	Neonatal Mortality Rate (per 1,000 live births) 2004	Infant Mortality Rate (probability of dying between birth and age 1 per 1,000 live births) Male 2000	Male 2007	Female 2000	Female 2007	Both Sexes 2000	Both Sexes 2007	Under-5 Mortality Rate (probability of dying by age 5 per 1,000 live births) Both Sexes 2000	Both Sexes 2007	Adult Mortality Rate (probability of dying between 15–60 per 100,000 population) Both Sexes 2007	Maternal Mortality 2005
Global average	28	56	48	52	45	54	46	78	67	183	400
Global median	14	31	23	25	19	28	22	33	25	176	130
Southeast Asia region average	35	62	50	61	48	61	49	84	65	220	450
South Asia											
Bangladesh	36	73	52	59	42	66	47	91	61	254	570
Bhutan	30	74	61	63	52	68	56	106	84	233	440
India	39	66	54	68	55	67	54	91	72	215	450
Maldives	24	44	27	42	25	43	26	55	30	94	120
Nepal	32	63	43	63	43	63	43	85	55	280	830
Pakistan	53	91	79	77	66	84	73	106	90	204	320
Sri Lanka	8	22	20	14	13	18	17	23	21	155	58
Other countries											
Brazil	13	31	22	25	18	28	20	32	22	159	110
China	18	25	16	35	22	30	19	37	22	115	45
Malaysia	5	12	11	10	9	11	10	14	11	143	62
Singapore	1	3	2	2	2	3	2	4	3	64	14
South Africa	17	58	48	53	44	56	46	74	59	520	400
Thailand	9	13	7	10	6	11	6	13	7	212	110

Source: http://www.who.int/whosis/en/, accessed on 14 October 2009.

Table 6.3   Expenditure on Health in South Asian and Other Countries as Share of GDP (per cent)

Country/Region	Year						
	2000	2001	2002	2003	2004	2005	2006
South Asia							
Bangladesh	3.1	3.2	3.1	3.1	3.1	2.8	3.1
Bhutan	5.4	5.7	4.5	4.1	4.2	4	4.5
India	4.3	4.6	4.8	4.8	4.9	5	4.9
Maldives	6.8	6.8	6.6	7.2	7.8	12.4	10.1
Nepal	5.4	5.3	6.1	5.8	5.7	5.8	5.7
Pakistan	2.5	2.3	2.3	2.2	2.2	2.1	2
Sri Lanka	3.7	3.8	3.8	3.9	4.2	4.1	4.2
Other countries							
Brazil	7.2	7.6	7.7	7.5	7.7	7.9	7.5
China	4.6	4.6	4.8	4.8	4.7	4.7	4.5
Malaysia	3.3	3.5	3.5	4.7	4.5	4.2	4.3
Singapore	3.4	3.7	3.7	4.2	3.7	3.5	3.4
South Africa	8.1	8.4	8.3	8.4	8.5	8.7	8.6
Thailand	3.4	3.3	3.7	3.9	3.5	3.5	3.5

Source: http://www.who.int/whosis/en/, accessed on 14 October 2009.

are higher than the global averages and mortality rates in other developing countries (Table 6.2). Most of the South Asian countries lie in the bottom half of countries for these social indicators, though there has been improvement in all the countries during 2000–7.

The poor status of these health indicators is in part a reflection of the low priority given to healthcare by most of the governments in South Asia. As shown in Table 6.3, health expenditures as a proportion of GDP are low, at around 3–5 per cent of GDP, but comparable to that in other developing countries. However, the main difference between most South Asian countries and other developing countries (shown in Table 6.4 for comparison) is the low share of government spending in total healthcare expenditure. This is particularly the case for India, Nepal, Bangladesh, and Pakistan where government spending constitutes a meagre 20–30 per cent of total healthcare expenditure, while its share stands at around 40–50 per cent in other developing countries. Private healthcare expenditure is not only significant but has also grown during 2000–7 in some of the larger South Asian countries, accounting for around three-fourth of total expenditure in India, Bangladesh, Nepal, and Pakistan in 2007.

The composition of healthcare spending in South Asia reflects the growth of private players in healthcare delivery and also the low priority and inadequate resources devoted to this sector by some of the governments in

Table 6.4   Characteristics of Healthcare Expenditure in South Asian and Other Countries

Country/ Region	Public–Private Composition of Healthcare Expenditure (%)						Out-of-pocket in Private Health Expenditure (%)		Share of External Resources in Health Expenditure (%)	
	2000		2003		2006		2000	2006	2000	2006
	Public	Private	Public	Private	Public	Private				
South Asia										
Bangladesh	26.5	73.5	28.7	71.3	36.8	63.2	88.1	88.3	19.4	14.6
Bhutan	74.5	25.5	68.7	31.3	68.6	31.4	100	100	26.5	48.2
India	22.2	77.8	18.5	81.5	19.6	80.4	92.1	94	0.6	0.7
Maldives	75.8	24.2	79.3	20.7	84.1	15.9	100	100	2.8	0.3
Nepal	24.9	75.1	26.1	73.9	30.5	69.5	91.2	85.2	15.2	15.7
Pakistan	20	80	16.6	83.4	16.4	83.6	98.2	97.9	0.9	3.2
Sri Lanka	47.9	52.1	41.3	58.7	49.2	50.8	83.3	85.8	0.3	1.2
Other countries										
Brazil	40	60	41.3	58.7	47.9	52.1	62.7	64	0.5	0.1
China	38.3	61.7	36.2	63.8	42	58	95.6	92.9	0.1	0.1
Malaysia	52.4	47.6	56.4	43.6	45.2	54.8	75.4	73.3	0.6	0
Singapore	36.8	63.2	34	66	33.6	66.4	97	94	0	0
South Africa	42.4	57.6	40.1	59.9	41.9	58.1	18.9	17.5	0.3	0.8
Thailand	56.1	43.9	66.6	33.4	64.4	35.6	76.9	76.6	0	0.3

Source: http://www.who.int/whosis/en/, accessed on 14 October 2009.

this region. Only in the case of the Maldives and Bhutan has the share of government spending in healthcare been significant, reflecting their small size and the limited scope in these markets for private players. The relatively higher share of government in total healthcare expenditure in the case of Sri Lanka reflects that country's more socially oriented policies and the policy thrust given to healthcare, as is also reflected in that country's better performance on social indicators such as mortality rates.

As shown in Table 6.4, the bulk of private spending on healthcare is out-of-pocket, indicating the very low levels of insurance penetration in this region. Although this is broadly comparable to that in other developing countries, given the fact that private spending constitutes a larger share of health expenditures in South Asia and within this most is out-of-pocket, this implies that both social as well as private health insurance cover is very limited. There has also been little change in this regard, with the share of private expenditure, and within that out-of-pocket payments remaining largely the same over the past few years. Hence, what emerges from the health sector expenditure characteristics is that in most of the countries in South Asia, access to healthcare is largely a function of ability to pay, that is, income level and economic background, with obvious implications for equity and human development outcomes. This dependence on private out-of-pocket spending when placed against the poor performance on social and physical infrastructure parameters is also indicative of this inequitable distribution of healthcare availability and quality of services.

Table 6.4 also highlights the significance of external resources as a source of health expenditure in some of the countries in this region, notably, Bangladesh, Bhutan, and Nepal. This reflects multilateral and donor funds received in the health sector, and captured in government spending on healthcare. Thus, some of the governments in this region are dependent on external funding for capacity building, health sector projects and initiatives, and technical assistance.

Overall, the status indicators suggest that there is a growing private sector participation in the health sector in South Asia, and thus there is scope for private investment and trade opportunities within the region. The indicators also highlight the need for increased resources to be devoted to healthcare, whether internal or external, to address the infrastructural gaps in this sector, and thus the potential commercial and cooperation possibilities in healthcare in South Asia. The indicators also highlight the commonality of interests that exist within the region in terms of improving basic health indicators, increasing availability of hospitals, doctors, nurses, and improving access to healthcare and equity in healthcare delivery. Again, this is indicative of regional collaboration prospects in this sector.

Health Policy Trends and Reforms

It is difficult to get a comprehensive perspective on policy trends and reforms that have been undertaken in the health sector in South Asia. This not only reflects the wide range of activities and services that constitute this sector, but also the relatively low priority given to healthcare in national policies and the lack of an integrated approach to this sector in the region. However, from the scattered information and various vision statements and proposals that are available on health policies and health system profiles for the countries in this region, what emerges clearly is that private participation, both domestic and foreign, has been encouraged in healthcare delivery.

The most important segment where private participation has been viewed as important is hospitals. Table A.16 in the Annexure (at the end of the book) shows that hospitals have been opened to FDI participation up to 100 per cent in most of the countries. The operating terms and conditions are also very liberal, with full repatriation of profits and income, minimal licensing and registration requirements, and also incentives in the form of tax holidays and import allowances in some countries. Most also do not put conditions on the form of participation. This is thus a segment where the governments in this region are keen to create an environment that is conducive to investors.

Policy related information on other segments of the health sector is more difficult to obtain for the countries in this region. However, some of the other important segments that are highlighted by the available official and policy literature, and which are in some way pertinent to a discussion on regional opportunities in health services include drugs and pharmaceuticals, medical devices and technology, and health insurance. Although pharmaceuticals and medical devices pertain to healthcare products rather than services, the existing regimes in these segments have a bearing on the scope for collaboration and cross-border investment opportunities in related services such as R&D, clinical trials, and testing. Health insurance is directly related to prospects in medical value travel. Table A.17 in the Annexure shows that health insurance tends to be a closed segment, reflecting the closed insurance sector in these countries. The policy orientation towards pharmaceuticals and medical devices is mixed, with the larger countries having open regimes to attract investment and develop contract manufacturing opportunities.

The main problem that governments in this region are facing is the dual task of financing and providing services. They have increasingly abdicated the responsibility of delivering services to the private sector and in some cases, also actively encouraged private participation. In recent years, public-private partnerships are also being considered to increase the effectiveness of public expenditure on health. It has been recommended by experts and multilateral funding agencies that the South Asian governments unbundle curative and preventive services and contract out services through competitive processes to private healthcare providers to improve health outcomes in this region.[1]

[1] See Bonu and Rani (2008).

Intra-regional Trade and Collaboration

Healthcare is one sector where the potential for regional integration and cooperation has been well recognized and also highlighted from the very beginning. The SAARC Social Charter contains various provisions which pertain to health related objectives in the region. For instance, one of the general provisions of this charter calls for the 'promotion of health as a regional objective' and for sharing information, capacity building, and a coordinated approach to health related issues in the region. The general provisions also recognize that the 'health of the population of the countries of the region is closely interlinked and can be sustained only by putting in place coordinated surveillance mechanisms and prevention and management strategies.'[2]

Article IV of the SAARC Social Charter, which specifically focuses on health issues, states that the member governments will 'strive to protect and promote the health of the population in the region', in particular 'addressing the problems of primary health issues and communicable diseases in the region.' This article also calls for sharing of knowledge and expertise among the countries with regard to disease prevention, management, and treatment, sharing of capacity for manufacture of drugs, taking a coordinated stand on issues pertaining to health in international fora, and adopting regional standards on drugs and pharmaceutical products. References to inclusive growth, equity, social development, use of information and communication technology, and improved public administration in the Social Charter also have a bearing on the provision of health services and health outcomes in the region. Hence, it is evident from these explicit and implicit references to health related goals and outcomes that the member governments share common concerns in this sector and also see scope for cooperation in various aspects of healthcare.

Regional initiatives and recent developments, undertaken by governments, as well as by the private sector, highlight some of the segments where regional opportunities exist. One such opportunity segment is cross-border investment in hospitals. Several leading Indian hospitals have entered other markets in the region, mostly through joint ventures with local partners, and through other arrangements, such as wholly owned subsidiaries, and management contracts. A few such examples highlight the regional potential for cross-border investment.

Apollo Hospitals has entered into several overseas investment ventures and management contracts with overseas hospitals, mainly to tap catchment

---

[2] See SAARC Secretariat (2009).

areas from which it receives patients.[3] These overseas facilities provide specialized and high-end treatments such as cardiac surgeries, joint replacements, and transplants. In the South Asian region, Bangladesh and Sri Lanka have been the markets of most interest.

Apollo's first overseas investment was in Colombo where it set up a 350-bed super-specialty hospital, driven by the large number of patients who were visiting the Apollo Hospital in Chennai. Initially, Apollo tried to manage operations and facilitate investment, but as investment from other parties was not forthcoming, it decided to enter as the primary investor. Apollo held a 47 per cent share in the project while the International Finance Corporation held a small equity stake, and local investors held a 35 per cent stake. Apollo's Colombo facility attracted patients who had earlier gone to Thailand, Australia, and India for treatment. However, this project had to be abandoned following the takeover by a Sri Lankan businessman. Recently, however, the Apollo Group has approached the Sri Lankan government to re-enter that market and is contemplating a majority stake of 51 per cent this time.[4]

Apollo has also taken on an operations management contract for a 330-bed tertiary care hospital in Dhaka. It has entered into a joint venture with its Bangladeshi partner, STS Holdings, Dhaka. The objective of this project is to cater to the large number of patients traveling to India and other neighbouring countries for treatment. According to newspaper reports, Indian hospitals are increasingly looking at entering Bangladesh through joint ventures and standalone entities, given that country's growing market and affluent population, economic stability, and the large number of Bangladeshi medical value travellers who are at present seeking treatment in other countries such as Thailand. Apollo's success in securing some of these overseas projects through competitive bids is due to the fact that it provides an integrated set of services, including human resource recruitment and management, medical equipment sourcing, and also has reasonable consulting fees.[5]

Likewise, Kolkata's BM Birla Heart Research Centre is interested in establishing its presence in Chittagong and Dhaka. A hospital is being set

[3] Apollo is also considering markets in the Middle East, UK, Mauritius, South Africa, Nigeria, Ghana, Fiji, Central Asia, and the Caribbean. Apollo is increasingly weighing the options of managing hospital assets without owning them versus investing and owning these assets.

[4] See http://www.livemint.com/2008/04/30154503/Apollo-to-invest-Rs-1K-cr-for.html, accessed on 14 September 2009.

[5] See Oberholzer-Gee et al. (2007).

up in Dhaka while management is being taken over from a hospital in Chittagong. AMRI Hospitals, Kolkata, is similarly considering setting up a branch in Bangladesh. These hospitals are interested in tapping the patient base in Bangladesh which is coming to Kolkata and other cities in India for treatment. Cultural and linguistic similarities and geographic proximity make Bangladesh an attractive market for overseas ventures for Indian hospitals in the eastern part of the country. The BM Birla Group is also considering setting up a hospital in Bhutan given that country's dire need for state-of-the-art facilities in healthcare.

There are several other ventures by leading Indian hospitals that also illustrate regional opportunities and interest among private players for cross-border investment and collaboration in the hospital segment. For instance, Manipal has a 700-bed hospital in Pokhara. It also runs a hospital in Kathmandu University, as part of a joint educational programme under which students from Nepal can come to India to complete part of their qualifications. Recently, the Bhutanese government has expressed interest in attracting investment from Indian hospitals. According to media sources, the Hinduja Group in India is considering setting up a hospital in Sri Lanka, in response to a request from the Sri Lankan government.[6] Growing private equity financing and initial placement offers in healthcare have also created opportunities for investment in healthcare in recent years.

Another promising segment where private players see commercial opportunities is in medical value travel. The regional South Asian market, in particular medical value travelers from Pakistan, Bangladesh, Nepal, and the Maldives, have been identified as one of the four strategic segments for promoting medical value travel exports by Indian hospitals, given the underdeveloped facilities and unavailability of specialized treatments in these markets.[7] Such patients would find medical care in India attractive due to cost, quality, cultural, and geographic proximity considerations.

The Manipal Hospital in Bangalore receives patients from over 30 countries, including Sri Lanka, Bangladesh, Nepal, and Pakistan among the SAARC nations. Apollo Gleneagles Hospital in Kolkata receives patients from Nepal and Bangladesh, and Apollo Chennai receives patients from

---

[6] See http://www.thehinduusinessline.com/2005/06/19/stories/2005061900410500. htm, accessed on 14 September 2009.

[7] The other three segments are the Indian diaspora who would come to their home country for medical treatment, countries with rationed healthcare such as the UK and Canada where waiting periods can be long, and the uninsured in markets such as the US who might prefer low cost quality treatment in India. See Obherholze-Gee et al. (2007).

Sri Lanka. Wockhardt Hospitals is a treatment destination for patients from South Asia and other regions. Pakistan is seen as a potential source market for patients seeking high-end treatment at a reasonable cost. There have been several high profile cases of Pakistani children seeking specialized cardiac treatment at Indian hospitals. The Bhutanese government sends patients to Kolkata and Delhi and pays for their treatment.

In view of the promising prospects for medical value travel and the growing internal market in India, Bangalore-based Narayana Hrudayalaya hospital has plans to build a nation-wide chain of 5,000-bed health cities in the major state capitals of India, such as in Jaipur, Ahmedabad, Hyderabad, and Ranchi. It aims to have 20,000 beds within the next five years, by 2013, with a total investment of US$ 100 million (Rs 400 crore).[8] The facilities will include separate suites for international patients, and specialized hospitals for cancer, eye, and for women and children. Narayana Hrudayalaya is targeting patients from the South Asian and other regional markets. Some of its hospitals have already established referral arrangements with hospitals and agents in the source countries and tied up with travel operators to provide an integrated set of services to medical value travellers.

There is some evidence of telemedicine links between major hospitals in India and establishments in other countries in this region, mainly for tele-consultation and telediagnostic services. Some identified potential opportunities are in remote monitoring of patients in other SAARC countries and telepsychiatry. GE's subsidiary in Delhi provides telemedicine services to hospitals in Nepal. Wipro is considering setting up a telemedicine centre in Colombo, which would provide front-end services while back-end reporting would be done by specialists based in India. But on the whole, telemedicine has still not taken off in the region and requires more investment in high-end training and use of specialized equipment, as well as acceptance of telemedicine as a form of healthcare delivery within the region.

Several governmental initiatives have also been undertaken in the region to promote cooperation in healthcare. In view of the common disease profiles and afflictions affecting the South Asian countries, regional centres have been identified by member governments to undertake work on disease control and joint research. The SAARC Tuberculosis Centre (STC), which was established in Kathmandu in 1992, is involved in the prevention and control of TB in the region. It coordinates the efforts of the National TB Control Programmes of member countries. There have been regional

---

[8] See http://www.livemint.com/2008/02/06232413/AIG-JPMorgan-buy-25-stake-in.html, accessed on 29 September 2009.

consultations on health issues which have focused on combating communicable diseases such as TB, malaria, waterborne diseases, and AIDS. There have been training programmes to fight major diseases such as malaria, TB, diarrhoeal diseases, leprosy, and maternal and child health issues which are a common concern in the region. The SAARC member governments have also entered into regional projects with multilateral development agencies such as the Canadian International Development Agency (CIDA), the World Health Organization (WHO), the UN Fund for Population Activities (UNFPA), and UNAIDS for capacity building, research, analysis, and technical cooperation. There has also been some discussion at a regional governmental level on traditional systems of medicine and the need for regional cooperation in this regard to meet the basic health needs of the people. As the South Asian countries share many traditional health practices and have resources that are required in common across the countries, the need to explore complementarities in this area and to develop a regional health tourism package have been highlighted.

There are some other segments where opportunities have been identified and some initiatives have been taken or contemplated. In the medical devices segment, there are regional opportunities for production, sales, distribution, and testing of medical devices. The GE office in Bangalore, which produces medical products, also delivers services to Bangladesh and Sri Lanka. According to the company, there is potential to introduce cost effective, affordable, and quality healthcare solutions in South Asia. There is some interest in medical education and exchange within the region. For instance, India's Manipal Group, in collaboration with the Government of Nepal, set up a college and hospital in 1994, where undergraduate training is provided and can be followed up with post-graduate training at Manipal's centre in India. Other issues that have been discussed include cooperation in medical expertise and pharmaceuticals, harmonization of standards and certification procedures, affordable access to pharmaceuticals produced in the region, mental health research, and information and expertise sharing through regional conferences, seminars, exchange of health professionals and academics, and joint research programmes.

Challenges and Constraints

Although there is potential for expanding intra-regional commerce, investment, and collaboration in healthcare, there are also numerous constraints that limit integration in this sector. There are challenges at both the governmental and private sector levels.

One of the main constraints in exploiting regional opportunities in healthcare is the attractiveness of the market for the private sector, vis-à-vis other markets. Key private sector players in South Asia, namely, Indian hospitals that have ventured into other SAARC markets or are catering to patients from the rest of the region, have attractive opportunities within India given the large domestic healthcare market which is growing at 15–20 per cent per year and an increasingly affluent population to cater to within India. Hence, they find the Indian market to be more attractive than the regional market in terms of growth opportunities for both medical value travel and new investments. In addition, there are uncertainties in terms of political and regulatory environments that are associated with investments in other SAARC countries. Expanding hospital chains within India, even in second and third tier cities, or setting up integrated health cities within India may be a more attractive proposition than catering to the regional market. As discussions with some leading corporate Indian hospitals reveal, the cost of promoting health tourism or setting up investments in other SAARC countries may be too high to warrant a regional focus. This may perhaps explain why despite all the hype about the potential in medical value travel and forays by Indian players in other neighboring countries, the actual regionalization of healthcare remains quite limited. As noted by one respondent from a leading Indian hospital, if patients from other SAARC countries are interested in getting treated in India, this would be welcome, but the hospital would not necessarily invest in attracting this segment in a big way as there are ample growth opportunities within India.

There are also specific challenges that affect the scope for medical value travel within SAARC. Factors such as delays in getting visas and absence of processes for granting expedited medical visas, delays in obtaining approvals for getting overseas treatment, poor airline connectivity, and inadequate and poor local support infrastructure, constrain the scope for medical value travel. There are also financing issues, including the lack of insurance portability and absence of regional insurance products which result in the use of informal channels for payment and constrain medical value travel. There are also cultural and linguistic problems and translation requirements when dealing with patients from other SAARC countries despite considerable affinity among the countries in this region. More recently, medicolegal cases have been rising with growing awareness in the region, raising jurisdictional issues over cases of malpractice and insurance cover.

At a governmental level, the main constraint to expanding medical value travel is that there is no government policy regarding regional cooperation in this segment. Despite recognition of commonalities among the countries, there has been no effort to develop joint medical value travel products at a regional level. Medical value travel has been seen as an extension of general tourism campaigns, as in the case of the Incredible India campaign, where major hospitals have been linked with tourism, but there is nothing specifically tailored to promote medical value travel from SAARC countries.

Several challenges have emerged in the context of regional investment projects in healthcare. These relate to managing partnerships with local stakeholders, issues of mobility of healthcare professionals, investment regulations, and domestic lobbies in the host country. Apollo's experience in Colombo well highlights some of these challenges. Apollo's first entry into the Sri Lankan market was not successful. Apollo invested around Rs 10 crores in its Colombo hospital. There was a mismatch of expectations between Apollo and its partner, a problem that is common in joint venture arrangements (the form taken by most international ventures in hospitals). The Apollo Group had difficulty carrying out its operations with a minority stake. It was finally forced to sell its 33.22 per cent stake in Apollo Hospitals to Sri Lanka Insurance Corporation (SLIC), which had the largest stake in this venture, following differences with SLIC over stake ownership.[9]

Apollo's ventures in Dhaka and Colombo have also faced difficulties over staffing. Indian hospitals have been recognized for their quality of infrastructure as well as professionals. Local staffing is seen as a potential risk to the quality of healthcare delivery and dilution of the corporate brand name. However, staffing of regional establishments with home country doctors has not been easy and has not always been well-received by the host country. It has proven difficult to relocate doctors and health administrators from India to other markets in the region, coupled with the fact that the availability of highly qualified health professionals is also constrained within India. There has also been resistance by professionals in the host countries to the hiring and relocation of Indian doctors. There have been challenges due to ethnicity, such as in the case of Sri Lanka, where patients and local staff may not be comfortable with Indian doctors due to their stand on ethnic issues, and it may take the local medical council six months to register an Indian doctor. In addition, the usual concerns about the safety of investment in politically unstable markets, such as Nepal, repatriation issues, and worker indiscipline and unionization have also hampered investments in healthcare within the region. For example, recently, a Maoist trade union called an indefinite closure of the

---

[9] Based on discussions with healthcare industry persons.

Manipal Teaching Hospital, run by the Manipal College of Medical Sciences in Pokhara, Nepal. The All Nepal Health Workers' Association and the Manipal Non-teaching Staff Union closed down all departments except emergency services in the hospital. Such problems have arisen earlier as well when employees have gone on strike.

Similar constraints also affect the scope for telemedicine within the region, although prospects in this segment have been highlighted by health academics and practitioners, especially as linked with medical value travel. Indian companies that could potentially set up telemedicine centres in other SAARC markets and provide local services may not be interested in the region, given the large and growing domestic market in India and the low margins in the region. There is also opposition from domestic lobbies, such as the local radiology fraternity and commercial industry bodies, to such foreign establishments. Infrastructure constraints in terms of cost of bandwidth, quality of image delivery, lack of home devices, and problems of data security and potential breach of patient confidentiality are also highlighted by practitioners, notwithstanding telecommunication reforms and investment in high speed bandwidth and encryption by governments.[10] Acceptance of telemedicine by patients in the region is another constraint. For instance, Apollo had wanted to start a telemedicine link at its hospital in Dhaka but teleconsultation was not accepted and this initiative did not materialize. There is also the constraint of human resources as there is a shortage of trained specialists even for the local market, making it difficult for telemedicine providers to focus on the regional market. Overall, telemedicine links within South Asia remain limited. They are mainly confined to a few private enterprises and have not been taken up at the governmental level, even though there are e-health initiatives and government subsidized programmes for ICT in healthcare in most countries in this region.

Other factors, such as difficulties in regional mobility of professionals, difficulties in organizing regional seminars and conferences, and lack of recognition of qualifications have also been highlighted by health industry experts as constraints in tapping regional prospects in healthcare. In particular, delivery of healthcare services through the movement of professionals depends on recognition of the medical professionals. But as of now, there is no formal mechanism for recognition of medical professionals'

---

[10] It is still not practical to perform surgeries remotely. Although data privacy is not yet a major issue in the region, awareness is growing, raising issues of liability and jurisdiction.

qualifications among the SAARC countries, although all the countries have similar regulations to govern the practice of medicine and dentistry, and also provide scope for reciprocal recognition of qualifications of other countries.[11] There has also been a lack of a regional perspective and absence of strong inter-governmental efforts, notwithstanding some of the regional consultations and initiatives discussed earlier. Overall, while health services present promising regional opportunities, a variety of infrastructural, human resource, regulatory, perception-related, logistical, and cultural barriers limit the realization of these opportunities.

Multilateral and Other Commitments in Health Services

The health services sector is one of the least committed sectors under the GATS. It is covered under two headings—professional services and health and social services. Professional health services pertain to medical and dental services, veterinary services, and services provided by midwives, nurses, and other healthcare personnel. Health and social services pertain to hospital services, other human health services, and social services.

Among the South Asian member countries of the WTO, only India, Nepal, and Pakistan have undertaken commitments in some aspect of health services. Bangladesh, the Maldives, and Sri Lanka have not scheduled either professional health services or health services infrastructure. The commitments and offers made in health services (professional and other) by the South Asian countries are summarized in Table 6.5.

It is evident from Table 6.5 that by and large there has been very little willingness among the South Asian countries to negotiate health services under the GATS. Even where this sector has been scheduled, the coverage has been rather limited to mainly hospital services. India has made the most extensive commitments in this sector among the South Asian countries and its offers significantly improve upon its Uruguay Round (UR) commitment, in that they cover more sub-sectors and also remove and liberalize limitations initially inscribed in its UR schedule. For instance, several sub-sectors which were not originally scheduled by India in the UR have been included in the initial or conditional offer, and limitations in the form of foreign equity ceilings have been relaxed in the offers. Pakistan has

---

[11] The Indian Medical Council Act does notify medical degrees from Bangladesh, Nepal, Sri Lanka, and Pakistan under the reciprocal arrangement provision which also means that these other countries recognize medical qualifications from notified Indian colleges and universities. But the status with regard to the recognition of qualifications in dentistry and nursing among the countries is not clear.

similarly improved on its UR commitment by including more sub-sectors in its offer. Nepal has made mostly full commitments except in the case of mode 3 where it has inscribed limitations on foreign equity participation and form of commercial presence.

An examination of these commitments suggests that the South Asian countries view health services as a sector where market access has to be conditional on meeting certain social obligations, such as bringing in latest

Table 6.5 Commitments and Offers in Health and Related Services by South Asian Countries

Sector/ Sub-sector	Uruguay Round Commitments	Conditional Initial Offer	Revised Offer
Bangladesh	**April 1995**		
Health services not scheduled or offered			
India	**April 1995**	**12 January 2004**	**24 August 2005**
Professional Services			
Medical and dental services	Sector not scheduled	1. None for provision of services on provider to provider basis such that the transaction is between established medical institutions covering areas of second opinion to help in diagnosis of cases or in the field of research 2. None 3. Limitations: - Only through incorporation with a foreign equity ceiling of 74 per cent - The latest technology for treatment will be brought in - FIPB approval 4. Unbound except as indicated in the horizontal section	No change
Veterinary services	Sector not scheduled	Sector not scheduled	1. None 2. None 3. Limitation of FIPB approval 4. Unbound except as indicated in horizontal section

(Contd . . .)

(*Table 6.5 contd . . .*)

Sector/ Sub-sector	Uruguay Round Commitments	Conditional Initial Offer	Revised Offer
Services provided by midwives, nurses, physiotherapists, and para-medical personnel	Sector not scheduled	1. None for provision of services on provider to provider basis such that the transaction is between established medical institutions covering areas of second opinion to help in diagnosis of cases or in the field of research 2. None 3. Limitations: - Only through incorporation with a foreign equity ceiling of 74 per cent - the latest technology for treatment will be brought in - FIPB approval - Public funded services may be available only to Indian citizens or price differential for other citizens 4. Unbound except as indicated in the horizontal section	No change

Health Services

Hospital services	1. Unbound 2. Unbound 3. Foreign equity ceiling is 51 per cent, only through local incorporation 4. Unbound except as given in the horizontal commitments	1. None, provided transaction is between two established medical institutions, covering areas of second opinion for diagnostics or research 2. None 3. Foreign equity limit increased to 74 per cent; FIPB approval required for foreign investors with prior collaboration; only through local incorporation; subject to inflow of latest technology for treatment; different conditions for publicly funded services 4. No change	1. No change 2. No change 3. No change 4. No change except restrictions removed for charitable purposes

(*Contd . . .*)

(Table 6.5 contd . . .)

Sector/ Sub-sector	Uruguay Round Commitments	Conditional Initial Offer	Revised Offer
Maldives **Health services not scheduled**	**April 1995**		
Nepal	**(Date of submission:** **30 August 2004)**		
Professional Services			

Veterinary
services
	1. None
	2. None
	3. None except only through
	   incorporation in Nepal and
	   with maximum foreign
	   equity capital of 51 per cent
	4. Unbound		

Health Services			

Hospital services	1. None
	2. None
	3. None except only through
	   incorporation in Nepal and
	   with maximum foreign
	   equity capital of 51 per cent
	4. Unbound except as
	   indicated in the horizontal
	   section
	Medical experts can work
	with the permission of the
	Nepal Medical Council for a
	maximum of one year		

Pakistan **Professional Services**	**April 1995**	**30 May 2005**	
Medical and dental services	1. Unbound 2. None 3. Subject to regulatory provisions 4. Unbound	1. No change 2. No change 3. No change 4. No change	

Veterinary
services
(excludes services
provided by
public
institutions)
	Sector not scheduled	1. Unbound
		2. None
		3. - Market access limitations
		   economic needs test
		   - National treatment
		   limitation: residency
		   requirement
		4. Unbound	

(Contd . . .)

(*Table 6.5 contd . . .*)

Sector/ Sub-sector	Uruguay Round Commitments	Conditional Initial Offer	Revised Offer
Services provided by midwives, nurses, physiotherapists, and para-medical personnel (excludes services provided by public institutions) Health services	Sector not scheduled	1. Unbound 2. None 3. None 4. Unbound	
Hospital services	1. Unbound 2. None 3. Subject to regulatory provisions 4. Unbound	1. No change 2. No change 3. None 4. No change	
Sri Lanka Sector not scheduled	**April 1995**	**September 2003**	

Source: Based on WTO member countries' GATS Commitment and Offer Schedules.

technology, ensuring quality services and accountability, and differentiating between health services for public as opposed to commercial purposes. Hospital services emerge as an important segment that the South Asian countries are willing to negotiate. All three countries, which have scheduled health services, have committed to opening up the hospital services segment, albeit to varying degrees in terms of foreign equity participation. All have inscribed conditions to ensure appropriate, accountable, and quality investment in the hospitals segment. It is also interesting to note that there is a general thrust on allowing institution based delivery of services, such as between providers in two countries, rather than direct delivery of services by providers to consumers in the other country.

If one were to juxtapose these characteristics against the intra-regional initiatives and opportunities that have been witnessed in health services in South Asia, then one can infer that the countries in this region may be willing to negotiate issues, such as intra-regional investment in hospitals and collaboration among regional health establishments for research, charitable, training, and academic exchange purposes. There are also no restrictions imposed on medical value travel (consumption abroad of hospital services), and hence this is another segment where there may be preparedness to negotiate on issues, such as arrangements between medical establishments and on common products such as marketing the region as a medical value travel destination. Several of the bilateral and regional agreements signed by the South Asian countries with countries outside the region include health services. Issues of cooperation, movement of professionals, and foreign investment have been discussed in this sector. Overall, the multilateral as well as regional/bilateral commitments made in health services indicate that the South Asian countries are likely to have a common approach and objectives, thus providing sufficient ground for regional negotiations in this sector.

Looking Ahead

There is a general view that the health services sector is one of the most promising areas for regional integration and the preceding discussion clearly shows that there are many opportunity areas. However, as also highlighted, there are numerous challenges that affect regional prospects in this sector. Given these challenges, as well as the nature of this sector where there is a mix of social and commercial objectives, a gradual approach would appear to be a feasible regional strategy. This would include pilot-based initiatives and cooperation in selected segments coupled with specific efforts to alleviate some of the constraints mentioned earlier, and to promote regional commercial opportunities and social objectives.

There are broadly three segments that need to be targeted regionally. These include commercial opportunities in medical value travel; cross-border investment; and capacity building and regulatory cooperation. Regional discussions would need to focus on facilitating cross-border investments, particularly in hospitals and potentially telemedicine centres; facilitating regional mobility of patients; instituting mechanisms to make the region more attractive as a destination for medical value travellers both within the region and for tourists from other regions; and initiating joint efforts in research, training, and capacity building not only in vision statements and documents but in practice through tie-ups between selected centres and establishments.

In the context of medical value travel, one important area to address would be insurance and cross-border payment arrangements. For instance, one could consider a regional insurance product which includes an overseas package for treatment in other countries. As international insurance premia are high, an insurance policy initiated within the region, such as in India, but with an understanding among the countries for treatment in the region, is a possible mechanism that could help promote medical value travel within the region. According to one leading Indian health practitioner, there is scope to institute a regional medicare system where reimbursements are scheduled transparently and rates are fixed for different procedures and treatments for each country in the region. Medical value travel would also get a boost in the region if regional insurance players recognize payments in each other's markets and there are bank-to-bank guarantees in the region. As a first step, Indian insurers could take a lead in this initiative and treatment could be limited to the Indian market, with a different fee structure for regional medical value travellers.[12] Pilot schemes could be introduced for specialized elective treatments and procedures, which may not be available in the home country of the patient. Some potential segments would be transplant surgery, infertility medicine, joint replacements, and treatments for cardiac, eye, dental, urological, and gastrointestinal problems. Thus, it would be useful for governments, insurance companies, and hospitals in the region to explore the possibility of cross-border insurance arrangements, common insurance products with agreed rates for treatment within the region, and supplementary financial arrangements through formal channels. The experience of other regional blocs such as in MERCOSUR, which have entered into regional payment arrangements to promote medical value travel, could be instructive in this regard.

In addition to facilitating payments, other issues, such as visas, transport, supporting logistics in the destination country, and follow-up services would also need to be discussed to promote medical value travel in the region. There is for instance, a need to streamline medical value travel related visas. According to an earlier study on Bangladeshi patients traveling to India for treatment, due to the more onerous documentation requirements associated with a medical visa, patients often went on a tourist visa and made use of informal channels of payment. This also resulted in an underestimation of the magnitude of medical value travel within the region as the purpose of travel was often not revealed for visa purposes (Rahman 2001). Streamlining documentation requirements and reducing the processing time for medical travel related visas would increase patient mobility in the region. There is also the issue of related support services such as accommodation, which is subject to high taxes and rents. While the multiplicity of taxes and high tax rates are a general constraint to promoting tourism (as highlighted in Chapter 5), governments could perhaps consider reducing the burden of such levies in the case of healthcare related tourism. It will also be important to take an integrated perspective of medical value travel, including instituting follow-up facilities in the home country of the patient in the form of stand-alone centres and tie-ups between

[12] There would, however, be some inherent limitations in the regional medical value travel market as there would be less scope for the insurance companies to increase prices and their insurance model would need to be more service delivery-based as opposed to revenue-led given the lower paying capacity in this region compared to the other regions.

establishments in the host and home countries for the purpose of pre- and post-treatment consultations, telemedicine facilities, and relaxing restrictions on cross-border practice of physicians and specialists. Like tourism, healthcare tourism could benefit from a coordinated marketing and promotion campaign by the countries in South Asia, such as marketing specific health tourism products, wellness tourism, and alternative treatments.

Most of these efforts to promote medical value travel would need to be initiated by private enterprises with support from the government on issues such as visas, approvals, and registration requirements. Governments and private sector players will need to take a regional perspective on medical value travel, so as to enable a structured movement of regional patients to identified centres of excellence, also enabling better utilization of super-specialists and high-end equipment available in the region. But as noted earlier, such a regional perspective is lacking, and regional players, particularly those in India may not have sufficient incentives to focus specifically on the South Asian countries as a target market.

Another area that should receive more attention is facilitation of cross-border investments in hospitals and telemedicine establishments. As highlighted earlier, there are investment-related bottlenecks which constrain this potential. Investment regulations for setting up hospitals within the region need to be streamlined and the approval process made speedier. Associated restrictions on movement of doctors from the source country of investment, special registration and approval requirements for foreign doctors, and restrictions on their practice need to be relaxed as such conditions affect the ability of the investing hospital to signal quality and attract local patients. Mobility of professionals as linked with investment presence needs to be liberalized if cross-border investment ventures are to be facilitated. Again, private sector initiatives must be supported by government measures on visas, licensing, registration, repatriation of income and profits, and provision of a stable investor friendly environment not only in healthcare but also generally. With a more favourable business environment and more SAARC-oriented policies, there is scope for regional establishments in the health sector.[13] There can also be government sponsored investments, where some of the member governments can actively invite investments from leading hospitals in the region and also work out arrangements with the source countries for staffing these establishments.[14]

[13] According to industry sources in India, there are around 10 potential players like Apollo who could establish themselves in the regional market.

[14] The Government of Bhutan, for instance, is interested in getting specialists from India to work in existing facilities in Bhutan.

There is a lot that could be done through inter-governmental dialogue on the capacity building and regulatory front and to implement some of the proposals that remain on paper. There is scope for research and development with multi-centre and multi-country studies focusing on common diseases that afflict the region and lifestyle diseases, such as heart disease, diabetes, new areas such as stem cell research, and public health issues. There could be teams of researchers working across the countries and common protocols on research could be developed, and data could be shared and validated. There is also scope for joint initiatives in public health for education, research, training, and awareness raising purposes. For such joint efforts to take off, country-specific evaluations will be needed to identify the centres of excellence. Given the lack of fiscal resources to devote to healthcare in this region, it would be important to draw upon both public and private enterprises for such joint initiatives through public-private partnerships.

Another pre-requisite for greater regional cooperation is increased interaction of the medical community, and among training institutions and hospitals in the region. Interaction could take the form of conferences, workshops, and exchange of health professionals to enable sharing of knowledge, best practices, latest research, discussion of common shortcomings and objectives in the health sector, and dissemination of information regarding regional facilities and services. Such interactions would be critical for removing perception related barriers which hinder regional trade in health services and to arrive at common instruments for promoting healthcare within the region. Short-term exchange programmes for doctors and students across identified research centres and training institutions could facilitate capacity building in specific domains and provide exposure to treatments that are not available in some of the countries. Educational and research institutions could also be linked through regional scholarships provided by governments and also by leading hospitals to promote medical studies in the region. Joint training could take place in areas, such as nursing and paramedical services. Such initiatives could help in addressing the shortage of human resources and problems of quality.

There is also need for regulatory cooperation among the SAARC countries on the issues of degree recognition and standards and accreditation of medical establishments. Such efforts towards quality assurance would help in brand building and in marketing the region as a destination for medical travelers. It would also be helpful in facilitating cross-border staffing of hospitals, exchange of students and professionals, and regional insurance and payment arrangements for medical value travel. This would require cooperation among professional associations, private players, and regulatory bodies across the countries in this region. However, one must recognize that standardization of training within the region will be difficult given the fact that even within India, which is the dominant SAARC country in healthcare, there is lack of standardization in medical education.

There are a variety of other areas where governments in this region could increase cooperation and enter into public-private partnership arrangements to improve the quality and reach of healthcare delivery. One of these is the promotion of ICT for health. The Indian Space Research Organization (ISRO) provides satellite connectivity within SAFTA. It is possible for hospitals and training institutions within South Asia to enter into telemedicine arrangements with establishments in the other countries, with government support, and to provide cross-border healthcare through satellite connectivity (which would not be constrained by infrastructure and security concerns unlike broadband delivery). Private telemedicine firms can be involved in such a regional initiative. Some countries in the region, such as the Maldives, provide good scope for telemedicine given their island topography and focus on ICT for development. Another potential area is clinical trials. Given the racial diversity and the common diseases and afflictions in the region, the large population base in South Asia provides opportunities for carrying out Stage 3 and 4 clinical trials. Many of these cooperation efforts in health services would also have implications for trade in health products, such as pharmaceuticals and medical equipment within the region.

Overall, there is lot of ground for private and governmental initiatives, and consultations in the health sector and the range of measures required is quite wide. These include measures pertaining to investments in physical infrastructure, human resource development, harmonization of standards, streamlining regulatory frameworks, communication and dissemination within the region, and developing an integrated approach to realizing both social and commercial opportunities in healthcare. There are also many synergies across the different opportunity segments, with investments driving medical value travel and vice versa, facilitating management tie-ups and joint ventures, telemedicine possibilities, and movement of professionals. There are also synergies with trade and investment in health sector products, such as medical equipment, pharmaceuticals, and manufacturing. The region offers scope for economies of scale and resource pooling in many areas of healthcare.

But while the opportunities are many and the measures required are also quite evident, there will be two major challenges to health services integration in this region. The first is the lack of a regional vision in healthcare due to the dynamics of the regional market, which make the main provider market, India, more focused on the internal market as opposed to the regional market. The second challenge is political instability which is a deterrent to investment flows, to the mobility of patients and health professionals, and even development initiatives in ICT and infrastructure sharing in the health sector. But if approached with a long-term vision, the health sector is one area where regional cooperation can go a long way towards building political and social goodwill between countries. Cases of emergency paediatric and very specialized surgeries carried out for Pakistani patients in Indian hospitals have attracted a lot of media attention in both India and Pakistan. Visa facilitation on humanitarian grounds can play an important role in furthering relations and building public opinion for greater engagement among the South Asian countries, particularly between India and Pakistan.

7

Education Services

Addressing Cross-cutting Impediments

Like healthcare, investment in human capital is essential for long-term growth, productivity improvement, and equity. In recent years, there has been a growing trend towards internationalization of education, in particular higher and professional education, with the private sector leading this growth. Today, a large number of students study abroad and international student mobility has increased by over 2 million since 2000 (Agarwal 2009). Many private institutions have established themselves in other countries to tap the growing global demand for education, and new forms of engagement through twinning and partnership programmes, distance learning, franchises, and subsidiaries have emerged.

South Asia is an important contributor to the growing global demand for education, given its sizeable young population and growing middle class. The region accounts for a large number of internationally mobile students, who go to countries, such as Malaysia, Singapore, the US, and the UK for higher education. It is also witness to growing domestic private sector participation in education and foreign presence through partnerships and twinning arrangements.[1] These trends are a reflection of the funding and capacity constraints affecting this region with demand outgrowing supply in education services at all levels of the education sector. As in the case of healthcare, one finds a paradoxical mix of the first world and the third world, with low enrolment, low literacy rates and poor quality, combined with some well-known and globally reputed educational institutions that provide professional and highly skilled manpower to the rest of the world.

The large and growing regional market for education potentially provides opportunities for commercialization and collaboration to private education providers and governments within the region across various segments

[1] Independent campuses and large-scale investments are rare.

of the education sector, especially in professional and technical education and in research and development. While there is some work on this sector for some of the countries in this region, including their engagement with the rest of the world, there is little analysis from a regional perspective about the prospects for trade, investment, and collaboration in education services in South Asia. It is thus worth examining whether there are potential gains from such intra-regional engagements in this sector to address the objectives of expanding capacity, attracting investments, and improving quality and access to education services. This chapter highlights these opportunities and some of the associated challenges, focusing primarily on higher education.

The chapter begins with an overview of key educational status and attainment indicators for each of the countries of South Asia. It places South Asia in a comparative perspective vis-à-vis other developing countries to highlight the challenges facing this region in education services. It also provides an overview of trends in educational attainment indicators over time to highlight the extent to which progress has been made in this region. This is followed by policy trends and regulations in this sector to indicate the extent to which education services have been opened up to private participation and foreign investment and the regulatory frameworks prevailing in this sector. The chapter then discusses the status of intra-regional trade, investment, and collaboration initiatives in education services which is followed by an outline of the key challenges to such engagement within the region. The chapter then discusses the multilateral and other commitments made by the South Asian countries in education services to highlight how important this sector is in their trade engagements with other countries, as well as their overall preparedness for liberalization. Finally, the chapter proposes some steps that could be taken at the governmental and the private sector levels to exploit regional complementarities and opportunities in education services and highlights the cross-cutting issues that would need to be addressed.

Trends and Current Status of Education Services

The South Asian region in general performs poorly on educational status indicators, though there is considerable variation among them with Sri Lanka and the Maldives for the most part outperforming the others. Table 7.1 provides the basic educational status and attainment indicators for the countries in South Asia. As is evident, India, Bangladesh, Pakistan, and Nepal exhibit progressively lower enrolment rates at the secondary and tertiary levels compared to other developing and developed countries,

Table 7.1 Indicators of Education Status in South Asia and Other Countries (2007, unless otherwise indicated)

Country	Population (mn) 2008	Gross Enrolment Rate (%), Pre-primary, Total	Net Enrolment Rate (%), Primary Level, Total	Net Enrolment Rate (%), Secondary Total	Gross Enrolment Rate (%), Tertiary, Total	Drop-out Rate (%), Primary	Pupil–Teacher Ratio, Primary	Pupil–Teacher Ratio, Secondary
South Asia								
India	1,140	47.08	89.81	–	13.48	34.21	40.2	32.7
Bangladesh	160	10.49	87.98	41.48	6.98	45.19	44.75	25.24
Pakistan	166	46.87	66.16	32.09	5.19	30.32	39.95	41.86
Sri Lanka	20.2	–	99.70	–	–	1.19	23.81	19.52
Bhutan	0.7	1.47	77.87	38.16	5.23	15.6	29.18	22.83
Nepal	28.6	37.71	74.55	42.24	8.96	38.43	40.02	–
Maldives	0.3	96.31	96.17	69.42	0.2	–	14.52	–
World	6,692	33.28	87.13	–	25.95	–	30.59	23.92
Other Countries								
Brazil	192	62.42	92.58	76.96	30.01	24.37	23.86	18.55
Malaysia	27	57.11	97.49	68.73	29.75	10.66	15.75	16.99
China	1,325.6	41.88	–	–	22.05	–	17.68	16.37
South Africa	48.7	51.13	87.47	71.85	–	–	30.98	29.02
Thailand	67.4	–	–	–	–	–	17.72	21.01
Singapore	4.8	–	–	–	–	–	20.42	16.96
United States	304.1	61.11	91.48	88.23	81.62	4.15	13.80	14.56
United Kingdom	61.4	73.36	97.20	91.33	58.99	–	17.24	14.01

Source: World Bank Data. Available at http://web.worldbank.org/WBSITE/EXTERNAL/DATASTATISTICS/0,,contentMDK:20535285~menuPK:1390200~pagePK:64133150~piPK:64133175~theSitePK:239419,00.html; http://web.worldbank.org/WBSITE/EXTERNAL/TOPICS/EXTEDUCATION/0,,contentMDK:20573961~menuPK:282404~pagePK:282404~piPK:148956~theSitePK:282386,00.html, accessed on 20 March 2010.

although they are broadly comparable at the pre-primary and primary levels. This drop in enrolment rates, combined with the high drop-out rates in almost all the countries, indirectly reflects problems of retention, quality, and capacity constraints in the education sector. The relatively high student–faculty ratio at both the primary and secondary levels in the three larger countries, India, Bangladesh, and Pakistan further reflects the human resource constraints affecting this sector.

The low educational status indicators in part reflect inadequate funding of the education sector, in particular the inability of the governments to provide adequate financial resources to augment capacity and quality. As shown in Table 7.2, the share of education expenditure in GDP, as well as the share of education in total government expenditure, is lower than that in comparable developing countries in other regions. The region spends less than the global average of 4.2 per cent of GDP on education. Higher

Table 7.2   Public Expenditure on Education

Country	Public Expenditure on Education as % of GDP	Public Expenditure on Education as % of Total Government Expenditure	Public Expenditure per Pupil as a % of GDP per Capita (All Levels)	Public Expenditure on Education as % of GDP (Average 2003–8)	Education Expenditure as % of GDP	Higher Education Expenditure as % of GDP
South Asia						
Bangladesh	2.39	13.99	13.27	2.41	2.3[f]	0.75[f]
Bhutan	5.1	17.17[e]	29.15[b]	6.2	5.6[b]	
India	**3.18[f]**	10.73[c]	**14.04[f]**	3.37	3.8[f]	0.70[f]
Maldives	8.06	12.03	**24.78[f]**	7.86	7.1	
Nepal	3.78	14.89[c]	13.03[b]	3.45	3.81[f]	0.40[f]
Pakistan	2.91	**12.18[f]**	12.03[c]	2.42	1.84[f]	0.29[f]
Sri Lanka	–	–	–	–	3.1[e]	0.50[e]
Others						
South Africa	5.13	16.2	18.41[a]	5.27		
Malaysia	**4.67[f]**	25.2[d]	22.61[d]	6.39	6.81[g]	1.96[g]
Thailand	**4.52[f]**	25.02[f]	16.56[d]	4.3	4.72[g]	0.92[g]
Brazil	**4.95[f]**	**16.18[f]**	16.08[e]	4.5	3.86[d]	0.66[d]
United Kingdom	**5.64[f]**	**11.91[f]**	**25.78[f]**	5.47	6.08[f]	1.33[f]
United States	**5.7[f]**	**14.76[f]**	**23.89[f]**	5.63	7.70[f]	3.05[f]

Source: UNESCO Institute of Statistics. Available at http://stats.uis.unesco.org/ unesco/TableViewer/document.aspx?ReportId=143&IF_Language=eng, accessed on 25 March 2010; Agarwal (2009: 55, Table 14).
Notes: [a]1999, [b]2000, [c]2003, [d]2004, [e]2005, [f]2006, and [g]2001.
Average calculation = sum of (public exp on education (% of GDP))/n; n = years for which data is available.

education spending in overall public spending, and specifically in public spending on education, is also quite low by global standards. Thus there are financial constraints and there is inadequate prioritization of education in government expenditures.

The trend in educational indicators over time further indicates that although there has been improvement in some areas, such as in raising literacy rates or gross enrolment rates at some levels, by and large the extent of these improvements is rather limited. Table 7.3 shows the trends in enrolment and expenditure over the 1990–2007 period in each

Table 7.3 Education Sector Indicators in the South Asian Countries (1990, 2000, 2007 unless otherwise indicated)

Indicator	Year	Bangladesh	Bhutan	India	Maldives	Nepal	Pakistan	Sri Lanka
Gross primary enrolment rate (%)	1990	80	–	98.6	134.1	114	69[b]	113
	2000	78[b]	78[d]	94.1	134.5	117.9	69.3	113[b]
	2007	93.8	–	89.81	114.2	121	84.8	111[d]
	2008		106		112			
Gross secondary enrolment rate (%)	1990	20.2	–	44.5	56[b]	33	25.1	77
	2000	44	46[d]	46.2	54	35	29[d]	75[b]
	2007	43[d]	56[f]	54.0[b]	–	48	32.4	–
Gross tertiary enrolment rate (%)11	1990	4.1	–	6.2	–	4.1	3.5	5
	2000	5	3.1	9.6	–	4	5[d]	5[b]
	2007	7.0[e]	5.2	13.5	–	–	5.2	–
Primary drop-out rate (%)	1990	–	–	–	–	–	–	–
	2000	–	19	41.0	–	–	–	–
	2007	45.2	16[d]	34.21	15.6	38.43	30.32	1.19
Pupil–faculty ratio, primary	1990	63	–	47.0	–	39	44[b]	29
	2000	47[d]	31[d]	40.0	23	43	33	28[b]
	2007	45		40.2	15	40	40	22[d]
	2008	44	30	–	13	38	41	–
Public expenditure as % of GDP	1990	1	–	4.0	4	2	3	3
	2000	2	7[d]	4.0	8[d]	3	2	3[b]
	2007	2	5[f]	3.18	8	4	3	–
	2008	2.39	5.09	–	8.05	3.78	2.90	–
Literacy rate (%), 15–24	1990	35.32[a]	–	48.22[a]	96.0	32.98[a]	–	–
	2000	47.49[d]	52.81[d]	61.01[c]	96.3	48.59[c]	–	90.68[c]
	2007	53.5	–	66.00	97.0	56.5	54.15[e]	90.81[e]

Source: EdStats, World Bank, UNESCO Institute of Statistics. Literacy rates: http:// web.worldbank.org/WBSITE/EXTERNAL/TOPICS/EXTEDUCATION/ EXTDATASTATISTICS/EXTEDSTATS/0,,contentMDK:21605891~menuPK: 3409559~pagePK:64168445~piPK:64168309~theSitePK:3232764,00.html, accessed on 20 March 2010.

Note: [a]1991, [b]1995, [c]2001, [d]2005, [e]2006, and [f]2008.

of the South Asian countries. It indicates that most of the countries have witnessed very marginal improvements in key education sector indicators and often there has actually been deterioration in key areas, such as public expenditure, primary enrolment rates, and student–teacher ratios. Sri Lanka and the Maldives are the best placed within the region, with higher primary enrolment rates, lower drop-out rates, and lower student–faculty ratios.

Such limitations notwithstanding, the South Asian countries have witnessed considerable growth in their education systems in terms of enrolment numbers and number of educational institutions and universities. Several common features emerge as a result of this growth. The most important of these is the privatization of education and the growing contribution of private education providers in the past 10–15 years in almost all the South Asian countries, particularly in the higher education segment. Meanwhile, the public sector's contribution has declined and capacity constraints in this segment have grown.

Another important feature that characterizes the education sector in most South Asian countries is the dualism in the financing structure between the public and private segments. The private education system tends to be relatively expensive while the public education system is characterized by very low tuition fees and is highly subsidized by the government. This financing structure has resulted in problems of cost-recovery and difficulties in funding capacity increases in the public education system. The latter has in turn resulted in an inequitable education system and a marked disparity between the public and private segments, with growing demand and insufficient capacity in the lower cost public education system, and a more rapidly growing higher cost private education system which mainly caters to the higher income groups. Statistics from some of the countries reflect these common trends.

The Indian higher education system has seen tremendous growth, from 25 universities to 398 universities and from 700 to 18,064 colleges between 1950 and 2007, and from an enrolment of 0.1 million to 11.2 million over the same period. There is an out-turn of 2.46 million graduates per year (Agarwal 2009: 15, Table 6).

This makes India's higher education system the third largest in the world after China and the US. Today, India has the largest number of higher education institutions in the world (though the average size of each institution is small, indicating a high degree of fragmentation). The private segment has been the primary contributor to this growth.

Pakistan has also witnessed rapid growth in the higher education system. The number of public sector higher education institutions has grown from 676 in 1999–2000 to 841 by 2006–7, while the number of private higher education institutions has expanded from 146 to 414 over the same period. Enrolment increased from around 4.75 million to close to 6.5 million during this period (Agarwal 2009: 23, Table 8). As in the case of India, a bulk of this increase has been in the private sector.

There has been rapid privatization of the education system in Bangladesh as well, following the enactment of the country's Private University Act in 1992. The pace of enrolments in private universities has accelerated, from a mere 6,200 students in 16 private universities in 1997 to over 44,000 students in 52 private universities in 2003. Today, 43 per cent of overall university enrolment is in 54 recognized private universities (Agarwal 2009: 33). However, enrolment in private education still remains lower than that in public institutions even though the public system has witnessed a continuous decline in standards and has failed to keep pace with growing demand.

Nepal has similarly witnessed an expansion in private sector capacity with the opening up of this segment. This has been further aided by the provision of government grants to private educational institutions. The public education system has tended to lag behind the private sector which has mainly catered to higher income students.

Sri Lanka differs from the other larger countries in South Asia in that the involvement of the private sector in education tends to be more limited. While Sri Lanka has seen growth in the number of private institutions that have been allowed, the number offering degrees are few. Moreover, the general view is that the private providers should mainly meet the needs in areas which the government cannot fulfil and should provide subsidies to poor students. Hence, the private education system is seen as a supplement to the public education system, which does not prevent equitable access to education, a stance that is consistent with Sri Lanka's historical thrust on education, its near universal literacy, and high level of participation in secondary education.

In contrast to the other South Asian countries, the Maldives and Bhutan, given their small size, have very small education systems and have not experienced similar growth in enrolment rates or the number of providers. Bhutan's education system is at a nascent stage. There is currently no private sector involvement in the country's higher education and demand is met completely by the Royal University of Bhutan or through education at overseas institutions. The Maldives, like Sri Lanka, has very high adult literacy rates and high primary and secondary enrolment rates. It is, however, different from the other countries in that it has no university and thus higher education is obtained either through overseas training or through a limited number of degree granting public institutions, and over 80 registered private institutions that offer certificate and diploma courses in professional fields within the country (Agarwal 2009: 47). Increasingly, the Maldives has been facing skill shortages in key sectors, such as tourism and hospitality, which is mainly being met through inflows of foreign skilled workers. Hence, there is growing demand for training in selected areas and private institutions are expected to cater to this need.

Despite these privatization trends, capacity constraints in the education sector have grown, resulting in more and more students from South Asia going overseas for higher education. Today, the region is an important source for international students. In 2005, around 200,000 students from the region (including Afghanistan) were studying abroad and this number has been growing over the years despite capacity expansion in all the countries. The outward mobility ratio (share of mobile students to the total number of students in a country's higher education system), that is, the outflow of students as a proportion of the domestic capacity in higher education, is high for the smaller countries such as Bhutan (15), Maldives (33), and Nepal (5.3), reflecting their small education base (Agarwal 2009: 64, Table 19).

India accounts for 70 per cent of the outward mobility of students in South Asia. Around 140,000 Indian students went abroad to study in 2005 and the country imported higher education to the tune of US$ 3.5 billion in 2004. More than 20,000 Pakistani students went abroad for higher studies in 2005 and this number has been rising by 13–15 per cent per year. Likewise, in 2005, around 14,500 Bangladeshi students and 9,000 Nepalese students were studying abroad and around 1,000–1,500 Maldivian students were estimated to be overseas (Agarwal 2009: 64, Table 19). Similarly, due to the shortage of higher education opportunities in Sri Lanka, a large number of the country's students go overseas for higher studies. The main markets for South Asian students are the English speaking countries—the US, UK, Australia, Canada and others, such as Malaysia, Singapore, and several other developing countries, including India.

Overall, the picture that emerges is of a region which is unable to meet the demand for education due to its growing population, as reflected in rising student–faculty ratios, a region which is unable to devote sufficient resources to the education sector as reflected in declining or stagnant public expenditure allocated to this sector in overall GDP, and growing reliance on private providers and overseas institutions, and a region which is unable to address issues of quality and governance as reflected in relatively high drop-out rates in most of the countries. Hence, the region faces resource, capacity, and regulatory challenges in the education services sector. There is concern that despite liberalization of the education sector and steps to enhance capacity and quality, capacity expansion has not been rapid enough resulting in growing skill shortages.

Policies and Regulatory Trends

The South Asian region mirrors policy and regulatory trends seen in the rest of the world. As highlighted earlier, one of the main developments has been the privatization of education, which has also been the global trend. In addition to encouraging domestic education providers, another important regulatory development in education services in South Asia has been the opening up of the sector to foreign providers. This trend has potential regional ramifications.

Foreign Participation

There are many foreign educational institutions that are operating in South Asia, through twinning or partnership arrangements, local campuses, franchises, and certificate or diploma granting programmes. There is also some outward presence by the educational institutions in this region, mainly from India, which have set up their operations abroad in places like Dubai, Malaysia, and Singapore in order to serve the local student population and also students from the region, who are studying abroad in these markets.

In India, according to a 2005 study, there were 131 foreign education providers, mostly operating through twinning and collaborative programmes with local partner institutions (Agarwal 2009: 21). Most of these partnerships were with US and UK universities, in professional programmes, such as business and hotel management. Foreign providers in India have also been engaged in recruiting students from the region for study in their home campuses abroad. However, there are few franchise operations and no foreign campuses to date in India. The latter could change with the passage of a Foreign Higher Education Providers Bill that is pending Parliamentary approval. This bill, if passed into legislation, would allow 100 per cent FDI in India's higher education sector, including establishing foreign university campuses. It has, however, aroused considerable debate in India about the likely implications for domestic providers and for quality, standards, pricing, and equity, as well as the supporting domestic regulatory reforms that would be required to put local providers on an even playing field.

In Pakistan, foreign provision of education has been deemed to be important for enhancing capacity and competitiveness in the higher education system. Both public and private foreign institutions are allowed to operate in Pakistan and collaboration between foreign and local education providers is encouraged by the Higher Education Commission. There are eight collaborative degree programmes in Pakistan (not all of them approved) as well as programmes run by reputed foreign institutions with local partners, with only minimal regulation. There are also three campuses of some US schools which offer bachelor's and master's programmes in professional courses such as business studies (Agarwal 2009: 28–9). Pakistan has put emphasis on establishing high quality institutions in science and technology, in partnership with reputed foreign institutions, with staffing of foreign faculty and administrators and technology parks and incubators for enhancing linkages with industry.

Likewise, the other countries in South Asia have also promoted internationalization of the higher education sector. In Bangladesh, internationalization has resulted in a proliferation of private institutions (albeit of variable quality) that have partnership arrangements and joint ventures with foreign providers. In Sri Lanka, there are several higher education degree programmes that are offered by foreign universities in partnership with Sri Lankan institutions, as well as foreign institutes which offer higher education qualifications. Similarly, there are partnerships between domestic educational institutions and foreign ones in the Maldives to address the growing needs in the tourism and hospitality sector. The degree of internationalization in Nepal and Bhutan, in comparison to the other South Asian countries, remains comparatively limited. It has mainly been in the form of foreign assistance for setting up local educational institutions or for developing capacity in local universities.

Regulatory Challenges and Concerns

The privatization and internationalization of education services in South Asia has in turn given rise to several regulatory concerns and challenges, akin to those seen globally. These concerns relate to issues of quality assurance, standards, pricing, equity, and access and stem from the financing constraints and the growing segmentation between public and private providers mentioned earlier. For instance, in Pakistan, one of the main challenges is that public sector institutions, though equitable, lack in quality, while the private institutions that are of high quality, are often unaffordable for most people. The same holds true in the case of India and Bangladesh. There has been considerable debate in some of the countries regarding public versus private education providers and the implications of private (including foreign) providers for costs, quality, and equity.[2]

The countries in this region also suffer from problems of regulatory enforcement and monitoring. Although all the countries have put in place regulatory arrangements to govern the private sector, many of the domestic and foreign providers and partnership arrangements are outside the regulatory framework and are functioning without regulatory approvals. There are examples of domestic private institutions, as in the case of Pakistan, which have cheated students by advertising themselves as accredited branches or affiliates of US universities. In the case of Bangladesh, national regulatory authorities have not been able to control the growth of unrecognized affiliations and partnerships. Such regulatory weaknesses have led to concerns about the management and governance of institutions, and consumer protection.

Table A.18 (see Annexure at the end of the book) highlights key regulatory and policy developments in the region in the education sector. It shows that education services in South Asia are undergoing changes in terms of reorganization of departments and regulatory bodies. It is evident that the governments in this region are tackling federal and sub-federal issues, as well as issues of inter-departmental and inter-institutional coordination to ensure quality, relevance, inclusiveness, and effective overall management of the education system. Some of the countries are undergoing important developments in this sector, such as the Foreign Higher Education Providers Bill in India mentioned earlier. It is also evident that there is separate emphasis in several South Asian countries on technical and scientific education, with the establishment of separate bodies to focus on these segments. Table A.19 in the Annexure further highlights the degree to which the four larger South Asian countries—India, Bangladesh, Pakistan, and Sri Lanka—have opened up their higher education sectors and the entry and operational conditions imposed on foreign education providers under mode 3, or commercial presence as termed under the GATS. These indices show that the education sector is relatively open in all the countries, though the extent of liberalization varies in terms of the incidence and nature of restrictions on the form of participation, taxes, authorization requirements, and minimum investment conditions imposed on foreign education providers. The degree of openness is broadly similar across all the countries.

[2] See, for example, Wadood (2006).

Although there are information limitations in education services, Table A.18 (see Annexure) and Table 7.4 clearly highlight the fact that this is a sector where there are prospects for international participation in South Asia, including potentially, regional engagement. Moreover, the concerns and regulatory approaches appear to be broadly similar, reflecting similarities across the countries in terms of their educational status and the institutional and other challenges which they face.

Intra-regional Collaboration and Initiatives

The congruence of interests and approaches, policy trends, and regulatory concerns highlighted earlier, provides a potential basis for regional cooperation in South Asia, especially in areas, such as technical and scientific education, and in professional courses. At present, there is already some limited intra-regional engagement in education services, mainly in the form of student mobility within the region and through cross-border establishment of franchises and subsidiaries in other countries within the region.

Regional Student Mobility

As discussed earlier, the South Asian region is an important contributor to the global mobility of students. To some degree, part of this student mobility is also within the region, primarily to the Indian market, and mainly from the smaller countries in the region. India hosts international students, mainly from developing countries in Africa and Asia, including South Asia. In 2003–4, over 12,000 international students, including 7,830 South Asian students (including Afghanistan), were enrolled in Indian universities and institutions, although this number has declined from 13,707 in 1993–4 (Agarwal 2009: 65–6, Table 21). India is one of the main markets for Nepali students pursuing higher studies on a self-financing basis. Bhutan also sends its students for higher education mainly to India and to a lesser extent to other English speaking countries, such as Australia, Canada, and the UK. India is also one of the main destinations for Maldivian students studying abroad on scholarships or through self-financing. India received 320 Bangladeshi students in 2003, down from 736 in 1993–4, though it is likely that there are actually a larger number of Bangladeshi students in India. Data on outward mobility of South Asian students to top destinations for higher education show that India ranks among the top five host countries for students from Nepal and Bhutan. Most of these students come for training in professional courses, such as IT and management. For instance, there are well-established IT training institutions, such as Aptech, which have special programmes (Aptech's India Window Programme) to deliver IT courses to foreign students from Asia and Africa.[3] There are also lesser known, aspirant business schools, such as the Aryans Business School (ABS), a business and technology school in Chandigarh, which is targeting students from SAARC countries for admission at affordable prices in various professional courses (MBA, MCA, BBA, BCA, BSc in IT, and e-MBA), followed by placements. The school has made visits to Nepal and Bangladesh to assess the requirements of students in those countries and to tie-up with potential educational institutions there.[4]

Apart from India, the other South Asian countries are comparatively not so important as destination markets for students seeking higher education in the region. Bangladesh plays host to a very limited extent. For instance, some of the private universities in Bangladesh are host to foreign students from other developing countries, including Sri Lanka and Nepal. In 2005, Pakistan and Bangladesh hosted 748 and 389 foreign students, respectively, but the breakdown in terms of the number of students originating in other South Asian countries is not available.

Table 7.4 shows the number of students from South Asia as well as other regions going to India for higher education during 2001–4. The numbers clearly indicate that Asian countries followed by African countries account for a majority of the foreign students studying in India. Asia accounted for over 50 per cent of all overseas students in 2001, of which the South Asian countries (excluding Afghanistan) constituted over 40 per cent of all overseas students.

Although South Asia continues to be the most important source region for inflows of international students into India, it is worth noting that the number of students coming to India from other South Asian countries has been declining, with the region's share falling to around 30 per cent in 2004. This reflects India's declining attractiveness as a destination market for higher education for South Asian students, given

---

[3] The Indian government has empanelled Aptech for its ITEC/SCAAP programme for international students. Under this programme, Aptech conducts courses in Delhi for participants from many developing countries, including some in South Asia. The Government of India funds this programme and also provides a monthly stipend and airfare to the participants. See http://www.aptech-globaltraining.com/html/itec.htm, accessed on 24 February 2010.

[4] See http://www.thaindian.com/newsportal/business/chandigarh-business-school-opens-doors-for-saarc-countries_10069637.html#xzz0bd4xhPNG, accessed on 24 February 2010.

Table 7.4 Inward Student Mobility from South Asia and Other Regions to India, 2001–4

	Number of Students					% of All Students				
	2000	2001	2002	2003	2004	2000	2001	2002	2003	2004
International (or internationally mobile) students from Africa	2,558	2,969	2,369	1,893	1,694	36.61	38.11	29.09	24.46	22.32
Students from Africa, country not specified	6	2	5	–	–					
International (or internationally mobile) students from North America, Central America, and the Caribbean	275	323	418	343	468	3.94	4.15	5.13	4.43	6.17
Students from North America, country not specified	–	–	–	–	–					
International (or internationally mobile) students from South America	–	4	14	10	551	–	0.05	0.17	0.13	7.26
Students from South America, country not specified	–	–	–	–	544					
International (or internationally mobile) students from Asia	4,004	3,866	4,314	4,452	4,749	57.30	49.62	52.97	57.53	62.58
Students from Bangladesh	–	576	545	372	319	–	14.90	12.63	8.36	6.72
Students from Bhutan	520	175	254	227	174	12.99	4.53	5.89	5.10	3.66
Students from Maldives	18	10	14	34	20	0.45	0.26	0.32	0.76	0.42
Students from Nepal	772	821	873	801	681	19.28	21.24	20.24	17.99	14.34
Students from Pakistan	9	5	3	3	1	0.22	0.13	0.07	0.07	0.02
Students from Sri Lanka	485	383	504	391	351	12.11	9.91	11.68	8.78	7.39
Students from Asia, country not specified	512	3	6	6	–	12.79	0.08	0.14	0.13	–
International (or internationally mobile) students from Europe	120	180	251	138	127	1.72	2.31	3.08	1.78	1.67
Students from Europe, country not specified	–	–	2	–	–					
International (or internationally mobile) students from Oceania	31	44	45	40	–	0.44	0.56	0.55	0.52	–
Students from Oceania, country not specified	–	–	–	–	–					
International (or internationally mobile) students (Total)	6,988	7,791	8,145	7,738	7,589	100	100	100	100	100

Source: http://www.atlas.iienetwork.org/page/135351/, accessed on 16 March 2010.

Table 7.5 Inward Student Mobility from Different Countries in Asia to
Pakistan, 2003

	Total (in numbers)	Share
International (or internationally mobile) students from Asia	262	100
Students from Afghanistan	116	44.27
Students from Bangladesh	8	3.05
Students from China	17	6.49
Students from Indonesia	2	0.76
Students from Iran, Islamic Republic of	12	4.58
Students from Iraq	1	0.38
Students from Japan	1	0.38
Students from Jordan	12	4.58
Students from Korea (Democratic People's Republic of)	1	0.38
Students from Myanmar	1	0.38
Students from Nepal	2	0.76
Students from Oman	1	0.38
Students from Palestinian Autonomous Territories	33	12.60
Students from Saudi Arabia	7	2.67
Students from Syrian Arab Republic	15	5.73
Students from Tajikistan	3	1.15
Students from Turkey	17	6.49
Students from United Arab Emirates	5	1.91
Students from Yemen	8	3.05

Source: http://stats.uis.unesco.org/unesco/TableViewer/document.aspx? ReportId=136
&IF_Language=eng&BR_Topic=0, accessed on 7 April 2010.

the growing affluence within the region with more students capable of
affording higher education in the West, as well as the growing number
of competing destinations within Asia, such as Malaysia and Singapore.

Though the number of foreign students in the other South Asian countries is very small, the pattern is similar. As seen in Table 7.5, Asian countries
are the main source of foreign students in Pakistan, the most important
origin country being Afghanistan (also a SAARC member). However,
inflows of students from the other SAARC countries are negligible.

Regional Investment

Another important means of intra-regional engagement in education services, again mostly in higher and professional education services, is through
investments in the form of local branches, franchises, subsidiaries, and tie-
ups with local partner institutions. As in the case of student mobility, where

student flows were primarily from the other countries to India, here too, the flows are largely one-way, with investments flowing from Indian educational institutions to the other South Asian countries. To date, however, these investments are rather limited in terms of sectoral orientation as well as the range of institutions. They are mostly confined to the areas of medical education and information technology and a few Indian institutions such as Manipal, NIIT, and Aptech. At the school level, there are few such investment ventures, one of these being the Delhi Public School franchise in Kathmandu.

One of the most prominent examples of regional investment and collaboration in education is the Manipal College of Medical Science (MCOMS), Pokhara, which was established in Nepal in collaboration with the Government of Nepal in 1994, and is affiliated to Kathmandu University. This is a well-recognized institute and is listed in the WHO Directory of Medical Schools and the International Medical Education Directory of Educational Commission for Foreign Medical Graduates (ECFMG). The institute has also been recognized by the Medical Councils of Nepal, Sri Lanka, Bangladesh, Mauritius, India, and the California Medical Board. It offers undergraduate and postgraduate degree programmes in medicine, dentistry, nursing, pharmacy, allied health, and other disciplines to address the shortage of medical and dental faculties with specialty training in Nepal. Manipal University and Kathmandu University have also signed an agreement for academic cooperation.

In the information technology area, NIIT, the Indian software and training company has opened learning centres in several countries in South Asia.[5] It has centres in Nepal, Sri Lanka, Bhutan, and Bangladesh, for instance, often with multiple centres in the same city, including second tier cities. Some of these branches are managed directly by NIIT while others are in partnership with local institutions. NIIT's partner in Kathmandu and Patan is CIS Pvt. Ltd. while its branch in Pokhara is managed directly by NIIT. The institute has 12 training centres in Bangladesh, not only in Dhaka but in smaller towns, such as Uttarpara and Narayanganj.

Another important Indian IT education company, Aptech, has also forayed into the regional market to provide IT training and software solutions through the franchisee route. Recently, it was exploring opportunities to venture into Sri Lanka in the IT education and animation business market. It has plans to take the Maya Academy of Advanced Cinematics (MAAC) animation brand to Sri Lanka (having acquired this academy to strengthen

[5] NIIT has over 1,900 computer education centres in over 26 countries.

its animation portfolio).[6] Aptech's international division has established its presence in Bangladesh through multiple centres and accounts for 40 per cent of the IT training market in that country. Aptech's overseas (and Indian) centres also have twinning programmes with overseas universities, such as for a bachelor's degree in information technology, wherein following two years of study at Aptech centres, including those in other South Asian countries, students may be eligible for a one year programme at the overseas university.[7]

Apart from these few examples of globally spread institutions like Manipal, NIIT, and Aptech, there is little information available on other regional investments by South Asian education and training institutes. This in part indicates the absence of international players in the region, particularly in countries other than India. It also reflects the relative lack of interest in the South Asian market compared to other regions such as West or Southeast Asia.[8]

Collaborative Ventures and Inter-governmental Cooperation

The importance of eradicating illiteracy and realizing universal primary education has been highlighted in several SAARC summit declarations. Commitments have been made and even a SAARC Literacy Year was declared as far back as 1996. The focus in the initial years was in areas of technical cooperation, such as in science and technology, health, culture, rural development, and agriculture. In 1998, the SAARC governments specifically included education as an agreed area of cooperation. Several issues have since then been highlighted in regional discussions with regard to cooperation in education services.

SAARC heads of state have called for regional initiatives and sharing of best practices and experiences in order to better utilize the region's resources, raise the quality of education, and undertaking strategic interventions in training, management, and performance evaluation. For example, the 12th SAARC Summit noted the importance of investing in human resources for the future development of South Asia and thus the need to set up a

[6] See http://www.siliconindia.com/shownews/Aptech_looks_to_enter_Sri_Lanka_-nid- 65406.html/1/1, http://www.thehindubusinessline.com/2010/02/12/stories/ 2010021252040500.htm; http://www.aptech-globaltraining.com/html/itec.htm (accessed on 24 February 2010).

[7] Aptech has such an alliance with the Southern Cross University, which is an internationally recognized Australian government university. See http://www.aptech-globaltraining.com/html/itec.htm, accessed on 26 March 2010.

[8] Some such examples are BITS which has set up a campus in Dubai, or Bhavan's International or Delhi Public School, which have franchises in the Middle East and in Singapore.

network of centres of higher learning and training and skill development institutes across South Asia and the critical role that could be played by the SAARC Human Resource Development Centre. Other issues that have been discussed include the promotion of higher and vocational education in the region and mutual recognition of educational institutions so as to realize the goal of a common regional educational standard. The concept of open learning and distance education and capacity building has also been discussed at various summits. It has been suggested that a SAARC Forum of Vice Chancellors of Open Universities be established in the region to build on existing expertise through the sharing and joint development of programmes and credit transfers for specific programmes. Heads of states have also urged the development of distance education outside the open university system by drawing on information technology and the need to utilize institutional facilities in education on a regional scale and possibly creating a consortium of open universities in the region.[9] There have also been initiatives to evolve common educational standards through uniform teaching aids and methods of instruction. Some agreement has been reached on minimum qualifications for a bachelor's degree and on the criteria for recognition of degrees awarded by universities in the region.

Notwithstanding such declarations and initiatives, to date, there is little on the ground and the scale of cooperation remains limited. There are a few examples of inter-governmental collaboration in partnership with industry, particularly in the area of IT training and support. For example, the Government of India is funding a 2.5 million Ngultrum 'Total Solutions' project in Bhutan. The aim of this project is to help create a knowledge-based Bhutanese society by providing access to IT and IT solutions to a large proportion of Bhutan's population, including government officials, teachers, entrepreneurs, and rural children. Under this project, ICT-enabled schools, computer labs, and computer stations would be set up in rural Bhutan over the next five years. The industry partner is NIIT, which is lending support to the Total Solutions project to improve computer skills in the country through a huge IT literacy programme. The Bhutanese government has also held discussions with IT majors, such as Infosys, seeking their support for developing IT infrastructure in the country.[10]

[9] See declarations at various SAARC summits, available at http://www.saarc-sec.org/data, accessed on 2 December 2009.

[10] See http://in.news.yahoo.com/20/20100214/372/tbs-niit-to-help-people-of-bhutan-improv.html, accessed on 24 February 2010; http://www.bbs.com.bt/PM%20and%20NIIT%20Chairman%20meet%20to%20discuss%20IT%20project.html, accessed on 24 February 2010.

A recent important development in inter-governmental cooperation is the establishment of the South Asian University (SAU) in New Delhi. This idea had first been mooted at the 13th SAARC Summit in November 2005 with the aim of providing world class facilities and professional faculty to students and researchers from SAARC countries. Subsequent to this, an inter-governmental agreement was signed for establishing this university at the 14th SAARC Summit in April 2007 and finally the establishment of this university and India's financial commitment to this initiative (at US$ 239.9 million or 79 per cent of the total cost of the full establishment until 2014) was approved by the Indian Parliament in 2008. The proposed university would also try to harmonize academic standards and accreditation norms in teaching, research, and curriculum in the region.[11]

The SAU is expected to become operational in the second half of 2010 with a postgraduate academic programme and some 5,000 students. It would grant diplomas, certificates, and degrees. This step has been described as the 'largest visible sign of transformation of SAARC from declaratory to implementation'. The SAU would be the first international university to be set up in India, with link campuses in the other SAARC member countries. The real estate cost of Rs 750 million has been borne by the Indian External Affairs Ministry and contributions for other expenses are to be determined on a participatory basis. The role of the SAARC governments would be to provide annual subsidies while full autonomy would be granted to the university. Thus, the SAU is conceived as a government-funded private education institution.[12] It is of course too early to comment about the SAU but it is a clear reflection of India's asymmetric commitment within SAARC.

There are some other initiatives to establish regional institutions, though information is too scanty to enable an analysis of their likely impact. For example, there is a plan to make the Nalanda University into a modern international university which will cater to issues pertaining to South Asian countries. The plan is to upgrade the university to an international centre for excellence in the field of education and to promote

[11] See 'India Moves to set up South Asian University', October 2008 available at http://timesofindia.indiatimes.com/articleshow/msid-3659792.prtpage-1.cms, accessed on 1 January 2010.

[12] See http://economictimes.indiatimes.com/News/News_By_Industry/Services/Education/South_Asian_Univ_to_offer_science_arts_courses_together/rssarticleshow/3227901.cms and http://www.saarc-sec.org/main.php?t=2.9.6, accessed on 1 January 2010.

regional cooperation and understanding within South Asia.[13] Bilateral cooperation initiatives also exist, such as between Bangladesh and Sri Lanka, wherein both countries have stated their intent to cooperate in several service sectors, including education.

There are also regional scholarship schemes. The Indian government has introduced the SAARC Fellowship and Scholarship Scheme to promote interaction among students, academics, and researchers from SAARC countries. Under the SAARC Scholarship Scheme, six fellowships and 12 scholarships are offered each year to the nationals of SAARC member countries in the areas of economics, education, environment, agriculture, mass communication, language and literature, sociology, transport engineering, applied economics, master of business administration, biochemistry, social work, food technology, and home science. Only those courses are offered for which there are no adequate facilities in the member countries. In addition to the scholarship, one Chair is also awarded to a member country on a rotation basis. The SAARC Secretariat decides the terms and conditions of these awards.[14]

There has also been discussion among the member governments to create a South Asian regional network on knowledge, research, and innovation which would connect all the countries in the region. This network would be aimed at tapping the synergies that exist at the regional level in terms of information sharing, expertise and knowledge in universities and non-university teaching and research centres, and various knowledge institutions. It has also been proposed to set up a regional high bandwidth, high speed internet based network to bring together knowledge workers in a variety of disciplines and help build regional databases to address the problems of the region through joint research and initiatives.[15]

Multilateral Commitments

Trade in education services under the GATS is covered under five categories— primary education, secondary education, higher education, adult education, and other education services. During the Uruguay Round, only 29 member countries made commitments in education services. Thus the

[13] This initiative has the support of other countries such as China, Japan, Singapore, Thailand, Cambodia, and Vietnam. See http://www.indiaedunews.neet/Inocus/November_2009/Nalanda_International_University_on_SAARC's_fast_track_9459/, accessed on 30 December 2009.

[14] See http://india.gov.in/overseas/passport.php, accessed on 4 January 2010.

[15] See http://web.worldbank.org/WBSITE/EXTERNAL/COUNTRIES/SOUTHAS IAEXT/0.,contentMDK:21746367~pagePK:146736~piPK:146830~theSite:223547,00. html, accessed on 1 January 2010.

sector was not a thrust area for negotiations in the WTO. This is also true for the South Asian countries. Barring Nepal which acceded only recently to the WTO and had to undertake more extensive service sector commitments, none of the other member countries from this region have scheduled education services in the Uruguay Round of GATS negotiations. This implies that the South Asian countries, notwithstanding their autonomous liberalization of this sector, would like to preserve their policy flexibility by excluding this sector from their scheduling commitments. India and Pakistan have, however, tabled education services in the subsequent request-offer negotiations, reflecting the fact that these countries have received requests in this sector from other WTO member countries and have also become more willing to negotiate this sector given their autonomous liberalization of education services since the Uruguay Round. Sri Lanka, Bangladesh, and the Maldives have, however, not changed their stance in education services (Table 7.6).

The commitments and offers vary in nature. India has been the most restrictive, offering only higher education, with various regulatory conditions imposed on foreign education providers. Nepal on the other hand has made commitments in three segments of education services, but has placed foreign equity participation limits and also phased in liberalization by gradually relaxing this limit. The negotiating stance of both these countries suggests that even where education services have been tabled by the South Asian countries, there has been an attempt to preserve regulatory autonomy in the interests of consumer protection and quality assurance. Pakistan is an exception in that it has not only tabled three segments in education services but also made unrestricted offers in modes 1, 2, and 3. Overall, the South Asian countries reflect a reluctance to multilaterally commit to full-fledged liberalization in education services so as to safeguard their concerns in this sector. However, where commitments or offers have been made, these are not highly restrictive.

Education services are not explicitly an important sector in the trade and cooperation agreements signed by the South Asian countries with countries outside the region. A few of the regional and bilateral agreements signed by the countries in South Asia cover education services. Some of these agreements also address areas that have a bearing on education services, including areas such as research and development services, IT training, mutual recognition, and human resource development. Most significant among these are the India-Singapore CECA and the Pakistan-China FTA. But on the whole, education services are not a high priority sector for the South Asian countries in their extra-regional agreements in the multilateral context.

Table 7.6 Status of Multilateral Commitments and Offers in Education Services by the South Asian Countries

Sector/Sub-sector	Uruguay Round Commitments	Conditional Initial Offer	Revised Offer
Bangladesh	**April 1995**		
Education services not scheduled or offered			
India	**April 1995**	**12 January 2004**	**24 August 2005**
Higher education services	Sector not scheduled	Sector not scheduled	1. None subject to the regulations as applicable to domestic providers in country of origin 2. None 3. None but subject to condition that fees charged can be fixed by appropriate regulatory authority and not lead to charging capitation fees or profiteering. FIPB approval required for foreign investors having prior collaboration 4. Unbound except as in the horizontal section
Maldives	**April 1995**		
Education services not scheduled or offered			
Nepal	**Date of submission: 30 August 2004**		
Higher education services/ adult education services/ other education	1. None 2. None 3. None, except only through incorporation in Nepal and with maximum foreign equity capital of 51 per cent and except for education services funded from state resources. Foreign equity participation will be increased to 80 per cent after five years from the date of accession 4. Unbound except as indicated in the horizontal section		
Pakistan	**April 1995**	**30 May 2005**	

	April 1995	September 2003
Higher education services (excludes public funded institutions)	Sector not scheduled	1. None 2. None 3. None 4. Unbound
Adult education	Sector not scheduled	1. None 2. None 3. None 4. Unbound
Other education services		1. None 2. None 3. None 4. Unbound

Sri Lanka   **April 1995**   **September 2003**

Education services not scheduled or offered

Source: Based on WTO member countries' GATS Commitment and Offer Schedules.

Areas for Regional Cooperation

The preceding discussion indicates that there are several factors which provide a good basis for greater intra-regional engagement and cooperation in education services in South Asia. The systems of higher education, where regional cooperation and commerce are likely to be concentrated, are quite similar. The academic systems, administrative structures, teaching and examination systems, and overall ethos of the education sector are broadly similar across the countries in South Asia. Enrolment rates tend to be low in higher education and the region is characterized by an elitist education system. Also, as is evident, government policies and efficacy in regulating quality tend to be weak in all the countries and there has generally been a rapid unplanned growth in higher education.

There are several broad segments or issues in the education services sector which could be addressed regionally. These include cross-border mobility of students within the region (which as noted has been declining in recent years), cross-border investments in the education sector through franchises, joint ventures, subsidiaries, and twinning and collaborative arrangements, distance education and ICT-based programmes, and harmonization of standards as well as mutual recognition of selected degrees, programmes, and institutions within the region. In each of these areas, initiatives are required to address some cross-cutting impediments to regional cooperation and commercial relations.

As highlighted earlier, one of the most promising areas is the pursuit of higher education by SAARC students within the region, mainly at Indian higher education institutions. While the ability of key host countries in the region, such as India, would in large part depend on their domestic capacity and quality, several issues need to be addressed to ease mobility of students within the region. One key issue is the visa regime for students who travel to another SAARC country to pursue training or higher education. This could be eased, at least for selective programmes, courses, and institutions. Today, foreign students coming on a self-financing basis or under scholarships are often required to go through cumbersome visa regulations and documentation requirements when coming to India for studies. Likewise, regional mobility of researchers and faculty and pooling of training resources from within the region are constrained by visa restrictions. The visa terms and conditions and the degree of restrictiveness also vary across different source countries in SAARC (with more liberal conditions for students from Nepal and Bhutan in the case of India). In the case of some degrees, 'No objection certificates' may be required from the Indian government. The visa issue has been a very important one, in that Pakistan had made its support for the South Asian University campus in India conditional on resolving issues pertaining to the free movement of students, teachers, faculty, and visiting professors. Although the Indian Prime Minister had announced the unilateral liberalization of visas for students, teachers, professors (and other groups such as patients and journalists) at the 14th SAARC Summit, this has not been implemented in practice.

In addition to addressing visa issues, another step which could facilitate regional mobility among students is the introduction of more regional scholarship schemes, funded by governments and by industry or industry associations for selected programmes and courses in SAARC countries. For instance, industry associations such as the National Association of Software and Services Companies (NASSCOM) in India, the Sri Lanka Association of Software and Service Companies (SLASSCOM) in Sri Lanka, or major IT firms could fund scholarships for SAARC students. They could also tie-up with universities and training institutions in the region for students enrolled in IT and computer application courses, and could also provide employment opportunities on completion of training.

The second area where regional cooperation needs to be enhanced is in facilitating cross-border investments, by easing regulations for setting up educational establishments and by encouraging more twinning and partnership programmes. Although the sector is relatively open, the governments could streamline regulatory approval processes further and help investors identify programmes, courses, and local partner institutions, with the aim of raising domestic standards, improving curricula, and encouraging partnerships with local institutions. Investments could also be facilitated with a broader view than merely encouraging commercial presence by regional players. For instance, investments in the education sector could be used to encourage twinning programmes and joint courses, hence also encouraging cross-border student flows within the region. Governments could also encourage SAARC-based companies investing in sectors outside of education services, such as in IT or healthcare, to provide financial, technical, and infrastructural support for government education initiatives in these sectors. Thus investment liberalization in other services could serve as a basis for regional companies to provide education and training inputs through customized courses and programmes, and tie-ups with local institutions. Regional investment in education and training services can also help in spurring research and development in areas of common interest to the region and for capacity building of researchers and trainers.

Governments in the region could actively encourage local and regional institutions to partner in joint research and development activities in fields, such as literature, history, medical science, agriculture, biotechnology, and natural sciences.

A third segment with regional prospects is distance education and ICT-enabled training. Distance education is of common interest to all the countries in this region as a means to providing greater accessibility to education and raising literacy. Since some countries in the region have considerable experience in providing distance education through open universities and through industry-government partnerships, this experience could be drawn upon by the less experienced countries. Again, IT and telecom industry partners could help the region's governments in such initiatives by extending the technical and infrastructural support and investments required in these sectors and thus provide the basis for such educational collaboration. Countries could also learn from the experiences of other SAARC members with regulation and monitoring of long distance providers. Public-private partnership models could also be explored.

Last but not least, there is need for regulatory cooperation among the SAARC countries on issues of mutual recognition, accreditation, and equivalence of standards and degrees. Some steps have been taken by establishing minimum qualifications, but more needs to be done through discussions among regulatory bodies, professional associations, governments, and private players in the region. It may be useful to tier educational and training institutions in different fields, programmes, and courses, so as to prioritize those where regional cooperation would be most beneficial, and to facilitate the steps mentioned earlier, in terms of investments, partnerships, distance education, or joint research, for the selected fields and courses. Over time, with experience and greater convergence of standards, the list of institutions and programmes can be gradually expanded. To the extent that several countries in the region have opened up their education sector to foreign providers, the associated development of their regulatory frameworks would also help their move towards regional harmonization of standards.

Thus, the range of private and governmental initiatives that could be undertaken to promote cooperation in education services is quite extensive. However, none of these initiatives can take off on a large scale unless the cross-cutting issues of visas, mutual recognition, and regulatory frameworks are addressed. Governments also need to be cognizant of the synergies between investments in other sectors and the education sector and the potential spin-off benefits from opening up in other areas for promoting cooperation in education services. A possible step would be to move beyond the establishment of a South Asia University to create a South Asia Higher Education Area (SAHEA) along the lines of the Europe Higher Education Area so as to deepen regional integration in education services. Given the social cum commercial objectives in this sector, a gradual approach would be desirable, including initiatives covering specific programmes and institutions and pilot projects and over time expanding the scale and scope of cooperation. India would need to play an important role given its dominant position in this sector within the region.

8

South Asia's Multilateral and Regional Commitments in Services

The opportunities and challenges to services integration in South Asia have been highlighted in the previous chapters for five different service sectors. If these opportunities are to be realized and the challenges are to be addressed, then the scope of any prospective agreement on services in South Asia, as well as the nature of the commitments made by the SAARC member countries under such an agreement, will play an important role. To some extent, the prospects for regional integration in services in South Asia can be inferred by examining the multilateral commitments and negotiating positions of the SAARC member countries in the service sector, as well as their stance on services liberalization under other bilateral and extra-regional agreements. The following discussion provides this comparative analysis of service sector commitments by the South Asian countries in different negotiating forums.

The chapter begins with priority issues for the South Asian countries in multilateral trade negotiations in general, with specific regard to the service sector. This is followed by an overview of the commitments made by the member countries of this region in the GATS negotiations and assesses the extent to which they have been willing to commit multilaterally, how these commitments compare with their unilateral liberalization in the service sector, and overall what their GATS commitments indicate about their domestic preparedness and negotiating stance in different services and modes of supply. The chapter then assesses these countries' service sector commitments in the context of various bilateral and extra-regional agreements and how the latter compare with their multilateral and unilateral liberalization of services trade and investment. Based on this comparative analysis of liberalization undertaken, as well as committed to in various forums, the chapter finally discusses the prospects for regional liberalization of services under an expanded SAFTA.

Participation in the WTO[1]

The South Asian countries have participated in the multilateral trading system to varying degrees. The four larger countries of Bangladesh, India, Pakistan, and Sri Lanka are founder members of the WTO since its establishment on 1 January 1995. Earlier they were members of the GATT. Among the smaller countries, the Maldives became a WTO member on 31 May 1995, Nepal subsequently acceded to the WTO on 23 April 2003, while Bhutan commenced its process of accession to the WTO in September 1999 but a government decision on WTO membership is still pending.

All the South Asian countries have been affected by the multilateral trading system in terms of market access for their key commodity exports and also in terms of their own commitments to liberalize tariff and non-tariff barriers. Bangladesh, India, Pakistan, and Sri Lanka have been actively engaged in the on-going Doha Development Round discussions across various sectors and issues, including the negotiations on agriculture, non-agricultural market access, and services, IPRs, aid, and development, albeit in varying capacities and to varying degrees. All of them have a keen interest in seeing a successful conclusion to the Doha Round, given the latter's likely implications for their trade and development objectives, including those of food and livelihood security, poverty alleviation, employment creation, and market access, among others. While many issues and concerns have been common among the countries, given differences in their size and levels of development, there have been resulting differences in their obligations and affiliations to various sub-groups under the WTO. This in turn has resulted in important differences in the nature of their participation and their priorities and concerns in the WTO negotiations.

In the agriculture negotiations, issues of food security, rural development, and livelihood concerns have been the priority areas for all the South Asian countries. In addition, as members of the G-22, India and Pakistan have also been involved in the negotiations on agricultural tariff cut formulas, and India in particular, has been a key player in the discussions on special safeguard measures and the removal of domestic support for agricultural products in developed countries. As members of the G-33 and G-90, Sri Lanka and Bangladesh, respectively, have focused on issues of food and

[1] South Asian Journal Conference, 29–30 April 2006, Islamabad, Group XIV, Coordinator Rajesh Mehta, available at http://www.southasianmedia.net/conference/conference_envisioning/vision_goup_xiv.htm, accessed on 17 September 2009; and South Asia in the WTO, concept note, Institute of Policy Studies of Sri Lanka, Colombo and Friedrich Ebert Stiftung, Colombo.

livelihood security issues and on the implications of removing export subsidies for net food-importing developing nations.

In the context of Non-Agricultural Market Access (NAMA) negotiations, the main focus area for India, Pakistan, and Sri Lanka has been the tariff reduction formula and the resulting tariff cuts on industrial products in these countries. India has also been actively engaged in the discussions on anti-concentration provisions and the sectoral zero-by-zero proposal. The LDC countries of Bangladesh, Nepal, and the Maldives are exempt from tariff reduction commitments and thus have been primarily concerned with issues of preference erosion and special and differential treatment. Hence, while the larger and more advanced countries in South Asia have been concerned about the market access implications of the NAMA negotiations and the fall-out for their domestic industries, the smaller less developed countries of the region have mainly been interested in retaining their preferences and extending them through other means, such as duty quota free access.

Interest in the GATS Negotiations

The South Asian countries have also been proactive players in the GATS discussions, in line with the growing role of the service sector and its growth potential in their economies, the significance of services for their infrastructural and institutional development, and the importance of certain services and modes of delivery in their export baskets. It is perhaps in the service sector that the South Asian countries have had a clear offensive agenda, centred around the issue of mode 4, or movement of natural persons, reflecting the significance of labour exports as a source of foreign exchange earnings and remittances for these countries.

Several of the South Asian countries have expressed their dissatisfaction with the existing commitments in mode 4 which do not address the categories and skills of interest to developing countries and continue to apply discretionary and non-transparent barriers to movement of service providers from developing countries. India and Pakistan have been active players in the 'Friends of Mode 4' grouping and have pushed for greater and more transparent market access in this mode, and the expansion of mode 4 commitments to cover categories, such as independent professionals and contractual service suppliers that are of interest to developing countries. India had also submitted a model schedule for undertaking mode 4 commitments. However, such proposals and templates for liberalization have not succeeded in either altering the scope and depth of commitments and subsequent offers in mode 4 or in addressing the various regulatory mechanisms affecting mode 4. India has also pushed for liberalization of commitments in mode 1 and has contributed to a collective proposal for liberalizing this mode, in order to pre-empt future protectionism in outsourcing, where India is a leading player in the global market.

The larger South Asian countries have also come under considerable pressure from leading developed countries to liberalize their key service sectors. They have been recipients of requests from the developed countries to open up services, such as telecommunication, banking, insurance, legal, accountancy, education, environmental, and retail distribution services, particularly through commercial presence, or mode 3. The thrust of these requests has been to relax limits on foreign equity participation in various services, to remove restrictions on the form of foreign commercial presence, and to streamline regulations and improve their transparency. However, as the following discussion and summary tables reveal, by and large, there has been a general reluctance on the part of the South Asian countries to commit liberally across a wide range of services or to improve upon their Uruguay Round services commitments during the subsequent request-offer discussions that have been underway since 2000. Most of them have not submitted initial or revised offers to improve upon their earlier Uruguay Round commitments, though they have unilaterally undertaken considerable liberalization in their service sectors (as highlighted in the previous chapters). Overall, the South Asian countries have had an offensive as well as defensive approach to services negotiations.

Multilateral Commitments in Services

An examination of the GATS commitments made by the South Asian countries clearly reflects the modest scope and conservative nature of their multilateral undertakings, especially when compared with the autonomous liberalization that they have undertaken in various service sectors. As shown later in this chapter, of the 12 GATS sectors that can be scheduled for negotiations, only Nepal has scheduled more than half, with 11 sectors committed. India and Pakistan rank second in terms of the scope of their GATS commitments, with six services scheduled. The other member countries have scheduled three or fewer services for commitments. The wider scope of Nepal's commitments reflects its later accession to the WTO and therefore the resulting compulsions to undertake more extensive obligations than the existing members.

However, what is more revealing is that of the many sub-sectors that could potentially be committed to under the GATS, the number of sub-sectors is less than 50 for all the countries. Most of the countries have committed in very few sub-sectors indicating that even within the limited number of sectors that they have scheduled, they are prepared to commit in very few segments (Figure 8.1). Thus, not only is the coverage across services limited, it is also limited within individual services that are scheduled. Overall, there is clearly unwillingness to liberalize services multilaterally.

There has been some improvement in the commitment stance in the request-offer process, though not uniformly. Of the three countries that tabled initial offers during the Doha Round of service negotiations, there was a moderate increase in the number of overall service sectors scheduled by

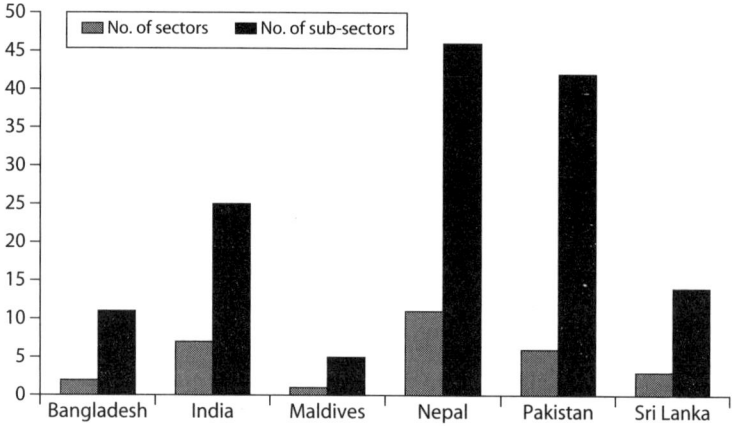

Figure 8.1 Number of Service Sectors and Sub-sectors Committed in the GATS by South Asian Countries

Source: Based on WTO Council for Trade in Services, Uruguay Round GATS Schedules of Commitments for the selected countries.[2]

[2] World Trade Organization, Council for Trade in Services, 'India: Schedule of Specific Commitments', GATS/SC/42, Geneva, 15 April 1994; World Trade Organization, Council for Trade in Services, 'Communication from the Maldives: Schedule of Specific Commitments under the GATS', GATS/SC/101, Geneva, 30 August 1995; World Trade Organization, Council for Trade in Services, 'The Kingdom of Nepal: Schedule of Specific Commitments', GATS/SC/139, Geneva, 30 August 2004; World Trade Organization, Council for Trade in Services, 'Pakistan: Schedule of Specific Commitments', GATS/SC/67, Geneva, 15 April 1994; World Trade Organization, Council for Trade in Services, 'Sri Lanka: Schedule of Specific Commitments', GATS/SC/79, Geneva, 15 April 1994.

Pakistan and India and a doubling of the number of sub-sectors committed in the case of Pakistan. India's initial conditional offer shows only a marginal increase in the number of sectors and sub-sectors. However, it is the only South Asian country to have tabled a revised offer, with a more than doubling of the number of sub-sectors committed in the initial offer. Thus, for both these countries, there has been some willingness to expand the scope of commitments with increased number of service sectors and sub-sectors, particularly the latter. One can infer that there is greater preparedness to expand commitments within already scheduled services rather than tabling more services for negotiations. The latter may reflect the fact that there are continuing sensitivities in the non-scheduled services and that the countries prefer a progressive approach to liberalization, by learning from their experience of liberalizing particular services and then extending this liberalization gradually. There is also a signaling dimension to the offers. It is interesting to note that although Sri Lanka has tabled an initial conditional offer, there is virtually no change compared to its Uruguay Round commitment (Figure 8.2). This probably reflects its intent to remain engaged in the Doha Round services negotiations but to make no substantive improvements in its commitments at this time. Bangladesh and the Maldives have not made any offers and thus their commitments in services remain highly limited.

While Figures 8.1 and 8.2 provide an idea of the scope of services commitments by the South Asian countries, to truly gauge the significance of this liberalization, one needs to examine the nature of the commitments made. Table 8.1 provides a comparative picture of the degree of liberalization undertaken by the South Asian WTO member countries. It is based on an examination of the latest schedule of either commitments, or where relevant, offers (initial or revised). It includes only sector-specific commitments or offers by the countries, not general or horizontal commitments, across the four modes of service delivery. Based on an analysis of these commitments and offer schedules, the liberalization undertaken is categorized as: (a) Opened, (b) Partially liberalized, and (c) Closed. The 'opened' category refers to cases where a country has scheduled no limitations on market access or national treatment, that is, scheduled 'None' in its commitment. The 'partially liberalized' category refers to cases where a country has placed some kind of limitation (for example, licensing and regulatory requirements, foreign equity limitations, and economic needs tests) on its market access and national treatment commitments. The 'closed' category refers to the case where a country has not scheduled the sector or sub-sector, that is, scheduled 'unbound' for market access and national treatment. The resulting table based on this categorization is quite revealing.

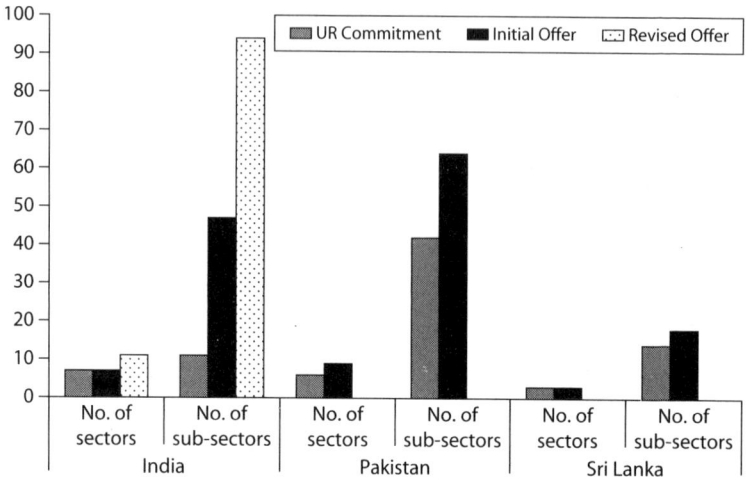

Figure 8.2   Progressive Liberalization of Services by South Asian Countries
                 in the GATS

Source: Based on WTO, Council for Trade in Services, Uruguay Round GATS
Schedules of Commitments, initial conditional offers, and revised offers for the
selected countries.[3]

Table 8.1 indicates that there are both similarities and differences in
the nature and scope of commitments made by the South Asian member
countries under GATS. The most commonly and most liberally committed sectors are telecommunication services and computer and information
services. Barring the Maldives, the remaining five countries have made

[3] World Trade Organization, Council for Trade in Services, 'India: Schedule of Spe-
cific Commitments', GATS/SC/42, Geneva, 15 April 1994; World Trade Organization,
Council for Trade in Services, 'Communication from the Maldives: Schedule of Spe-
cific Commitments under the GATS', GATS/SC/101, Geneva, 30 August 1995; World
Trade Organization, Council for Trade in Services, 'The Kingdom of Nepal: Schedule of
Specific Commitments', GATS/SC/139, Geneva, 30 August 2004; World Trade Orga-
nization, Council for Trade in Services, 'Pakistan: Schedule of Specific Commitments',
GATS/SC/67, Geneva, 15 April 1994; World Trade Organization, Council for Trade in
Services, 'Sri Lanka: Schedule of Specific Commitments', GATS/SC/79, Geneva, 15 April
1994; World Trade Organization, Council for Trade in Services, 'India: Conditional Initial
Offer', TN/S/O/IND, Geneva, 12 January 2004; World Trade Organization, Council for
Trade in Services, 'Pakistan, Conditional Initial Offer on Services', TN/S/O/PAK, Geneva,
20 May 2005; World Trade Organization, Council for Trade in Services, 'Sri Lanka, Con-
ditional Initial Offer on Services', TN/S/O/LKA, Geneva, 8 September 2003; World Trade
Organization, Council for Trade in Services, 'India, Revised offer on Services', Geneva, 12
August 2005.

Table 8.1   Nature of GATS Commitments by South Asian Countries

	□ Opened	▨ Partially liberalized		▩ Closed		
Sector	Sub-sector	Country	Mode 1	Mode 2	Mode 3	Mode 4
PROFESSIONAL SERVICES	1. Legal services	Bangladesh	Closed	Closed	Closed	Closed
		India	Closed	Closed	Closed	Closed
		Maldives	Closed	Closed	Closed	Closed
		Nepal	Opened	Closed	Closed	Closed
		Pakistan	Closed	Opened	Partially liberalized	Closed
		Sri Lanka	Closed	Closed	Closed	Closed
	2. Accounting, auditing, and book-keeping services	Bangladesh	Closed	Closed	Closed	Closed
		India	Opened	Opened	Closed	Closed
		Maldives	Opened	Opened	Partially liberalized	Closed
		Nepal	Opened	Opened	Partially liberalized	Closed
		Pakistan	Closed	Closed	Partially liberalized	Closed
		Sri Lanka	Closed	Closed	Closed	Closed
	3. Medical and dental Services	Bangladesh	Closed	Closed	Closed	Closed
		India	Partially liberalized	Opened	Closed	Closed
		Maldives	Closed	Closed	Closed	Closed
		Nepal	Closed	Closed	Closed	Closed
		Pakistan	Closed	Opened	Closed	Closed
		Sri Lanka	Closed	Closed	Closed	Closed
	4. Services provided by mid-wives/nurses, physiotherapists, and para-medical personnel	Bangladesh	Closed	Closed	Closed	Closed
		India	Partially liberalized	Opened	Closed	Closed
		Maldives	Closed	Closed	Closed	Closed
		Nepal	Closed	Closed	Closed	Closed
		Pakistan	Closed	Opened	Closed	Closed
		Sri Lanka	Closed	Closed	Closed	Closed
COMPUTER AND RELATED SERVICES	1. Consultancy services related to installation of computer hardware	Bangladesh	Opened	Opened	Opened	Closed
		India	Opened	Opened	Partially liberalized	Closed
		Maldives	Opened	Opened	Opened	Closed
		Nepal	Opened	Opened	Partially liberalized	Closed
		Pakistan	Closed	Closed	Closed	Closed
		Sri Lanka	Closed	Closed	Closed	Closed
	2. Software implementation services and data processing services	Bangladesh	Closed	Closed	Closed	Closed
		India	Opened	Opened	Closed	Closed
		Maldives	Opened	Opened	Partially liberalized	Closed
		Nepal	Opened	Opened	Partially liberalized	Closed
		Pakistan	Opened	Opened	Opened	Closed
		Sri Lanka	Closed	Closed	Closed	Closed
	3. Database services	Bangladesh	Closed	Closed	Closed	Closed
		India	Opened	Opened	Opened	Closed
		Maldives	Opened	Opened	Partially liberalized	Closed
		Nepal	Opened	Opened	Partially liberalized	Closed
		Pakistan	Opened	Opened	Opened	Closed
		Sri Lanka	Closed	Closed	Closed	Closed

(*Contd . . .*)

(*Table 8.1 contd . . .*)

Sector	Sub-sector	Country	Mode 1	Mode 2	Mode 3	Mode 4
TELECOMMUNICATION SERVICES	1. Fixed line voice telephone services	Bangladesh	▒		▒	▓
		India	▓		░	
		Maldives	▒		▒	▒
		Nepal			░	▒
		Pakistan		░		
		Sri Lanka	▓			
	2. Cellular telephone services	Bangladesh	░		▒	▒
		India	▓		▒	▒
		Maldives	▒	▒	▒	▒
		Nepal			▒	▒
		Pakistan				▒
		Sri Lanka			░	▒
CONSTRUCTION SERVICES	1. General construction work for buildings	Bangladesh	▒		▒	▒
		India	▒			▒
		Maldives	▒		▒	▒
		Nepal	▒		▒	▒
		Pakistan	▒		▒	▒
		Sri Lanka	▒		▒	▒
	2. General construction work for civil engineering	Bangladesh	▒		▒	▒
		India	▒			▒
		Maldives	▒		▒	▒
		Nepal	▒		░	▒
		Pakistan	▒		░	▒
		Sri Lanka	▒		▒	▒
DISTRIBUTION SERVICES	1. Commission agents services	Bangladesh	▒		▒	▒
		India			░	▒
		Maldives	▒		▒	▒
		Nepal			░	▒
		Pakistan	▒	▒	▒	▒
		Sri Lanka	▒	▒	▒	▒
	2. Wholesale trading services	Bangladesh	▒		▒	▒
		India			░	▒
		Maldives	▒		▒	▒
		Nepal	▒		▒	▒
		Pakistan	▒		░	▒
		Sri Lanka	▒		▒	▒
	3. Retailing services	Bangladesh	▒		▒	▒
		India	▒		▒	▒
		Maldives	▒		▒	▒
		Nepal	▒		▒	▒
		Pakistan	▒		░	▒
		Sri Lanka	▒		▒	▒
EDUCATION SERVICES	1. Higher education services	Bangladesh	▒		▒	▒
		India	░		░	▒
		Maldives	▒		▒	▒
		Nepal			░	░
		Pakistan				▒
		Sri Lanka	▒		░	▒

(*Contd . . .*)

(*Table 8.1 contd . . .*)

Sector	Sub-sector	Country	Mode 1	Mode 2	Mode 3	Mode 4
ENVIRONMENTAL SERVICES	1. Sewage Services	Bangladesh				
		India				
		Maldives				
		Nepal				
		Pakistan				
		Sri Lanka				
	2. Refuse disposal services	Bangladesh				
		India				
		Maldives				
		Nepal				
		Pakistan				
		Sri Lanka				
	3. Sanitation and similar services	Bangladesh				
		India				
		Maldives				
		Nepal				
		Pakistan				
		Sri Lanka				
FINANCIAL SERVICES	1. Insurance—life	Bangladesh				
		India				
		Maldives				
		Nepal				
		Pakistan				
		Sri Lanka				
	2. Insurance—non-life	Bangladesh				
		India				
		Maldives				
		Nepal				
		Pakistan				
		Sri Lanka				
	3. Banking services—acceptance of deposits	Bangladesh				
		India				
		Maldives				
		Nepal				
		Pakistan				
		Sri Lanka				
HEALTH AND RELATED SOCIAL SERVICES	1. Hospital services	Bangladesh				
		India				
		Maldives				
		Nepal				
		Pakistan				
		Sri Lanka				

(*Contd . . .*)

(*Table 8.1 contd . . .*)

Sector	Sub-sector	Country	Mode 1	Mode 2	Mode 3	Mode 4
TOURISM SERVICES	1. Hotels and restaurants	Bangladesh	▓	▓	▒	▓
		India			▒	▓
		Maldives	▓			
		Nepal			▒	
		Pakistan				
		Sri Lanka	▓		▓	
	2. Travel agencies and tour operator services	Bangladesh	▓		▓	▓
		India			▒	
		Maldives	▓			▓
		Nepal			▓	
		Pakistan				▓
		Sri Lanka		▓		
TRANSPORT SERVICES	1. Maritime transport— international freight and passenger movement	Bangladesh	▓		▓	▓
		India	▒		▓	▓
		Maldives	▓		▓	▓
		Nepal	▓		▓	▓
		Sri Lanka	▓		▓	▓
	2. Pipeline Transport Services	Bangladesh	▓		▓	▓
		India	▓		▓	▓
		Maldives	▓		▓	▓
		Nepal	▓		▓	▓
		Pakistan	▓		▓	▓
		Sri Lanka	▓		▓	▓

Source: Based on WTO Council for Trade in Services, individual country schedules of GATS commitments.[4]

commitments in telecommunication services and four out of the six countries have made commitments in computer and information services.

Another relatively liberally committed sector is tourism services. The fact that most countries have not only scheduled these services but also made liberal commitments in them not only reflects sector-specific characteristics which make these services more amenable to liberalization but also the autonomous opening up and deregulation of these services in the

[4] World Trade Organization, Council for Trade in Services, 'India: Schedule of Specific Commitments', GATS/SC/42, Geneva, 15 April 1994; World Trade Organization, Council for Trade in Services, 'Communication from the Maldives: Schedule of Specific Commitments under the GATS', GATS/SC/101, Geneva, 30 August 1995; World Trade Organization, Council for Trade in Services, 'The Kingdom of Nepal: Schedule of Specific Commitments', GATS/SC/139, Geneva, 30 August 2004; World Trade Organization, Council for Trade in Services, 'Pakistan: Schedule of Specific Commitments', GATS/SC/67, Geneva, 15 April 1994; World Trade Organization, Council for Trade in Services, 'Sri Lanka: Schedule of Specific Commitments', GATS/SC/79, Geneva, 15 April 1994.

South Asian countries in recent years. The commitments are wide ranging and tend to cover several segments within these sectors. The commitments are for the most part full, that is, no restrictions are placed for modes 1 and 2 but are mostly partial, that is, some limitations have been placed in the case of mode 3 or foreign commercial presence. Pakistan interestingly is the only country to have made fully liberal commitments on commercial presence across these services (as well as in education services). Mode 4 remains unbound and thus outside the purview of multilateral liberalization.

The South Asian countries have made moderately liberal commitments in the health, construction, and accountancy services sectors. Once again, modes 1 and 2 are by and large fully liberalized while mode 3 is subject to partial liberalization, including limitations on FDI, form of commercial presence, and approval and authorization requirements. As before, mode 4 remains uncommitted. These are thus indicative of services where there has been some degree of opening up in these economies but there is unwillingness to commit extensively or liberally due to lack of preparedness and remaining sensitivities in these services regarding the fall-out of liberalization, such as on prices, local employment, and local service providers (as in the case of accountancy services).

Across most of the South Asian countries, the most restricted services are distribution, transport, and financial services, and to some extent education, legal, and environmental services, where there has been least scheduling and mostly partial or unbound commitments even when scheduled. Amongst the modes, mode 1 and 2 tend to be more liberally committed compared to modes 3 and 4. Once again, domestic sensitivities regarding liberalization and its implications for aspects, such as employment in the case of retail distribution, or for the public sector providers in the case of financial, education, and environmental services, or for local firms as in the case of legal services, possibly underlie the very restrictive stance reflected by the South Asian countries in these services.

It is worth examining how well these GATS commitments reflect the unilateral policy liberalization in the South Asian countries, that is, to what extent the South Asian countries have been willing to bind in their existing regimes, especially with respect to foreign commercial presence. What emerges clearly is that the South Asian countries have not been willing to lock in the status quo in terms of their current policy regimes. The countries have maintained FDI limitations against their commitments even in areas where they have in practice completely liberalized FDI regulations, and in areas where FDI policies are still not fully liberal, they have for the most part placed limitations which are more restrictive than those they apply in practice. For instance, although India has completely opened up its cellular phone segment, its commitment on mode 3 is only partial under the GATS. The FDI ceiling on basic communication services is lower under the GATS than it is in practice. Thus the stance is more conservative in the GATS and the multilateral commitments fall short of the unilateral liberalization undertaken in even the most liberalized services, such as telecom or computer services. Moreover, there has been limited scheduling of some services, such as energy or transport, even though these have been opened up. Thus, clearly, the South Asian countries have tried to maintain their policy space in the GATS and have not used it as a means to push through further liberalization in their service sectors and appear to follow the course of first liberalizing unilaterally, realizing the benefits and challenges, and then committing multilaterally.

It is also worth assessing the nature and scope of the requests to the South Asian countries to improve upon their earlier commitments in the context of the ongoing request-offer negotiations, and to what extent they have acceded to these requests. Almost all the countries have received requests from the developed countries across a wide range of services, including telecommunications, environmental, financial, transport, energy, business, and transport services. These requests have mostly focused on market access under modes 1, 2, and 3. For example, requests to Bangladesh cover 10 out of 12 possible services, and 127 sub-sectors out of a potential 161 sub-sectors. India has received requests from all major developed countries as well as developing countries in a wide range of services. The thrust of these requests is on accessing the Indian market through commercial presence, with a majority of the requests targeted at the financial and telecommunication services sectors. It has also received plurilateral requests in 14 sectors, including all the major services, following the initiation of plurilateral negotiations after the Hong Kong Ministerial. Pakistan has also received many initial and later collective requests in several services which mainly ask for the removal of market access and national treatment limitations in modes 1, 2, and 3.

However, there has been little improvement offered by most of the South Asian countries in response to these requests. Bangladesh has not tabled any offer. Pakistan made an initial offer in May 2005, which basically increases foreign equity limits to 60 per cent from 51 per cent in most cases, and restrictions in modes 1–3 have been removed in many services. Sri Lanka has made an initial offer but this does not add any sectors and only makes some improvements in the three sectors scheduled earlier, mainly in mode 3. Of all the countries, India has made the most significant changes over its Uruguay Round commitments. Although its initial offer of January 2004 was not that different, the revised offer tabled by it in August 2005 significantly expanded the scope of the earlier commitments by increasing the number of sectors and sub-sectors offered and it also removed many commercial presence restrictions in important services. As a key player in services negotiations, India also signaled its willingness to come forward in services negotiations, in the hope of receiving improved revised offers in its sectors of modes of interest, though this did not materialize. Nevertheless, for all the South Asian countries, including India, even the improved offers by and large remain more restrictive than the status quo, especially with regard to commercial presence, though the wedge between commitments and the existing policy has been reduced.

Bilateral and Extra-regional Commitments in Services

Some of the South Asian countries are also members of bilateral and extra-regional trade and economic cooperation agreements that cover services. Table 8.2 provides an overview of all such agreements, their current status, and the nature of services coverage under them. As is evident from this summary table, most of these agreements cover services in the form of cooperation agreements rather than through concrete liberalization commitments. All the agreements which only involve countries from within the South Asian region are shaded in blue.

As can be seen from Table 8.2, services are at a relatively incipient stage in terms of coverage and status of negotiations under these agreements and in most cases, the coverage is quite narrow. Transport services and trade facilitation related services, such as ports, cargo, transport, and transit services are the most commonly covered areas, particularly in the various bilateral agreements involving India and the LDC members of SAARC. Hence, there is a clear emphasis on the role of services in facilitating merchandise trade within the region and also generally.

There are, however, two agreements, both of which are with countries outside the region that cover services more extensively and involve liberalization commitments that go beyond those committed or offered under the GATS. These are the Pakistan–Malaysia FTA and the India–Singapore Comprehensive Economic Cooperation Agreement (CECA). BIMSTEC, a sub-regional agreement of which Bangladesh, India, and Sri Lanka are members, has also made progress in several service sectors, though the focus is limited to cooperation issues.[5] Under the Pakistan–Malaysia FTA,

---

[5] See Boxes 8A.1 and 8A.2 in the Appendix to this chapter for details on the services commitments and provisions in both these agreements and the extent to which these agreements go beyond the GATS.

Table 8.2 Services Cooperation and Liberalization in Bilateral, Sub-regional, and Extra-regional Agreements by South Asian Countries

Country/ Countries	Type of Agreement	Year of Agreement/ Negotiations	Status	Coverage of Services	Other Issues
Bangladesh –USA	Trade and Investment Framework Agreement (TIFA)	Talks started in 2002	Three rounds of negotiations on b/w 2002 and 2005. Talks in stalemate now over IPR issues and duty free exports		
Bangladesh – Russia	None yet	Talks on to sign FTA	Talks on for cooperation in areas of power sector, agriculture, commerce, and cultural issues	Power sector	
Bangladesh– India	FTA	1 April 2006	Valid for 3 years and then consider extension	Cooperation in area of transport—agree to sign mutually beneficial agreements for sharing of waterways, roadways, and railways to boost commerce	
Bhutan– Bangladesh	Agreement on Trade		Under negotiation	Cooperation in areas of trade facilitation, identification of specific ports of entry and exit in both countries for commerce, MFN on many goods	
Bangladesh –Pakistan	FTA	Talks on from 2006	• Under negotiation • Joint Business Council has met • was to be concluded by September 2006 • stalled due to political uncertainty in both countries	Seeking SAFTA+ commitments from both countries (more flexible RoO rules than under SAFTA, more cooperative sensitive list than under SAFTA) Mostly in area of transportation: • Direct shipping links • Enhancing transport of passengers and cargo by air • Exploring investments in tourism and allied sectors — cooperation in tourism agreement signed in February 2006 • Creating a Joint Fund to undertake investment-promotion activities and linkages among export processing agencies of the two countries	Cooperation Agreements in Agriculture, Export Promotion and Product Standardization & Quality Assurance

					Investment
Bhutan–India	Agreement on Trade, Commerce, and Transit	28 July 2006	Signed and in force	Essentially covers cooperation in the area of transportation and customs clearance with India agreeing to allow transit of exports and imports into Bhutan on a duty free and custom free basis	
Pakistan–Malaysia	FTA	Signed on 8-11-2007	Signed and approved—in force	Has a specific section of services signed along with FTA (see Annexure for details)	
Pakistan–China	FTA	Signed on 24 November 2006	Signed and approved—in force	Yes—agreement on services signed on 22-2-2009. To be made effective during first half of 2009. Pakistan will further open 102 sub-sectors under 11 major sectors out of the 12 WTO-defined sectors and China will further open its 28 sub-sectors under six major sectors	
				Specifically, Pakistan will relax its shareholding restrictions on China's investments in sectors of construction, telecom, finance, distribution, healthcare, environmental protection, tourism, transportation, research and development, and IT education Chinese service providers in those sectors will be allowed to hold 60 to 99.99 per cent stake, compared with the cap of 40 to 51 per cent of foreign investment	
				Pakistan has agreed to grant more favourable treatment to Chinese companies in certain conditions	
				Solely China-funded businesses are possible, particularly in courier, telecom, and tourism	
				Fifty-six sectors, including five major sectors of distribution, education, environment, transportation, entertainment, and sports, will be open to Chinese providers for the first time. Chinese investors will also have access to service markets in sub-sectors like legal affairs, accountancy, architecture, printing and publishing, and veterinary	

(*Contd . . . .*)

(*Table 8.2 contd . . .*)

Country/ Countries	Type of Agreement	Year of Agreement/ Negotiations	Status	Coverage of Services	Other Issues
				Pakistan will also provide better conditions to facilitate personnel flow	
				The sectors that China will open mainly include mining, environmental protection, health care, tourism, sports, transportation, translation, real estate, computers, and marketing consultancy	
Pakistan–US	Bilateral Investment Treaty		Under negotiation		
Pakistan–Sri Lanka	FTA	Fully effective from 12 June 2005	Fully effective	Nothing significant	Mainly tariff concession and elimination on goods
Pakistan– Afghanistan	FTA/Trade and Economic Cooperation Agreement	Not yet effective — talks on	Under consideration	Cooperation in transportation: Already effective under the ATTA (Afghanistan Transit Trade Agreement) renamed the Pakistan–Afghanistan transit Agreement. Pakistan and Afghanistan would not levy customs duty, taxes, dues, or charges of any kind whether national, provincial, or municipal on goods in transit regardless of their destination. Extension of railway link between Chaman and Spin Boldak was discussed in 2006 and in January 2009 with the aim of establishing better communication and development of physical infrastructure. This would help in enhancing trade facilities between the two countries.	
Pakistan– GCC	FTA under consideration	Under negotiation from 2006		Nothing significant concluded yet	
Pakistan– Indonesia	FTA and PTA under negotiation	Under negotiation	Framework for Comprehensive Economic Partnership signed in 2005	FTA keen to cover trade facilitation issues, banking, marine and air transport, and technical know-how sharing	

Agreement	Type	Signed/Operational	Status	Details
Pakistan–Iran	PTA	Signed on 4 March 2005, operational from 1 September 2006	Fully effective	Only covers goods—negotiations on to improve customs procedures, trade facilitation, and banking improved transport links
Pakistan–Mauritius	PTA	PTA signed on 30 November 2007	FTA under consideration	Boosting trade in services, bringing down NTBs, improving air links and visas for business travellers
Indo-Nepal	Trade and Transit Treaty	Signed in 1999, effective till 2006 and has been renewed for another seven years		Largely pertaining to trade facilitation, easing of border measures and granting Nepal duty and customs free transit of its trade through the Indian territory, access to ports and so on
India–Singapore	CECA	Signed on 29 June 2005	Under implementation	Extensive coverage of services (see Appendix for details)
India–ASEAN	FTA	August 2008	• FTA negotiations underway • Early Harvest Scheme chalked out	Coverage of services integral part of FTA – GATS + commitments sought from both sides. Stated areas of cooperation in services: media and entertainment, health, financial, tourism, construction, business process outsourcing, and environmental Cooperation in science & technology and human resource development also envisaged Facilitating movement of business people also envisaged • Trade facilitation • Mutual recognition arrangements, conformity assessment, accreditation procedures, and standards and technical regulations • Non-tariff measures • Customs cooperation • Trade financing • Business visa and travel facilitation

(*Contd . . .*)

(Table 8.2 contd . . .)

Country/ Countries	Type of Agreement	Year of Agreement/ Negotiations	Status	Coverage of Services	Other Issues
India–Maldives	Trade agreement	1981	Nothing significant	Nothing significant – overarching trade facilitation measures outlined	
Sri Lanka–Iran	Trade and cooperation agreements	2004		Cooperation agreements in areas of environment, health, and visa matters	
APTA (Bangladesh, India, LAO PDR, China, Korea, Sri Lanka)	APTA as an initiative of ESCAP, is a preferential tariff arrangement that aims at promoting intra-regional trade through exchange of mutually agreed concessions by member countries	1975	Tariff negotiations underway	Mainly tariff concessions on goods and preferential RoO rules as of now Extension of talks to include trade facilitation, services, etc., being scheduled for APTA 3 Ministerial Council in Korea on 22 October 2009	
BIMSTEC (Bangladesh, Bhutan, India, Nepal, Sri Lanka, Thailand, Myanmar)	Economic Cooperation Sub-grouping	1997	Talks underway for cooperation in 13 priority sectors lead by member countries in a voluntary manner— trade & investment, technology, energy, transport & communication, tourism, fisheries, agriculture, cultural cooperation, environment and disaster management, public health, people-to-people contact, poverty alleviation, and counter-terrorism and transnational crimes	Areas that have made headway: Tourism—Kolkata Declaration 2005 • Increased cooperation in transportation by air, land and water • Promote heritage, culture, adventure, eco, and MICE tourism • Simplification of frontier procedures and other formalities • Share best practices • Come out with a concrete plan of action • Setting up of BIMSTEC Tourism Fund, BIMSTEC Tourism Information Centre, explore cooperation with SASEC, develop joint tour packages Trade and investment—The National Chambers of Commerce has urged for speedier negotiations on services within the BIMSTEC FTA.	

Energy—Declaration of 1st BIMSTEC Energy Ministers
Conference, 2005
• Vision of BIMSTEC Trans Power Exchange and Grid
  Connections, Common Regulatory Framework, Trans
  BIMSTEC Gas Pipeline, Promotion of hydropower
  projects, promote use of non-conventional sources of
  energy, technical cooperation

Culture—Cooperation to promote better understanding
of cultural issues and to promote socio-economic
development

Source: Based on the various bilateral and regional agreements signed by individual SAARC member countries.

Pakistan has relaxed its ceiling on foreign equity participation, raising it from 51 per cent in its GATS offer to 60 per cent under the FTA. It has also scheduled additional sub-sectors in construction, telecommunication, and tourism services and has also scheduled additional sectors, such as recreational and sporting services and transport services across various segments in these services. The recently signed agreement between Pakistan and China similarly undertakes more extensive commitments compared to the GATS.

Likewise, under the India–Singapore CECA, India has improved upon its GATS commitments by scheduling additional sectors and sub-sectors and relaxing limitations inscribed in its GATS schedules under CECA. It has, for instance, extensively scheduled additional business and professional services, such as management and consulting, taxation advisory, and rental/leasing services. India has also scheduled commitments in internal freight services under air transport services, which are not covered in its GATS commitments. The CECA also has a special clause on air services which urges the Indian and Singaporean governments to conclude open skies agreements and includes a cooperation chapter on education and media, as well as a chapter on e-commerce. Issues of recognition of degrees, inter-institutional collaboration, and regulatory cooperation are also covered under this agreement. Thus, the India–Singapore CECA not only involves more significant liberalization compared to the GATS but also takes a much more comprehensive approach to the service sector.

Overall, it is evident that services are still not a primary focus area in the context of other agreements signed by the South Asian countries either within the region or outside. Most of these agreements primarily address cooperation and transit issues and few concrete commitments relating to trade in services.[6] The only two agreements with significant depth in service sector negotiations, namely, the Pakistan–Malaysia FTA and the India–Singapore CECA discussed earlier, are with partners outside the sub-region. Among other sub-regionals, BIMSTEC has made more progress in several key service sectors but the nature of negotiations is currently restricted to cooperation and has not progressed in the trade mode. It is also worth noting that the two larger countries in this region, India and Pakistan, are increasingly entering into agreements that involve service

---

[6] See Table 8A.1 (in the Appendix to this chapter), which summarizes key aspects of various sub-regional and bilateral agreements assigned by SAARC countries and how these compare to the GATS.

sector liberalization, cooperation in services, and other cross-cutting issues in services. The latter is indicative of their growing interest in services and willingness to commit bilaterally and regionally in services, beyond what they are willing to commit multilaterally. The LDCs in South Asia, however, are primarily interested in a very limited set of services, mainly those pertaining to trade facilitation and border infrastructure services. Bilateral agreements among the SAARC member countries mainly focus on transport and infrastructure related cooperation issues in the service sector.

Broad Prospects for Services Integration under SAFTA

The preceding analysis reveals several facts about the South Asian countries' approach to services liberalization, which are likely to be reflected in their regional approach to services liberalization under an expanded SAFTA. First, the analysis suggests that South Asian countries prefer autonomous liberalization to undertaking multilateral obligations, although they are likely to be more forthcoming in bilateral or regional agreements than under the GATS. Second, the South Asian countries would like to preserve their flexibility to roll back policies if so required and to cautiously observe the outcome of liberalizing unilaterally before committing multilaterally. Third, commercial presence is the most sensitive mode for all countries in this region, where they have preferred to maintain the most policy space by committing more conservatively than the prevailing policy environment permits. Fourth, although the South Asian countries would like to remain active participants in services negotiations, only the larger countries, India and Pakistan, have been willing to improve their commitments in any significant manner or to undertake more extensive commitments in the context of other agreements. Among them, India has sought to make more substantive improvements in its commitments mainly reflecting its own offensive interests in this sector. Finally, all agreements that are more extensive in their coverage of services involve countries outside the region and none of the intra-regional agreements have a comprehensive approach to service sector issues.

What can one infer about the prospects for liberalization of services under SAFTA based on this analysis? Perhaps the most important inference to draw from this discussion is that it may be premature to expect a very comprehensive and liberalization oriented approach to the inclusion of services under SAFTA, at least in the initial years. The approach may initially need to centre around issues of collaboration, regulatory cooperation, transport and trade facilitation, and may involve to a limited extent only some services where there is common interest among the countries or where the existing policies and commitments undertaken are already quite liberal, such as in tourism, information technology, and possibly telecommunication services (following some intra-regional discussions on regulations and standards). It is also likely that there would be asymmetry in the nature of obligations undertaken by the SAARC member countries, and thus a differential approach, as in the case of goods, may be warranted with India and Pakistan undertaking more obligations and the LDCs committing in a narrower range of services and perhaps in a more limited manner within those services. India is likely to be the main country with an interest in seeking greater market access in the other markets within the region, particularly in sectors where it has proven its relative competence and where Indian investors are already present. It is, however, unlikely that significant market access will be obtained, even in those areas where cross-border investments and initiatives already exist within the region, given the general conservativeness with which most countries in South Asia have committed in the service sector.

Overall, it would be realistic to expect a progressive approach to services liberalization under SAFTA. India would have to be the key player pushing services negotiations in the region by committing more without necessarily seeking reciprocal access, while simultaneously pushing forward discussions on cross-cutting issues such as investment, labour mobility, regulation, and standards among others. Such issues would need to be addressed for any long term meaningful intra-regional integration in services. Thus, a special and differential treatment approach could be adopted under a regional agreement in services, as has been done in the case of SAFTA for goods. One basic problem, however, needs to be noted in this regard. Given the fundamental asymmetries in the region, it is India that would be the main source of investment in the service sectors of the other SAARC member countries. Hence, if regional services integration is to yield benefits, commitments would need to be forthcoming from the lesser developed countries in SAARC in order to attract investments in key services from India or the other larger member countries. Such access could potentially be reciprocated by India and the other larger countries in the region, by offering quid pro quo access in services or goods and by addressing issues, such as non-tariff barriers, trade facilitation, and regulatory cooperation.

Appendix 8A

Examples of FTAs signed by SAARC countries with other partners that have a significant services component and commitments in addition to those made under the GATS framework:

Box 8A.1 Service Commitments and Provisions in the Pakistan–Malaysia FTA

Pakistan–Malaysia FTA: Significant deviations in Pakistan's services commitments in comparison to its 2005 offer under the GATS Doha Round of negotiations; commitments have gone beyond the Doha Round revised offer by Pakistan

- In most sectors where a foreign equity participation limit has been placed, Pakistan has offered Malaysia up to 60 per cent foreign equity participation as against 51 per cent in its GATS offer.
- Additional sub-sectors have been scheduled in construction, telecommunication, and tourism services.
- Additional sub-sectors in tourism include, for example, theme park attraction services and convention centres to Malaysian capital with up to 60 per cent equity participation.
- Additional sectors scheduled:

  Recreational, cultural and sporting services:
  - Libraries, archives, museums
  - Sporting services (cricket, football, and hockey)—allowing commercial presence

  Transport services:
  - Railway services—passenger transportation/freight/container terminal/supporting services—permitting market access in modes 1, 2, and 3 with 60 per cent equity participation
  - Road transport service—passenger/freight/rental of commercial vehicles/maintenance and repair of road transport equipment/supporting services—opening up modes 1, 2, and 3 with foreign equity participation of 60 per cent
  - Services auxiliary to all modes of transport

Box 8A.2   Services Commitments and Provisions in the India–
Singapore CECA

Indo-Singapore CECA: Significant deviations in India's services commitments in
comparison to its 2005 revised offer under the GATS Doha Round of negotiations; its commitments under the CECA go beyond its Doha Round revised offer

- Additional sub-sectors scheduled in professional services (advisory taxation
  services), rental/leasing services
- Other business services scheduled extensively—sale of leasing services of
  advertising space of time, management and consulting, especially relating
  to legal consultancy, services incidental to electricity distribution, convention services, specialty design services, and photographic services
- Education and environmental services that India has offered in its revised
  conditional GATS offer have not been scheduled in the CECA
- Additional sub-sectors scheduled under recreational services (library services and archive services)
- India has scheduled commitments in internal freight transport by air
  although air services have not been scheduled in the GATS. The CECA
  also has a special clause on air services urging both governments to conclude open skies agreements.
- The CECA has a specific chapter on 'Cooperation in Education' between
  the two countries: Both countries shall facilitate collaborations between
  the Indian Institutes of Technology (IIT) and/or Indian Institute of Science (IISc), and universities in Singapore, such as proposed collaboration
  between IIT Mumbai and the National University of Singapore, and IIT
  Chennai and the Nanyang Technological University of Singapore, to offer
  post-graduate research and education, with industrial linkages to multinational and local companies based in India and Singapore. MRAs—The
  degrees specified by the University Grants Commission (UGC) of India
  and awarded by an approved university or an institute deemed to be a
  university under the UGC or an Institution of National Importance of
  India and similarly, degrees awarded by the universities in Singapore shall
  be recognized for the purposes of qualifying the holder to be considered
  for admission to the universities of both countries. Also setting up of a
  joint committee on education to oversee implementation of the CECA
  and explore other areas of cooperation as they may emerge.
- The CECA has a specific chapter that highlights the importance of e-commerce and permits the supply of services by electronic means
- Cooperation agreement in the area of media that includes issues like the
  setting up of a policy and regulatory framework, regulating content and
  sharing technical know-how in the areas of print and broadcast media

Other points:

- Although several bilateral trade and economic cooperation agreements have been signed between individual member states of SAARC, most are in the range of cooperation and transit agreements and do not have concrete commitments relating to trade in goods and services.
- The only two agreements with significant depth in service sector negotiations are with partners outside the sub-region.
- Among other sub-regionals, BIMSTEC has made more progress in several key service sectors but the nature of negotiations is currently restricted to cooperation and has not progressed in the trade mode.

Table 8A.1 Status of Bilateral and Regional Commitments in Services

	Has/is negotiated/ing other bilateral/regional trade agreements with services components. If YES, number and name of these agreements	Extent of commitment in negotiations on services (coverage of sectors and sub-sectors)	Nature of the commitments undertaken in services	Are the services commitments GATS + ?
Bangladesh	YES—3			
	1. Proposed Bangladesh–USA TIFA (Trade and Investment Framework Agreement)	1. Energy	1. Not clear as negotiations not concluded	
	2. Proposed Bangladesh–Russia FTA	2. Energy, culture	2. Not clear as negotiations not concluded	
	3. Proposed Bangladesh–Pakistan FTA	3. Shipping, air transport, tourism, education, health	3. Not clear as negotiations not concluded	
Bhutan	NO			
India	YES—7			
	1. Framework Agreement on Comprehensive Economic Cooperation between ASEAN and India	1. Media & entertainment, health, finance, tourism, construction, BPO, R&D, environment, and movement of professionals (mode 4)	1. Not clear as negotiations not concluded	
	2. Indo-Singapore CECA	2. Above 68 sub-sectors scheduled by India in all GATS sub-sectors	2. Modes 1 and 2 liberalized substantially across most sub-sectors. Mode 3 restrictions limited to foreign equity limits, adherence to pertinent domestic regulations, approval from respective regulatory bodies and, in a few cases, incorporation Mode 4 relatively closed	2. GATS +
	3. Framework agreement for establishing FTA between Thailand and India	3. Tourism, IT and BPO, and air transport	3. Not clear as negotiations not concluded	
	4. Proposed India–Malaysia CECA	4. Medical, healthcare & diagnostic services; advertising services, audio-visual services, education, computers & IT, telecommunications, financial, tourism & travel, transport (air and maritime); architectural, engineering & construction; distribution, accounting & taxation, movement of natural persons (mode 4)	4. Not clear as negotiations not concluded	

	Agreement	Sector coverage	Status	
	5. Proposed India–Mauritius CECPA	5. Distribution, tourism & travel, auditing, professional services, and computer & IT	5. Not clear as negotiations not concluded	
	6. India–Korea CEPA	6. IT & software services, construction & engineering services; audio-visual & entertainment services; telecommunications; transportation; financial; and tourism	6. Market access in key sectors realized, including movement of natural persons in professional services. Liberalization committed in mode 3 in key services.	6. GATS +
	7. Proposed India–EU FTA	7. Telecommunications, IT & computers, air transport, and other services	7. Not clear as negotiations not concluded	
Maldives	No			
Nepal	No			
Pakistan	YES—6			
	1. Proposed Pakistan–Bangladesh FTA	1. Shipping, air transport, tourism, education, and health	1. Not clear as negotiations not concluded	
	2. Pakistan–Malaysia FTA	2. Extensive coverage of 66 sub-sectors	2. Modes 1 and 2 relatively liberalized. Mode 3 liberalization subject to foreign equity limitations in few sectors and mode 4 remains relatively closed	2. GATS +
	3. Pakistan–China FTA	3. Fifty-six sectors including five major sectors of distribution, education, environment, transportation and entertainment, sports, and business services	3. Not clear as negotiations concluded but schedule not made public yet	
	4. Proposed Pakistan–Afghanistan Trade and Economic Cooperation Agreement	4. Energy—gas pipeline, communications	4. Not clear as negotiations not concluded	
	5. Proposed Pakistan–Indonesia PTA	5. Banking, marine, and air transport	5. Not clear as negotiations not concluded	
	6. Pakistan–Mauritius PTA	6. Not clear	6. Not clear as negotiations not concluded	
Sri Lanka	YES—1			
	1. Sri Lanka–Iran Trade and Cooperation Agreements on Health and Environment	1. Health, environment, and visa matters	1. Not clear as negotiations still in the realm of cooperation only	

Source: Based on selected bilateral and regional agreements signed by individual SAARC member countries.

9

The Way Forward

Identifying Drivers and Negotiating Frameworks

The discussion of various services in the earlier chapters highlights the potential mutual benefits from enhanced cooperation and increased regional services trade and investment flows in South Asia. As is evident, regional integration opportunities in South Asia span across all kinds of services. There are opportunities in infrastructural services as highlighted by the telecommunication and energy service sectors, in commercial services as highlighted by the tourism service sector, and also in social services as highlighted by the health and education service sectors. These opportunities span all four GATS modes of services delivery. Although only a small set of representative services have been discussed in this book, similar potential exists in a variety of other services, such as entertainment, information technology, cultural, environmental, and banking services, to name a few. The discussion also highlights the synergies and complementarities that exist across different modes and services, with positive implications for regional integration efforts at large, going beyond the service sector.

The potential gains from services integration in South Asia arise from an interesting mix of asymmetries, complementarities, and commonalities across the countries in the region. Asymmetries and complementarities in size, levels of development, technical and institutional capacity, private sector enterprise, and financial and human resources create scope for resource flows between the countries in the region. These differences can be leveraged and these gaps can be addressed. At the same time, commonalities in objectives and interests arising from the infrastructural, income, and regulatory status of countries in the region create scope for cooperation as well as increased trade and investment ties in various services to address common goals of physical and social infrastructure development, employment creation, universal service provision, equity, and poverty alleviation.

Yet, as the discussion indicates, there has been virtually no progress in services integration. There are very few concrete programmes and projects that have been undertaken, although numerous dialogues have taken place, numerous working groups have been formed, and numerous initiatives have been envisioned. Even where inter-governmental cooperation has progressed and resulted in successful outcomes, it has been limited to bilateral arrangements, which have been narrow in scope, piecemeal in nature, and not part of any long-term integrated strategy for cooperation. Sub-regional and plurilateral initiatives have also not succeeded in the region despite support from various development agencies, such as the Asian Development Bank and the World Bank. There is comparatively much more that has happened on account of private sector initiative, especially in less regulated sectors such as healthcare and tourism, which are not dominated by public sector entities. But even here, the engagement is largely bilateral, limited in scope, and not underpinned by any long-term strategy for regional cooperation in these services or governmental efforts to create a climate that is conducive to regional investment and trade flows.

Given this past experience in services, can one then expect SAFAS to make a significant difference to regional integration in services in South Asia? To answer this question, one needs to focus attention on three issues. First, one needs to identify the main drivers of services integration in South Asia, so as to arrive at a well thought out and structured strategy for promoting services trade in the region. Second, one needs to recognize the barriers that constrain regional services trade, which would either need to be overcome or worked around when pursuing services integration in the region. Third, one needs to recognize the problems with the approach taken thus far under SAARC, which has prevented the realization of concrete outcomes, so that a more workable and realistic strategy can be formulated for regional services integration in the future.

The discussion that follows provides a detailed account of the possible sectoral and cross-sectoral strategies for negotiating services under SAFTA. It draws upon the earlier discussion on individual services and trends in services trade, investment, and intra-regional opportunities and challenges to define these strategies and highlights issues that would need to be addressed in order to achieve a convergence of interests among the member countries and to address common challenges in services within the region.

Identifying the Drivers of Regional Services Integration

There are four mutually interdependent drivers of services integration in South Asia. These are: infrastructure gaps that exist in the region; the presence of a dynamic private sector; social, cultural and historical ties; and the institutional and human resource capacity requirements.

Services integration in South Asia is necessitated by the huge infrastructure gap that exists in key service sectors, such as telecom, power, transport, logistics, and healthcare, and the consequent need for financial, managerial, and technical resources that are locally relevant and attuned to local conditions to bridge this gap. The existence of these shortages, combined with common concerns confronting countries in the region, as well as differences among them in their levels of development, stage of liberalization, private sector maturity, and regulatory capabilities, create scope for regional cooperation in the development and management of infrastructure. Physical and social infrastructure creation is not only a necessity in all the countries of the region but it also provides an opportunity to align country level objectives with regional objectives, such as through the establishment of a regional power grid, cross-border investments in health and educational infrastructure, creation of regional transport corridors and associated road networks, or sub-regional development of tourism infrastructure. There are huge potential externalities with regard to employment creation, socioeconomic development, trade in goods, and overall economic relations in the region.

The presence of a dynamic private sector in several countries of the region is another important driving force for regional services integration. The private sector has become increasingly important in the region, not only in the traditionally less regulated services but also in sectors that have undergone liberalization in recent years. This creates opportunities for increased private sector investment in South Asia, through wholly owned subsidiaries, joint ventures, management and technical tie-ups, and even public-private partnerships across countries, which can be supported by a consortium of private sector companies in particular services and through dialogues among industry associations in the region. Once again, there is scope to align national objectives with regional goals of encouraging investments, creating employment, promoting services exports, and promoting private sector participation in services through regional cooperation in services.

A third driving force is the social, cultural, and heritage bonds that tie the countries in the region, which can be leveraged to promote commercial and non-commercial relations in services. Sharing of common history, languages, boundaries, and recreational and cultural interests creates commercial and non-commercial opportunities in a wide range of services, including tourism, sports, media, entertainment, healthcare, education, transport, and financial services. Again, national objectives of promoting cultural integration, social cohesion, services exports, investment, employment, and diversification of the services sector can be aligned with regional integration efforts.

A fourth important driver of services integration in South Asia is the need to address capacity gaps with regard to human resources and institutions in the region. There is a need to develop soft skills and managerial, technical, and professional expertise in many services. There is also a need to establish regulatory bodies or improve their functioning, to design and adapt regulatory frameworks to changes in the economic and policy environments, and to establish and harmonize standards in many services. There is scope for cross-country learning, transfer of knowledge and best practices, data and information gathering and sharing, and joint studies on services to address both human resource and institutional capacity gaps in the region. Once again, regional efforts can be aligned with national goals of institutional capacity building and skill development in services.

Key Channels for Effecting Services Integration

An identification of these main drivers of services integration also makes evident the key channels through which this integration would need to be effected. *Mobility of production factors* in the form of financial and human resource flows and *mobility of consumption factors* in the form of consumer flows are the main channels for realizing services integration in South Asia. These are not necessarily independent channels.

Factor and consumer mobility can enable countries in the region to realize economies of scale by harnessing the regional endowment and consumer base. For example, investment inflows coupled with increased consumer mobility in tourism services can enable the smaller countries in the region to develop their tourism infrastructure and cater to the larger domestic market, thus realizing economies of scale in the tourism industry. The prospects of a large regional consumer base can in turn help attract further investment into the sector. Factor and consumer mobility can also enable countries in the region to specialize in different parts of the value chain in certain services, thus creating scope for intra-industry trade in services and a diversified services export basket in the region. For example, specialization in different parts of the value chain could take place in sectors like IT services where lower value added tasks could be outsourced from the more advanced countries like India to other countries in the region. Such differentiation would be made possible by investments from Indian companies in these other markets, in the process also expanding regional exports of IT-ITeS services and helping in the development of this sector.

Investment is perhaps the most important means of fostering regional integration in services. This is evident from the preceding discussion on selected services, where investment emerges as the main form of intra-regional engagement and an important objective in most inter-governmental efforts. Investment has a bearing on all the drivers mentioned earlier. It is a means of addressing infrastructure gaps, of promoting private sector participation, leveraging linguistic and cultural affinities, and enabling the development of institutional and human resource capacity. For example, increased intra-regional investment is critical to realizing goals, such as the establishment of a regional power grid and exploitation of hydropower resources to promote energy security. Investment, whether public or private or PPP-based is critical for the development of transport corridors and road networks to facilitate goods trade. It is required for the establishment and management of health and educational institutions to improve access to social infrastructure, and the establishment of telecom grids and cable networks within the region to improve connectivity and develop capabilities in related areas like IT. As is evident, the associated benefits are many, not only in services but also in other areas. Thus, investment is critical for promoting regional integration in services and also more generally in South Asia. Further, recent liberalization and regulatory reforms in services in the South Asian countries provide the basis for expanding intra-regional investment flows through cross-border participation of the private sector and public-private partnerships in services.

Mobility of people, from the production as well as the consumption side, is the other critical channel for furthering services integration. Investment flows must be complemented by intra-regional mobility of manpower, in particular technical and professional manpower and business visitors. Likewise, intra-regional mobility of consumers is needed to integrate the regional market across a wide range of services, including tourism, education, healthcare, entertainment, recreational, and cultural services. Such mobility is essential for leveraging the large consumer base that exists in South Asia, and can help some of the smaller countries attract investments from regional investors by enabling economies of scale which their fragmented domestic markets would not otherwise support. Thus, people mobility for service delivery, particularly as linked to investment flows, and people mobility for services consumption is needed for meaningful integration in services.

Possible Approach to Services Integration

It has been said time and again that regional integration has been a failure in South Asia and there is no reason to expect otherwise in the case of the service sector. This failure has mainly been blamed on the complex political economy of the region, in particular, the strained relations between the two big players, India and Pakistan. But one could argue that in large part the problem has also been due to the very approach that has been taken to integration. There has been a tendency to declare ambitious projects and targets without addressing fundamental problems constraining the channels outlined earlier for effecting this integration. Action plans, documents, and summit declarations have been made without heed to investment regulations, institutional and regulatory capacity, or people mobility, all of which are the means of translating action plans and declarations into actual outcomes. Thus, first and foremost, the approach to services integration needs to be realistic and phased, focusing more on tangible economic cooperation. There need to be clear timetables for deliverables, over the medium term and over the long term. Without concrete timelines and deliverables, any discussion on services will remain only at the drawing board level, as has been the case in the past. This time table would also need to vary depending on the sectors and issues under consideration, with some services possibly being put on a fast track where there are fewer sensitivities or complex regulatory issues and thus greater ease of negotiations.

It will be important to address the fundamental constraints to services integration. As highlighted earlier, pooling of factor and consumption markets will be the main channel for services integration. Hence, regional discussions will have to focus on all the cross-cutting issues that have a bearing on factor and consumer mobility in the region. The most important among these cross-cutting issues are the streamlining of investment regulations, improving the business environment, enhancing institutional and regulatory capacity, ensuring regulatory cooperation, and enhancing people mobility. Without addressing these issues it will not be possible to translate action plans and declarations into actual outcomes. Specific initiatives will need to be undertaken at the regional level on each of these issues, which would need to be complemented by reforms and policy initiatives at the country level.

In the context of investments in the region, one of the main constraints has been procedural and administrative delays, lack of transparency, and uncertainties stemming from economic and political instability and policy changes. Regional discussions in this regard could thus specifically focus on speedier clearances and approval procedures in general; fast track procedures for regional investors with prior collaboration or expertise in the country or sector; fast track clearances in identified services which are largely commercial in nature and where there are fewer sensitivities; provision of regular and updated information on the regulatory framework governing investment in different services through government websites and reports; and information on bidding processes and award of contracts.

It would also be useful to consider a regional investment treaty and double taxation treaties among the countries to remove existing barriers to investment in the region. This regional investment framework would need to address issues of investment facilitation, investor protection, dispute settlement, and contract enforcement so as to ensure greater ease, transparency, and commitment in regional investments. A common investment framework would help in developing investment policies and associated regulations in a coordinated manner and enable harmonization of rules and procedures, and mutual recognition of standards and technical specifications in services within the region.

Clearly, these efforts will need to be complemented by national efforts and must be seen by the individual countries as part of an overall drive towards improving their business environment, to attract not only regional investors but investors at large. According to the *Doing Business in South Asia 2007* report, the countries in the region perform poorly on a variety of business environment parameters, including key parameters like business registration, access to credit, investor protection, contract enforcement, and licensing policies.[1] Barring India none of the other South Asian countries features among the top 10 reformers with regard to the business environment. Thus, regional efforts to increase procedural transparency and improve the operationalization of investments cannot be independent of national efforts to reform the business climate.

Regional efforts will also need to focus on facilitating cross-country mobility of persons, in the context of service delivery and in the context of services consumption. Hence, there needs to be discussion about streamlining visa procedures and requirements for selected categories of persons

---

[1] See World Bank (2007).

within the region. If investments are indeed critical to services integration in the region, then mobility of people relating to investment flows must be given priority in any labour mobility discussions. Efforts could be oriented towards simplifying visa procedures and expediting visa approvals for categories, such as business visitors, intra-corporate transferees, and professionals and academics against bonafide approved or prospective investment projects, institutional tie-ups, and exchange arrangements. Likewise, streamlined processes and speedier approvals could be introduced for special categories of services consumers, such as medical value travellers students, leisure travellers, and transit travellers. There are, no doubt, security concerns in relaxing visa regulations between some of the countries. But even in these cases, mobility restrictions could be streamlined for a limited set of persons, those associated with commercial presence or where other regulatory approval processes are involved. Similarly, mobility restrictions could be streamlined for those services which have been identified as high priority or fast track sectors.

Related issues, such as transport connectivity will also need to be addressed, such as by identifying selected bilateral and sub-regional projects to develop road and rail transport links and joint investments in these projects, signing of open skies agreements between countries in the region, and developing transit hubs in the region. Integration of the regional transport network, providing transit facilities for the landlocked nations of Bhutan and Nepal, creating land corridors through member countries to link remote parts of the region, and related procedural issues have received attention under sub-regional projects on transport logistics and trade facilitation.[2]

It is evident that neither investment facilitation nor people mobility facilitation, even on a selective basis, can proceed without institutional and regulatory cooperation in specific services and also more generally. As already highlighted in the context of a regional investment treaty, discussions are required on establishing of standards, and a mutual recognition of these standards. Discussions are required not only among governments

[2] Some examples of such cooperation include the approval of a SAARC Regional Multimodal Transport Study, the construction of a key transport corridor between Agartala and Akhaura via a rail link, an agreement for cross-border truck movement between India and Bangladesh to improve cross-border operations at Petrapole and Benapole, initiation of various feasibility studies on road and rail links in the sub-region consisting of Bangladesh, India, Nepal, and Bhutan, and reviews of various transit agreements and development of operational frameworks for bilateral or trilateral agreements in the region. See Asian Development Bank (2007b).

but also among regulatory bodies, professional associations, industry associations, research institutions, and civil society in the region in order to share information, exchange best practices, collect data, conduct joint feasibility and impact analysis studies, identify priority areas for a services agreement, develop soft skills, and create regional templates for investment or immigration related initiatives.

Thus a multi-pronged approach is required, where regional efforts are complemented by national efforts, where the key issues of investment and people mobility are prioritized, and related institutional efforts are undertaken at various levels. Similarly, a phased and prioritized approach is required with regard to sectoral coverage, a point also noted several times earlier. It would be useful to first liberalize the least contentious services, such as tourism or IT where success is more likely and where there are fewer regulatory complexities that could delay efforts. Pilot projects could be launched in these services, ideally on a plurilateral and sub-regional basis. There are, for example, initiatives that have already been agreed upon in the tourism sector, such as the Buddhist tourism circuit under the South Asia Sub-regional Economic Cooperation (SASEC) programme. Such identified projects could be taken up on a priority basis and related issues of mobility, transport connectivity, tourism infrastructure development, and investments worked out. A pilot-based approach in selected services which goes beyond bilateral arrangements could provide the much needed confidence and practical experience to engage in larger and more complex regional projects, such as in the energy or telecom sectors. Successful outcomes in some areas could also have a positive demonstration effect in other services and provide the impetus for launching initiatives in other areas.

A similar phased and prioritized approach could be taken with regard to country participation in services discussions. It may be useful to proceed on issues and sectors and sub-sectors where there is a minimum core group of three or more member countries who are interested in participating as it may not be practical to wait for buy-in from all the countries in the region. This group could be expanded over time as outcomes are realized among a smaller set of countries and there is learning by doing. An attempt could also be made to build on existing bilateral agreements and other plurilateral agreements that are common to some of the countries in the region (such as BIMSTEC) to use discussions under those as a basis for negotiations under the SAARC Framework Agreement on Trade in Services (SAFAS). Thus an open approach to services integration could be adopted as has been done in groups like ASEAN.

Agreement Architecture and Negotiating Modalities

From a scheduling and regional commitment perspective, the approach outlined and the key channels for effecting services integration highlighted earlier will need to be kept in mind. The GATS scheduling framework with sectoral and horizontal schedules and a positive list approach could be adopted.

Given the need to phase in services integration, a progressive approach should be followed to scheduling. While there should be substantial sectoral coverage under SAFAS, initial scheduling can be limited to a few agreed services which have been identified for high priority and fast track negotiations within the region. However, countries can always schedule additional services that extend beyond this agreed list even in the initial stages. Market access commitments should ideally reflect existing policies, thus binding in the prevailing regulatory and policy environment, and where possible, going beyond by providing more favourable conditions at the regional level. But at a minimum, they should be GATS plus. Discriminatory measures should be removed as far as possible, unless there are clearly specified grounds for imposing such measures, such as national security, consumer protection, or availability of government subsidies and other incentives for social and developmental reasons. Special and differential treatment should be provided for LDCs in the region, in terms of either providing longer implementation periods for the commitments, or allowing narrower coverage of sectors and sub-sectors in the scheduling process. It may not be useful to encourage special and differential treatment in terms of greater restrictions being maintained against the commitments made as much of the potential benefit of scheduling a sector would be negated, especially for the LDCs which could gain from increased investment flows from other countries in the region.

Investment, people mobility, government procurement, subsidy, taxes, and other cross-cutting issues would need to be addressed in the horizontal commitment schedules. To make progress on some of the more contentious issues amongst these, such as on movement of natural persons, it may be worth considering a request-and-offer approach to liberalizing temporary movement for select categories of service providers or professionals in select disciplines. The same could be undertaken for horizontal market access commitments for investment and government procurement policies, where procedural issues could be simplified for select services and streamlined institutional provisions could be incorporated into the relevant sectoral schedules.

The architecture of the regional agreement on services needs to be flexible and incremental on the one hand, while also having mechanisms to ensure commitment to the regional liberalization process on the other. In particular, the agreement must include provisions for transparency, safeguard measures, and review mechanisms. Given the fact that lack of transparency and uncertainty about the policy environment are identified as a major constraint in regional services trade and investment, there need to be transparency provisions under SAFAS, which require the countries to provide information on current rules and regulations as well as providing prior information on proposed changes in these policies. There must also be in-built mechanisms to undertake periodic reviews of commitments and their implementation status to encourage compliance and progressive liberalization. Safeguard measures are also required to provide some cushion to countries in case of emergencies which may necessitate temporary withdrawal of commitments.

Concluding Thoughts

In sum, any regional services agreement must be broad-based and flexible, yet ensure sufficient depth of commitments in at least a selected set of services to begin with, eventually expanding the scope of commitments to more services. A regional services agreement must also address key cross-cutting issues both in terms of the architecture of the agreement itself and generally outside the agreement, through on-going cooperation efforts and discussions in various forums. Only then can SAFAS become a vehicle for social and economic development in the region.

There are four critical steps that are pre-requisites for successful regional integration in services in South Asia. Progress in these areas must to some extent precede the finalization of any services agreement and must constitute an integral part of the work agenda both in the lead up to and during the SAFAS negotiations. The first important step is to improve the information base on services not only for individual member countries but also in terms of their bilateral trade and investment flows with other South Asian countries, so as to enable a more informed view about the service sector and its intra-regional status. Only a proper understanding of the significance and nature of services in bilateral relations and the barriers affecting trade and investment flows in individual services and markets can enable meaningful negotiations and the framing of a suitable architecture for the resulting agreement.

A second important step would be to undertake more regional discussions on regulatory and institutional issues, so as to facilitate cross-country learning in the development of regulatory frameworks and enable an eventual move towards greater harmonization in the region. The latter is particularly important in the context of people and capital mobility, which would be the critical modes for services delivery within the region across a wide range of services. In order to arrive at an understanding on issues, such as visas, taxes, and standards, which would form the basis for greater labour and capital mobility within the region, discussions on regulatory frameworks and standards would be a necessary condition.

A third critical step which would need to underpin much of the regional efforts in services (and also in goods) would be the development of the regional transport services infrastructure and trade facilitation measures. The importance of this issue is well recognized within SAARC in the context of the goods trade, but its importance for promoting movement of consumers, service providers, investors, and business visitors, which are all integral to services trade and investment flows, also needs to be underscored. Improved air and land connectivity within the region and transit agreements among groups of countries can greatly facilitate regional services integration, supported of course by regulatory cooperation on taxes, investment, standards, visas, and the other cross-cutting issues highlighted earlier.

A final critical step would be to engage in capacity building efforts regionally. This would take the form of joint research and development activities, joint projects in selected services, such as healthcare, environment, education, renewable energy, and tourism, regional training and development of human resources, sharing and exchange of ideas and information, and sharing of best practices. Such efforts may also enable the countries in the region to arrive at common positions in areas, such as energy, environment, or healthcare and to project a unified position in other negotiating forums.

Epilogue
Political Economy Challenges

Although the preceding chapters have highlighted the many opportunities for services integration in South Asia and also outlined various strategies and approaches to realize this integration, the discussion has downplayed the challenges that will arise in this process given the complex political economy dynamics within South Asia. This downplaying has to some extent been deliberate as the aim throughout this book has been to focus on the opportunities in services integration, rather than getting mired in the usual pessimism that characterizes discussions on South Asia and SAARC, mainly due to the strained political relations between the key players in the region. Such pessimism leads to neglect of potential positive outcomes and also results in inadequate focus on other constraints, such as regulatory, infrastructural, and capacity related constraints to integration in the region. Hence, the discussion throughout has tried to move beyond the politics of integration (though references to this were necessary in the context of several services and issues) and to take a relatively more objective look at the benefits and other challenges.

However, no discussion on South Asia can completely ignore the root problem of politics which confronts this region. Undoubtedly, the single biggest challenge to services integration in South Asia, and for that matter overall integration in South Asia, is the complex political economy of this region. Whatever has been proposed as the way forward in the earlier chapters cannot be de-linked from the political economy dynamics among the member countries. These political problems cut across all the areas that have been identified as critical pre-requisites for successful integration of services under SAFAS. For instance, the economic agenda of improving the mobility of service providers and people within the region, or improving land connectivity and developing transport corridors, or engaging in energy trade, cannot be insulated from these political realities.

There are two fundamental problems on the political economy front (apart from the poor political relations between India and Pakistan) that would impede progress in services integration in South Asia. The first of these is internal to most of the member countries, and in turn has a bearing on relations within the region and thus on the integration prospects. This concerns the political instability and fragility characterizing many of the SAARC member nations. Several governments in the region are faced with (or have been faced with) internal conflicts on ethnic, religious, and social grounds, hurting their legitimacy and their ability to implement institutional, structural, and regulatory reforms and to make the requisite investments in social and physical infrastructure with long-term objectives in mind. Failure to progress in these supporting areas at the national level, in turn, makes it difficult to realize the pre-requisites for regional integration. This is also likely to limit the scope and depth of any liberalization undertaken in a regional services agreement. Weak governments and lack of internal social and political cohesion also make it difficult for the member governments to invest in cooperation and relation building efforts with other countries in the region, the problems witnessed in Indo-Pakistan and Indo-Nepal relations being cases in point. Lack of internal cohesion has also bred mistrust within and among nations in the region, thus undermining one of the very foundations for regional integration. These problems also reflect themselves in lack of political will to deepen regional integration, which, as pointed out by many studies, has been the Achilles heel of SAARC.

The second fundamental problem in the region is the structural and geo-political asymmetry among the countries in South Asia. Although the large differences in endowments, economic size, trade baskets, and strategic importance of the member countries in this region do create scope for complementarities among the member countries in terms of trade and investment flows, they also pose challenges in terms of the distribution of benefits from regional integration and also create differences among the member countries in terms of their strategic interests within the region. As highlighted earlier, India dominates in services growth, trade and investment flows, competitiveness trends, and overall significance within the region. Hence, any services agreement is bound to reflect these asymmetries. Moreover, India's growing global importance as an emerging economy and its presence in forums, such as the G-20 create scope for conflicting positions and strategic interests with the other member countries of the region and could potentially divert India's focus from South Asia towards other regions and alliances.

Overall, South Asian integration is constrained by the strong divisions that exist within and among some of the member states, which undermine the very concept of a cohesive and integrated region. Belief in economic integration itself may be wanting among member countries. Hence, progress based on inter-governmental efforts alone is unlikely. Parallel efforts among industry, civil society, and academics through continual dialogue and institutional cooperation at various levels are essential to build confidence, remove distrust, and develop the will to proceed with regional integration in the long run. In the context of a services agreement, a careful balancing of interests and sensitivities is required, such as through a special and differential treatment of the smaller countries in the region, by trading off concessions across different sectors and issues, and through cooperation in other areas which are of common interest.

Although it is difficult to say which should precede the other, political will or integration, perhaps it is time to look at integration, however, limited in scope and however tentative the steps, as a means to cementing better relations and creating goodwill among the member countries of SAARC. As services integration relies much more on factor mobility and people-to-people contact in comparison to integration in goods, it provides a great opportunity for building the much needed trust and goodwill among the member countries of SAARC through a variety of channels, including increased business-to-business contacts, better understanding among the peoples of these countries due to increased intra-regional travel, and greater stake of companies and investors in ensuring political and economic stability within the region. For once, it may be worth examining the role that service industries and associations in the region could play as opposed to politicians in providing the much needed boost to regional cooperation in South Asia.

Annexure

FDI Policy and Regulatory Status

Telecommunication Services

Table A.1 Status of FDI Policy in the Telecommunications Sector in South Asian Countries

	Source	Provisions/Limitations on FDI
Bangladesh	National Telecommunications 1998	• Investment from sources outside the country may be arranged through supplier credit, joint ventures, BLT/BOT/BOO/BTO agreements, etc., in addition to the usual loans and grants from international organizations, as well as through bilateral agreements with other countries in conformity with the industrial policy of the government. • Foreign investors are encouraged to demonstrate their commitment to Bangladesh by forming joint ventures with local companies and within the telecommunication sector. Government will consider equity participation of up to 100 per cent of the overall shareholdings of the telecommunication operating company.
Bhutan	FDI Policy Rules and Regulations 2005	Telecommunications not opened to FDI.
India	DIPP	1. FDI up to 100 per cent in telecom manufacturing, ISPs without gateways, infrastructure provider (IP)-I, call centres, and IT-enabled services. 2. FDI up to 74 per cent in ISPs with gateways, IP-II, and radio paging. 3. FDI up to 74 per cent (automatic up to 49 per cent, FIPB approval above 49 per cent) in all other telecom services—basic and cellular, unified access services, national/international long distance, V-Sat, public mobile radio trunked services (PMRTS), global mobile personal communications services (GMPCS), and other value-added telecom services.
Nepal	Telecommunications Policy 2004	Foreign investment shall be attracted in the telecommunication sector, subject to minimum 20 per cent local participation through joint ventures in basic telephone and mobile telephone services.
Maldives	Investment Bureau	Telecommunications not open to FDI
Pakistan	Investment Bureau	Government permission not required except for licenses. 100 per cent foreign equity ownership. Repatriation allowed (all telecom services). Minimum amount to be invested—US$ 0.15 million.
Sri Lanka	Investment Bureau	Allowed up to 100 per cent foreign equity participation. These services are regulated and subject to approval by various government agencies. The screening mechanism is non-discriminatory and, for the most part, routine.

Source: Various countries telecommunications regulatory bodies/ministry websites/telecommunications policies.

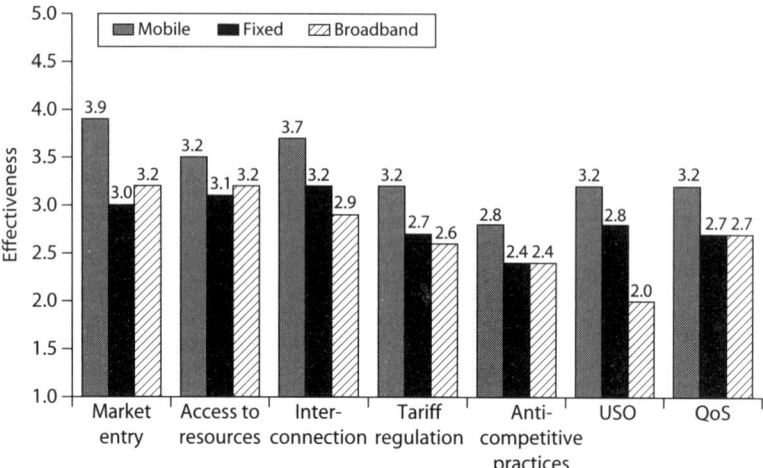

Figure A.1   Telecom Regulatory Environment Scores for Pakistan, 2008
Source: Reproduced from Wilson (2008).

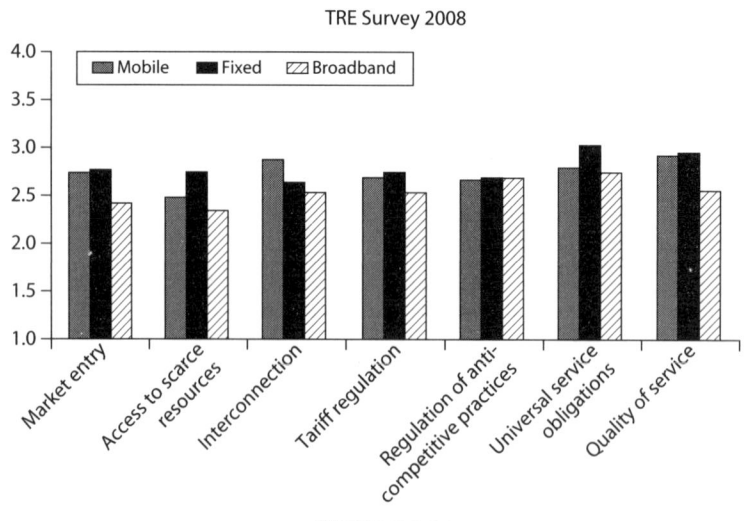

Figure A.2   Telecom Regulatory Environment Scores for Sri Lanka, 2008
Source: Reproduced from Knight-John (2008).

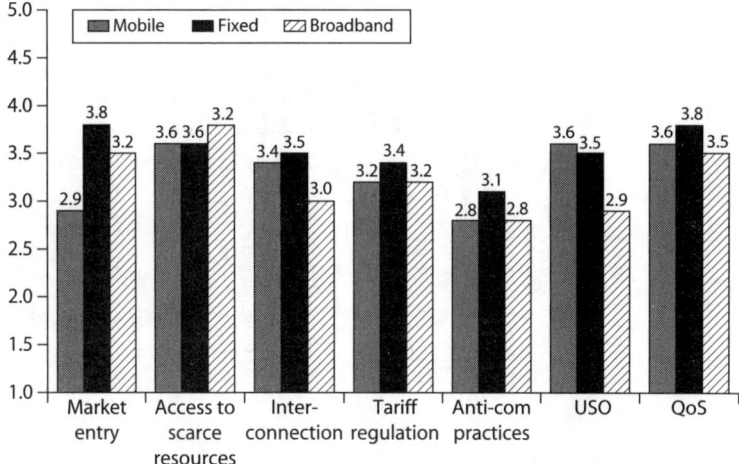

Figure A.3   Telecom Regulatory Environment Scores for Maldives, 2008
Source: Reproduced from Galpaya (2008).

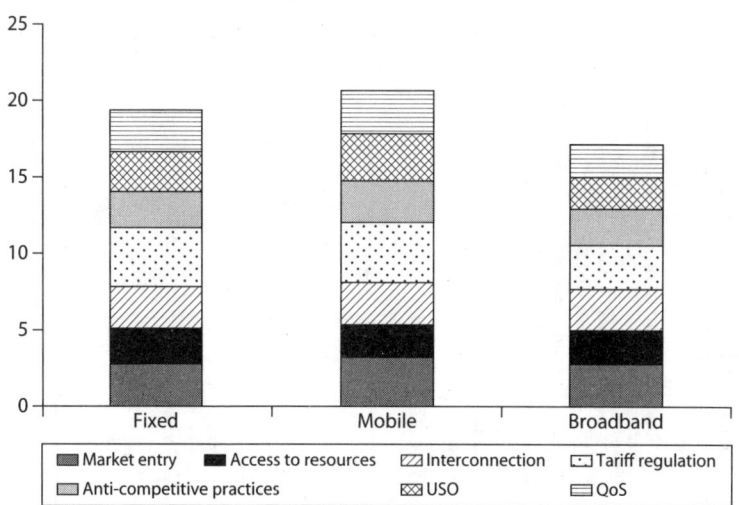

Figure A.4   Telecom Regulatory Environment Scores for India, 2008
Source: Reproduced from Malik (2008).

Energy Services

Table A.2 Policy and Regulatory Status in Energy Services in Bangladesh

Type of Energy	FDI Permission	Conditions on FDI	Private Participation	Power Sector Reforms/Regulatory Authority	Import Policy for Related Resources	Others
Electricity	Allowed	Incentives such as tax holidays and repatriation of profits for foreign investors	Allowed	• Energy policy was prepared and adopted in 1996 • A separate organization termed as Power Cell was created to design, facilitate, and monitor reform measures • Segregation of power generation, transmission, and distribution functions into separate services • Corporatization and commercialization of emerging power sector entities • Policy has also been designed to promote small-scale generation in the private sector, particularly to serve non-grid areas, pockets of continued power shortage, and provide opportunity for sale of excess power from captive generation to consumers in the neighbouring areas • Bangladesh Energy Regulatory Commission to frame rules and regulation to ensure transparency in the management, operation, and tariff determination in the electricity, gas, and petroleum sector and to protect consumer and industry interest and promote competitive market • Introduction of cost reflective tariff for financial viability of the utilities and promoting efficient use of electricity • Development of demand management, including energy efficiency measures to conserve energy • Development of alternative/renewable energy sources	• Petroleum oil and all kinds of oil obtained from bituminous mineral crude & LPG— importable by Bangladesh Petroleum Corporation. However, in the private sector, it is importable with the approval of the Ministry of Power, Energy & Mineral Resources and prior permission from the Ministry of Commerce • Coal/Hard Coke—In case of import of coal and hard coke in both private and public sector, pre-shipment inspection certificate shall be obtained from an internationally reputed surveyor to the effect that the quantity, weight, and quality (standard) of the item are found as declared and quantity of sulphar should not be above 1 per cent • Nuclear reactors and their parts— Importable by Bangladesh Atomic Energy Commission only with the clearance of the sponsoring ministry	Biomass (primarily wood, crop residues, and animal waste) is a significant non-commercial energy source in Bangladesh, estimated to account for over half of the country's energy consumption
Petroleum	Allowed		Allowed			
Natural Gas	Allowed		Allowed			
Hydropower	Allowed		Allowed			
Others (nuclear, wind, etc.)	Not allowed in nuclear energy					

Sources: http://www.boi.gov.bd/sector_brief.php#natural; http://www.bpdb.gov.bd/vision%20statement.htm; http://www.banglaembassy.com.bh/FDI%20in%20Bangladesh.htm; Import Policy Order 2006–9, available at http://www.mincom.gov.bd/acts.php (accessed on 4 November 2009).

Table A.3 Policy and Regulatory Status in Energy Services in Bhutan

Type of Energy	FDI Permission	Conditions on FDI	Private Participation	Power Sector Reforms/ Regulatory Authority	Import Policy for Related Resources	Others
Electricity Petroleum Natural Gas Hydropower	51 per cent	• All foreign investment only in local currency • Investment cap of US$ 0.5 million for services sector and US$ 1 million for manufacturing sector • BOOT (build, own, operate, and transfer) system • According to BOOT, the foreign investor could operate a power project for 30 years with a possible extension of another 15 years		• No specific energy policy to provide guidance to the energy sector in Bhutan • Department of Energy is responsible for the formulation of energy and power sector policy, plans, programmes, and guidelines/regulations, feasibility studies related to hydropower development, Detailed Project Reports (DPRs) for sustainable development of hydropower projects • Bhutan Electricity Authority, an autonomous regulatory agency, regulates the electricity sector	• Bhutan has no identified petroleum reserves or a refinery for crude oil processing. The Royal Government of Bhutan has a long-term agreement with the Government of India for the supply of petroleum products • Bhutan imports most of its finished products of petroleum and related oils (diesel, petrol, kerosene, lubricating oils, and liquid petroleum gas) from India • To minimize the dependency on fuel imports several policy measures taken by the government, including encouraging use of electricity by exempting import tax on electric domestic appliances and subsidizing electricity tariff for domestic use	For India, it is 70 per cent; talks going on to increase it to 100 per cent
Others (nuclear, wind, etc.)						

Source: http://eneken.ieej.or.jp/data/2598.pdf; http://www.dailynews.lk/2009/01/28/fea03.pdf; https://www.bhutantimes.com/modules/newbb/viewtopic.php?viewtopic.php?topic_id=2627&forum=10; http://www.bhutantimes.bt/index.php?option=com_content&task=view&id=856&Itemid=1; http://www.bhutanmajestictravel.com/news/2007/bhutan-imported-petroleum-and-related-products-worth-us-472-billlion.html (accessed on 9 November 2009).

Table A.4 Policy and Regulatory Status in Energy Services in India

Type of Energy	FDI Permission	Conditions on FDI	Private Participation	Power Sector Reforms/ Regulatory Authority	Import Policy for Related Resources
Electricity	• 100 per cent (generation, transmission, and distribution)	Automatic route subject to provisions of the Electricity Act, 2003	Allowed	• National Electricity Policy (The Electricity Act, 2003) has put in place a highly liberal framework for generation • No requirement of licensing for generation • The requirement of techno-economic clearance of CEA for thermal generation project is no longer there • For hydroelectric generation also, the limit of capital expenditure, above which concurrence of CEA is required, would be raised suitably from the present level • Captive generation has been freed from all controls • Open access in transmission has been introduced to promote competition amongst the generating companies who can now sell to different distribution licensees across the country • The Electricity Act, 2003 enables competing generating companies and trading licensees, besides the area distribution licensees, to sell electricity to consumers when open access in distribution is introduced by the State Electricity Regulatory Commissions • Concept of multiple licensees in the same area of supply through their independent distribution systems • Central Electricity Regulatory Commission to regulate the tariff of generating companies owned or controlled by the central government, to regulate the inter-state transmission of energy, including tariff of the transmission utilities, to promote competition, efficiency, and economy in the activities of the electricity industry • The State Electricity Regulatory Commission determines tariff for generation, supply transmission, and wheeling of electricity : wholesale/bulk /rental/ within the state	• As per the present import policy, coal can be freely imported (under Open General License) by the consumers themselves considering their needs and exercising their own commercial judgments • The import of petroleum products, being canalized items, can be done by public sector oil company, the Indian Oil Corporation

Petroleum	• For refining 49 per cent in case of PSUs with approval of FIPB • 100 per cent in case of private companies, foreign companies do not need clearance from FIPB but need to inform RBI • For non-refining—100 per cent • 100 per cent FDI permitted through automatic route for marketing of petroleum products • 100 per cent FDI permitted through automatic route for petroleum product pipelines	• For refining FIPB (in case of PSUs) and automatic (in case of private companies), subject to sectoral policy and no divestment or dilution of domestic equity in the existing PSUs • For non-refining automatic, subject to sectoral regulations issued by the Ministry of Petroleum and Natural Gas • Marketing of petroleum products • Minimum investment of US$ 450 mn in exploration and production or refining or pipelines or terminals and other conditions as laid down by the Ministry of Petroleum and Natural Gas	Allowed
Natural gas	• 100 per cent allowed in natural gas exploration • 100 per cent for natural gas and LNG pipelines	• Subject to exploration policy • Subject to FIPB approval	Allowed	Petroleum and Natural Gas Regulatory Board Bill enacted, Regulatory Board constituted
Hydropower	100 per cent for natural gas and LNG pipelines	Automatic route	Allowed	No independent regulatory body
Others (nuclear, wind, etc.)	Not allowed in atomic energy			

Source: http://coal.nic.in/eximp.html; http://ssaindia.net/FdiPolicy.htm; http://siadipp.nic.in/policy/changes/press7_00.htm; http://dipp.nic.in/manual/FDI_Manual_text_Latest.pdf; http://www.powermin.nic.in/JSP_SERVLETS/internal.jsp; http://www.indiamart.com/sell-in-india/indian-import-policy.html; http://www.investmentcommission.in/oil_&_gas_exploration.htm (accessed on 3 November 2009).

Table A.5 Policy and Regulatory Status in Energy Services in Maldives

Type of Energy	FDI Permission	Conditions on FDI	Private Participation	Power Sector Reforms/ Regulatory Authority	Import Policy for Related Resources	Others
Electricity	Full foreign ownership of investment projects is allowed in all sectors and activities			• The Maldives Electricity Bureau (MEB), chaired by the Ministry of Trade and Industries (MTI), regulates the State Electric Company Ltd. (STELCO) and the private power providers • STELCO is entirely a state-owned organization responsible for the generation, distribution, and supply of electricity to customers throughout Maldives	• Maldives imports all its fuel in refined form and in very small quantities, which makes this form of fuel even more expensive	• Maldives has no conventional energy resources (for example, oil and gas) that it can utilize to meet its energy needs • It utilizes imported petroleum fuels to meet all of its energy needs
Petroleum						
Natural gas						
Hydropower						
Others (nuclear, wind, etc.)						

Source: http://www.sari-energy.org/PageFiles/Countries/maldives_Energy_detail.asp; http://books.google.co.in/books?id=c-fV6ohJVBcC&pg=PA87&lpg=PA87&dq=import+policy+maldives&source=bl&ots=Q5DNyscKUC&sig=DMFVusgcY5QqQkBOgf0YlPQUrgw&hl=en&ei=6Hv2SuvnKNSWkAWJitWjAw&sa=X&oi=book_result&ct=result&resnum=5&ved=0CBAQ6AEwBA#v=onepage&q=import%20policy%20maldives&f=false (accessed on 9 November 2009).

Table A.6 Policy and Regulatory Status in Energy Services in Nepal

Type of Energy	FDI Permission	Conditions on FDI	Private Participation	Power Sector Reforms/ Regulatory Authority	Import Policy for Related Resources	Others
Electricity	100 per cent	• No licensing required to set up 'Energy Based Industry'	Allowed	• Department of Electricity Development as the single window for power development	• All commercial fossil fuels (mainly oil and coal) are either imported from India or from international markets routed through India	• Except for some lignite deposits, Nepal has no known oil, gas, or coal deposits
Petroleum	100 per cent	• Registration of 'Industry' is required	Allowed	• For all the projects/industries involving FDI, the Department of Industries is the relevant authority	• Nepal has allowed the import and sale of petroleum products by the private sector in an effort to help ease fuel supplies in the Himalayan nation	• Fuel imports absorb over one-fourth of Nepal's foreign exchange earnings
Natural gas	100 per cent		Allowed	• Electricity Tariff Fixation Commission (ETFC) is the sole authority for electricity tariff and other charges levied to the customers against services rendered through generation, transmission, and distribution of electricity by the licensee	• Interested private companies can import fuel from any part of the world and sell at their own prices	
Hydropower	100 per cent		Allowed			
Others (nuclear, wind, etc.)	Not allowed					

Source: http://www.doind.gov.np/pdf/pmanual.pdf; http://www.nepalmonitor.com/2009/01/fdi_in_nepals_hydropower.html; http://www.s ari-energy.org/Publications/REP/Regulation/NepalStatus.pdf; http://www.sari-energy.org/PageFiles/Countries/Nepal_Energy_detail.asp; http:// www.business-standard.com/india/news/nepal-ends-noc-monopoly-over-petrol-import-sale/39661/on (accessed on 4 November 2009).

Table A.7 Policy and Regulatory Status in Energy Services in Pakistan

Type of Energy	FDI Permission	Conditions on FDI	Private Participation	Power Sector Reforms/ Regulatory Authority	Import Policy for Related Resources	Others
Electricity Petroleum Natural gas Hydropower Others (nuclear, wind, etc.)	100 per cent in infrastructure sector	Min. investment US$ 0.3 mn	Local companies encouraged to form joint ventures with foreign companies	• In 1994, the government formulated a power policy and invited for the first time, independent power producers (IPPs) to invest in the generation part of the power sector • IPPs get involved in disputes and litigation with the government over the rates set in their PPAs with Water and Power Development Authority (WAPDA) • Establishment of National Electric Power Regulatory Authority (NEPRA), under NEPRA Act, 1997, an autonomous regulatory agency, to ensure transparent and judicious economic regulation in the power sector • Private Power and Infrastructure Board (PPIB), established in 1994, to facilitate private investors • Unbundling of WAPDA's vertically integrated Power Wing into separate generation, transmission, and distribution companies (as in the 1998 WAPDA Act) in 1998 • WAPDA has now been reorganized into four thermal generation companies called GENCOs, nine distribution companies called DISCOs, and one National Transmission and Dispatch Company (NTDC) • The hydroelectric power development and operation functions remain with WAPDA • Pakistan Electric Power Company Private Limited (PEPCO), a separate agency within WAPDA, is made responsible for the restructuring and preparation for privatization for the generation and distribution companies in due course through the Privatization Commission • The process of separating out various entities and corporatization is in progress • While unbundling has been completed, the various entities created from WAPDA still lack independence from WAPDA and from one another; the distribution companies are still financially integrated with WAPDA	• Petroleum sectors allowed to import secondhand plant, machinery and equipment, actually required for their projects • Petroleum oils and oils obtained from bituminous minerals crude importable by oil refineries only • Motor spirit, including aviation spirit, kerosene, including kerosene-type jet fuel, other medium oils, and preparations/light diesel oil, gas oils/ high speed diesel oil, and other fuel oils importable by approved oil marketing companies	

Source: http://www.pakboi.gov.pk/invest.pack.htm; http://www.sari-energy.org/PageFiles/Countries/Pakistan_Energy_detail.asp#reforms; Import Policy Order, available at http://www.epb.gov.pk/v1/tradepolicy/pdf/0775-31072006-ipo.pdf (accessed on 5 November 2009).

Table A.8 Policy and Regulatory Status in Energy Services in Sri Lanka

Type of Energy	FDI Permission	Conditions on FDI	Private Participation	Power Sector Reforms/ Regulatory Authority	Import Policy for Related Resources	Others
Electricity Petroleum Natural gas Hydropower Others (nuclear, wind, etc.)	Allowed	• Min. investment US$ 500,000 for small-scale power generation projects • US$ 12,500,000 for large-scale projects in petroleum and petroleum product, power generation, transmission, and distribution	Permission granted for private sector developers to develop and implement power generation projects through the following renewable energy technologies: biomass power generation, technologies using waste sugarcane as renewable energy, wind power technology, power-generating technology using municipal solid waste	• The electricity supply industry is dominated by state-sector institutions, namely, the Ceylon Electricity Board (CEB) and Lanka Electricity Company (Pvt.) Ltd. (LECO) • CEB is expected to be unbundled vertically and horizontally to form one generation company, a single transmission and bulk-power trading company, and several distribution companies • A regulatory structure in the form of the Public Utilities Commission of Sri Lanka (PUCSL) is already in place, for all physical infrastructure sectors, inclusive of the electricity and petroleum industries • The Electricity Reform Act No. 28, 2002 was enacted in December 2002 to regulate and restructure the electricity industry in Sri Lanka • To use only coal and LNG for all future long-term thermal power generating plants	• The Island is still to strike oil and is totally dependent on imports for its entire requirement of oil	

Source: http://www.boi.lk/2009/pdf/Incentives.pdf; http://mope.gov.lk/uploads/policy/policyen.pdf; http://www.sari-energy.org/ PageFiles/Countries/Sri_Lanka_Energy_detail.asp#reforms (accessed on 5 November 2009).

Tourism Trade

Table A.9 Regulatory and Policy Environment in Tourism Services in Bangladesh

Category	FDI Policy	FDI Restrictions	Licensing / Registration Issues	Taxes and Levies	Others

Hotels	100 per cent	No Restriction	• Hotel owner to apply within two months of opening to the controller for registration and classification of hotel
			• Registration requirements include:
			  • Satisfying prescribed norms of health, hygiene and comfort
			  • Medical fitness of staff
			  • Structurally safe and adequately protected building against fire, etc.
				• Multiplicity of taxes
				• High rate of taxes
					• Government has taken steps to establish, Special Tourist Zones (STZs) at Cox's Bazar, Sundarbans, and Kuakata
					• Government has taken initiative to exploit the eco-tourism potential of the country for sustainable tourism development

Tour and travel operators	100 per cent	No Restriction	• Travel agency should hold appointment as agent from the national airline of Bangladesh and at least one foreign airline with authority to quote air fares, make reservations, issue tickets, national and international handling of tours etc. • Transacts business of Taka 50 lakh or more in a year		

Source: http://bdlaws.gov.bd/pdf/637____.pdf; http://www.mocat.gov.bd/notice_details.php?ID=8&CATEGORY=1; http://www.discoverybangladesh.com/meetbangladesh/investment.html; http://www.mocat.gov.bd/policies/Bangladesh_Travel_Agencis_(Registration_&_Control)_Rules%20and%20Ordinance%201977.pdf (accessed on 8 November 2009).

Table A.10 Regulatory and Policy Environment in Tourism Services in Bhutan

Category	FDI Policy	Route	Restrictions/Facilities on FDI	Licensing/Registration Issues	Taxes and Levies	Others
Hotels	• Up to 70 per cent of the equity • Draft FDI Economic Policy 2009 recommends international companies to have 100 per cent equity in four and five star hotels in Bhutan	• FDI Registration (FDIR) Certificate to be issued by the Ministry of Trade & Industry	• The minimum size of investment (total project cost) US$ 500,000 • Investments governed by sector-specific policies and procedures • Foreign investors accorded the same treatment, including investment incentives and exemptions, as accorded to local investors	• Hotels in the country will soon be graded on a star rating, based on a new classification system introduced by the Tourism Council of Bhutan (TCB) • Earlier there existed the letter system, introduced in 1999, which categorized hotels as class A, B, and C class	• Hotels have to compromise on quality due to high duty levied on capital goods • In certain cases, the government has provided duty exemption on certain items such as kitchen equipment, bedding, and furniture • Royalties are applicable for tourism industry	• Lack of online transaction and credit card facilities hampering hotel business • Most hotels are unable to provide 'high-value service' due to the non-availability of trained and professional human resources within the country • According to Tourism Council of Bhutan records, the single largest complaint from visitors to Bhutan is poor quality of services in hotels

Source: http://www.mof.gov.bt/index.php?deptid=14&id=84; http://bhutan-360.com/hotels-to-be-rated-with-stars/; http://www.bhutanobserver.bt/2009/bhutan-news/08/hoteliers-raise-concerns.html; http://www.bhutanmajestictravel.com/news/2009/the-hotel-industry-in-bhutan-is-booming.html (accessed on 5 November 2009).

Table A.11 Regulatory and Policy Environment in Tourism Services in India

Category	FDI Policy	Route	Restrictions on FDI	Licensing / Registration Issues	Taxes and Levies	Others
Hotels	100 per cent	Automatic	For foreign technology agreements, automatic approval is granted if: • Up to 3 per cent of the capital cost of the project is proposed to be paid for technical and consultancy services • Up to 3 per cent of the net turnover is payable for franchising and marketing/ publicity fee • Up to 10 per cent of gross operating profit is payable for management fee, including incentive fee	• Every state in India has in general a Registration of Tourist Trade Act (the Tourist Trade Act) • The Tourist Trade Act requires all hotels, travel agents, tour operators, tourist guides, tourist taxi operators, and dealers of notified articles and other persons engaged in tourist activities in each particular state to register themselves under the Tourist Trade Act	• Multitude of central and state taxes like expenditure tax, luxury tax, etc. • High rate of taxes • Highest import duty on imported liquor used in hotels	• Ministry of Tourism provides incentives for the construction of hotels in the budget category and the heritage basic category by way of subsidy • Hotels in Delhi set up before 2010 have been granted infrastructure status with special tax concessions
Tour and travel operators	Same as hotels	Same as hotels	Same as hotels		• Taxation of the gross service amount leads to double taxation and increases the burden for tourists	

Source: http://www.sebi.gov.in/dp/indianlof.pdf; http://www.tourism.gov.in/annualreportE08-09.pdf; http://dspace.iimk.ac.in/ bitstream/2259/544/1/107-113+srinivas.pdf; http://magazine.indiabizclub.com/tourism-hotels/regulatory-policy-of-indian-hotel- industry/ (accessed on 7 November 2009).

Table A.12 Regulatory and Policy Environment in Tourism Services in Maldives

Category	FDI Policy	Route	FDI Restrictions	Licensing/Registration Issues	Taxes and Levies
Hotels	100 per cent		• All foreign nationals investing in tourism shall sign an agreement with the Ministry of Tourism	• Maldives Tourism Act (Law No. 2/99) provides for the determination of zones and islands for the development of tourism in Maldives: the leasing of islands for development as tourist resorts, the leasing of land for development as tourist hotels and tourist guest houses, the leasing of places for development as marinas, the management of all such facilities, and the operation of tourist vessels, diving centres and travel agencies, and the regulation of persons providing such services	• Tax for each tourist per day of stay at a tourist resort, tourist hotel, tourist guest house, or tourist vessel
Tour and travel operators				• No person shall provide travel agency services in Maldives except after obtaining a license issued by the Ministry of Tourism • A license to provide travel agency services shall be issued to parties that satisfy the following conditions: (a) where the party is a company or other business organization, the provision of travel agency services is included as an object in the memorandum of association of that company or business organization (b) where the party is a foreign company or business organization, it is registered at the Ministry of Trade and Industries as a company or business organization carrying on business in Maldives (c) the (physical) presence of an office operated in compliance with guidelines provided in regulations made under this Act, and the services determined by the Ministry of Tourism to be necessary at such office are made available from the travel agency • No person shall act as a tour guide in Maldives except after obtaining permission from the Ministry of Tourism in accordance with regulations made by that ministry • Every person acting as a tour guide shall, whilst acting in the course of business as a tour guide, attach to his attire in a manner identifiable to others the permission issued to him	

Source: http://www.tourism.gov.mv/article.php?aId=8; http://www.maldiveisle.com/tourismactofmaldives.htm; http://www.investmaldives.org/downloads/documents/FIL.pdf (accessed on 11 November 2009).

Table A.13 Regulatory and Policy Environment in Tourism Services in Nepal

Category	FDI Policy	Route	FDI Restrictions	Licensing/Registration Issues	Taxes and Levies	Others
Hotels	100 per cent, not permitted in tourist lodging	• Permission of the Department shall be required to be obtained for foreign investment of technology transfer	• Nepal encourages foreign investment as joint venture operations with Nepalese investors or as 100 per cent foreign-owned enterprises • Foreign investments are permitted up to 100 per cent equity share holding in medium and large-scale industries • In cottage and small industries permission may be granted to use foreign technology in the form of investment	• Hotel, Lodge, Restaurant, Bar and Tourist Guide Regulation, 2038 B.S. (1981 AD) specifies minimum facilities in terms of number of rooms, electricity, laundry, decoration of rooms with Nepalese art and culture, etc.	• Tourists are required to pay value added tax (VAT) and tourism tax on invoice where applicable (for example, hotel bills, restaurants, etc. VAT is 10 per cent, and tourism tax is 2 per cent of the total bill)	• The government accords high priority to tourism development and plans to create the necessary environment and infrastructure to strengthen the tourism industry • A major strategy in meeting the demand for hotel rooms in Nepal is to encourage increased private foreign investment, including private foreign investment for the development of tourist infrastructure such as 4 and 5 star hotels and resorts
Tour and travel operators	Travel agency and trekking agency not permitted			• A person who desires to take tourist guide license shall have tourist guide training and certificate of hotel management from a tourism training centre		

Source: http://www.nepalvista.com/travel/visa.html#3a; http://www.catmando.com/gov/industry/fipd/fipd10.htm; http://www.catmando.com/gov/industry/fipd/fipd15.htm; http://www.tourism.gov.np/foreignInvestmentAndTechTransferAct1992.php; http://www.tourism.gov.np/hotel_lodge_rest_tour_guide_regulation2038eng.php (accessed on 8 November 2009).

Table A.14 Regulatory and Policy Environment in Tourism Services in Pakistan

Category	FDI Policy	Route	FDI Restrictions	Licensing/Registration Issues	Taxes and Levies	Others
Hotels	100 per cent		• Minimum investment US$ 0.15 mn		• Any plant, machinery or equipment, which is not manufactured locally, and is used for tourism, hotels, or tourism-related projects is importable at a custom duty of 5 per cent and zero rated sales tax • The hotel tax is levied at the rate of Rs 7.5 per cent ad valorem of room rent per lodging unit per day, for the categories, such as on 60 per cent of the total number of lodging units in hotels charging Rs 100 or above but not exceeding Rs 400 per day	• Tourism sector is treated as an industry by virtue of Ministry of Industries and Production Circular No. 1-129/99-INV-IV dated 2nd August, 1999 • Deemed export status granted to tourism industry including hotels
Tour and travel operators	100 per cent		• Min. investment US$ 0.15 mn			

Source: http://www.pakboi.gov.pk/invest.pack.htm; http://www.tahseenbutt.com/investment_in_pakistan.html (accessed on 7 November 2009).

Table A.15 Regulatory and Policy Environment in Tourism Services in Sri Lanka

Category	FDI Policy	Route	Restrictions on FDI	Licensing/Registration Issues	Taxes and Levies	Others
Hotels	Allowed		• For small scale projects minimum investment is US$ 500,000 • For expansion of an existing non-BOI company engaged in the hotel industry (3 star and above), minimum investment is US$ 5,000,000		• A Tourism Development Levy is imposed on the turnover of every institution licensed under the Tourist Development Act, No. 14 of 1968 • Hotel services are categorized in luxury rate (20 per cent) category for VAT purposes	• Tourism is categorized under small-scale infrastructure projects • Tourism in Sri Lanka is forecasted to be the 4th highest revenue earner by 2010 • Given the high returns estimate and its importance to the country's future economic growth, a focused incentive plan to develop this lucrative market is in place
• Tour and travel operators	• 100 per cent	• Up to 40 per cent will be approved by the Board of Investment (BOI) • Foreign investment in excess of 40 per cent (and up to 100 per cent) will be approved by BOI on a case-by-case basis in consultation with the relevant authorities		• The regulatory authority of all tourism-related developments is the Sri Lanka Tourism Development Authority (SLTDA) • It is involved in establishing, updating and regulating industry standards in the travel and tourism industry, registering and licensing tourist service providers, inspecting and monitoring tourist establishments and service providers, and formulating and regulating prices charged for tourist services • No tourist enterprise or tourist service shall carry on business unless it is registered with the authority • Tourist guides, chauffeur tourist guides, and travel agents are offered varied types of training to ascertain their competence at the job • The Sri Lankan Institute of Tourism and Hotel Management has been set up to equip young men and women in the multifaceted field of hospitality and travel industry		

Source: http://www.sltda.gov.lk/boi_incentives; http://www.boi.lk/2009/pdf/Incentives.pdf; http://www.sltda.lk/registration_of_tour_guides; http://www.sltda.lk/classification_of_tourist_hotels; http://www.sltda.gov.lk/sites/default/files/section_16_act.pdf; http://www.sltda.gov.lk/sites/default/files/Tourism_%20Act_%202005.pdf; http://www.pwccn.com/webmedia/doc/633784183988549499_aptn22_may2009_sl.pdf (accessed on 10 November 2009).

Health Services

Table A.16 Status of FDI Policies in Hospitals

Country	FDI	Entry Route	Restriction on Form of Participation	Discriminatory Provisions w.r.t. Domestic Providers/Other Restrictions/Facilities
Bangladesh	No restriction on foreign equity participation limit, 100 per cent in any undertaking allowed			No restriction on repatriation of profits and income by foreign companies
Bhutan	Not allowed Recently talks of opening health sector to FDI			
India	100 per cent	Automatic approval	No	
Maldives	100 per cent		Wholly owned /JV	Foreign investments registered with the Invest Maldives required to pay annual royalty to the government. Royalty fee is 3 per cent of gross income or 15 per cent of profits, whichever is higher, for majority foreign-owned companies. For others, royalty is 1.5 per cent of income or 7.5 per cent of profits, whichever is higher. No restrictions on repatriation of earnings or profits, no foreign exchange restrictions
Nepal	Up to 100 per cent			Except industries that affect security and public health, no other industries need to obtain any license or permission for establishment and operation. Just need to be registered with the concerned department
Pakistan	100 per cent	Automatic	No	100 per cent foreign equity allowed if the amount of foreign equity investment in the company/project is at least US$ 0.3 million FDI allowed on repatriable basis Equal treatment for domestic and foreign investors
Sri Lanka	Remain restricted and subject to case-by-case approval for foreign equity exceeding 49 per cent	Approval is required from the Board of Investment (BOI) prior to the establishment of a foreign business venture in Sri Lanka		BOI has separate incentive programmes to promote regional development, with the aim of establishing new factories or service companies (such as hotels, hospitals, or training institutes) in regions outside Colombo. Incentives include 10–20 year tax holidays for investments in northern and eastern provinces and 2–10 year tax holidays for investments located in other provinces. In addition, imports of machinery and equipment exempted from both customs duty and value added tax. Minimum investment levels apply Generally, treatment of foreign investors is non-discriminatory.

Sources: Websites for Boards of Investment and other online official sources for all the countries.

Table A.17 Status of Policies in Other Segments of Health Services

Country	FDI/Imports/ Exports	Industrial Licensing/Other Policies	Entry Route	Restriction on Form of Participation, Discriminatory Provisions, Other Conditions
Bangladesh				
Drugs and pharmaceuticals	Very restricted imports, locally-manufactured drugs mostly prohibited from imports	Local firms allowed to contract manufacture for domestic distribution only with locally-present MNCs.	Sales of drugs by foreign firms in the domestic market permitted only if local manufacturing presence	
Health insurance				
Bhutan				
Medical devices	Proposed FDI policy allows 100 per cent FDI in medical equipment and specialized health			
Health Insurance	Not allowed			
India				
Drugs and pharmaceuticals	100 per cent	Not required	Automatic route FDI proposals for the manufacture of licensable drugs and pharmaceuticals and bulk drugs produced by recombinant DNA technology, and specific cell/tissue targeted formulations will require prior government approval.	The venture should not attract compulsory licensing. Should not involve use of recombinant DNA technology.
Medical devices		Some medical devices have been notified in the Drugs Act.		
Health insurance	26 per cent	Required from Insurance Regulatory and Development Authority (IRDA).	While FDI approval is automatic, a license must first be obtained from the Insurance Regulatory and Development Authority.	Joint venture In July 2004, the GoI announced its intention to increase the FDI cap to 49 per cent, but this change first requires parliamentary approval of an amendment to the Insurance Regulatory and Development Authority (IRDA) Act. In December 2008, the GoI introduced this amendment bill in the upper House of the Parliament. However, introduction of the bill is the first step in a lengthy process and an increase in the FDI limit to 49 per cent would take effect only after approval from both Houses of Parliament.

Maldives Health insurance	100 per cent (general insurance, not specific to health)	Wholly owned /JV
Pakistan Diagnostic centres/pathology	100 per cent	Automatic 100 per cent foreign equity is allowed if the amount of foreign equity investment in the company/project shall be at least US$ 0.3 million
Medical devices Telemedicine	National telemedicine forum established.	
	Negligible imports Many private companies providing 'medical subscription' services to big hospitals in the West, but no regulation of this	
Drugs and pharmaceuticals	100 per cent	Automatic Government permission not required except specific licenses from the Ministry of Health.
Sri Lanka Health insurance	100 per cent (general insurance, not specific to health insurance).	

Sources: Websites for Boards of Investment and other online official sources for all the countries.

Education Services

Table A.18 Policy and Regulatory Developments in Education Services in South Asia

Country	Degree of Openness, Conditions for Operators, Regulatory Framework
India	• The Foreign Education Bill, if passed, will allow 100 per cent FDI by universities, automatic route, opening gates to top universities from across the world. But no rules or regulations in place yet for foreign universities to be recognized under UGC.
	• Stanford, Harvard, Wharton, and the European Business School INSEAD have shown interest in setting up India campuses.
	• On 15 March 2010, the central government unanimously approved the Foreign Educational Institutions Regulation of Entry and Operations (Maintenance of Quality and Prevention of Commercialization) Bill 2010. This Bill proposes to allow foreign education providers to set up campuses in India and offer degrees and diplomas to students. It still needs to be ratified by both Houses of Parliament before it can become law. It was tabled in the Lower House in May 2010.
	• All formal educational institutes in India to be run as not-for-profit centres under a society (Societies Registration Act, 1860) or a public trust (Registration Act, 1908).
	• All K12 institutes have to be affiliated to an education board—either central boards like ICSE and CBSE or state boards.
	• Of late several schools have been seeking affiliations with various international boards.
Bangladesh	• MoE is aiming to move towards a devolved system of governance within the current administrative structure. In this system the central government will be responsible for formulating policies, financing, setting quality standards, and monitoring and evaluation etc., while the lower levels of government will be responsible for administering the system. MoE is empowering officials at the district and upazila levels to take greater responsibility in monitoring school performances and ensuring public disclosure of information (for example, SSC passing rates, teacher absenteeism, and class sizes) related to school quality.
	• To ensure appropriate financial controls, MoE is implementing a Financial Management Reform Programme (FMRP). This is intended to increase accountability and transparency in the use of resources.
Sri Lanka	• Foreign investments in education will be approved limited to 40 per cent. Foreign ownership in excess of 40 per cent will be approved on a case-by-case basis by the BOI.
	• Higher educational institutions governed by the Act of Parliament (Universities Act No.16 of 1978).
	• UGC under the Ministry of Higher Education is the apex body of universities in Sri Lanka
	• SLIATE governed by Act No. 29 of 1995 is the apex body in charge of non-university higher technological education in Sri Lanka

Bhutan	• For services—the minimum size of investment is US$ 500,000 and the foreign investors can hold up to 70 per cent. • The MoE having mandate for the overall development of the tertiary education system in the country is responsible for formulating policies and regulating tertiary education institutes through planning and funding, registration and licensing, and quality assurance. • Under the ministry the Department of Adult and Higher Education with Tertiary Education Division under it has the overall responsibility for all tertiary education activities. • The Registrar for Tertiary Education (chaired by the Minister for Education) together with the Board for Tertiary Education are envisaged to provide an oversight and direction to the tertiary education institutes through the same mechanism as mentioned earlier in the following manner: funding, registration and licensing, and quality assurance. • Government aims to provide an enabling environment for private sector investment, including FDI in the tertiary education sector by introducing clearer procedures, providing financial incentives, providing favourable procedures for hiring of foreign faculty, and entry of foreign students
Pakistan	• The state dispenses its responsibility in education through direct service delivery as well as regulating non-state interventions in the sector; however, the largest proportion of service delivery in Pakistan remains with the public sector even as the private sector is growing. • The role of the federal government would be confined within its stewardship of facilitation, coordination, and in ensuring standards of education nationally. • A national policy formulation will always need to be moderated at the federal level with direct and continuing consultations with the provinces and local governments. Therefore, the federal government should not generally and essentially engage directly in implementation of projects. As a consequence directly funded projects of the provincial governments should be designed on a participatory basis and steered with togetherness of oversight and not in isolation with each other. • Higher education is exclusively and autonomously dealt with by the Higher Education Commission. • Inclusive education (special education) is dealt by a separate ministry. Science and technology is being dealt by the Ministry of Science and Technology and Technical Education and vocational training is being pursued in NAVTEC which resides in the Prime Minister's Secretariat.
Nepal	• Educational management will be done in the pattern of federal decentralization in such a way as to make local bodies responsible in all the aspects of educational processes, including education plan at the local level. These will be responsible for the grouping of schools, coordination, resource mobilization, operation, and preparation of guidelines and the fixing of quality targets. The school management committee will be responsible for the management and operation of schools. • By giving emphasis on school based management, arrangements will be made to make them accountable to local bodies. • Arrangements will be made to make economic and other works transparent by social auditing along with the making of schools autonomous and responsible for good governance, management, resource mobilization, and quality promotion.

(Contd . . .)

(*Table A.18 contd . . .*)

Country	Degree of Openness, Conditions for Operators, Regulatory Framework
Maldives	• Under the present government's restructuring, higher education and training, which had fallen under the purview of the Department of Higher Education and Training of the former Ministry of Higher Education, Employment and Social Security, is now under the Ministry of Education. The Ministry of Education is now responsible for both school level and tertiary education in Maldives.
	Administration of overseas scholarships still remains in the newly restructured Higher Education Ministry under the new name of the Ministry of Human Resources, Youth and Sports.
	• The newly created Department of Higher Education (DHE) in November 2008 under the Ministry of Education is the government agency now responsible for overall development of the tertiary education system in the country. The department is expected to undertake this task through policy formulation, planning and funding, registration and licensing, and quality assurance.
	• In the absence of an education or higher education act, state higher education institutions have so far been established through Presidential directives. The two state higher education institutions are governed through their respective councils.

Source: Author's compilation based on official documents, Ministry of Education, websites of individual SAARC member countries, and miscellaneous country and multilateral agency reports.

Table A.19 Indices of Restrictions on Foreign Commercial Presence in Education Services in Bangladesh, India, Pakistan, and Sri Lanka, 2009

Restriction	Criteria	Score	Weights	Bangladesh 2009	India 2009	Pakistan 2009	Sri Lanka 2009
Foreign equity limits	Foreign ownership not permitted	1	0.37	0	0	0	0
	Foreign ownership permitted	0					
Min. investment requirement	Min. investment requirement condition is attached with FDI approval	1	0.07	0	0	1	1
	No min. investment requirement condition is attached with FDI approval	0					
Joint venture arrangements	Foreign institution entry is allowed only through joint ventures with domestic institutions	1	0.07	0	1	1	1
	No requirement for a foreign institution to enter through a joint venture with an institution	0					
Regulatory body	There does not exist an independent regulatory body	1	0.07	0	0	0	0
	There exists an independent regulatory body	0					
Limit on number of foreign providers	Limit on the number of foreign providers allowed to establish campuses in the country	1	0.07	0.5	0.5	0.5	0.5
	No limit on the number of foreign providers but there are registration and authorization requirements to establish a campus in the country	0.5					
	No restrictions on either number or registration and authorization requirements	0					
Local enrolment in international schools	Restrictions on local student enrolment in international schools established domestically	1	0.07	0	1	0	0
	No restrictions on local student enrolment in international schools established domestically	0					
Recognition of qualifications	Degrees from foreign institutions established domestically are not recognized	1	0.07	0	0	0	0.5
	Degrees from foreign institutions established domestically are recognized partially or on a case-by-case basis	0.5					
	Degrees from foreign institutions established domestically are fully recognized	0					
Acquisition of immovable property	Acquisition of immovable property is not permitted	1	0.07	0.5	0.5	0.5	0.5
	Acquisition of immovable property is permitted but with certain conditions/extra fees	0.5					
	Acquisition of immovable property is permitted without any restriction	0					

(*Contd* . . .)

(*Table A.19 contd* . . .)

Restriction	Criteria	Score	Weights	Bangladesh 2009	India 2009	Pakistan 2009	Sri Lanka 2009
Corporate tax laws	Tax rates are much higher than the average	1	0.07	0.75	0.5	0.75	0.75
	Tax rates are moderately higher than the average	0.75					
	Tax rates are average of Asia level	0.5					
	Tax rates are moderately lower than the average	0.25					
	Tax rates are much lower than the average	0					
Discriminatory tax treatment	Tax rates for foreign firms are more than 15 per cent higher than the rates for domestic firms	1	0.07	0	0.5	0	0
	Tax rates for foreign firms are more than 11–15 per cent higher than the rates for domestic firms	0.75					
	Tax rates for foreign firms are more than 6–10 per cent higher than the rates for domestic firms	0.5					
	Tax rates for foreign firms are more than 1–5 per cent higher than the rates for domestic firms	0.25					
	Tax rates are equal for foreign and domestic firms	0					
	Mode 3 Trade Restrictiveness Index		1	0.1225	0.28	0.2625	0.2975

Source: Based on various online resources and policy documents available at respective country governments, multilateral agencies, and other private organization websites.

Notes: 1. The creation of restrictiveness indices for education service is inspired by the Australian Productivity Commission Staff Working by Nguyen-Hong and Wells. However, some more regulations appropriate for the education sector are added to better understand the regulatory environment prevailing in these countries.

2. There are various ways of allocating weights to different parameters used in calculating restrictiveness indices, such as researcher's judgment, and factor analysis.

3. The weights used in this table are based on the researcher's judgment. In doing this, more weight is allocated to FDI limits and other parameters are re-weighted accordingly. There is a problem with the availability of information for some of the parameters used in the table as precise information is not available. In such a situation, inferences are drawn from the available information. Some degree of subjectivity cannot be ruled out in exercising this judgment.

4. Some of the regulations for India and Pakistan are given scores based on the draft education bills of these countries.

Bibliography

Adams, R.H. Jr. 2003. 'International Migration, Remittances and the Brain Drain: A Study of 24 Labor-Exporting Countries', World Bank Policy Research Working Paper No. 3069, World Bank, Washington, DC.

Adkoli, B.V. 2006 'Migration of Health Workers: Perspectives from Bangladesh, India, Nepal, Pakistan, and Sri Lanka', *Regional Health Forum*, 10 (1): 49–58.

Agarwal, P. 2009. *Privatization and Internationalization of Higher Education Services in the Countries of South Asia: An Empirical Analysis*. New Delhi: Indian Council for Research on International Economic Relations. Available at www.saneinetwork.net/pdf/SANEI_VIII/7.pdf, accessed on 31 December 2009.

Agarwal, P. 2006. 'Higher Education in India: The Need for Change', Working Paper No. 180, Indian Council for International Economic Relations (ICRIER), New Delhi.

Ahmed, S. and E. Ghani. 2008. 'Making Regional Cooperation Work for South Asia's Poor', Policy Research Working Paper 4736, World Bank, South Asia Region, South Asia Regional Programs Unit, Washington, DC.

Ahsan, A. 1988. 'Third Asian Summit', *SAARC Perspective*, 2 (3): 55.

Ali, R. 2007. 'Energy Resources and Regional Economic Cooperation in SAARC Countries', mimeo.

Aly, J.H. 2007. 'Education in Pakistan: A Revised White Paper', Ministry of Education. Available at http://planipolis.iiep.unesco.org/upload/Pakistan/Pakistan%20National%20Education%20Policy%20Review%20WhitePaper.pdf, accessed on 27 December 2009.

Amarawickrama, H.A. 2004. 'Sri Lankan Electricity Supply Industry: A Critique of Proposed Reforms', Surrey Energy Economics Discussion Paper Series, July, University of Surrey.

Asian Development Bank (ADB). 2008a. *Emerging Asian Regionalism: A Partnership for Shared Prosperity*. Manila: Asian Development Bank.

———. 2008b. *South Asia Economic Report: Foreign Direct Investment in South Asia*. Manila: Asian Development Bank.

———. 2008c. *Key Indicators for Asia and the Pacific 2008* (39th Edition). Manila: Asian Development Bank. Available at http://www.adb.org/Documents/Books/Key_Indicators/2008/pdf/Key-Indicators-2008.pdf , accessed on 9 September 2009.

————. 2007a. *Information Highway Project in South Asia Targets ADB Approval in 2007*. Manila: Asian Development Bank. Available at http://www.adb.org/ media/Articles/2007/12086-asians-highways-projects, accessed on 17 November 2008.

————. 2007b. 'Preparing the South Asia Subregional Economic Cooperation Transport Logistics and Trade Facilitation Project', Regional Technical Assistance Report, Project No. 39454, Asian Development Bank, Manila.

————. 2006a. 'Preparing the South Asia Subregional Economic Cooperation in Tourism Development Project', Technical Assistance Report, Project No. 39399, Asian Development Bank, Manila.

————. 2006b. *Regional Cooperation Strategy and Program: South Asia (2006–08)*. Manila: Asian Development Bank. Available at http://www.adb.org/ Documents/CSPs/South-Asia/2006/CSP-SA-2006.odf, accessed on 22 February 2010.

————. 2005. 'South Asia Subregional Economic Cooperation (SASEC): Progress and Next Steps', first meeting of the Information and Communications Technology (ICT) Working Group, Asian Development Bank, Manila. Available at http://www.adb.org/Documents/Events/2005/SASEC/SASEC-II/SASECII-session-5.pdf, accessed on 14 December 2009.

————. 2004. 'South Asia Subregional Economic Cooperation (SASEC)', first meeting of the Information and Communications Technology (ICT) Working Group, Asian Development Bank, Manila. Available at http://www.adb.org/ Documents/Events/2004/SASEC/First_Mtg_ICT/SASEC-1st-Proceedings. pdf, accessed on 14 December 2009.

Asian Development Bank and UNCTAD. 2008. *Quantification of Benefits from Economic Cooperation in South Asia*. New Delhi: Macmillan India Ltd.

Asia Forum on Information and Communication Technology Policies and e-Strategies. 2003. *Maldives-Country Report*, October, Kuala Lumpur.

Asia Pacific Forum on Telecommunications Policy and Regulation. 2003. 'Nepal Country Paper', July, Chiang Rai.

Asia Pacific Telecommunity (APT). 2005. 'Review of the SATRC Activities', presentation made at the Eighth SATRC Meeting, August, Bhutan.

————. 2004. 'SATRC Action Plan 2004', APT/SAP04, Bangkok.

Athukorala, P. and K. Sharma. 2006. 'Foreign Investment in a Least Developed Country: The Nepalese Experience', *Transnational Corporations*, 15 (2): 125–46. Available at http://www.unctad.org/en/docs/iteiit20062a1_en.pdf, accessed on 27 December 2009.

Balasooriya, A., Q. Alam, and K. Coghill. 2006. 'The Effectiveness of the Telecommunications Regulatory Regime: The Case of Sri Lanka Telecom', *Public Administration and Development*, 26: 383–93.

Banga, R. and B. Goldar. 2004. 'Contribution of Services to Output Growth and Productivity in Indian Manufacturing: Pre and Post Reforms', Working Paper No. 139, Indian Council for Research on International Economic Relations (ICRIER), New Delhi.

Banik, N. 2006. 'How Promising is SAFTA?', *Asia-Pacific Trade and Investment Review*, 2(2): 143–50.

Baysan, T., A. Panagariya, and N. Pitigala. 2006. 'Preferential Trading in South Asia', World Bank Policy Research Working Paper 3813, World Bank, Washington, DC.

Berman, S.D. 2008 'ICT-Based Distance Education in South Asia', *International Review of Research in Open and Distance Learning*, 9 (3): 1–6.

Board of Investment. 'Education and Skills Development', Government of Sri Lanka. Available at http://www.boi.lk/2009/education.asp, accessed on 27 December 2009.

Bonu, S. and M. Rani. 2008. 'South Asia, Health Systems of', *International Encyclopedia of Public Health*, Six-Volume Set. Boston: School of Public Health, Boston University.

Bose, S. 2007. '"Energy Politics" India-Bangladesh-Myanmar Relations', Special Report, No. 45, Institute of Peace and Conflict Studies, New Delhi.

Brunet, S., J. Bauer, T. De Lacy, and K. Tshering. 2001. 'Tourism Development in Bhutan: Tensions between Tradition and Modernity', *Journal of Sustainable Tourism*, 9 (3): 243–63.

Bureau of Economic, Energy and Business Affairs, Department of State, USA. 2009. '2009 Investment Climate Statement—Maldives', February. Available at http://www.state.gov/e/eeb/rls/othr/ics/2009/117868.htm, accessed on 12 February 2009.

Bureau of Economic, Energy and Business Affairs, Department of State, USA. 2009. 'Investment Climate Statements 2009', various country reports. Available at http://www.state.gov/e/eeb/rls/othr/ics/2009/, accessed on 27 December 2009.

CEO Conclave. 2006. 'Regional Telecom Taking Flight', *SAARC Communication Industry's Own Discussion Forum*, Voice&Data (voicendata.com), A Cybermedia Publication, December.

Chanda, R. 2010. 'Constraints to FDI in Hospital Services in India', *Journal of International Commerce, Economics and Policy*, 1 (1): 121–43

———. 2009a. 'Mobility of Less Skilled Workers under Bilateral Agreements: Lessons for the GATS Mode 4 Negotiations', *Journal of World Trade*, 43 (3): 479–506.

———. 2009b. 'Opportunities and Risks in Liberalizing Trade in Services: Case Study of India', in Saman Kelegama (ed.), *Trade in Services and South Asia*, pp. 23–68. Colombo: Institute for Policy Studies and Friedrich-Ebert-Stiftung; New Delhi: Sage Publications.

Chanda, R. 2008a. 'Low-skilled Workers and Bilateral, Regional, and Unilateral Initiatives: Lessons for the GATS Mode 4 Negotiations and Other Agreements', UNDP, Geneva.

———. 2008b. 'The Skilled South Asian Diaspora and Its Role in Source Economies', Institute of South Asian Studies (ISAS) Working Paper No. 34, National University of Singapore.

———. (ed.). 2006a. *India's Trade in Services: Prospects and Strategies*. New Delhi: Wiley Publishers.

———. 2006b. 'Intermodal Linkages in Services Trade', OECD Trade Policy Working Paper No. 30, Paris.

Chanda, R. 2005. 'Trade in Services and South Asia: An Aggressive Agenda', in CENTAD (ed.), *South Asian Yearbook of Trade and Development*, pp.105–208. New Delhi: New Concept Information Systems.

———. 2004a. 'Movement of Natural Persons from South Asian Countries', written for EINTAD project, *CUTS*, Jaipur.

———. 2004b. 'Movement and Presence of Natural Persons: Issues and Proposals for the GATS Negotiations', *South Centre*, Geneva.

———. 2002a. *Globalization of Services: India's Opportunities and Constraints*. New Delhi: Oxford University Press.

———. 2002b. 'Trade in Health Services', in Nick Drager and Cesar Vieira (eds), *Trade in Health Services: Global, Regional, and Country Perspectives*, pp. 35–44. Washington, DC: Pan American Health Organization, Program on Public Policy and Health, WHO.

———. 2002c. 'Trade in Health Services', *Bulletin of the World Health Organization, The International Journal of Public Health*, 80 (2): 158–63.

Chanda, R. and G. Sasidaran. 2009. 'Understanding India's Regional Initiatives with East and Southeast Asia', *Asian-Pacific Economic Literature*, 23 (1): 66–78.

———. 2008a. 'GATS and Developments in India's Service Sector', chapter 7, in Suparna Karmakar, Rajiv Kumar, and Bibek Debroy (eds), *India's Liberalization Experience—Hostage to the WTO*, pp. 169–212. New Delhi: Sage Publications.

———. 2008b. 'Understanding India's Regional Initiatives within Asia', Institute of South Asian Studies (ISAS) Working Paper No. 48, National University of Singapore.

Chandra, R. and R. Kumar. 2008. 'South Asian Integration Prospects and Lessons from East Asia', Working Paper No. 202,Indian Council for Research on International Economic Relations (ICRIER), New Delhi.

Chandran, S. 2009. *Expanding Cross-LoC Interactions: Perspectives from India*. New Delhi: Institute of Peace and Conflict Studies.

Chengappa, S. 2006. 'Move Over IT and BT, Make Room for MT', *The Deccan Herald*, 29 May. Available at http://healthcarekpo.com/index2. php?option=com_content&do_pdf=1&id=9, accessed on 29 September 2009.

Chi Kin Yim. 2005. 'Healthcare Destinations in Asia', HKU 406, Asia Case Research Centre, The University of Hong Kong, Homg Kong.

Chitrakar, Ramesh C. 2008. 'Potential for Trade in Services: Country Study-Nepal', Centre for Economic Development and Administration, Tribhuvan University, Kirtipur, presentation at New Delhi, 6–7 February.

Chowdhury, Iftekar Ahmed. (2009. 'India, Pakistan and Bangladesh: "Trilaterilism" in South Asia?', ISAS Brief No. 129, National University of Singapore, Institute of South Asian Studies, Singapore.

CII-McKinsey. 2002. *Healthcare in India: The Road Ahead*. New Delhi: CII.

Connell, J. 2006. 'Medical Tourism: Sea, Sun, Sand, and … Surgery', *Tourism Management*, 27: 1093–100.

CUTS International. 2008. 'Domestic Preparedness for Services Trade Liberalization: Are South Asian Countries Prepared for Further Liberalization?', Working Paper No. 3/2008, CUTS, Jaipur.

Das, D. 2008. 'South Asia's Integration with the Rest of Asia: A Survey', in *Asian-Pacific Economic Literature*, pp. 25–40. Canberra: Blackwell Publishers.

Das, Ram Upendra. 2009. 'Regional Economic Integration in South Asia: Prospects and Challenges', RIS Discussion Paper No. 157, Research and Information System for Developing Countries, New Delhi.

De Alwis, R. 2008. 'Promoting Tourism in South Asia', *Financial Times*, 14 September.

De, Prabir. 2009. 'Regional Cooperation for Regional Infrastructure Development: Challenges and Policy Options for South Asia', RIS Discussion Paper No. 60, Research and Information System for Developing Countries, New Delhi.

Dhungel, K.R. 2008. 'Regional Energy Trade in South Asia: Problems and Prospects', *South Asia Economic Journal*, 9 (1): 173–93.

Dihel, N. and B. Shepherd. 2007. *Modal Estimates of Services Barriers*. Paris: OECD. Available at http://fiordiliji.sourceoecd.org/vl=4684505/cl=27/nw=1/rpsv/cgi-bin/wppdf?file=5l4kxgnx0v6k.pdf, accessed on 12 November 2009.

Directorate General of Civil Aviation. 2007. *Bilateral Air Services Agreements*. New Delhi: Government of India.

D'Sami, B. 2001. 'Migration Patterns and Challenges for Indians Seeking Work Abroad: A Special Focus on South India', National Forum of Migrant Workers' Rights, Chennai.

DTI-GTZ, Federal Ministry for Economic Co-operation and Development. 2007. 'Borderless Health Services Delivery: IT Matters Tele-Health', Health Brief No. 7, German Development Center. Available at http://www2.gtz.de/dokumente/bib/07-1663.pdf, accessed on 7 October 2009.

Economist Intelligence Unit. 2007. *World Investment Prospects to 2011: Foreign Direct Investment and the Challenge of Political Risk*. New York: Columbia Program on International Investment.

Board of Investment of Sri Lanka. 2009. 'Education and Skills Development'. Available at http://www.boi.lk/2009/education.asp, accessed on 23 November 2009

The Economic Times. 2008. 'Apollo to Invest Rs. 1k Crore for Setting up 15 Hospitals', 30 April. Available at http://economictimes.indiatimes.com/articleshow/2998212.cms, accessed on 12 October 2009.

Energy Information Administration. Various Years. 'Country Analysis Briefs for South Asian and Data'. Available at www.eia.doe.gov, accessed on 30 October 2009.

Equations. 2006. 'ADB's SASEC Tourism Development Plan and its Potential Impacts on India's NE', A Briefing Paper, Equitable Options for Tourism, 15 December. Available at http://www.equitabletourism.org/stage/files/file Documents350_uid10.pdf

Export–Import Bank of India. 2004. 'BIMST-EC Initiative: A Study of India's Trade and Investment Potential with Select Asian Countries', Occasional Paper No. 100, EXIM Bank, Mumbai.

————. 2002. 'Sri Lanka: A Study of India's Trade and Investment Potential', Occasional Paper No. 92, April, EXIM Bank, Mumbai.

Frost and Sullivan. 2009. 'Telecom Companies Capital Expenditure', report for South Asia and the Middle East, Mumbai. Available at http://www.frost.com/prod/servlet/press-release.pag?docid=189275765, accessed on 2 October 2009.

Galpaya, H. 2008. *Telecom Regulatory and Policy Environment in the Maldives: Results of the 2008 TRE Survey.* Maldives: LIRNEasia.

Gautam, V. 2008. *Healthcare Tourism: Opportunities for India.* Mumbai: Export Import Bank of India, Quest Publishers.

Government of Bangladesh. 2009. *Government Tourism Policy of Ministry of Civil Aviation and Tourism.* Bangladesh: Ministry of Civil Aviation and Tourism.

Government of India. 2007. 'Trade in Education Services—A Consultation Paper on Higher Education in India and GATS: An Opportunity', in *Preparation for the Services Negotiations at the WTO.* New Delhi: Trade Policy Division, Department of Commerce.

Government of Maldives. 2006. *Maldives Telecommunications Policy 2006–2010.* Male: Ministry of Communication, Science, and Technology.

————. 2001. *Maldives Telecommunications Policy 2001–2005.* Male: Ministry of Communication, Science, and Technology.

————. 1999. *Tourism Act of Maldives,* Law No. 2. Male: Government of Maldives.

Government of Nepal. 2001. *The Hydropower Development Policy 2001.* Singhadurbar: Ministry of Water Resources.

Government of Pakistan. 2009. *Incentives for Investment in Tourism Sector in Pakistan.* Islamabad: Ministry of Tourism.

———— 2003. *De-Regulation Policy for the Telecommunication Sector.* Islamabad: Ministry of Information Technology, IT and Telecommunication Division. Available at www.moitt.gov.pk

Government of Sri Lanka. 2006. *National Energy Policy and Strategies of Sri Lanka.* Colombo: Ministry of Power and Energy.

Gunawardene, N. 2007. 'lk, Sri Lanka', *Digital Review of Asia-Pacific, 2007–08*, pp. 296–303. Ottawa: IDRC. Available at http://www.digital-review.org/uploads/files/pdf/2007-2008/2007_C27_lk_Sri_Lanka_296_303.pdf?93d8e68695e76f3bf28837adbeb3725c=e68fc0eb62b31b653ba40beaf1d7295a, accessed on 30 September 2009.

Healthlink Worldwide. 2006. 'Improving Health, Connecting People: The Role of ICTs in the Health Sector of Developing Countries', Working Paper No. 7, Afri-Afya and the Institute for Sustainable Health Education and Development, UK.

Hirantha, S.W. 2004. 'From SAPTA to SAFTA: Gravity Analysis of South Asian Free Trade', paper presented at the European Trade Study Group (ETSG) 2004 Programme, Nottingham, September.

Hoekman, Bernard and Aditya Mattoo. 2008. 'Services Trade and Growth', chapter 1 in Juan A. Marchetti and Martin Roy (eds), *Opening Markets for Trade in Services.* Cambridge: Cambridge University Press.

Hussain, R.M. 1999. 'SAARC 1985–1995: A Review and Analysis of Progress', in E. Gonsalves and N. Jetly (eds), *The Dynamics of South Asia: Regional Cooperation and SAARC*, pp. 21–39. New Delhi: Sage Publications.

Ibrahim, Z. 2004. 'Country Status Report—Maldives', for the APT training course, Kobe, Japan, February.

India Brand Equity Foundation. 2009 'Telecommunication Market and Opportunities', Report by Evalueserve, Gurgaon.

Indian Institute of Management Ahmedabad. 2000. 'Regional Cooperation in South Asia: Benefits of Integrating the Primary Energy and Electricity Markets', chapter 8 in *Development and Climate: An Assessment for India.* Denmark: UNEP Collaborating Centre on Energy and Environment (UCCEE).

Institute of Policy Studies (IPS). 2008). *First South Asia Economic Summit Statement* (28–30 August). Colombo: IPS.

———. 2007. *Study on Potential for Trade in Services under the SAFTA Agreement: Sri Lanka* (July). Colombo: IPS.

Institute of Policy Studies and Friedrich Ebert Stiftung. 2006. *South Asia in the WTO: Concept Note.* Colombo: IPS.

International Labour Organization (ILO). 2008. *Global Employment Trends Report.* Geneva: ILO.

International Monetary Fund (IMF). 2007. *Direction of Trade Statistics Yearbook 2007.* Washington, DC: Statistics Department, IMF.

International Organization for Migration (IOM). 2008. *World Migration Report.* Geneva: IOM.

Jayasuriya, S. and M. Knight-John. 2002. 'Sri Lanka's Telecommunications Industry: From Privatisation to Anti-Competition?', Centre on Regulation and Competition, Working Paper Series, January, Manchester, UK.

Jetley, R. and I. Lodhi. 2009. Presentation on 'Civil Nuclear Energy in South Asia: Some Geo-Political Implications', 30 July, Institute of South Asian Studies, National University of Singapore, Singapore. Available at http://www.isasnus.org/events/activities/20090730%20-%20Dr%20Rajshree%20Jetly.pdf, accessed on 16 September 16 2009.

Karmakar, S. 2005. 'India-ASEAN Cooperation in Services—An Overview', Working Paper No. 176,Indian Council for Research on International Economic Relations (ICRIER), New Delhi.

Kelegama, S. and R. Adhikari. 2002. 'Regional Integration in the WTO Era: South Asia at Crossroads', Discussion Paper, South Asia Watch on Trade, Economics and Environment and CUTS Centre for International Trade, Economics & Environment, Kathmandu and Jaipur.

Knight-John, M. 2008. *Telecom Regulatory and Policy Environment in Sri Lanka, Results of the 2008 TRE Survey.* Colombo: Institute of Policy Studies.

———. 2007 'Telecommunications Sector and Regulatory Performance in Sri Lanka: A Tale of Missed Opportunities?,' study done for LIRNEasia, Institute of Policy Studies of Sri Lanka, Colombo.

Krueger, E., R. Pinto, V. Thomas, and T. To. 2004. 'Impacts of the South Asia Free Trade Agreement', La Follette School of Public Affairs, Policy Analysis Workshop, Public Affairs 869, Spring, University of Wisconsin-Madison, Madison.

Lallana, E. 2004. 'An Overview of ICT Policies and e-Strategies of Select Asian Economies', Asia-Pacific Development Information Programme, UNDP, Bangkok.

Lama, M.P. 2004 'Energy Cooperation in South Asia', Follow-up of the SAARC Decisions Concerning SAFTA and Energy Cooperation, Centre for Policy Dialogue, Dhaka.

Lama, M.P., Mohan M. Sanju, and Q.K. Ahmad. 2002. 'Reforms and Power Sector in South Asia: Scope and Challenges for Cross-Border Trade', report prepared under the South Asia Network of Economic Research Institutes (SANEI), October.

Lethbridge, J. 2007. 'A Global Review of the Expansion of Multinational Healthcare Companies', Public Services International Research Unit, University of Greenwich14 September.

———— 2004. 'Changing Healthcare Systems in Asia', Public Services International Research Unit, University of Greenwich, 10 December.

Maldives EFA 2000 Assessment Group. 1999. 'Education for All: The Year 2000 Assessment', Maldives Country Report, Male, 31 October 31. Available at http://www.unesco.org/education/wef/countryreports/maldives/contents.html, accessed on 27 December 2009.

Malik, P. 2008. 'Telecom Regulatory and Policy Environment in India: Results and Analysis of the 2008 TRE Survey'. Available at http://lirneasia.net/wp-content/uploads/2009/07/TRE_India_Final_Nov16.pdf

Malla, S. (2008) 'Towards a Regional Energy Market in South Asia', prepared for South Asia Centre for Policy Studies, Dhaka, May.

————. 2005. 'SACEPS Task Force Report on Energy Cooperation in South Asia', prepared for South Asia Centre for Policy Studies, Dhaka.

Malla, B.B. 2001. 'Nepal Electricity Authority and its Role in Regional Power Trade', Kathmandu, 19 March.

Manning, C. and A. Sidorenko. 2007. 'The Regulation of Professional Migration in ASEAN: Insights from the Health and IT Sectors', *World Economy*, 30 (7): 1084–113.

Marchetti, J. and M. Roy. 2008 *Opening Markets for Trade in Services: Countries and Sectors in Bilateral and WTO Negotiations*. Cambridge: Cambridge University Press.

Mehta, R. 2006. 'WTO and South Asia', South Asian Journal Conference, Group XVI, Islamabad, 29–30 April. Available at http://www.southasianmedia.net/conference/conference_envisioning/vision_goup_xiv.htm, accessed on 25 August 2009.

Ministry of Education, Government of Nepal. 2007. 'Three Years Interim Plan (2064/65 BS – 2066/67)' Available at http://moe.gov.np/new/userfiles/file/plans_policies/eng/Three%20Years%20Interim%20Plan.pdf, accessed on 23 November 2009.

Mirza, Z. 2004 'Trade in Health Services in Pakistan: A Country Case Study, Key Findings and Reflections', presentation at the Interregional Workshop on Trade and Health, 12–13 October.WHO/South East Asia Regional Office, New Delhi.

Mishra, S.K. 2007. 'E-Health Initiatives in India', Expert Group Meeting on 'Regional Trends in Health Services and Their Impacts on Health Systems Performance in the Asian and Pacific Region', 9–11 October, Bangkok.

Moinuddin, M. 2008. 'Rethinking Regionalism in South Asia: Prospects and Strategic Implications of SAFTA', Discussion Paper, Yokohama National University, Japan.

Mortensen, J. 2008. 'International Trade in Health Services Assessing the Trade and the Trade-Offs', DIIS Working Paper No. 2008/11, Danish Institute for International Studies, Copenhagen.

Mukherji, I.N. 2000 'Charting a Free Trade Area in South Asia: Instruments and Modalities', presented at the Second Conference of the South Asia Network of Economic Research Institutes (SANEI), 26–9 August, Kathmandu.

Mukherji, I. 2004. 'Towards a Free Trade Area in South Asia: Charting a Feasible Course for Trade Liberalization with Reference to India's Role', RIS, Discussion Paper No. 86, Research and Information System for Developing Countries, New Delhi.

Murugan, A. 2008. 'Medical Tourism: Opportunities and Challenges in Tamil Nadu', presented at a conference on 'Tourism in India—Challenges Ahead', 15–17 May, Indian Institute of Management, Kozhikode.

Nag, S.R. 2008. 'Regional Cooperation and Integration Prospects in Asia', RIS Discussion Paper No.131, Research and Information System for Developing Countries, New Delhi.

National Tourism Statistics and Annual Reports, various countries, various years.

Newberry, D. 2007. 'Power Sector Reform, Private Investment and Regional Cooperation', in *South Asia: Growth and Regional Integration*, pp. 144–70. Washington, DC: World Bank.

Organization for Economic Co-operation and Development (OECD). 2001. *Trends in International Migration*, Annual Report. Paris: OECD.

Oberholzer-Gee, Felix, Tarun Khanna, and Carin-Israel Knoop. 2007. *Apollo Hospitals-First world Health Care at Emerging-Market Prices*. Cambridge: Harvard Business School.

Pakistan Telecommunication Authority. 2008. *Economic Performance of Industry*. Islamabad: Pakistan Telecommunication Authority.

Panagariya, A. 2007. 'Trading Choices of South Asia', in World Bank, *South Asia: Growth and Regional Integration*. Washington, DC: World Bank.

———. 2003. 'South Asia: Does Preferential Trade Liberalization Make Sense', *World Economy*, 26 (9): 1279–91.

Pant, B. and B.D. Sigdel. 2004. 'Attracting Foreign Direct Investment: Experiences and Challenges', Nepal Rastra Bank (NRB), Working Paper 1.

Pitigala, N. 2005. 'What Does Regional Trade in South Asia Reveal about Future Trade Integration? Some Empirical Evidence', World Bank Policy Research Working Paper 3497, World Bank, Washington, DC.

Pokharel, S. 1998. 'Energy in Nepal', 17th World Energy Council, Houston, 13–18 September.

Rahman, M. 2001. 'Bangladesh–India Bilateral Trade: An Investigation into Trade in Services', prepared under the South Asia Network of Economic Research Institutes (SANEI) Study Programme, Centre for Policy Dialogue, Dhaka.

Rahman, R. 2007. 'The State, the Private Health Care Sector and Regulation in Bangladesh', *The Asia-Pacific Journal of Public Administration*, 29 (2): 191–206.

Raihan, A. 2007. 'Potential for Trade in Services under SAFTA: Bangladesh Country Study', submitted to SAARC Secretariat as part of the Work Programme of the SAARC Network of Researchers on Global Financial and Economic Issues, New Delhi.

Ramesh, M. 2005. 'Hindujas Plan Hospital in Sri Lanka', *The Hindu Business Line*, 18 June.

Raychaudhuri, A. and P. De. 2007. 'Assessing Barriers to Trade in Education Services in Developing Asia-Pacific Countries: An Empirical Exercise', Asia-Pacific Research and Training Network, Trade Working Paper Series No. 34, UNESCAP, Bangkok. Available at http://www.unescap.org/tid/publication/ aptir2470_ajitava_prabir.pdf, accessed on 31 December 2009.

Raza, M.A. 2007. 'The Energy Charter Treaty and Its Role in Central and South Asia', presentation, Harriman Institute, Columbia University, New York, 13 November.

Reserve Bank of India (RBI). 2008. *Direction of Trade Data in RBI Handbook of Statistics on the Indian Economy*. Mumbai: RBI.

———— *Handbook of Statistics on the Indian Economy*. Mumbai: RBI. Available at http://www.rbi.org.in/scripts/PublicationsView.aspx?id=8701, accessed on 21 January 2009.

Research and Information System for Developing Countries. 2008. *SAARC Regional Study on Potential for Trade in Services under SAFTA*. New Delhi: RIS.

————. 2008. 'SAARC Regional Study on Potential for Trade in Services under SAFTA', preliminary draft for discussion at the SAARC Regional Workshop on Trade in Services, RIS, New Delhi.

————. 2007. 'Potential for Trade in Services under SAFTA: Country Report of Pakistan', submitted to SAARC Secretariat as part of the Work Programme of the SAARC Network of Researchers on Global Financial and Economic Issues, RIS, New Delhi.

————. 2003. 'Energy Cooperation in South Asia: Potential and Prospects', RIS Policy Brief No. 8. RIS, New Delhi.

Research and Information System for Developing Countries and Institute of Southeast Asian Studies (2004), 'Towards and Asian Economic Community: Vision of a New Asia', (ed.) Nagesh Kumar, New Delhi: RIS.

Reinfield, M.A. 2003. 'Tourism and the Politics of Cultural Preservation: A Case Study of Bhutan', *Journal of Public and International Affairs*, 14 (Spring): 1–26.

Rimchen, P. 2007. 'Bhutan Study Paper on Potential for Trade in Services under SAFTA Agreement', prepared for Research and Information System for Developing Countries, Thimpu.

Rodriguez-Delgado, J. 2007. 'SAFTA: Living in a World of Regional Trade Agreements', IMF Working Paper WP/07/23. IMF, Washington, DC.

Royal Government of Bhutan. 2004. 'Bhutan Information and Communications Technology Policy and Strategies' (BIPS), Thimpu, July.

South Asian Association for Regional Cooperation (SAARC). 2008a. 'Report of the Inception Workshop for the Study on Potential for Trade in Services under SAFTA Agreement', Regional Consultation Meeting on Draft Study, SAARC/ RCM/TIS/3, New Delhi, 6–7 February.

————. 2008b. *Revised SAARC Plan of Action on Telecommunications*. Kathmandu: SAARC Secretariat.

————. 2008c. 'SAFTA Ministerial Council: Third Meeting', Report of the Thirteenth Meeting of the Committee on Economic Cooperation, SAARC/ SMC.03/6, New Delhi, 3 March.

————. 2004. *Agreement on South Asian Free Trade Area (SAFTA)*. Islamabad: SERC. Available at http://www.saarc-sec.org/data/agenda/economic/safta/ SAFTA%20AGREEMENT.pdf, accessed on 25 August 2009.

SAARC, Research and Information System for Developing Countries. 2007. 'Inception Workshop for the Study on Potential for Trade in Services under SAFTA Agreement', New Delhi, 10–11 May.

SAARC Energy Centre. 2007. *SAARC Energy Newsletter*, various articles, II (1). Islamabad: SERC.

SAARC Secretariat. 2009. *Social Charter of the South Asian Association for Regional Cooperation*. Kathmandu: SAARC Secretariat.

Sahoo, P. 2006. 'Foreign Direct Investment in South Asia: Policy, Trends, Impact and Determinants', ADB Institute Discussion Paper No. 56, Asian Development Bank, Manila.

Salam, Justice Mohammed Abdus. 2005. 'An Introduction of the Bangladesh Telecommunication Regulatory Commission', presentation at Asia Pacific Forum on Telecommunications Policy and Regulation, Singapore.

Salt, J. 2006. 'International Migration and the United Kingdom', Report of the United Kingdom SOPEMI Correspondent to the OECD, UK.

Samarajiva, R. 2009. 'Choices-Regional Roaming', *Lanka Business Online*, 7 April. Available at http://www.lankabusinessonline.com/fullstory. php?nid=2109193520#, accessed on 13 October 2009.

————. 2008. 'Choices-Real SAARC', *Lanka Business Online*, 18 July. Available at http://www.lbo.lk/fullstory.php?nid=1871648785#, accessed on 13 October 2009.

SAWTEE. 2008. 'Nepal's Export potential in Services', submitted to Enhancing Nepal's Trade Related Capacity, Ministry of Industry Commerce and Supplies and UNDP, SAWTEE, Kathmandu.

Sharma, S. 2006. 'Focusing on Regional Tourism Markets: Prospects and Challenge for Nepal', Policy Paper 28, prepared for Economic Policy Network, Government of Nepal and Asian Development Bank, Kathmandu. Available at http:// www.mof.gov.np/economic_policy/pdf/Focusing_Regional.pdf, accessed on 2 December 2008.

Sharma, K. and Prema-chandra Athukorala. 2006. 'Foreign Investment in a Least Developed Country: The Nepalese Experience', *Transnational Corporations Journal*, 15 (2). Available at http://www.unctad.org/en/docs/iteiit20062a1_ en.pdf, accessed on 2 December 2008.

Shreshtha, R.M. 2008. 'Hydropower Development in Nepal: Issues, Opportunities and Challenges', presented at the 3rd NRN Regional Conference, Bangkok, 24–5 May.

Siddiqui, T. 2008. 'Developing Integrated Energy Policies in South Asia', SAARC Energy Centre, Report No.1, SERC, Islamabad: SERC.

Sigimura, M. 2008. 'International Student Mobility and Asian Higher Education', Sophia University, presented at the 2009 World Conference on Higher Education, Macau, China, 24–26 September.

Singh, N. 2006. 'Services-Led Industrialization in India: Assessment and Lessons', Working Paper Series, Department of Economics, University of California at Santa Cruz, December.

Song, Hong. 2005. 'Increased Connectivity in Asia: Empirical Evidence and Issues', in *Asian Economic Cooperation and Integration: Progress, prospects, and Challenges*. Manila: Asian Development Bank.

South Asia Trade and Investment Network (SATIN). 2008. 'Regional Trade in South Asia—Towards Stronger Linkages and Growth', Executive Summary and Special Focus on adding Services to the South Asia Free Trade Agreement, Policy Paper. Commonwealth Business Council and SAARC Chamber of Commerce and Industry, Kathmandu.

Srivastava, L. and N. Mishra. 2007 'Promoting Regional Energy Cooperation in South Asia', *Energy Policy*, 35: 3360–8.

Subbarao, P. Srinivas. 2008. 'A Study on FDI in Indian Tourism', paper presented at 'Conference on Tourism in India-Challenges Ahead', Vishakhapatnam, 15–17 May.

Sundar, S and K. Deb. 2000. *Restructuring and regulation of infrastructure in South Asia*. Sri Lanka: South Asian Forum on Infrastructure Regulation.

Tamang, B. 2007 'Overview of Bhutan-India Cooperation in the Power Sector', presentation, Department of Energy, Ministry of Economic Affairs, Thimpu, 29 October.

Tham, S.Y. 2008. 'ASEAN Open Skies and the Implications for Airport Development Strategy in Malaysia', ADB Institute Working Paper No. 119, Asian Development Bank Institute, Tokyo.

Thapa, B., A. Sharma and R. Gupta. 2007 'Prospects for Energy Integration', *Himal Southasian*, April.

Thinley, K. 2009a. 'Higher Education in the Kingdom of Bhutan', Tertiary Education Division, Government of Bhutan, Thimpu. Available at http://portal. unesco.org/geography/en/files/10897/12351203545Bhutan.pdf/Bhutan.pdf, accessed on 27 December 2009.

———.2009b. 'A Country Report: Higher Education in the Kingdom of Bhutan, Cherishing Dreams and Confronting Challenges', Ministry of Education, Royal Government of Bhutan. Available at http://portal.unesco.org/geography/en/ files/10897/12351203545Bhutan.pdf/Bhutan.pdf, accessed on 23 November 2009.

Tongia, R. and V.S. Arunachalam. 1998. 'Natural Gas Imports by South Asia: Pipelines or Pipedreams?', Department of Engineering and Public Policy, Carnegie Mellon University, Pittsburgh.

UNCTAD. 2008. *Handbook of Statistics 2008* (online version). Available at http:// stats.unctad.org/handbook/ReportFolders/ReportFolders.aspx

———. 2007. *Trade and Development Report 2007: Regional Cooperation for Development*. Geneva: UNCTAD.

———. 2004. *World Investment Report*. Geneva: UNCTAD.

UNCTAD and Japan External Trade Organisation. 2008. *South-South Trade in Asia: The Role of Regional Trade Agreements*. Geneva: UNCTAD.

UNDP. 2008. 'South-South Regionalism and Trade Cooperation in the Asia-Pacific Region', Asia-Pacific Trade and Investment Initiative, UNDP Regional Centre in Colombo, UNDP RCC, Colombo.

UNESCAP. 2009a. 'Energy Trade and Transboundary Energy Cooperation', chapter 5 in *Energy Security and Sustainable Development in Asia and the Pacific*. Bangkok: UNESCAP.

———. 2009b. 'Energy Supply and Use', chapter 28 in *Statistical Yearbook for Asia and the Pacific 2008*. Bangkok: UNESCAP.

———. 2003. 'Investing in Bhutan, Foreign Investment Policy and Regulations', Part 4, *Trader's Manual for Least Developed Countries: Bhutan*. Available at http://www.unescap.org/tid/publication/t&ipub2297_part4.pdf, accessed on 27 December 2009.

UNESCO, National University of Education Planning and Administration (India), Ministry of Human Resource Development, GoI. 2009a. 'Facing Global and Local Challenges, The New Dynamics for Higher Education—Sri Lanka Country Report', South, South-West and Central Asia Sub-regional Preparatory Conference for 2009 World Conference on Higher Education, New Delhi, 25–6 February. Available at http://portal.unesco.org/geography/en/files/10905/12353682765Sri_Lanka.pdf/Sri%2BLanka.pdf, accessed on 25 November 2009.

———. 2009b. 'Facing Global and Local Challenges: The New Dynamics for Higher Education- Maldives Country Report', South, South-West and Central Asia Sub-regional Preparatory Conference for 2009 World Conference on Higher Education, New Delhi, 25–6 February. Available at http://portal.unesco.org/geography/en/files/10906/12353684495Maldives/Maldives, accessed on 23 November 2009.

United States Agency for International Development (USAID). 2008a. 'Hydropower in South Asia-Potential Resource for Energy Exports', South Asia Regional Initiative for Energy Cooperation and Development, New Delhi. Available at www.sari-energy.org, accessed on 12 March 2009.

———. 2008b. 'South Asia Regional Initiative for Energy Cooperation and Development: Annual Report', USAID, Washington, DC. Available at www.sari-energy.org, accessed on 12 February 2009.

———. 2008c. 'South Asia Regional Initiative for Energy Cooperation and Development: Midterm Evaluation Report', USAID, Washington DC. Available at www.sari-http://www.sari-energy.org/ProjectReports/RegionalEnergySecurity_RegionalReport_Complete.pdf, accessed on 12 March 2009.

———. 2006. 'Regional Energy Security for South Asia, Regional Report', SARI/Energy Program, USAID, Washington, DC. Available at http://www.sari-energy.org/, accessed on 12 March 2009.

———. 2005. 'Economic and Social Benefits Analysis of Power Trade in the South Asia Growth Quadrangle Region', South Asia Regional Initiative for Energy Cooperation and Development, USAID, Washington, DC.

————. 2000. 'Viability of Power Exports from Bangladesh to India', prepared for the Government of Bangladesh. USAID, Washington, DC.

Ure, J. 2004. 'FDI in Telecommunication Services in Asia', high-level policy seminar on 'Services FDI and Competitiveness in Asia', UNCTAD and ASEAN, Ritsumeikan University, Kyoto, 2–4 March.

Velde, Dirk Willem Te. 2008. 'Regional Integration, Growth and Convergence: Analytical Techniques and Preliminary Results', draft note, Overseas Development Institute, London.

Venugopal, K. 2003. 'Telecommunication Sector Negotiations at the WTO: Case Studies of India, Sri Lanka and Malaysia', ITU/ESCAP/WTO Regional Seminar on Telecommunications and Trade Issues, Bangkok, 28–30 October.

Vora, N. and Shweta Dewan. 2009. 'Indian Education System Long Way from Graduation', IDFC, SSKI, India Research. Available at http://www.educomp. com/DataImages/Downloads/Education%20Sector%20-%20Jan09.pdf, accessed on 27 December 2009.

Vucetic, V. and V. Krishnaswamy. 2009. 'How Can South Asia Promote Energy Trade', chapter 10 in Ejaz Ghani and Sadiq Ahmed (eds), *Accelerating Growth and Job Creation in South Asia*. New Delhi: Oxford University Press.

Wadood, Syed Naimul. 2006. 'The Public–Private University Debate in the Higher Education Sector in Bangladesh', Department of Economics, North South University, Dhaka. Available at http://mpra.ub.uni-muenchen.de/10888/, accessed on 26 November 2009.

Weerakoon, D. 2008. *SAFTA: Current Status and Prospects*. Colombo: IPS.

Weerakoon, D. and J. Thennakoon. 2008. 'The South Asian Free Trade Agreement: Which Way Forward?', *Journal of South Asian Development*, 3 (1): 135–50.

Wilson, J. 2008. 'Telecom Regulatory and Policy Environment in Pakistan: Results of the 2008 TRE Survey', Pakistan Country Report, Lahore.

————. 2007. 'Liberalizing the Telecommunications Sector: Making Pakistan an Information Economy', Final Report, LIRNEAsia Six Country Multi-component Study 2006–7, Lahore.

World Bank. 2008a. 'Potential and Prospects for Regional Energy Trade in the South Asia Region', Energy Sector Management Assistance Program, South Asia Regional Cooperation Program, World Bank, Washington, DC.

————. 2008b. 'Trade and Transport Facilitation in South Asia: Systems in Transition', Volume I: Summary and Main Report, Report No. 44-61-SAS, Sustainable Development Unit, South Asia Region, World Bank Office, New Delhi.

————. 2007. *Doing Business in South Asia*. Washington, DC: World Bank.

————. 2006. 'India–Bangladesh Bilateral Trade and Potential Free Trade Agreement', Bangladesh Development Series, Paper No. 13, World Bank Office, Dhaka. Available at http://www.worldbank.org.bd/bds, accessed on 9 September 2009.

World Economic Forum. 2009. 'Travel and Tourism Competitiveness Reports'. Available at http://www.weforum.org/en/initiatives/gcp/TravelandTourism Report/index.htm, accessed on 8 November 2009.

World Tourism Organization. 2008. *World Tourism Barometer*, 6 (3).

World Trade Organization, Council for Trade in Services. 2005a. 'Pakistan, Conditional Initial Offer on Services', TN/S/O/PAK, Geneva, 20 May.

———. 2005b. 'India, Revised Offer on Services', Geneva, 12 August.

———. 2004a. 'The Kingdom of Nepal: Schedule of Specific Commitments', GATS/SC/139, Geneva, 30 August.

———. 2004b. 'India: Conditional Initial Offer', TN/S/O/IND, Geneva, 12 January.

———. 2003. 'Sri Lanka, Conditional Initial Offer on Services', TN/S/O/LKA, Geneva, 8 September.

———. 1995. 'Communication from the Maldives: Schedule of Specific Commitments under the GATS', GATS/SC/101, Geneva, 30 August.

———. 1994a. 'India: Schedule of Specific Commitments', GATS/SC/42, Geneva, 15 April.

———. 1994b. 'Pakistan: Schedule of Specific Commitments', GATS/SC/67, Geneva, 15 April.

———. 1994c. 'Sri Lanka: Schedule of Specific Commitments', GATS/SC/79, Geneva, 15 April.

World Trade Organization (WTO). Various Years. *International Trade Statistics*. Geneva: WTO. Available at http://www.wto.org/english/res_e/statis_e/its2009_e/its09_toc_e.htm, accessed on 24 October 2008.

World Trade Review. 2009. 'Traditional Medicine in South Asia: Untapped Export Potential', *Opinion*, 9 (14). Available at http://www.worldtradereview.com/news.asp?pType=N&iType=C&iID=210&siD=14&nID=48210, accessed on 29 September 2009.

World Travel and Tourism Council (WTTC). 'Tourism Impact Data Forecasting Tool'. Available at http://www.wttc.org/, accessed on 8 November 2009.

———. Economic Impact Analysis 2009—South Asia'. Available at http://www.wttc.org/bin/pdf/temp/southasia.html, accessed on 12 December 2008.

Yoosuf, A. Sattar. 2004. 'South-East Asia Regional Perspective', presentation at Interregional Workshop on Trade and Health, WHO/SEARO, WHO South East Asia Regional Office, New Delhi, 12–13 October.

Zainudeen, A. 2006 'Telecom Use on a Shoestring: The Case of Bangladesh', WDR Dialogue Theme 3rd Cycle, Discussion Paper WDR0601, LIRNEasia, World Dialogue on Regulation for Network Economies, Denmark. Available at regulateonline.org, accessed on 7 October 2009.

Zaman, A. 2008. 'Revving up Energy Trade in South Asia', *Financial Express*, 13 August (online edition).

Zita, K. 2003 'Nepal', USTDA South Asia Communications Infrastructure Conference, New Delhi, 21–3 April.

Website Links

http://www.americanchronicle.com/articles/view/88220

http://www.aptech-globaltraining.com/html/itec.htm

http://www.aptech-globaltraining.com/html/itec.htm

http://archives.indiainfoline.com/news/innernews.asp?storyId=114336&lmn=1

http://aric.adb.org/indicator.php (Asian Development Bank, Asia Regional Integration Centre Integration Indicators Database)

http://www.asiatradehub.com/bangladesh/tax.asp

http://www.asiatradehub.com/pakistan/tax1.asp

http://www.atlas.iienetwork.org/page/135351/

http://www.avrefdesk.com/two_letter_airline_codes.htm

http://www.bangladesh-bank.org/ (Bangladesh Bank)

http://www.bangladesh.gov.bd/ (National Web Portal of Bangladesh)

http://www.bangladesh.gov.bd/bddemo/index.php?option=com_content&task=vi ew&id=82&Itemid=157

http://www.banglaembassy.com.bh/FDI%20in%20Bangladesh.htm

http://www.bbs.com.bt/PM%20and%20NIIT%20Chairman%20meet%20 to%20discuss%20IT%20project.html

http://bdlaws.gov.bd/pdf/637___.pdf

http://www.bea.gov.bt/index.php?

http://bhutan-360.com/hotels-to-be-rated-with-stars/

http://www.bhutan.gov.bt/government/newsDetail.php?id=1429%20&%20cat=2

http://www.bhutanmajestictravel.com/news/2009/the-hotel-industry-in-bhutan-is-booming.html

http://www.bhutanmajestictravel.com/news/2007/bhutan-imported-petroleum-and-related-products-worth-us-472-billion.html

http://www.bhutanobserver.bt/2009/bhutan-news/08/hoteliers-raise-concerns. html

http://www.bhutantimes.bt/index.php?option=com_content&task=view&id=12 33&Itemid=79

http://www.bhutantimes.bt/index.php?option=com_content&task=view&id=85 6&Itemid=1

https://www.bhutantimes.com/modules/newbb/viewtopic.php?topic_ id=2627&forum=10

http://www.biman-airlines.com/

http://www.blonnet.com/2008/07/21/stories/2008072151151600.htm

http://www.blonnet.com/2008/05/18/stories/2008051851170300.htm

http://www.blonnet.com/2007/01/27/stories/2007012702000600.htm

http://www.boi.gov.bd/abt_ficci.php

http://www.boi.gov.bd/sector_brief.php#natural

http://www.boi.lk/2009/pdf/Incentives.pdf

http://www.boi.lk/2009/reserved_for_reguler.asp

http://books.google.co.in/books?id=cfV6ohJVBcC&pg=PA87&lpg=PA87& dq=import+policy+maldives&source=bl&ots=Q5DNyscKUC&sig=DM FVusgcY5QqQkBOgf0YlPQUrgw&hl=en&ei=6Hv2SuvnKNSWkAW-

JitWjAw&sa=X&oi=book_result&ct=result&resnum=5&ved=0CBAQ6AEwB
  A#v=onepage&q=import%20policy%20maldives&f=false
http://www.bpdb.gov.bd/vision%20statement.htm
http://www.btrc.gov.bd/
http://www.btrc.gov.bd/policy/Telecom_Policy_1998.pdf
http://www.business-standard.com/india/news/nepal-ends-noc-monopoly-over-
  petrol-import-sale/39661/on
http://www.catmando.com/gov/industry/fipd/fipd10.htm
http://www.catmando.com/gov/industry/fipd/fipd15.htm
http://www.cbr.gov.pk/newst/Rules/The%20Sales%20Tax%20Special%20
  Procedures%20Rules%202007.pdf
http://www.cbsl.gov.lk/
http://chronicle.com/article/Indias-Education-Minister/47891/
http://www.dailynews.lk/2009/01/28/fea03.asp
http://datastore.sltda.gov.lk/SLTDA/Reports/travel_agency/TravelAgency-
  BusinessReqirments.pdf
http://dgca.nic.in/pub/pub03-04/chap7/part7.htm
http://dipp.nic.in/ (Department of Industrial Policy and Promotion, Government
  of India)
http://www.discoverybangladesh.com/meetbangladesh/investment.html
http://www.doind.gov.np/pdf/pmanual.pdf
http://www.drukair.com.bt/
http://dspace.iimk.ac.in/bitstream/2259/544/1/107-113+srinivas.pdf
http://economictimes.indiatimes.com/News/News_By_Industry/Services/
  Education/South_Asian_Univ_to_offer_science_arts_courses_together/
  rssarticleshow/3227901.cms
http://www.education.nic.in/TechnicalEdu/FPEIbill2005.asp
http://www.eepc.gov.eg/fita/fiscalite_66.html
http://eneken.ieej.or.jp/data/2598.pdf
http://www.energybangla.com/index.php?
http://en.wikipedia.org/wiki/Pakistan_Telecommunication_Authority
http://www.epb.gov.pk/v1/tradepolicy/pdf/0775-31072006-ipo.pdf - Import
  Policy Order
http://www.eudelbangladesh.org/en/documents/investorguide/telecomsector.pdf
http://www.financialexpress-bd.info/
http://flyaow.com/citycoded.htm
http://www.flykingfisher.com/plan-book/schedule.aspx
http://www.getpakistan.com/home/about_pakistan/invpak.htm
http://www.gmgairlines.com/international-final.html
http://www.greeneconomyinitiative.com/news/183/ARTICLE/1675/2009-08-22.
  html
http://www.hec.gov.pk/InsideHEC/Divisions/QALI/QualityAssurance/
  UniversityAccreditation/ForeignCollaboration/Pages/welcome.aspx
http://home.airindia.in/SBCMS/WebPages/Home.aspx?CityId=Ind
http://www.indiaedunews.neet/Inocus/November_2009/Nalanda_International_
  University_on_SAARC's_fast_track_9459/

http://www.indianairlines.in/scripts/flightschedule.aspx
http://india.gov.in/overseas/passport.php
http://in.news.yahoo.com/20/20100214/372/tbs-niit-to-help-people-of-bhutan-improv.html
http://in.news.yahoo.com/32/20100125/1073/tsp-no-ipl-ever-says-pak-board.html
http://www.itu.int/ITU-D/ict/statistics/index.html (International
  Telecommunications Union, ICT Indicators Database)
http://www.itu.int/ITU-D/ICTEYE/Regulators/Regulators.aspx (International
  Telecommunications Union, World Regulatory Policies Database)
http://investinpakistan.org/investment-laws.php
http://www.investmaldives.com/home.htm
http://www.investmaldives.org/
http://www.investmaldives.org/downloads/documents/FIL.pdf
http://www.island.com.mv/downloads.php
http://www.jamiahamdard.edu/govschool.asp
http://www.jetairways.com/EN/IN/PlanYourTravel/Schedules.aspx
http://www.lankabusinessonline.com/fullstory.php?nid=912202156
http://www.livemint.com/2007/05/04124713/Bangladesh-proposes-import-of.
  html?d=1
http://www.livemint.com/2008/04/30154503/Apollo-to-invest-Rs-1K-cr-for.
  html
http://www.livemint.com/2008/02/06232413/AIG-JPMorgan-buy-25-stake-in.
  html
http://www.madaan.com/sectors.html
http://magazine.indiabizclub.com/tourism-hotels/regulatory-policy-of-indian-hotel-industry/
http://www.malaysiaairlines.com/uploads/en/downloads/common/MHAugust09.
  pdf
http://www.maldiveisle.com/tourismactofmaldives.htm
http://www.mgiworld.com/get.php/pdfs/doing_business/doingbusinsrilanka.pdf
http://www.mihinlanka.com/flight-schedule.htm
http://www.mincom.gov.bd/acts.php - Import Policy Order 2006-2009
http://www.mocat.gov.bd/notice_details.php?ID=8&CATEGORY=1
http://www.mocat.gov.bd/policies/Bangladesh_Travel_Agencis_(Registration_&_
  Control)_Rules%20and%20Ordinance%201977.pdf
http://www.moedu.gov.bd/ (Ministry of Education, Bangladesh)
http://www.mof.gov.bt/index.php?deptid=14&id=84
http://www.moics.gov.np/act_regulations/FITTA/FITTA_%201992.pdf

http://mope.gov.lk/uploads/policy/policyen.pdf
http://www.nationsencyclopedia.com/Asia-and-Oceania/Sri-Lanka-FOREIGN-INVESTMENT.html
http://www.nepalmonitor.com/2009/01/fdi_in_nepals_hydropower.html
http://www.nepalvista.com/travel/visa.html#3a
http://newsoutlookindia.com/item.aspx?670863

http://newsrilanka.com/2009/07/tourism-ministry-to-promote-%E2%80%98religious-tourism%E2%80%99-in-lanka/

http://newsrilanka.com/2009/07/jaffna-the-latest-tourist-destination/

http://www.nrb.org.np/ http://www.pakboi.gov.pk/invest.pack.htm (Nepal Rastra Bank)

http://www/nsc.gov.np/report.php

http://www.opfblog.com/8229/tax-proposals-for-pakistan-budget-2009-10/

http://www.pakboi.gov.pk/invest.pack.htm

http://www.pakboi.gov.pk/pdf/IG/12_17.pdf

http://www.pakboi.gov.pk/pdf/IG/28_31.pdf

http://www.pakistan.gov.pk/divisions/tourism-division/media/Travel%20 Agencies%20Rules%201977.pdf

http://www.piac.com.pk/WeeklyFlightSchedule.aspx

http://ppi.worldbank.org/ (World Bank, Private Participation in Infrastructure Database)

http://prayatna.typepad.com/education/2006/05/foreign_direct_.html

http://www.pta.gov.pk/annual-reports/report2001/reportfinal2000-2001.pdf

http://www.pwccn.com/webmedia/doc/633784183988549499_aptn22_ may2009_sl.pdf

http://www.reformingeducation.in/?p=109

http://www.reformingeducation.in/?tag=the-foreign-education-providers-regulation-bill

http://www.rma.org.bt/ (Royal Monetary Authority of Bhutan)

http://www.saarcenergy.org/web/

http://www.saarc-sec.org/data

http://www.saarc.sec.org/?t=2.8.3

http://www.saarc-sec.org/main.php?t=2.9.6

http://www.sari-energy.org/PageFiles/Countries/Pakistan_Energy_detail. asp#reforms

http://www.sari-energy.org/PageFiles/Countries/maldives_Energy_detail.asp

http://www.sari-energy.org/PageFiles/Countries/Nepal_Energy_detail.asp

http://www.sari-energy.org/PageFiles/Countries/Sri_Lanka_Energy_detail. asp#reforms

http://www.sari-energy.org/Publications/REP/Regulation/NepalStatus.pdf

http://www.sbp.org.pk/ (State Bank of Pakistan)

http://www.sebi.gov.in/dp/indianlof.pdf

http://www.siliconindia.com/shownews/Aptech_looks_to_enter_Sri_Lanka_-nid-65406.html/1/1,

http://www.sltda.gov.lk/boi_incentives

http://www.sltda.lk/classification_of_tourist_hotels

http://www.sltda.lk/registration_of_tour_guides

http://www.sltda.gov.lk/sites/default/files/section_16_act.pdf

http://www.sltda.gov.lk/sites/default/files/Tourism_%20Act_%202005.pdf

http://www.southasianmedia.net/conference/conference_envisioning/vision_ goup_vii.htm

http://www.southasianmedia.net/Magazine/Journal/9_energy_cooperation.htm
http://www.srilankan.aero/travelplanner/scheduling.asp
http://www.state.gov/outofdate/bgn/b/109308.htm (Bureau of South and Central
    Asian Affairs, Department of State, USA)
http://www.state.gov/e/eeb/rls/othr/ics/2009/117846.htm
http://www.state.gov/e/eeb/rls/othr/ics/2009/117868.htm
http://www.state.gov/e/eeb/rls/othr/ics/2009/117846.htm
http://www.state.gov/e/eeb/rls/othr/ics/2009/117442.htm
http://www.studyinsrilanka.com/higher_education.htm
http://stats.uis.unesco.org/unesco/TableViewer/document.
    aspx?ReportId=143&IF_Language=eng (UNESCO Institute of Statistics)
http://stats.unctad.org/Handbook/TableViewer/dimView.aspx
http://www.tahseenbutt.com/investment_in_pakistan.html
http://www.tahseenbutt.com/real_estate_pakistan.html
http://www.thaindian.com/newsportal/business/chandigarh-business-school-
    opens-doors-for-saarc-countries_10069637.html#xzz0bd4xhPNG
http://www.thehindu.com/thehindu/mag/2006/01/08/
    stories/2006010800430300.htm
http://www.thehindubusinessline.com/2010/02/12/stories/2010021252040500.
    htm
http://www.thehindubusinessline.com/2008/08/25/stories/2008082551910100.
    htm
http://www.thehinduusinessline.com/2005/06/19/stories/2005061900410500.
    htm
http://timesofindia.indiatimes.com/articleshow/msid-3659792.prtpage-1.cms
http://tonto.eia.doe.gov/country/country_time_series.cfm?fips=BG - Bangladesh
http://tonto.eia.doe.gov/country/country_time_series.cfm?fips=BT - Bhutan
http://tonto.eia.doe.gov/country/country_time_series.cfm?fips=IN - India
http://tonto.eia.doe.gov/country/country_time_series.cfm?fips=NP - Nepal
http://tonto.eia.doe.gov/country/country_time_series.cfm?fips=MV - Maldives
http://tonto.eia.doe.gov/country/country_time_series.cfm?fips=PK - Pakistan
http://tonto.eia.doe.gov/country/country_time_series.cfm?fips=CE - Sri Lanka
http://www.tourism.gov.bt/about-tcb
http://www.tourism.gov.in/
http://www.tourism.gov.in/annualreportE08-09.pdf
http://www.tourism.gov.in/guidelines/toguideline.pdf
http://www.tourism.gov.mv/article.php?aId=3
http://www.tourism.gov.mv/article.php?aId=8
http://www.tourism.gov.np/foreignInvestmentAndTechTransferAct1992.php
http://www.tourism.gov.np/hotel_lodge_rest_tour_guide_regulation2038eng.php
http://tsdb.wto.org/simplesearch.aspx
http://www.ugc.ac.lk/recognition-of-foreign-universities.html
http://www.unctad.org/en/docs/iteipc20038_en.pdf
http://www.unctad.org/en/docs/poiteiitm29.en.pdf

http://unstats.un.org/unsd/databases.htm (United Nations Online Statistical Database)

http://www.universityworldnews.com/article.php?story=20081127151417381

http://www.unwto.org/statistics/index.htm (World Tourism Organization, 2009 Online Statistics)

http://www.wafed-nepal.org/news/news02102009.html

http://web.worldbank.org/WBSITE/EXTERNAL/DATASTATISTICS/0,content MDK:20535285-menuPK:1390200-pagePK:64133150-piPK:64133175-th eSitePK:239419,00.html (EdStats, World Bank)

http://web.worldbank.org/WBSITE/EXTERNAL/TOPICS/EXTEDUCATION /0,,contentMDK:20573961-menuPK:282404-pagePK:148956-piPK:21661 8-theSitePK:282386,00.html

http://web.worldbank.org/WBSITE/EXTERNAL/TOPICS/EXTEDUCATION/ EXTDATASTATISTICS/EXTEDSTATS/0,,contentMDK:21605891-men uPK:3409559-pagePK:64168445-piPK:64168309-theSitePK:3232764,00. html

http://www.welcomenepal.com/corporate/473182689482-574861922369

http://www.who.int/whosis/en/

Index